KANT AND THE FATE OF AU

It has been argued that Kant's all-consuming efforts to place autonomy at
the center of philosophy have had, in the long run, the unintended effects
of leading to the widespread discrediting of philosophy and of undermining the notion of autonomy itself. The result of this "Copernican revolution" has seemed to many commentators the de-centering, if not the self-
destruction, of the autonomous self.

In this major reinterpretation of Kant and the post-Kantian response to
his Critical philosophy, Karl Ameriks argues that such a view of Kant rests on
a series of misconceptions. He demonstrates that the thought of Kant's
successors (such as Fichte and Hegel) was determined by a radical Enlightenment conception of autonomy developed by Karl Reinhold, and that this
conception entailed a serious distortion of Kant's more modest approach.
The influence of Reinhold continues to mar current interpretation of Kant.
By providing the first systematic study of the underlying structure of the
reaction to Kant's Critical philosophy in the writings of Reinhold, Fichte,
and Hegel, Karl Ameriks challenges the presumptions that dominate popular approaches to the concept of freedom, and to the interpretation of the
relation between the Enlightenment, Kant, and post-Kantian thought.

A landmark study, this book will be of particular interest to all students of
Kant as well as those in fields such as intellectual history, political theory,
and religious studies concerned with issues of autonomy and modernity.

Karl Ameriks is McMahon-Hank Professor of Philosophy at the University of
Notre Dame.

MODERN EUROPEAN PHILOSOPHY

General Editor
ROBERT B. PIPPIN, *University of Chicago*

Advisory Board
GARY GUTTING, *University of Notre Dame*
ROLF-PETER HORSTMANN, *Humboldt University, Berlin*
MARK SACKS, *University of Essex*

This series contains a range of high-quality books on philosophers, topics, and schools of thought prominent in the Kantian and post-Kantian European tradition. It is nonsectarian in approach and methodology, and includes both introductory and more specialized treatments of these thinkers and topics. Authors are encouraged to interpret the boundaries of the modern European tradition in a broad way and in primarily philosophical rather than historical terms.

Some Recent Titles:

KANT AND THE FATE OF AUTONOMY

Problems in the Appropriation of the Critical Philosophy

KARL AMERIKS
University of Notre Dame

CAMBRIDGE
UNIVERSITY PRESS

PUBLISHED BY THE PRESS SYNDICATE OF THE UNIVERSITY OF CAMBRIDGE
The Pitt Building, Trumpington Street, Cambridge, United Kingdom

CAMBRIDGE UNIVERSITY PRESS
The Edinburgh Building, Cambridge CB2 2RU, UK   http://www.cup.cam.ac.uk
40 West 20th Street, New York, NY 10011-4211, USA   http://www.cup.org
10 Stamford Road, Oakleigh, Melbourne 3166, Australia
Ruiz de Alarcón 13, 28014 Madrid, Spain

First published 2000

Printed in the United States of America

Typeface Baskerville 10.25/13 pt.   *System* MagnaType™[AG]

A catalog record for this book is available from the British Library.

Library of Congress Cataloging in Publication Data
Ameriks, Karl, 1947–
Kant and the fate of autonomy : problems in the appropriation of the critical
philosophy
/ Karl Ameriks.
p.   cm. – (Modern European philosophy)
Includes index.
ISBN 0-521-78101-9 (hb) – ISBN 0-521-78614-2 (pbk.)
1. Kant, Immanuel, 1724–1804 – Contributions in concept of freedom. 2.
Reinhold, Karl Leonhard, 1758–1823 – Contributions in concept of freedom. 3.
Fichte, Johann Gottlieb, 1762–1814 – Contributions in concept of freedom. 4.
Hegel, Georg Wilhelm Friedrich, 1770–1831 – Contributions in concept of
freedom. 5. Liberty – History – 18th century. 6. Liberty – History – 19th
century. I. Title. II. Series
B2799.L49 A48   2000
142'.3 – dc21
99-054675

ISBN 0 521 78101 9 hardback
ISBN 0 521 78614 2 paperback

CONTENTS

ACKNOWLEDGMENTS

This volume has been in the making for more than a decade, and over that time I have benefited in many ways from many more people than I can begin to do justice to here. I am deeply indebted to all the colleagues, students, friends, and fellow scholars who have helped me with philosophical issues concerning the period of "Kant and after." In notes throughout the volume and in remarks in the Introduction, I indicate many specific philosophical debts, but it is no doubt an incomplete accounting, and I apologize to those who are not given the credit they deserve.

Special thanks for making possible the completion of the volume are owed to Robert Pippin and Gary Gutting, who helped not only on countless specific points but also with their constant encouragement and the challenge of their relentless intellectual energy. My thanks also to Terry Moore at Cambridge University Press for his kind patience and guidance and to the Press's careful reviewers for their many insightful remarks.

The early work of Daniel Breazeale and Alexander von Schönborn was crucial for my first investigations of Reinhold. More recently, Manfred Kuehn, Manfred Frank, and Dieter Sturma have provided extensive help on numerous projects involving the understanding of the latest German research in this area; it has been an honor and an education for me to have been associated with them in common projects. I should also acknowledge the inspiring influence of the outstanding senior scholars who led me into this tradition: Karsten Harries, David Carr, Hans Frei, John Findlay, Cyrus Hamlin, Dieter Jähnig, Walter Schulz, and Gerold Prauss. Günter Zöller, Sally Sedgwick, Thomas Rockmore, Graciela de Peirris, Michael Friedman, Paul Franks, Alison Laywine, Stephen Houlgate, Carl Posy, Patricia Kitcher, Rudolf Makkreel, Henry E. Allison, Jerry Schneewind, Allen Wood, Daniel Dahlstrom, Fred Neuhouser, Tom McCarthy, Kenneth Westphal, Frederick Beiser, Pauline Kleingeld, Paul Guyer, Raymond Geuss, Marcia Baron, Marcelo Stamm, Alessandro Lazzari, Susan Shell, Georg Mohr, Rolf-Peter Horstmann, Volker Gerhardt, Christel Fricke, and Jane Kneller have helped by arranging or participating in meetings where their special contributions and questions provided a crucial stimulus for my final revisions. Many students have also helped through discussions on issues relating to this project, especially Eric Watkins, John Davenport, Patrick Kain, Tad Schmaltz, Jeff Hoover, Victor Krebs, Daniel Kolb, Michael Murray, Steven Naragon, and Hayden Anderson. In addition, Andrew Lamb and Patrick Frierson provided excellent assistance with the final preparation of the text.

I am very pleased to acknowledge institutional support for this project from a Fellowship Grant from the National Endowment for the Humanities (for 1998), as well as from special grants from the Alexander von Humboldt Foundation, the Earhart Foundation, and the Institute for Scholarship in the Liberal Arts at Notre Dame. A number of creative scholar-administrators have helped greatly in making it possible for me to have time to devote to this project, and I am especially indebted to Nathan Hatch, Mark Roche, Christopher Fox, and Stephen Watson for helping to arrange an extended leave for me for 1997–8. I would like to express my deep appreciation to the members of the Notre Dame philosophy department and the whole Notre Dame community for the extraordinarily supportive and stimulating environment that they have always provided for me and my whole family – and without them, without Geraldine and Michael and Kevin, all the work would have made no sense.

I gratefully acknowledge permission from the publishers to use materials from the following earlier publications. For Chapter 2: "Reinhold and the Short Argument to Idealism," in *Proceedings: Sixth International Kant Congress 1985*, ed. G. Funke and T. Seebohm (Washington: Center for Advanced Research in Phenomenology and University Press of America, 1989), vol. 2, part 2, 441–53. For Chapter 3: "Kant, Fichte, and Short Arguments to Idealism," *Archiv für Geschichte der Philosophie* 72 (1990): 63–85. For Chapter 4: "Fichte's Appeal Today: The Hidden Primacy of the

Practical," in *The Emergence of German Idealism,* ed. M. Baur and D. Dahlstrom (Washington: Catholic University of America Press, 1999), pp. 116–30; and "The Practical Foundation of Philosophy in Kant, Fichte, and After," in *The Reception of Kant's Critical Philosophy: Fichte, Schelling, and Hegel,* ed. S. Sedgwick (Cambridge: Cambridge University Press, 2000), pp. 109–28. For Chapter 5: "Understanding Apperception Today," in *Kant and Contemporary Epistemology,* ed. P. Parrini (Dordrecht: Kluwer, 1994), pp. 331–47; and "Kant and the Self: A Retrospective," in *Figuring the Self: Subject, Absolute, and Others in Classical German Philosophy,* ed. G. Zoeller and D. Klemm (Albany: SUNY Press, 1997), pp. 55–72. For Chapter 6: "Hegel's Critique of Kant's Theoretical Philosophy," *Philosophy and Phenomenological Research* 46 (1985): 1–35. For Chapter 7: "The Hegelian Critique of Kantian Morality," in *New Essays on Kant,* ed. B. den Ouden (New York: Peter Lang, 1987), pp. 179–212.

INTRODUCTION: KANT AND THE
FATE OF AUTONOMY

How it could happen that a whole epoch of philosophers, from
Reinhold to Hegel, was of the opinion that philosophy must be
deduced from one proposition – this has still remained unclear to
me, and I have as yet found no answer for it in the literature.[1]

Near the end of his life, a public challenge was issued to Kant in the
anonymous review of an obscure work, Johann Gottlieb Bohle's *Entwurf
der Transcendental-Philosophie* (Göttingen, 1798):

> *Kant* is the first *teacher* of Transcendental Philosophy and Reinhold the
> admirable *disseminator* of the critical doctrine; but the first true transcenden-
> tal philosopher is undeniably *Fichte*. For Fichte has realized what the *Critique*
> proposed, carrying out systematically the transcendental idealism which
> *Kant* projected. How natural therefore is the public's desire that the origina-
> tor of the *Critique* declare openly his opinion of the work of his worthy
> pupil![2]

1 Kurt Röttgers, *Kritik und Praxis* (Berlin: de Gruyter, 1975), p. 93, n. 28. The "one proposition" philosophy of Reinhold is discussed in detail in Chapter 2 below.
2 Quoted by Arnold Zweig, in his note on Immanuel Kant, Aug. 7, 1799, "Public Declaration
  concerning Fichte's *Wissenschaftslehre*," in *Correspondence/ Immanuel Kant*, ed. and trans. A.
  Zweig (Cambridge: Cambridge University Press, 1999), p. 560n.

1

In an unusual public reply, Kant issued an impassioned statement that insisted on distinguishing the latest fashions from "the common standpoint" of his own philosophy:

> Since the reviewer finally maintains that the *Critique* is not to be taken *literally* in what it says about sensibility and that anyone who wants to understand the *Critique* must first master the requisite *standpoint* (of Beck or of Fichte), because *Kant's* precise words, like Aristotle's, will destroy the spirit, I therefore declare again that the *Critique* is to be understood by considering exactly what it says and that it requires only the common standpoint that any mind sufficiently cultivated in abstract investigations will bring to it.[3]

In an obvious reference to "successors" such as Reinhold and Fichte, Kant pointedly added:

> There is an Italian proverb: May God protect us especially from our friends, for we shall manage to watch out for our enemies ourselves. There are indeed friends who mean well by us but who are doltish in choosing the means for promoting our ends. But there are also treacherous friends, deceitful, bent on our destruction while speaking the language of good will *aliud linqua promptum, aliud pectore inclusum genere* [who think one thing and say another], and one cannot be too cautious about such so-called friends and the snares they have set.[4]

Kant's warning remarks were widely ignored, but they merit our attention now more than ever. Developments in our own time have once again made a pressing issue of the task of properly sorting out the successors to his Critical philosophy, of finding a way through what Kant called "the snares" that were set immediately after him. In this study I offer a series of investigations that set out a new reading of the main contours of Kant's era, a reading that aims to make understandable and, to a considerable extent, to vindicate Kant's suspicion that his work would be seriously misunderstood by those who seemed to stand closest to it.

The sharp rise and fall of the appreciation of Kant's Critical philosophy is a first-order historical mystery. In the 1780s it quickly achieved extraor-

---

3 Ibid., p. 560. Kant's letter was published in the *Intelligenzblatt* of the *Allgemeine Litteratur-Zeitung*, and is in *Kant's gesammelte Schriften* (Berlin: Preussische Akademie der Wissenschaften/ de Gruyter, 1900–), vol. 12, p. 371. Quotations from the sentence prior to this one, and also from the next sentence after the passage quoted (the very end of the letter), are discussed below Chapter 1, n. 15 and n. 20. See also Kant's already very negative remarks about Fichte's philosophy in his letter to Tieftrunk, April 5, 1798.
4 Kant, *Correspondence*, p. 560.

dinary prominence, and yet by the 1790s it was overshadowed to such a degree in his own land that the very ideas that Kant had put at the center of philosophy – the new "transcendental" notions of "deduction," "idealism," and "autonomy" – took on a meaning that he could no longer recognize. I believe this strange development has a significance that goes far beyond details in the history of philosophy; it affects the understanding of concepts that are still central to leading trends in systematic philosophy, and it has ramifications for our own era's conception of itself as an heir to the Enlightenment. Beyond the problem of Kant's shifting popular reputation and the evaluation of his technical achievements, there is the general issue of the fate of his most central thought, autonomy. There can appear to be a tragic irony in Kant's role here. Just as modern religious apologists have been understandably accused of inadvertently corrupting, through their sincere but faulty arguments, the very faith that they sought most earnestly to defend, it can be argued that Kant's all-consuming effort to bring autonomy to the center of philosophy (and life in general) has had, in the long run, the unintended effect of leading to a widespread discrediting of philosophy (in its traditional special role) as such, and to an undermining of the notion of autonomy itself. The philosophical "Copernican revolution," which supposedly put the activity of human subjectivity at the center of everything, has seemed to many current thinkers to have led ultimately to the de-centering, if not the self-destruction, of the autonomous self.[5]

I will be arguing that although these developments have serious and understandable grounds, they rest in large part on a series of misconceptions that can still be reversed. In other words, it is possible (albeit with some revisions, for the sake of the "common standpoint" that Kant wanted above all to defend) to take the most basic ideas of the Critical philosophy in a way that preserves rather than threatens our commitment to autonomy. Unfortunately, explaining how and why this should be done is a task that requires nothing less than a close historical account of several crucial but covered-over episodes in the twisting path of philosophy from Kant to Reinhold, Fichte, Hegel, and their followers in our own time. To leave room for even the barest essentials of this very complicated story of philosophy after Kant, my account here will have to leave for another

5 See the developments recounted in volumes such as *The Modern Subject*, ed. Karl Ameriks and Dieter Sturma (Albany: State University of New York Press, 1994); *Deconstructive Subjectivities*, ed. Simon Critchley and Peter Dews (Albany: State University of New York Press, 1996); and *Figuring the Self*, ed. David Klemm and Guenter Zoeller (Albany: State University of New York Press, 1997).

occasion the project of a detailed study of Kant's own full system.[6] And since the focus of my account will be on the philosophical *evaluation* of the most fundamental concepts of the era, it cannot aim to provide anything like a full-scale narrative of post-Kantian German philosophy. On the presumption that enough has already been written in recent years to make this once-exotic strand of thought familiar and even attractive to many English-language readers, I will be working "against the current" for the sake of beginning to stress *Critical problems* in popular post-Kantian developments. Why such a task has so far been so neglected is an interesting story in itself, one that requires a discussion of the divisions that have arisen within the camp of the followers of German philosophy.

A. ONE STORY OF THE DECLINE AND FALL OF ABSOLUTE AUTONOMY

A. 1. The Division of Philosophy after Kant

From the beginning of their era, the classical German philosophers all took on the mantle of champions of the philosophy of freedom. But freedom is a term that calls out for definition. Even if Kant is not entirely responsible for "the invention of autonomy,"[7] he certainly deserves the most credit for promoting the notion that in general our freedom should be understood specifically as autonomy. Kant's Critical philosophy led to, even if it did not complete, the absolutizing of this originally political and delimited notion. It was the first to argue for extraordinarily strong forms of autonomy throughout our *theoretical* and *practical* experience as well as in the higher-order *philosophical* system that explains both of these domains. For Kant, our freedom involves a capacity to be not merely an occasional uncaused or self-directed force; above all, it is a power whose action is ever present in an internally generated and law-governed way. The Kantian self is literally "auto-nomous," that is, defined by a *self-legislation* that is carried out on itself as well as by itself.

6 For a summary of my view of the basic character of Kant's system, see below Chapter 1, which draws upon and extends several of my earlier studies of Kant. Numerous references are provided to these studies, which I intend to collect and supplement soon in another volume giving a broader treatment of the problem of interpreting Kant's *Critiques*. I do not anywhere provide a detailed conceptual analysis of the central notion of autonomy itself or discuss the many interesting attempts to do so in recent literature. The term can obviously be given all sorts of meanings, and for my purposes there is enough to do in focusing simply on the most basic components of the word in Kant's original and fundamental discussion.

7 See J. B. Schneewind, *The Invention of Autonomy* (Cambridge: Cambridge University Press, 1997).

In current thought, this general idea is surely Kant's most popular contribution, and whatever else one thinks of his work, it seems that everyone now strives to account for autonomy in some way or other, either as an advocate making an attempt to provide a reconstruction of some aspect of it in Kant's own spirit, or at least as a diagnostician (e.g., MacIntyre) trying to reveal its deep problems. It is not, however, the direct advocates or enemies of this doctrine in our own time that are the main topic of this study. My interest in the "fate of Kantian autonomy" primarily concerns the forgotten background of current discussions in the complex sequence of appropriations that Kant's central doctrine suffered in the era of the Critical philosophy's very first readers, from Reinhold to Hegel – and the intriguing possibility that these neighborly "friends" of Kantian autonomy were the greatest danger to it. My main goal is to make understandable *how* they covered over its original meaning in Kant's own thought, where it still had several significant limitations, and *why* they went beyond Kant by *absolutizing* the call for autonomy in the name of a series of extravagant projects that still have a deep and unfortunate effect on our presumptions about current philosophical options.

My story is complicated by the fact that recently there has been a renaissance of interest in these very figures, and that it is not so much Kant but rather the first post-Kantians – above all Hegel, but also others, such as Fichte, Herder, Hölderlin, Schelling, Schlegel, and Schleiermacher – who have captured the attention of the most exciting thinkers currently writing on the era. Dieter Henrich, Charles Taylor, Stanley Cavell, Jürgen Habermas, Richard Rorty, Robert Brandom, Allen Wood, Charles Larmore, Manfred Frank, Raymond Geuss, Frederick Beiser, Robert Pippin, to name just a few (and to say nothing of earlier French and British figures such as Sartre and Isaiah Berlin) – are all united in making a loud and clear call for an exploration and defense of autonomy. But they do not conjoin with this call the old refrain "Back to Kant" – and several even go so far as to shout, rather than whisper, "Away from Kant!"

This is an odd development, given the fact that elsewhere Kant's own conception of autonomy has simultaneously become the direct focus of some of the most influential recent work in philosophy. The conception is central to John Rawls, and also, by no accident, to Christine Korsgaard, Barbara Herman, Thomas Hill, Onora O'Neill, Thomas Nagel, and Thomas Scanlon, to name just a few major ethicists with broadly similar Kantian views. A range of broadly similar perspectives emphasizing the study of Kantian autonomy can also be found in the work of figures as diverse as J. B. Schneewind, Harry Frankfurt, and Stephen Darwall, as well

as that of top interpreters and foreign scholars such as Henry Allison and
Gerold Prauss.

These two schools of thinkers – which I will call "post-Kantian" and
"pure Kantian"[8] (using quotation marks to distinguish them from their
eighteenth-century predecessors – and by "pure" here I mean not necessarily "authentic," but rather "purified" from what are taken to be out-of-
date and inessential "material" claims) – tend to take very different approaches to autonomy. There are occasional accommodating gestures
and exceptions, of course, but on the whole those who write on the
original post-Kantians are interested almost exclusively in how the idea of
autonomy was radically "improved" or corrected after Kant, while those
who write at length on Kant himself rarely have even a word (let alone a
good word) to say about the post-Kantians who now seem most fascinating
to so many scholars. What is going on? Both groups are composed of
outstanding intellects, and although the first is clearly more oriented
toward history than the other, there is nothing like the deep divide between continental and analytic approaches here. The "post-Kantians" include precise systematicians, and the "pure Kantians" occasionally in-
dulge in outstanding historical work.

It is also striking that there does not seem to be much of an ideological
difference between these two groups, for they are both composed of
thinkers who appear very sympathetic to broadly liberal political and
ethical agendas, and who would be very happy, for the most part, to make
a tight common front against any serious commitment to traditional
metaphysics (here Nagel is unusual in his group) or nonsecular values
(here Taylor is unusual in his group). And this is no accident, for both
groups understand "self-legislation" in large part as a rejection of anything outside "humanity." That is, in form they reject any philosophical
method claiming truths not tied to a relatively natural (in a broad sense)
"internal" procedure – such as an "equilibrium" reached by thinkers like
us, or a process of "consensus" or "solidarity" – that abstracts from special
intuitions and controversial metaphysical procedures. And with respect to
content they also tend to insist on denying any substantive principles that
may ultimately involve a domain beyond natural persons altogether. The
two groups thus reinforce one another quite naturally, so that it can look

8 The "pure Kantian" label here does not mean that these writers are fully orthodox in their
Kantianism, which is quite controversial, but signals that they tend to focus purely on Kant
rather than his successors. For more distinctions, see Onora O'Neill, "Kant's Ethics and
Kantian Ethics," in *Bounds of Justice* (forthcoming).

as if it is largely an accident that the members of the one group tend not to write books like those of the members of the other group. Thus it can appear that there is no deep meaning in the fact that Kant's interest in autonomy is charted out in systematic and largely analytic terms by one group of thinkers, who prefer doing that sort of thing, while other writers focus more on historical issues and on how the notion of autonomy was developed more concretely in later eras.

But surely this complementary and "progressive" picture is too simple, too Whiggish, too blind to the facts, even if it is close to a view that was often promulgated by the original post-Kantians themselves. Reinhold, then Fichte, then Hegel, all encouraged the thought that they were, above all else, "completing" the great revolution begun by Kant in the name of autonomy. And scholars such as Pippin and Wood have certainly unearthed many points of influence and similarity that make this claim at least understandable. But it is also clear that Kant himself mightily resisted making common cause with his successors, and that they in turn were often very bold in their criticisms of absurdities they claimed to find in his philosophy. Hence it makes sense to approach the divide in focus between the "post-" and "pure Kantians" by exploring the hypothesis that it reflects what is, after all, a deep and genuine division in orientation.

There are several considerations supporting this hypothesis. To focus on Kant's notion of autonomy in its own pristine terms, as "pure Kantians" do, clearly appears to involve emphasizing nonrelative and/or non-pluralistic[9] claims in a way that seriously conflicts with the views of many "post-Kantians." On the other hand, concrete intersubjectivity, the effect of historical and social factors that "post-Kantians" see as fundamental, can seem beside the point in the arguments of the "pure Kantians." No one would say that sociohistorical considerations are unimportant – they have a special value for everyone today, and even Kant has his own significant theory of this domain – but for the pure Kantian they clearly seem secondary in the process of philosophical analysis or, for example, in the construction of anything like a "categorical imperative procedure." And if this is true for practical reason, it would seem to be all the more clearly true for Kantian theoretical reason and its basic commitment to eternal

9 Charles Larmore's work is a helpful reminder of the possibility that there are significant kinds of "pluralism" that can go hand in hand with a deep objectivism and antirelativism. See his *The Morals of Modernity* (Cambridge: Cambridge University Press, 1996); and cf. Tzvetan Todorov, *On Human Diversity: Nationalism, Racism, and Exoticism in French Thought* (Cambridge, MA: Harvard University Press, 1993).

categories, whereas for the "post-Kantians" there is no hesitation (e.g., in Rorty) in invoking a kind of Hegelian historicism for the domain of "pure theory" as well.

These strong contrasts have remained remarkably undiscussed from a broadly inclusive perspective, perhaps because most philosophers in the two groups tend not to engage with one another in a significant variety of ways. Those who write on Kant alone usually lack motivation as well as time for looking closely at his successors. On the other hand, those who do focus on the successors have already crossed the Rubicon, and thus they tend simply to work out their own complicated version of the progressive post-Kantian story mentioned earlier (even if, for obvious chronological reasons, they at least are likely to be more familiar with Kant than Kantians are with Hegel, etc.).

To help overcome this divide, it can be useful to introduce another possibility here, a neglected perspective that will be the emphasis of this study – namely, that there is a story to be told about the development of philosophy after Kant that is both *significant* and largely (but not exclusively) a matter of *regress* rather than progress. It is rather surprising, but understandable, that more traditional Kantians have not done much to develop this kind of alternative to the prevalent "no story" and "story of progress" options. Those who work directly on Kant have not been much concerned with an historical account at all, because they tend to think that his intrinsic philosophical power is such that it does not matter very much what people wrote right after him – especially if they wrote in a notoriously difficult way, in a German that makes even Kant look easy by comparison.[10] What matters for them is simply the project of combining the core of Kant's original theory with the best systematic work of our own age. Similarly, the many scholars who now work on the period after Kant have not been interested in a nonprogressive account. There is an enormous amount for them to do simply to begin to make sense of their unusual terrain, and they are unlikely to have proceeded very far without already having some strong convictions that gold is to be found primarily in the post-Kantian texts and that it is worth all the hard work required to dredge it out.

10 Here cultural relativists might be amused by Wilhelm von Humboldt's opinion: "A version of philosophical style of quite peculiar beauty is also to be found among us in the pursuit of fine-drawn concepts in the writings of Fichte and Schelling, and, though only here and there, but then to truly gripping effect, in Kant." *On Language: The Diversity of Human Language-Structure and Its Influence on the Mental Development of Mankind*, trans. P. Heath (Cambridge: Cambridge University Press, 1988), p. 175.

My perspective is unlike that of either of these two dominant groups insofar as I have long found myself equally fascinated by the preeminent systematic value of Kant's philosophy and by the complex historical question of how we got from Kant's time to our present philosophical situation – especially given the complicated developments right after Kant as well as the repetition, in several obvious ways, of similar developments in our own time. Like the "post-Kantians," I believe it is very important to tell the story of how philosophy moved on after Kant, through various remarkable controversies and reversals, to Hegel and all that he made possible. But like the "pure Kantians," I look at these developments from a systematic perspective that is most sympathetic to the main contours of Kant's own work. Thus, unlike the "post-Kantians," I see a need to explain how there were important confusions, rather than mere "improvements" and "completions" in the works of Kant's immediate successors. And yet, unlike the "pure Kantians," I want to insist on the importance of attending to historical developments, and of reflecting on influential misunderstandings introduced after Kant. Such a fascination with the negative might seem retrogressive or morbid, but in fact it can be liberating, and is hardly unusual. Ever since Hegel and Nietzsche, there has been a growing delight in exposing the shortcomings of classical modern philosophy. A similar pleasure and opening for the future can come from beginning a genealogy of the first genealogists themselves. Moreover, from my own more traditional Kantian perspective, the peculiar misrepresentations introduced by the original post-Kantians remain a huge hidden obstacle to a genuine appreciation of Kant's philosophy today. Even "pure Kantians" are affected by these misconceptions when they remain too embarrassed to present the Critical philosophy whole and largely "without apology," and thus buy into the original post-Kantians' presumptions that Kant's metaphysics is too absurd to be worth exploring in its original meaning.

On this point, the "neglected perspective" cannot help but appear "untimely" in its contrast with the common "humanistic" front that was noted above and that dominates most current approaches to the Kantian era. That front tries to build alliances and to minimize embarrassment by suggesting that Kant himself need not be taken to have *any* serious metaphysical commitments. Things in themselves, transcendental freedom in a literal, metaphysical sense, existential assertions about God or an afterlife, suspicions about the nonultimacy of spatiotemporal descriptions – all that, it is sometimes proposed, is not part of Kant's own Critical project, but is rather an awkward husk imposed on his texts by careless readers.

Once this bowdlerizing move is accepted,[11] it can become relatively easy to forge many connections between Kant and the original post-Kantians (even if, for the reasons just given, they in fact have not been developed much), because these post-Kantians were also most concerned with wanting to make the way free for an explicitly "humanistic" transcendental philosophy. Much of the current renaissance of interest in these figures comes from a greater appreciation of this point, and from an overreaction to the fact that earlier interpretations had often confused the complicated terminology of the German idealists with ineradicable commitments to a transcendent metaphysics of the old speculative type. This confusion still manifests itself in such common English tendencies as that of attaching a basically skeptical meaning to the word "idealism," or of conflating "transcendental" and "transcendent" claims – thereby forgetting that in their original contexts these terms are more like antonyms than synonyms, since for Kant "transcendental" considerations concern what is needed inside our experience, whereas what is "transcendent" is wholly outside our experience.

However understandable its source may be, I will not criticize the "bowdlerizing" approach to Kant in detail here, but will merely note that it is not my own intention to take this popular route. Even if construing the Critical philosophy in largely antimetaphysical ways that already accommodate central ideas of later developments makes it easier to save Kant in the face of post-Kantian interests, I prefer to explore a reading of the Critical philosophy that starts by taking it warts and all. It is a challenging experiment to see what Kant still might have to offer us even if he is allowed to be very much caught up in the metaphysical doctrines alluded to earlier, the old ideas that so many current readers would prefer to jettison altogether. Accepting a strong metaphysical core at the heart of Kant's philosophy can yield several interpretive advantages, not the least of which is that it is an approach that might reveal something new simply because it is so rarely attempted any more. From the start, this approach also makes it easier at least to understand the harsh criticisms of the first post-Kantians, who all clearly presumed that there are strong metaphysical commitments expressed in Kant's texts. (It can be sorted out later whether they properly identified these commitments; but it is a bit much to suppose that these first readers could totally miss the "fact" that Kant didn't even have a serious transcendent metaphysics.) Another advantage

11 On the contrast between old and new ways of reading Kant, see P. F. Strawson, "The Problem of Realism and the A Priori," in *Kant and Contemporary Epistemology*, ed. P. Parrini (Dordrecht: Kluwer, 1994), pp. 167–74.

of the approach is that the presence of these commitments might help us to understand why there still remains such a distance between the "post-Kantians" and "pure Kantians." Even if it is not of interest to the "pure Kantians," the underlying metaphysical content of Kant's arguments, and especially claims about various substantive necessities, may well be part of what makes it very difficult for their use of Kant's texts to fit in smoothly with the concerns that animate the strongly antimetaphysical, and not merely nonmetaphysical, approach of the "post-Kantians."

There can also be considerable systematic value, and not merely an interpretive benefit, in keeping alive a metaphysical approach to Kant's texts. There is a remarkably strong presumption, common to "post-Kantians" and "pure Kantians" alike, that metaphysics is a weak and dying discipline, hence that it is all the better to keep it some distance from one's Germanic philosophical heroes. But although metaphysical arguments may not be of great interest to many of the current readers of Kant (a significant fact that was also true of his original readers), the state of metaphysics as such is not at all the embarrassment that its nonpractitioners commonly suggest. At the end of the twentieth century, hard-core naturalist materialists such as David Armstrong, theistic materialists such as Peter van Inwagen, theistic immaterialists such as Alvin Plantinga, and nontheistic nonmaterialists such as those inspired by Roderick Chisholm, as well as many other superb philosophers of logic and language, have brought the discipline into a clearer and more rigorous form today than it has ever had. For these philosophers, Kant's problem is not that he is too metaphysical but that he does not appear to be metaphysical enough, that he writes in terms that can seem too psychological and subjective, or simply too vague and inconsistent (not always an easy combination).[12] And yet, given Kant's intensive training in questions of the mainline metaphysical tradition, and the way that this clearly structures his Critical writings as well, it is highly unlikely that Kant's own massive work is wholly irrelevant to the neo-Leibnizian theories of the present age – even if that has been the common supposition of most of its friends and foes alike.[13]

12 For an especially clear expression of this view, see Michael J. Loux, *Metaphysics: A Contemporary Introduction* (London: Routledge, 1998), pp. 7–10. Loux's interpretation implicitly accepts the popular "short argument" reading of Kant that I discuss in Chapter 3 below (and that derives from Kant's first radical idealist readers) – and the immediate absurdities that Loux recounts in such a view provide one more *reductio*, I believe, for actually ascribing such a view to Kant. As Loux points out, if Kant really holds, for example, to the claim that all thought as such is merely subjective, then that claim itself loses any weight for us.

13 See *Lectures on Metaphysics/ Immanuel Kant*, ed. and trans. Karl Ameriks and Steve Naragon (Cambridge: Cambridge University Press, 1997); K. Ameriks, "Kant and Short Arguments

Fortunately, James van Cleve, Rae Langton, John Hare, and Robert M. Adams, among others, have recently done insightful work that indicates a growing analytic appreciation of ontological doctrines in Kant's system. The steady influence of systematicians such as Sellars, Strawson, and McDowell may also eventually generate more profitable mutual relations between the study of Kant and the rest of contemporary metaphysics (once the interest in their work moves beyond a concentration on intriguing but somewhat limited epistemological issues).

It is likely, however, that the antipathy to metaphysics that still animates most current readings of Kant is not based primarily in a fear of specific ties between Kant and the metaphysical literature of the now-standard contemporary sort (which can go in all sorts of directions) – especially since many of the most popular discussions of Kant tend to show little interest in details of this analytic literature. The "metaphysics" that mainly bothers "post-Kantians" and "pure Kantians" appears to have a much more specific and "internal" source, one that is familiar enough even if it does not map smoothly onto current research areas. The main source of the fear, I suspect, is simply the fact that, precisely for the kind of readers who tend to be most intrigued by Kant, it can *seem* to go directly against the founding "spirit" of Kant's "Copernican" turn to leave metaphysical room for *any* sort of "noumena," or even any strong ontological (and not merely "conceptual" or "epistemic" or "practical") claims. The spirit of that revolution is encapsulated in the simple thought that "objects must conform to our knowledge," rather than vice versa,[14] and this thought can be easily *taken* to imply (although by itself it certainly does not entail) that objects in any sense beyond our experience must be completely dismissed. This "Copernican spirit" is also directly connected to the interest in Kant's central notion of autonomy, for that notion can naturally be understood in terms of the thought that theoretical and practical laws must first of all conform to *us*, so that our *self*-legislation can maintain its

to Humility," in *Kant's Legacy: Essays in Honor of L. W. Beck*, ed. P. Cicovacki (Rochester: Rochester University Press, 2000); and K. Ameriks, "The Critique of Metaphysics: Kant and Traditional Ontology," in *The Cambridge Companion to Kant*, ed. Paul Guyer (Cambridge: Cambridge University Press, 1992), pp. 249–79.

14 Kant, *Critique of Pure Reason*, B xvi. All quotations of this work are from the Norman Kemp Smith translation (London: Macmillan, 1929), with the first and second editions designated as A and B, respectively, followed by page numbers. The context of this passage makes it clear that Kant's argument essentially involves a restriction to objects *of experience* and does not claim that objects *as such* must conform to our knowledge. It is precisely this restriction that allows him to claim that he has forever blocked "free-thinkers" and "materialists" from any ground for asserting that their positions hold for objects as such. See below at n. 16.

primacy. Here a lot depends, however, on exactly what can be meant by the "self" that Kant says is the source of laws. At this point, I can no longer put off indicating some of my reasons for approaching Kant – and even his notion of autonomy – in a way that goes against the grain of popular "Copernican" expectations.

A. 2. Kantian Autonomy as Metaphysical but Moderate, Not Absolute

Although there is, as has been noted, a natural tendency to understand the Kantian position in "humanistic" terms, enormous difficulties arise as soon as one tries to work this thought out concretely. In the moral realm, the main – and yet often forgotten – point that must always be kept in mind is that Kant is quite clear that laws of morality are not as such limited to human selves. Their necessity is tied to a source and meaning in considerations that are independent not only of spatiotemporal beings (and thus of all humanity) but even of finite persons as such. For Kant, what is truly good and right in itself is so for any rational being, even if it is also true that how human beings react to moral laws will involve the specific pressure of an imperative form, due to the fact that humans are creatures of sensibility and are not constructed in such a way that they invariably follow rational laws of action.[15] The most fundamental Kantian principles of value thus remain independent of space and time in their definition, even though in fact it is true that *we* understand and plan our actions always in terms of space and time. This means that the fundamental "self" that autonomously "generates" the basic laws of morality is *not defined* as a *human* self, even though we actually become aware of the laws only as exemplified in concrete spatiotemporal, that is, human contexts. Neither the grounding of the laws nor their ultimate scope can be a matter of any kind of temporal, let alone spatiotemporal, *action* (such as consensus formation limited to the specific conditions of finite beings like us). Why then even bother to say that they are laws "given" by us at all rather than that they are laws to which we must conform? The best answer, I propose,

15 See my "On Schneewind and Kant's Method in Ethics," *Ideas y Valores* 102 (1996): 28–53; some of the considerations there overlap with objections made by Thomas Nagel and Gerald Cohen to Christine Korsgaard's "constructivist" interpretation of Kant, in C. Korsgaard, *The Sources of Normativity*, with G. A. Cohen et al. (Cambridge: Cambridge University Press, 1996). Cf. below Chapter 1, n. 53; Patrick Kain, "Self-Legislation and Prudence in Kant's Moral Philosophy: A Critical Examination of Some Constructivist Interpretations" (Ph.D. dissertation, University of Notre Dame, 1999); and Larmore, *Morals of Modernity*.

has to do with the fact that such laws are still not external to our *essential nature*, which for Kant is our sheer rationality. In this way they in one sense have a significant "internal" source – they come from something "in" us, even if it is not *only* in *us* – whereas if they were grounded simply in a contingent fact such as a natural, political, or arbitrary religious power, they would have an external source. Moreover, it is evident that Kant understands this rational nature not as a matter of mystic insight or "mirrored presence" but rather in terms of an exercise of judgment, and thus, even if it is not strictly psychological, this nature has a normative "inner" meaning that reflects what there is that always remains "in us" as rational agents despite whatever variations there may be in external data.

This position involves what can be called a moderate understanding of our moral autonomy, one that contrasts with both extreme internal and external conceptions of moral authority. It contrasts with an extreme *internal* conception according to which the ground of such laws themselves (and not simply their discovery in our moral knowledge) is literally a function of the construction of human beings, be it in a whimsical individual way (which corresponds to a more popular meaning of "autonomy") or even in a highly structured and ideal communal manner (e.g., via considerations from something analogous to an "original position"). Such a conception would undermine the deep rationalist meaning of laws as strictly necessary in Kant's understanding of morality as self-*legislation*. The moderate position also contrasts with an extreme *external* conception that would give the rules of morality a constant form but only because of the incessant power of a natural or political or supernatural force. Such a conception would turn us into mere instruments rather than exemplifications of rational choice, and it would thus undermine the role of the individual self in Kant's view of morality as *self*-legislation. This moderate position might not seem to be as exciting as Kant's "Copernican" language originally suggests, but when one considers the historical and systematic positions that it excludes, including all naturalist and supernaturalist extremes, I think one can understand why Kant's notion of our practical autonomy still deserves attention, even if much of the enthusiasm for it in the past may have rested on misunderstandings and crude images of various kinds of bootstrapping (what Kierkegaard called flogging oneself to mimic real authority).

Parallel arguments can be found in the domain of theoretical autonomy, where Kant has a moderate position that again excludes extreme and naive internal and external conceptions of knowing. Given Kant's presumptions about a priori theoretical knowledge, the "self" that legislates the laws according to which we must know the objects of experience cannot literally be, as on an extreme internal view, the self in its distinctively human, that is, spatiotemporal qualities. A human self, a *Homo sapiens,* is defined as a particular kind of spatiotemporal object, so it cannot *as such* be the *source* of spatiotemporality itself. Moreover, as such a human self, it is even more evident that it also cannot (either individually or as a biological species) be the source of the more fundamental categories of the pure understanding, for these have a necessary general meaning that is broader and more basic than that of spatiotemporal concepts. This meaning is precisely what Kant himself stresses in pointing out the basic difficulty of his transcendental deduction, namely, how concepts with a source that is independent of space and time can still be shown to be valid for all that is within space and time. This meaning is also what allows Kant to use these concepts (e.g., in his account in the postulates of God's role as an object of moral belief) for *thinking* about the moral law as holding for persons conceived of in a way that is not limited to the spatiotemporal domain. And again, not only is the basic content of the laws here not limited to a spatiotemporal human self, but the way that it is "due" to us also cannot be understood as a spatiotemporal operation, since the grounding "self" must be supposed to be precisely the source of all such operations.

Such talk leads inevitably to the issue of how the "self" of theoretical autonomy is to be conceived positively if it is not to be thought of specifically as a merely human self. Kant's answer is that it is the self described as a transcendental structure ("transcendental subject") that is relevant here; what objects – that *we can know theoretically* – must conform to is a pure epistemic subject defined in terms of general forms of intuitive and conceptual intentionality. Since this structure provides "forms," it can provide laws, that is, strict general determinations. And since *for us* these theoretical laws are *known* only as laws for objects in space and time (when understanding and sensibility are united in the schematization of spatiotemporal principles), it is understandable why Kant would say that the "conforming" relationship is rooted in the subject rather than vice versa, in objects simply as such. For, if objects are introduced, as on an extreme external model, as simply things outside us and our powers, then, no matter how these objects might affect us in an empirical or nonempirical way, there is no reason why we should think that they absolutely must fit (although, for all we know they could happen to fit) our conceptions. But if "objects" are taken to mean "objects as they can be *known* in *our* experience," then it is no wonder that these might have to conform to however it is that we are internally structured to have experience. (Note that this is only an attempt to reconstruct the beginning of Kant's position, not to defend it, or to claim that, even given these first points, it is already clear that transcendental idealism is the only possible way to understand our experience of necessary relations.)

In the theoretical domain, one might still ask at this point, as was asked with respect to the practical domain, why such general structures are to be connected specifically with the term "self," especially if the popular "human" meaning for the term precisely cannot be the correct one. The answer here is the same as in the case of moral autonomy, namely that these structures can be said to involve a self (although Kant understandably tends rather to use the more formal and less psychological term "subject") since they are internal simply in the moderate sense of reflecting our relevant essence, in this case our epistemic essence as rational epistemic subjects capable of determining theoretical truths. These structures come from our "self" or are "due to us" in that they are not simply the result of anything understood solely as an outer – merely supernatural or natural – *force*. That is, in the act of knowing we are not a wholly incidental "copying" instrument of forces; "our" very own structure has to be reflected in the laws that arise for the objects we know. It is precisely in this extended sense that Kant refers to enumerating the principles of "common logic" as a matter of finding what lies within "my own self."[16] Obviously, he is not trying to reduce formal logic to individual psychology; rather, he is letting us know that he likes to use the word "self" at times to stand for a domain of features that is necessarily available to us and not forced upon us, because it lies within our own essence as rational beings. Thus, it is not subject to the caprice of whatever is beyond us, be it sheer contingent nature or something entirely supernatural. Again, this moderate reading may not seem as exciting as what one first imagines in hearing about a Copernican revolution whereby "we" structure the world, but it still does connect in specific ways with relevant notions of the self and of legislation, and it provides for a clear contrast with extreme empiricist and speculative rationalist models of explaining experience.

The moderate reading of Kantian autonomy shows there is a way to respect the evocative language of the "Promethean" image of Kant's Copernican revolution while avoiding the absurdities of taking its talk of self-legislation in literal human terms, and while also not going so far as to insist, as many neo-Kantians do, on a reading that makes human limits the

16 Kant, *Critique of Pure Reason*, A xiv.

limits of all that there can be in Kant's philosophy. On the moderate view, there is a natural way to understand Kant's basic notion of autonomy as committed not to an escape from metaphysics altogether but rather to some fairly substantive but very limited metaphysical claims about our rational essence as practical and theoretical beings. These are literally metaphysical claims because, at the very least, their validity is prior to physical conditions altogether.

By themselves, however, these claims do not yet amount to a metaphysics of an especially threatening kind, one that asserts that, in addition to experience (theoretical and practical) and the immediate conditions in the "rational self" for its laws, there might be some other mode of existence, such as God, an "afterlife," an "I know not what in itself" underlying matter, or a nonnatural power of causality of absolute spontaneity. Nonetheless, I would not object to pursuing the idea that Kant is best understood as ultimately committed to all the additional strong metaphysical claims that have just been listed. Fortunately, such a general project does not have to be carried out at this point. For the "fate of autonomy," it is enough to focus merely on the issue of freedom, and on whether this central concept should be given a metaphysical reading in Kant.

Not surprisingly, my interpretation involves a moderate but nonetheless metaphysical and "untimely" position on this basic issue. The position is moderate in emphasizing how much Kant's antidogmatic epistemological considerations are aimed at exposing difficulties in traditional arguments for freedom.[17] The position is metaphysical in insisting on a reading of Kant as committed, despite his criticisms of all theoretical arguments, to a straightforward assertion – which is not at all the same as an "explanation" – of our absolute freedom (i.e., of our being uncaused causes).[18] The position is untimely simply because, in contrast to the "pure Kantians" of our era, it is willing to stress that such a metaphysical claim presents itself as central to the Critical philosophy – a philosophy that does, after all, speak repeatedly of such things as the "metaphysics" of morals, and its "grounding."

Many Kant interpreters seem concerned to avoid the main issue here. They prefer speaking in terms of Kant's holding only to hedges rather than to assertions, and to practical beliefs understood as *meaning merely*

17 See my *Kant's Theory of Mind* (Oxford: Oxford University Press, 1982; 2d ed., 2000).
18 This point was made, but perhaps not clearly enough, in my "Kant and Hegel on Freedom: Two Recent Interpretations," *Inquiry* 35 (1992): 329–47. Cf. Henry E. Allison's response, *Idealism and Freedom* (Cambridge: Cambridge University Press, 1997), p. 204, n. 46.

that we act "as if" we were free. In these interpretations, the issue of
freedom is sometimes bracketed altogether, since it is so tempting to
spend one's time writing about all the other intriguing aspects of the
Kantian theory, the details concerning the content and motivation of our
moral life. This can be a very profitable endeavor, but at some point this
kind of literature takes on the appearance of being written in the spirit of
those who prefer not to talk about the elephant in the room. At the least,
it plays down the fact that Kant's Critical philosophy at its very core was
committed – on whatever grounds, and with whatever strength – to taking
an assertive stand on the *existence* of absolute freedom. More than anyone
else ever had to before, Kant struggled mightily with this issue, for he had
to find some way to reconcile his unusually intense beliefs about strong
moral accountability – including especially the inadequacy of compatibilism – with his unusually strong commitment to Newtonian universal and deterministic laws. It is only natural to suppose that he thought he
had to have a literal metaphysical answer here, a substantive transcendental idealism that can leave room for existential claims about features such
as freedom in a sense that goes beyond all physical experience. This kind
of answer is certainly what his first readers, from Schleiermacher through
Hegel, supposed, and it is hard to believe that they were all wrong about
Kant's most basic intentions here.

A. 3. Metaphilosophical Complications

No doubt there are intrinsic difficulties with such a position – as there also
are for all the classic options on the problem of freedom. The main
concern for my study, however, is an interpretive issue, namely, what
happens on the hypothesis that such a metaphysical position is central to
Kant's own philosophy *and* that post-Kantian writing is primarily an attempt to work around this difficult issue. Such an approach to understanding the Critical era hardly seems irrelevant, given the well-known
central role of freedom in Fichte's philosophy and Fichte's central role as
a mediator between Kant's very first readers and the later reaction of
Hegel and others. The approach also seems very much worth taking
precisely because other interpreters, given the allergy to metaphysics that
I have been describing, have tended not to give it full attention.

The "fate of Kantian autonomy" is thus in large part a story about how
the original post-Kantians reacted to the metaphysical problem of absolute freedom, and about the question of whether they could hold onto
anything like Kant's original notion of autonomy without continuing to

accept the original metaphysical meaning of its ground. The retrogressive conclusion of my story will be the claim that the first post-Kantians gave answers to the problem that were usually much worse than whatever Kant himself had to offer – and that later "post-Kantians" have not removed these difficulties. However, even if the problem of our absolute freedom is central to the story of the development of philosophy in Kant and after, it is not the whole story; there are a host of other basic problems intersecting with the notion of autonomy. For example, in theoretical philosophy, there is the difficult issue of the nature of self-determination in apperception; in practical philosophy there is the difficult issue of finding a sustainable notion of self-satisfaction in radical moral commitment and development, and in metaphilosophy there is the general issue of justifying the autonomy of philosophy itself. Here my findings involve a more complex pattern. I will argue that on all these issues there are post-Kantian (original and current) confusions about autonomy that are closely tied up with other significant misconceptions about Kant and philosophy in general. At the same time, however, there definitely are significant contributions made by the post-Kantians, and I will give special attention to those aspects of their work that help to bring out some difficulties in Kant's work on these particular issues.

The main problem that I will be stressing in Kant's system has to do with the methodological issue of his complex attitude toward the status of arguments for freedom. For *interpretive* purposes, I will be emphasizing that the claim of absolute freedom is central to Kant's own conception of philosophy, and that in many ways he is clearer than his successors about the standards philosophy must meet in approaching that issue. My own *evaluative* position, however, leaves room for the complex view that Kant may have been mistaken about the metaphysics that his own ethical theory requires, and that, in any case, given his own admirable standards of argument, there are problems with his commitment to asserting the absolute freedom that he thought was needed. In particular, I believe matters might have been much easier for him if he had given more weight to the thought that, at a significant commonsense level as well as upon full theoretical reflection, compatibilism can survive as an acceptable view and as one that can be reconciled with the *content* of even Kant's demanding morality. This is not to say that in his mature work Kant himself would have accepted compatibilism in any ordinary sense. Rather, I am merely making a plea for what I understand would definitely be a revised Kantian position but not a radically revised one, for it would involve a moderate modification that still would not insist on banishing metaphysics alto-

gether or dispensing with the core of Kant's epistemological and normative doctrines. In the end, I see Kant's ethics as best defended in terms
that, ironically, Hegel emphasizes better than anyone else (terms that
bring out the concrete "conditioning" and reinforcing factors at the heart
of moral identity), even though on my view Hegel does not make a clear
presentation of the most relevant points within his own position (since he
fails to see the point of focusing on causal theories such as compatibilism)
or make a proper explicit comparison of it with Kant's.

I will not be setting out a case for compatibilism itself here. Rather, I
will be focusing simply on the fact that, contrary to the supposition of
most of the thinkers close to Kant himself, it is not obvious that noncom-
patibilism is intrinsically the best position on freedom. Moreover, non-
compatibilism raises especially severe general methodological problems
for Kant given his own conception of philosophy as having to answer to
common sense. The problems in the discussion of the specific issue of
freedom in Kant's Critical period are simply one vivid example of the
general difficulty of Kant's influential effort to find a philosophy that is at
once professionally solid, "scientific" in his special sense, and yet also fully
satisfying to what is taken to be our proper commonsense perspective.[19] A
Kantian solution to the problem of freedom in this extremely challenging
context has to meet two very different kinds of conditions. First, it has to
work out all the metaphysical technicalities in a way that puts it at least on
a par with all the other most sophisticated options; and second, it has to
do so in a way that does not insult what appears to be sacrosanct for the
"common standpoint." And yet, despite Kant's general respect for some
kind of notion of common sense as a limiting condition on philosophy, it
seems that he did not give adequate attention to the possibility that the
widespread compatibilist understanding of freedom, shared by his Leibnizian and Humean opponents among others, is at least as close to ordinary views as is his own adamantly noncompatibilist position.

The difficulty regarding practical freedom is closely related to a problem
with another basic aspect of Kant's doctrine of autonomy, namely his
influential idea that philosophy itself is autonomous. Kant provides not
only the definitive expression of the philosophy of autonomy; he is also a
major advocate of the idea of the autonomy of philosophy, and he is
unique in the way that he combines both of these concerns. He advocates

---

19 The broad and often unappreciated concern with common sense (or "natural consciousness") in this period is noted by Rolf-Peter Horstmann, *Die Grenzen der Vernunft* (Frankfurt:
Anton Hain, 1991), p. 40. This topic is explored in more detail in Chapter 1 below.

a metaphysical but moderate view on both doctrines. On the general doctrine of autonomy, he holds that the most distinctive feature of human beings is that they are self-legislating, but in a way that cannot be understood in simply natural terms or given a strict demonstration that establishes its crucial nonnatural component. In this way Kant stands between those who would reduce theoretical or practical spontaneity to some kind of mere relative freedom and those who say that there is some kind of demonstration or intuition, theoretical or practical, that actually discloses our more than relative freedom. In other words, for Kant what is most important about us is too momentous to be watered down but also too mysterious to be presumed to allow of direct evidence in any ordinary sense.

His doctrine of the autonomy of philosophy expresses a similarly moderate position between reductionism and dogmatism, for Kant does not allow philosophy to be entirely subsumed under other fields, nor does he think that it can work in complete independence of other knowledge. Kant stresses that philosophy, more than any other discipline, can and should govern itself. It cannot be a mere subsection of any of the natural sciences (or other disciplines, as he emphasizes in *The Conflict of the Faculties*), which are too specific and contingent in their detail, nor can it be a merely formal discipline, without concrete claims about the world of experience and the essences of individual beings. Philosophy thus cannot work in isolation from other branches of knowledge; it must presume and incorporate what seems irresistible to theoretical and practical experience. In addition, Kant sees that philosophy has come to a point where it must also acknowledge the framework of the modern scientific revolution as placing some kind of general limits on all that from now on can "come forth as legitimate metaphysics." Like ordinary theoretical and practical life, philosophy is only self-legislating and not self-creating, for it can only propose laws and structures for data that must be given to it and that cannot be deduced entirely from its own resources.

Kant's moderate philosophy of autonomy and his moderate view of the autonomy of philosophy itself are related. If philosophical truth were limited to being nothing more than science or common belief, it could never give adequate sustenance to the idea of absolute freedom that he takes to be crucial to autonomy in general. Fortunately, philosophy has resources within itself to generate metaphysical structures, such as transcendental idealism, which can provide a means for saving our ineradicable pre-philosophical interest in features such as freedom. Unlike many of the post-Kantians, however, Kant does not encourage the suggestion that philosophy, whatever its particular starting point, might be so strongly foundational, so capable of developing a system out of itself, that it could avoid first exploring and respecting the boundary conditions that are laid down with the development of modern natural science. This makes science for Kant much more of an initial and external constraint on philosophy than it was for Reinhold, Fichte, and even Hegel (whose interest in the natural sciences is not to be denied). For the Critical philosophy this means, for example, that the doctrine of determinism within nature, which Kant believed modern science requires, also requires philosophers not to proceed until they can reconcile their system with it. This leaves Kant with a special vulnerability but also a distinctive flexibility. With basic changes in science (which he could not envision, but which we now know are not merely possible but even actual) or even in our central "commonsense" conceptions (e.g., about equality), the constraints that precondition the Critical philosophy can take on a new configuration. One can thus imagine a series of "successor" Critical philosophies,[20] each incorporating these changes and carrying out improved attempts to outline the constitutive features of experience, newly conceived, in a manner that is parallel to Kant's earlier efforts, even if differing from the *Critique* on particular principles. I am suggesting that even our understanding of an issue such as compatibilism (understood as a position that does not deny the possibility of absolute, libertarian freedom but simply tries to proceed without insisting on it) might develop in such a way that it could trigger a kind of moderately revised Kantianism, a philosophy of autonomy that slightly modifies its underlying metaphysics while holding onto its core ethical content. Such a new Kantianism would be unlike that of the "pure Kantians" insofar as it would understand itself historically and would see itself as a dialectical refinement of crucial metaphysical dimensions of the original Critical philosophy. This is close to what "post-Kantians" want, but not quite. Kant, even after the experience of Hegel, can still remain Kant; necessity and metaphysics can still be maintained even with the recognition that our characterization of specific categories, including the notion of action, may have to be significantly improved over time.

But this is only my own imagined happy ending. The first post-Kantians had much more radical dialectical proposals. Rather than introducing flexibility, they wanted to construct a system that would be even more certain, expansive, and unified than Kant's own. Losing sight of the full

20 For an espousal of one version of such a flexible Kantianism, see Michael Friedman, "Kantian Themes in Contemporary Philosophy," *Proceedings of the Aristotelian Society*, supp. vol. 72 (1998): 111–29. Cf. below Chapter 1.

difficulty of proving autonomy at all, they wanted to leap ahead to insure the most complete autonomy for philosophy itself. But at critical points the old central problem came back time and again. Reinhold, Fichte, and Hegel each wanted a philosophy of freedom much more radical than Kant's, but for each of them one can find at least as many difficulties as Kant had in addressing the issue of freedom directly. The chapters that follow will trace these difficulties in detail.

B. A ROAD MAP TO THE MAIN STAGES OF KANT AND AFTER

This book has four main parts: Kant, Reinhold, Fichte, Hegel. Part I sets out a brief interpretation of Kant as holding to a relatively modest system, culminating in a doctrine of autonomy that does not entirely resolve the difficulty of grounding an absolute claim to freedom. Part II is the most distinctive feature of the volume (and includes the largest amount of previously unpublished material), an extended argument that it is Reinhold above all who determined the image of Critical philosophy, and that he did so in ways that continue to have deleterious effects on our whole understanding of modern philosophy. I offer historical hypotheses about the motivations behind the remarkable reception and development of Reinhold's extraordinarily ambitious and ill-founded first system, an *Elementarphilosophie* that aimed at preserving autonomy at all costs. Part III argues that Fichte's system can be understood as largely an attempt that takes over almost all of Reinhold's basic framework and modifications (and distortions) of Kant but incorporates them into a system of autonomy based more clearly (but not unambiguously) on practical considerations. Part IV then examines Hegel's system as another kind of continuation of Reinhold's project by more complex means, one that inherits many earlier misconceptions about Kant but also offers some corrective to the one-sidedness of the first post-Kantians. One significant development here is that, like Kant (but without clearly realizing that he is following Kant), Hegel moves beyond the unfortunate representationalist tendencies of Reinhold and Fichte, as well as their very influential predecessors, Jacobi and Hume.[21] By "representationalist," I mean any the-

---

21 This development is what eventually made possible the current Sellarsian appropriation of both Kant and Hegel by philosophers such as John McDowell and Robert Brandom. This very significant appropriation is not traced in this volume, but see Robert Pippin, "Introduction: Hegelianism?" in *Idealism as Modernism: Hegelian Variations* (Cambridge: Cambridge University Press, 1997), pp. 1–25. On Kant, cf. below Chapter 1, sec. B. 3; and A.

oretical philosophy that insists on starting from the perspective of a "veil of ideas," that is, the premise that what we *first know* are immediate private objects such as sense data (and thus remains obsessed with problems of skepticism about the external world). I take it that, although this point continues to be surrounded by misunderstandings, Kant was not a "representationalist" in this sense at all, although he does use the notion of representation in other ways – for example, in a common and quite harmless distinction between signs or thoughts from the things that they are about (see below Chapter 1, sec. B.3).

The four parts of the volume consist of eight essays altogether. The two main essays on Hegel are chapters that include virtually unmodified versions of earlier articles, while all the other essays, except for Chapter 3, consist primarily of new or heavily revised material. Part I consists of one chapter on Kant, which draws together many themes from my earlier Kant interpretations and connects them with some discoveries in the latest work on the first post-Kantian figures. This chapter does not attempt to provide a full defense of its reading of Kant, but it does lay out the fundamental points of what is meant to be an appealing and distinctive approach to Kant's entire Critical project. It emphasizes how an appreciation for the context of Kant's work reveals that, despite first appearances, his Critical system has a much more modest and defensible conception of philosophical systematicity than any found in his predecessors, the "classical moderns" from Descartes to Hume, or his successors, the German idealists who culminate with Hegel. I explain how this modest conception was misunderstood by all but a few of Kant's initial readers and how, as a consequence, it is still passed over by influential current interpreters, who often inappropriately align him with the skeptical problems of the classical representationalist tradition.

In providing a brief outline of Kant's system as a whole, I specify its major components in terms of a four-part structure that is also useful for bringing out contrasts with the much more ambitious idealist systems that succeeded it. With respect to their formal role, the four parts of Kant's system, and of each of its major subsystems, can be distinguished as: (1) its starting point, (2) its set of derived principles, (3) its interpretation of the domain of these principles, and (4) its account of the goal of the whole.

Collins, *Possible Experience: Understanding Kant's Critique of Pure Reason* (Berkeley: University of California Press, 1999), Chapter 5, "The Concept of Representation." One can appreciate Collins's especially clear formulation of this familiar point without going so far as to adopt his tendency not to use the term "idealist" for Kant at all.

With respect to their content, these four parts are: (1) an epistemic notion of experience as fundamentally judgmental, (2) a set of transcendental arguments concerning necessary conditions of this experience, (3) a metaphysical doctrine of transcendental idealism as an interpretation of the meaning of these conditions, and (4) a combined metaphysical and moral theory that shows how all these components together provide for the fulfillment of our underlying concern with autonomy. I go on to argue that although all of these parts, including its innovative common-sense starting point, were immediately and severely criticized, Kant's system holds up well against the extreme claims of the philosophies that succeeded it. The most influential part of the system, however, is its doctrine of autonomy, and this inherits the difficulties of the rest of the system while also introducing a special problem of its own because of Kant's final belief that freedom must be understood in a strong, or "transcendental" sense, and that it is revealed to us only as a "fact of reason." A full understanding of this idea requires an appreciation of Kant's special effort to defend his crucial strong conception of freedom in a way that meets metaphysical and popular demands at once. I conclude that this effort falls short of Kant's own highest standards – but also that it turns out that all later attempts in the idealist tradition to justify a doctrine of autonomy have difficulties that are at least as severe as Kant's, and are often much worse.

Part II is devoted to an extensive chapter on K. L. Reinhold, with an explanation of how his work determined the reception of the Critical philosophy from the very beginning. Reinhold's interpretation of Kant, followed immediately by the presentation of his own system, was the most influential philosophical event of its time (the classical period in Jena in the decade after Kant's *Critique*), and it continues to have significant indirect effects that have not been fully appreciated. Reinhold modified the Critical philosophy so that it looked as if it required what I will call a "strong foundational" program. This program would replace Kant's four relatively modest steps with four highly ambitious ones: (1) an absolutely certain basis in the mere notion of representation, (2) a fully "rigorous science" with exhaustive and absolutely necessary principles, (3) a "short argument" to idealism that makes the very thought of a thing in itself beyond experience totally "unthinkable," and (4) an insistence on freedom as an absolutely primitive, intuitive "fact." These four points are also characterized as Reinhold's insistence on a philosophy that is at once radically (1) public, (2) professional, (3) bounded (limited to human experience), and (4) oriented above all toward justifying and developing human autonomy. I explain how these Reinholdian modifications are understandable responses to points commonly raised against Kant, and also how they involve serious distortions of the Critical philosophy and lead to a system much more vulnerable than Kant's own. Given these problems, one cannot help but wonder how Reinhold's bold new system could have come about and been received so positively at first. I argue at length that a full appreciation of the cultural context of Reinhold's era and the force of his pro-Enlightenment sentiments can make the genesis and reception of his work at least understandable, even if all its innovations are unacceptable. I also argue that Reinhold is responding to, and in part responsible for, various strong foundationalist conceptions of philosophy that still play a major role not only in Kant interpretation but also, unfortunately, in indirectly determining our sense (as expressed, e.g., in the work of Richard Rorty) of the major options available for contemporary philosophy. This is a reason why it is especially important to keep in mind the alternative of a modest system more like Kant's original one.

Part III comprises three chapters on Fichte's philosophy, the first of which reproduces a relatively short article that contains *in nuce* the original guiding ideas for this present book-length study. This pivotal chapter begins with a highly concentrated version of the main points that are now laid out at length in the first two chapters of this study. After recapitulating the fundamental features of Kant's philosophy and Reinhold's reaction to it, the major section of the essay goes on to explain how Fichte's philosophy can be understood as a radicalization of Reinhold's revisions of Kant. Fichte holds onto Reinhold's formal insistence on the "strong program" of an absolutely unified foundational system, but he sees the difficulties that come from basing philosophy theoretically, as Reinhold did, on a notion of mere representation or a dogmatic intuition of freedom. He therefore can be understood as proposing a philosophy that aims to accomplish what Reinhold did in his four steps but now on the basis of practical considerations that involve completely dismissing things in themselves and taking strong moral claims to be the absolute source of all certainty. Fichte's "practical foundationalism" is thus an attempt to develop a thoroughly unified system from a basis that supposedly resolves the difficulties underlying not only Kant's conceptions of idealism and freedom but also Reinhold's modifications of them. Unfortunately, Fichte still takes over from Reinhold and his contemporaries (especially Jacobi) various misconceptions about Kant and theoretical philosophy that make his new approach much more problematic than Kant's own. Thus, when he goes on to radicalize Kant's special interest in practical reason, Fichte's theoretical misconceptions lead him to make claims that are even more vulnerable than Kant was to charges of having an inadequate basis for the commitment to an extremely strong notion of freedom.

The next two chapters discuss in more detail recent attempts to vindicate the practical and the theoretical dimensions of Fichte's philosophy as an improvement on Kant. Chapter 4 focuses on further documenting Fichte's "practical foundationalism" and on clarifying his notion of the radical primacy of the practical in a specifically moral sense. I point out reasons for concurring with recent views that in its conclusions and orientation Fichte has a basically "objective" philosophy that is not "one-sided" in any individual or psychological sense. At a methodological level, however, I add criticisms of Fichte and his followers for engaging in a hasty dismissal of theoretical considerations. In not considering the full range of metaphysical threats to claims of freedom, Fichte's method still remains "one-sided" in comparison with Kant's more balanced approach. The chapter ends with evaluations of important recent apologies for Fichte by Robert Pippin and Allen Wood. As an alternative to my reading of Fichte as a "practical foundationalist," Pippin stresses passages in Fichte that suggest that our activity in the general context of argumentative reasoning reveals a different kind of ground for philosophy in normative considerations that are not specifically moral. I offer a reading of these passages that notes their limitation to an opponent using a very restricted "mechanistic" approach. I also argue that these passages are connected in the text to two nearby claims (that "freedom precedes being" and that his determinist opponent has a merely instrumental view of reason) in a way that shows Fichte can still be read as implicitly relying, even here, on an argument involving controversial moral considerations. In defense of Fichte's practical way of basing philosophy on the "I," Wood's interpretation stresses different passages that suggest there is a dialectical process in developing our self-consciousness that can "demonstrate" our freedom and the existence of objects in a way that Kant could only "postulate." If successful, Fichte could achieve Reinhold's goals of improving on Kant by completely unifying philosophy and overcoming skepticism. Here again I point out weaknesses in Fichte's arguments and in the whole notion of a radically practical foundation for philosophy. I add some contextual and historical considerations, picking up on earlier points about Reinhold, to help explain why writers in Fichte's position were so desperately interested in finding a system that is "scientific" and "practical" at once, while leaving traditional metaphysics behind.

Chapter 5 focuses on the notion of the act of apperception, which has a central position in Kant's *Critique* and Fichte's appropriation of it in his account of the active nature of "self-positing" self-consciousness. I note a specific sense in which Kant's own extremely influential principle that all "our" representations are subject to an original unity of apperception seems to make a stronger claim than is intrinsically defensible or clearly needed for his own system. Stronger, that is, even more controversial, versions of this principle can be found in the work of important recent Kant interpreters such as Dieter Henrich, as well as in Fichte as interpreted recently by Frederick Neuhouser. I criticize their accounts of apperception as being vulnerable to even more difficulties than Kant's. I conclude by noting similar difficulties in recent attempts to utilize Kant's notion of apperception to answer Hume's skepticism. This chapter can be understood as a plea for a return to a very modest conception of apperception, one that does not exaggerate its place in Kant's work or overload it with the ambitious Fichtean goals of current interpreters.

The fourth and final part of this book consists mainly of two extensive essays on Hegel's relation to Kant. The first essay (Chapter 6) outlines and criticizes the fundamentals of Hegel's objections to Kant's theoretical philosophy, whereas the next essay (Chapter 7) concerns fundamental issues in Hegel's reaction to Kant's practical philosophy.[22] A brief final chapter provides a retrospective postscript on my interpretation of the era as a whole.

These chapters are all anticipated by brief remarks at the end of Chapter 3 that outline a way in which Hegel's system can also be understood as a radical variation on Reinhold's four-part modification of Kant's system. Unlike Fichte, Hegel does not invoke an entirely "practical foundation." Instead, he tries to get around Fichte's objections to metaphysics by dismissing the "one-sided" (i.e., excessively subjective) representationalist presuppositions about theoretical philosophy that Fichte carries over

---

22 Except for the addition of some introductory remarks and the corrections of some minor errors, printer's mistakes, and small adjustments in the format of references and partitions, I have left these essays on Hegel almost entirely in their original wording. They were originally conceived in the context of planning the overall project of this work, they are otherwise not easily accessible, and they have taken on a position in the literature for some time in this form. See, e.g., Paul Guyer, "Thought and Being: Hegel's Critique of Kant," in *The Cambridge Companion to Hegel*, ed. Frederick Beiser (Cambridge: Cambridge University Press, 1993), p. 205, n. 1; and Henry E. Allison, *Kant's Theory of Freedom* (Cambridge: Cambridge University Press, 1990), pp. 272–3. Hegel research has in the meantime made considerable progress, but I believe that the fundamental problems of the Kant-Hegel relation remain largely the same as before concerning the main issues of this book. See Chapter 8 below.

from Reinhold and others. Unfortunately, Hegel himself carries over from Fichte the Reinholdian supposition that Kant has (1) a starting point that is too contingent, as well as (2) a way of developing principles that is not absolutely necessary and (3) an idealism that does not go far enough in excluding as wholly "unthinkable" what is beyond experience. The result is (4) a philosophy that still aims to achieve a version of Reinhold's overly ambitious objective of a system that is completely unified, all-inclusive, and in that sense absolutely (rather than "moderately") autonomous.

In laying out Hegel's critique of Kant's theoretical philosophy, Chapter 6 focuses on objections to Kant's transcendental deduction and transcendental idealism. I note that, like many later interpreters, Hegel does not appreciate the distinctive and relatively modest character of these doctrines. Hegel's critique of the transcendental deduction misconceives Kant's starting point and procedure, and it appears to repeat some confusions about apperception found in Fichte's discussion. Hegel holds onto Reinhold's presumptions that philosophy requires a beginning that can be fully self-justified and developed in a manner that does not involve any contingent steps or any possible features of reality beyond what is absolutely necessary for the satisfaction of self-consciousness. Hegel also charges that Kant illegitimately seeks a "preliminary" study of knowing independent of knowledge itself – but this criticism appears to rest again on a conflation of Kant's procedures with those of his representationalist predecessors. Hegel treats Kant's claims about the limitations of our knowledge as if they were a presumption of his methodology, whereas in fact they arise only as metaphysical conclusions drawn from specific features of the limited idealism that Kant grounds at the end of his system. This point leads to an evaluation of Hegel's direct response to Kant's transcendental idealism. Hegel's criticisms here are divided into a global attack on the notion of a thing in itself and specific attacks on the arguments of Kant's Transcendental Dialectic. The global attack can be understood as one more effect of taking over a bad Reinholdian version of the Critical philosophy and of unfairly presuming that Kant's own notion of the thing in itself is vulnerable to the absurdities of the notion that Reinhold defines as "unthinkable." I offer a more limited criticism of Hegel's specific response to Kant's Antinomies and Paralogisms. Without defending Kant's own controversial claims to establish transcendental idealism, I note that Hegel tends to evade the specific problems of Kant's arguments and to substitute for them matters of interest for his own system, for example, the "dynamic" self-developing quality of mind.

I go on to give a more positive evaluation of the practical side of Hegel's philosophy. Like most recent interpreters, I agree that, despite Hegel's own protestations, the evaluation of this part of his work can be separated from most of the other, overly metaphysical aspects of his system. Hegel's critique of Kant's practical philosophy deserves special attention, both for its originality and relative independence from the misunderstandings of the other post-Kantians as well as for its special relevance to contemporary criticisms of Kantian moral theory. The structure of the discussion here makes use of Hegel's own characterization of the contrast between his approach and Kant's as involving three major issues: The possibility, content, and motivation of moral action. The major part of Chapter 7 focuses on the problem of motivation, which has played the key role in recent neo-Hegelian attacks on Kantian morality. I review Kant's discussion of the motivations of respect and love, and point out various ways in which he could reply to common criticisms that his conception of morality excludes the role of a wide range of appropriate emotions. Here it is important to understand how much Kant's theory develops in his later works by including a more detailed account of the way that moral commitments need to be and can be sustained by means of attitudes grounded in the hopes and effects involved with various religious and social factors. I argue that Kant's account in his *Religion* of how an ethical community can "move toward" a "kingdom of God" is a major influence on Hegel's work from the beginning. Kant's discussion of the postulates of pure practical reason, which ground our hope in such a kingdom, was a major issue in Tübingen, where Hegel and other major post-Kantians were trained. Hegel's own original dialectical and secular concept of autonomy turns out to have its roots in an attempt to find ways for escaping the paradoxes of Kant's account of how we need to go through a "revolution" in character in order to become good and to maintain a rational hope for a decent future. In giving an entirely this-worldly account of moral change and the sacrifices that morality demands, Hegel radicalizes the approach that characterized Reinhold and the first post-Kantians when they tried to appropriate the *Critique* in the service of the immediate practical objectives of the Enlightenment. Hegel's account has the advantage that it can explain moral attitudes in terms of the natural, social, and historical factors that seem relevant today; a disadvantage of the theory (in addition to its overconfident optimism) is that it relativizes freedom in way that in effect leaves Kant and the whole libertarian tradition behind even while it disingenuously maintains much of the language of that tradition.

In a final chapter I continue the discussion of the systematic role of the notion of freedom. On my reading, Kant himself is a strong libertarian, but he ultimately has inadequate grounds for his position, whereas Hegel is ultimately an antilibertarian, although he obscures this fact with conflicting types of rhetoric about freedom. Despite his confusing language, I see Hegel as offering an extremely strong challenge to Kant's libertarianism, and as introducing a view that could have been developed into an appealing form of compatibilism. From this perspective Kant's weakness is not, as is often supposed, that his strong metaphysical notion of freedom is itself incoherent or in direct conflict with the rest of his system; the problem is simply that his theory seems not clearly needed or desirable, for the reasons brought out in Hegel's discussion of moral change. By bracketing the idea of a radically evil noumenal self, and by focusing on deep modifications in one's self-conscious relation to a community, Hegel can more easily explain how a person can maintain identity through a process of "moral revolution" that is truly fundamental and not only an appearance of character alteration.

For these reasons, I believe that, like Kant himself, Kantians need to say much more about compatibilism if they are going to insist on rejecting it in the face of Kant's own theory of the law-governed nature of human experience. Although it is clear that in his Critical period Kant himself could never have accepted compatibilism, compatibilism looks more and more like a position that his value theory may have to live with (as Kant did in his earlier work), and it is worth considering closely, since even most neo-Kantians seem comfortable with holding onto the content of most of Kant's normative theory without insisting on the ultimate libertarian bases of his theory of action. Many neo-Kantians appear to reject libertarianism from the start as a wholly mysterious leap into bad metaphysics, but even without going this far – and instead accepting, as I do, that "transcendent" metaphysical claims, inside or outside Kant's philosophy, need not be sheer nonsense – it is still possible to use Kant's own commitment to a philosophy that would respect common sense, as far as possible, as a ground for backing off from an unqualified commitment to absolute freedom – even commitment to a kind that only insists that we must act "as if" free.

Criticisms from another direction can be made of Hegel's system, which has been praised for ultimately abstracting altogether from causal considerations of moral action. In contrast, I argue that rather than giving, as he should have, a clear explanation of why causal considerations are not threatening to morality from a compatibilist perspective, what Hegel actually does is present remarks that in some places suggest a straightforward determinist theory and at other places a straightforward libertarian theory. The main point of my concluding section thus brings back the main theme of this Introduction, namely that the whole discussion of moral action in Hegel as well as in the contemporary "pure Kantian" and "post-Kantian" literature would benefit from addressing the metaphysical issues such as freedom much more directly. Even if one ends up with allowing a compatibilist position that says in one sense we are free (qua carrying out actions that involve the direction of our own rational mind) while in another sense we may also be determined (qua instantiating events that fall under natural causal laws), this is better than supposing that we can put off altogether the assertion of possible truths about what our ultimate causal situation is, as opposed to expressing simply how we might feel we "have" to think about it "from a practical point of view" or when "abstracting" from causal factors for specific purposes. In the end, without endorsing all the specifics of Kant's metaphysics, I do strongly endorse his insistence that philosophers need to come to a clear statement on metaphysical issues such as freedom and to explain whether their positions in fact allow that all our action may be ultimately caused, no matter how it may appear to us in certain contexts. This point is itself compatible with seeing the road from Kant to Hegel, especially on the central issue of autonomy, as pointing to some significant ways to improve the original Critical project, even if most of the proposals that were made along the way, and that were most influential, involve serious misrepresentations of Kant as well as deep misunderstandings about the viable objectives of philosophy in general.

In these introductory remarks I have had to simplify matters enormously, and I realize that many controversial points have been left without substantiation. In the chapters that follow, I present considerably more documentation in the course of spelling out my explicitly pro-Kantian reading of what I take to be the most basic points of the whole complex post-Kantian period. I have tried to keep the study as short as possible, and this means that there remains an enormous amount of relevant material in this field that does not receive attention or even mention. (Some topics arising from the very latest scholarship on Hegel, for example, have had to be put off for another occasion.) At a certain point, trying to add more detail can be self-defeating. Near-thousand-page volumes on very small periods in this era are now becoming not uncommon, and although many of them are very useful, they also present obvious difficulties for their readers, obvious strains for finite eyes and brains. Very short studies –

individual articles or relatively superficial surveys – also have their uses and their serious limitations. Scholarship on this period is growing exponentially, but there remains the danger that we will be dominated by the limited genres of the narrow article and the bland or indigestible encyclopedic overview. This volume attempts something in between a straightforward, exhaustive narrative and a mere collection of highly specific studies. The chapters have been written so that in principle they can be read independently and in any order (with many cross-references so that one can skip around to discussions of related topics as one wishes), and in fact they were initially composed over a fairly long period of time that does not correspond to the order of presentation here. However, they are also designed to be read from start to finish, and to reinforce one another so that they can make a cumulative impression that adds up to one relatively compact and unified picture of the most basic components of the period as a whole, understood as a sequence of reactions to and modifications of the core of Kant's philosophy.

More specifically, my intent has been to focus on the central themes that make clear my own distinctive and critical way of understanding the whole period, namely as the dramatic rise, decline, and fall of the project of absolute autonomy. In this way readers have at least a provocative guide, one concrete proposal of a way to order the mass of historical complexities. There are obviously other grand narratives that can be offered, and I would hope that readers try to keep in mind the need to assess views of the whole as well as of the parts. Fortunately, there are already many masterful recent accounts of relatively specific topics in this period that readers can also fall back on and that have certainly been a great source of inspiration and information for me. Books by Beiser, Wood, Pippin, Allison, and Neuhouser (to name just a few with a large influence) have each focused intensely on various parts of the big story that I have been trying to construct for the period as a whole, and it is a misleading fact that most of my references to their work here happen to touch only on points of difference.

PART I

KANT

KANT'S MODEST SYSTEM

I want to have only a piece of the system of the whole of human cognitions, namely the science of the highest principles, and such a project is modest.

Metaphysik Mrongovius[1]

From a contemporary perspective, this remark, like Kant's Critical writings in general, can easily appear to suffer from a laughable fascination with systematicity, and to indicate an attitude that does serious injustice to both theoretical and practical realities by distorting issues in order to satisfy an obsession with formal principles. This common and harsh view of Kant has several understandable sources, no doubt, but I believe that a close look at the actual context of his work reveals that this kind of criticism distorts and covers over what are really the most distinctive features of the Critical philosophy. In contrast to most of his predecessors and successors, Kant's Critical work, as it was actually carried out, can be shown to be remarkably modest and sophisticated in its conception of the

1 *Lectures on Metaphysics/ Immanuel Kant*, ed. and trans. Karl Ameriks and Steve Naragon (Cambridge: Cambridge University Press, 1997), p. 111. *Kant's gesammelte Schriften* (Berlin: Preussische Akademie der Wissenschaften/ de Gruyter, 1900–), vol. 29, p. 748. Hereafter the latter work will be cited as *AA*.

systematic nature of philosophy – even if it does betray a weakness for
grand programmatic statements which led to unfortunate misunderstandings.

That there is a looseness in Kant's system is clear enough simply from
the fact that the best-known philosophers who came after him, the German idealists, all immediately castigated Kant for not at all setting up the
kind of absolutely certain and unified system that they believed philosophy clearly requires. Similarly, it takes only a little reflection to see that, in
contrast to the main traditions before him – the scholastics, the great
modern philosopher-scientists, and the all-leveling skeptics and radical
empiricists – Kant's philosophy has an unusual openness to a wide variety
of considerations and a special respect for universal common sense.
Nonetheless, from the perspective of much late twentieth-century
thought, the Kantian system often still appears to be a paradigm case of
the overambitious and artificial demands of traditional philosophy. My
hypothesis is that this perspective is due in large part to our own century's
casual attitude toward texts and history, and to a sequence of peculiar
turns in the development of the anarchic metaphilosophy that dominates
our fin de siècle: consider the ever-growing influence of Nietzsche, the
late Heidegger, and so-called postmodernism in continental thought; or,
in analytic schools, the rise of antiphilosophical forms of naturalism after
the collapse of grand programs such as positivism and the "linguistic
turn." In other words, the alleged problem here may be very much in the
eye of the beholder, and the result of an allergic overreaction to problems
of other systems of the past. An extra complication here is a major point I
will be emphasizing, namely, that there is a series of fateful and long-
forgotten misunderstandings in the original picture of the Critical philosophy itself that can be seen as indirectly responsible for much of the
growing discontent with systematic philosophy in general, and for the
continuing antipathy to what is taken to be the systematic form and
content of Kant's work in particular. Without being blind to weaknesses
that remain in the Critical philosophy, I believe it is possible to unearth a
"modest system" at its core, and to use Kant's own words to help explain
how the peculiarities of the immediate reception of that philosophy led to
serious misinterpretations that to this day block an appreciation for what
is truly of enduring value and current significance in the core moderate
features of Kant's idea of systematic philosophy.

Pursuing the first steps of this argument will raise a number of general
questions:

Why was modern philosophy concerned so much with system even before
   Kant?

What specific features are most relevant to Kant's own understanding of
   systematicity, especially if, as I am suggesting, it took on such a relatively
   "modest" form?

How is it that Kant's philosophy could be so criticized by some as not
   being systematic enough, and by others as trying to be much too
   systematic?

What were the main sources and consequences of the drive by Kant's
   idealist successors to make up for the lack of systematicity that they
   sensed in his philosophy?

A full answer to these questions would require, at the least, a thorough
analysis of Kant's entire work as well as a detailed narrative of the main
episodes in philosophy in the whole post-Kantian era. Such an account
would quickly become so lengthy that it would be obviously self-defeating.
Therefore, I have chosen the strategy of focusing on a few major problems,
and of repeatedly relating these to a basic pattern of issues that I see as
central to most thinkers of Kant's era, while using extensive references to
indicate where more details can be found. In this chapter, I will attempt to
do little more than to outline what seem to me to be the most important
points in Kant's own work that bear on the general systematic shape of his
philosophy. These points have been selected with an eye to helping make
intelligible the common structure in the immediate reception of Kant's
philosophy that will be described at length in the following chapters.

My discussions of these issues in Kant and in post-Kantian works will
concern questions of systematicity in both theoretical and practical philosophy, as well as the problem of the relation between these two branches
of philosophy. Not surprisingly, the status of natural science will take on a
central role in the understanding of the role and nature of the theoretical
branch of Critical philosophy, and the issue of freedom will play the
central role in the evaluation of its practical branch. I will not be presuming that there is a single answer to these questions in Kant's works; on the
contrary it will be important to trace his Critical opinions as they develop
to a high point of maturity in 1787–8, when he revises his first *Critique* and
writes his second. Throughout this process, Kant is also struggling to
define his very complex and subtle understanding of the relation between
philosophical reason and what can be called "common knowledge," that
is, the whole domain of what we are confident about in an informal way,

apart from technical philosophy and science. Although I will note that the
proper demands that Kant himself raises cause some difficulties for his
own system, I will contend that on the whole his treatment of the relation
of philosophy to what is outside of it provides a model that is still valuable
and superior to that of his major successors – once it is purified of the
distortions that were imposed upon it.

I will begin with a preliminary section (A) that offers a sketch of the
peculiar problem, within the overall framework of Kant's philosophy, of
the standing of all types of knowledge that, like philosophy itself, fall
between the extremes of rudimentary "common knowledge" and exact
scientific knowledge. Against this backdrop, I will go over again, in more
detail in the second and third sections, the historical context of Kant's
answer to the specific question of the scientific status of his own philosophy. These sections will focus on comparing Kant's conception of the key
requirement of systematicity with other very influential conceptions of it
(B) right before and (C) after him. In a final section (D) on changes in
the foundations of Kant's practical philosophy, I will explain how Kant
struggled to achieve a proper understanding of the unity of philosophy
and of the relation between the demands of metaphysics and common
sense.

Throughout, I will be arguing for a way of looking at Kant's philosophy
that takes its claim to "modesty" seriously and that can defend it as an
especially appropriate model in our own time for approaching the crucial
and often neglected issue of the role that philosophy can play as a mediator, rather than a guarantor, of common knowledge and science. While
the special strength of Kant's general approach lies in its deep appreciation of modern science, its weakness turns out to be the lack of a full
appreciation for the way that his own system raises a demand for a special
vindication of crucial presuppositions within its moral theory that go
beyond common knowledge. The strategy of Kant's successors was, by and
large, to construct systems that would aim to make up for this weakness by
trying to meet even more demanding conditions. An alternative reaction,
more in the spirit of Kant's own modest objectives, would be to relax the
foundationalist demands placed upon philosophy. My final suggestion
will be that a contemporary, flexible Kantian does best by reminding us
that that there are metaphysical considerations that philosophy must
address, but that it may be possible to carry out these considerations in a
variety of ways – for example, by explicitly leaving open libertarian and
nonlibertarian options.

A. PRELIMINARY OVERVIEW OF THE MODERN
CONTEXT OF THE CRITICAL PHILOSOPHY

The introductory observations of this first section fall into three brief subsections: (A. 1) a reminder of some basic options within the era of modern philosophy; (A. 2) a preliminary proposal about how to situate Kant's transcendental philosophy with regard to these options; and (A. 3) an elucidation of an important new problem – the problem of "in between knowledge" – that arose for this era and generated a complex Kantian response.

A. 1. Three Traditional Options

Any very brief characterization of the whole period of modern philosophy must be understood as meant with many implicit qualifications. The most obvious place to start in determining what is distinctive about modern philosophy is to focus on the remarkable phenomenon of modern science, and specifically on the new disciplines that arose with the Galilean revolution and the development of the exact science of Newtonian physics. This development by no means determined only one sort of possible philosophical reaction. I see three main lines of immediate reaction especially worth distinguishing: *skepticism, scientism,* and *classical modern systematic metaphysics*. The first two lines were encouraged by the very sharp contrast that arose between the highly theoretical and counterintuitive "scientific image" of modern physics and the range of other widespread options, especially the "manifest image" of common sense, the entrenched so-called common sense of the Aristotelian tradition, and the claims of primitive and radical empiricism.[2]

It is well known that the multiplicity of these images and the striking contrasts between them combined with other cultural developments at this time – for example, momentous religious conflicts and the new availability of ancient texts – to generate a deep and influential concern with skepticism.[3] Even when, as in Descartes, the skeptical position was not at

2 These images are emphasized in Wilfrid Sellars's very Kantian and aptly titled volume, *Science, Perception, and Reality* (London: Kegan Paul, 1963), a work that has strongly influenced philosophers concerned with Kant such as Richard Rorty, Jay Rosenberg, Robert Brandom, and John McDowell (see below at n. 34). As an exegete rather than a systematic philosopher, Sellars is one of the most reliable of Kant's readers – although most of his students have tended to follow his system more than his exegesis.
3 See, e.g., Richard Popkin, *The History of Skepticism from Erasmus to Descartes* (New York: Harper,

all presented in order to be endorsed, it hounded the modern era, at the very least until Hume – and precisely because the very rigor of modern thought disclosed more and more difficulties in finding non-question-begging philosophical responses to it. For my purposes, even philosophers who themselves are not at all skeptics can be seen as belonging to this group as long as they take – as so many still do (e.g., Stroud, Rorty, and Cavell) – the central function of philosophy as such, at least heretofore, to reside in nothing less than a discovery of, or an endless discussion about, the refutation of skepticism.

A second, "scientistic" option, which has become ever more popular in the aftermath of Hume, is to turn away from the frustrating issue of skepticism while accepting a sharp contrast between modern science and other images of reality, and then to take this contrast to signify nothing other than the sheer error of all nonscientific perspectives. On this option, philosophy becomes "scientism" when it goes beyond an intense but limited concern with science and the philosophy of science, and it embraces the radical view that responsible philosophy is *nothing other than* philosophy of science. "Scientism" was not a project well worked out in Kant's own time, but it took on a dominant position soon thereafter in positivist programs that viewed philosophy as little more than a codification of technical knowledge, knowledge accepted largely without question from ideal images of ongoing scientific disciplines.[4]

Familiar as these options have become, especially in our own time, most of classical (i.e., pre-Kantian) modern philosophy seems to have taken a third and quite different course. In rationalism and empiricism alike – in Descartes, Leibniz, Spinoza, as in Berkeley and (much of) Hume and Mill, among others – what one finds is not primarily a direct development of skepticism nor anything like a proto-Quinean physicalism. What one finds is rather the construction of intricate and massive "systems of the world," each set out with many of the formal features of the new highly systematic sciences of the Newtonian era, but with ontologies – for example, of monads or other special substances, or all-encompassing impressions – determined ultimately by philosophers alone, and in considerable contrast to the "furniture" that ordinary scientists take themselves to be discussing. Only with the decline of phenome-

---

1964); and Edwin Curley, *Descartes Against the Skeptics* (Cambridge, MA: Harvard University Press, 1978).

4 A sophisticated variation of this view is critically discussed in Michael Friedman's presidential address, "Philosophical Naturalism," *Proceedings and Addresses of the American Philosophical Association* 71 (1997): 7–21. See below at n. 23 and n. 31.

nalism and traditional idealism, and the growing anarchy of philosophical developments after the Second World War, has this remarkable option moved away from the center of the philosophical stage (even though it continues to draw highly accomplished practitioners).

A. 2. Kant's Transcendental Option

Where does Kant's philosophy fit in among these options? One could *try* to align it with any one of the three paths that have been noted, namely, the battle with skepticism, or the mere articulation of modern science, or the development of a pure philosophical ontology. In fact, many Kant interpretations have fixed on one or the other of the first two approaches, that is, the extremes of taking Kant to be basically a respondent to the skeptic (cf. Strawson, Wolff) or an apologist for the Newtonian science of his time (Körner and Weldon). I have often argued against these popular interpretive strategies,[5] and I would contend more positively now that it is most useful to think of Kant's transcendental approach as introducing a unique *fourth* basic option in response to the fundamental challenge set by the rise of modern science.

Like other options here, the Kantian *transcendental option* accepts as its starting point a *sharp apparent* contrast between common sense and modern science. However, what Kant goes on to propose is that, instead of focusing on trying to establish with certainty – against skepticism – that the objects of common sense exist, let alone that they have philosophical dominance, or, in contrast, on explaining that it is only the theoretical discoveries of science that determine what is objective, one can rather work primarily to determine a positive and balanced philosophical relation between the distinct frameworks of our manifest and scientific images.

This is, I believe, how the basic propositions of Kant's first *Critique* can best be understood. That book defends principles involving philosophical concepts, such as causality and substance, that can be taken, in different ways, as necessary framework presuppositions relevant both for ordinary empirical judgments – so that we can, for example, properly understand that a boat is moving a certain way, in objective space and time, only if we place it in relation to some general and "transcendentally" necessary principles of experience – as well as for the fundamental axioms of modern

5 See K. Ameriks, "Kant's Transcendental Deduction as a Regressive Argument," *Kant-Studien* 69 (1978): 273–87. This is not to deny that Kant was highly concerned with Humean skepticism, specifically about "reason."

physics, as Kant goes on to try to show in detail in his *Metaphysical Foundations of Natural Science*. Kant's investigations can be seen as trying, among other things, to clarify the basic meaning and metaphysical presuppositions of Newtonian axioms, and yet, since his investigations first provide a general ground for causality, they do not simply take the objective truth of the scientific principles themselves as an absolute first premise. On this strategy, one also does not aim basically at refining a special philosophical ontology for the natural world (there are complications here, for I would not deny that Kant has some important ontological concerns, and even is committed to more than what is "natural"), that is, a "new system" – to repeat a Leibnizian phrase that Kant echoed in his own early career – that competes with the entities posited by science itself. Instead, one tries to explain how the peculiar objects of modern science can cohere with the ordinary sensible judgments that we make, as well as with whatever general metaphysical commitments turn out to be unavoidable for us. In the end, particular statements about houses and boats are to be considered as backed up by reference to items that are instances of general laws covering in an exact way all sorts of theoretical entities, entities that human beings are not expected even to be *able* to perceive directly – as Kant noted with respect to small particles and magnetic fields.[6] The whole framework of these entities can be taken not to replace but just to provide a precise ground of explanation for – while also remaining epistemically dependent upon – the domain of "common knowledge" and everyday "judgments of experience" that we always need to make about the macro-objects of ordinary perception. Here one always needs to keep in mind that the terms "knowledge" (*Erkenntnis*) and "experience" (*Erfahrung*) have very specific meanings for Kant. Unlike the standard English philosophical use of the term "knowledge," Kant's term "knowledge" signifies a "lower" kind of "cognitive state" that involves a grounded or putative truth claim but not necessarily an actual truth (see A 58/B 83, "Knowledge is false, if . . . ," and see below at n. 30 and n. 41). Kant's term "experience," on the other hand, usually has a "higher" meaning than in ordinary English, since it designates what is already a cognitive state, and not a simple psychological event, a crude mere "representation" (or "idea") that is not complex enough even to be able to have a truth value.

Although his focus is on "experience" and "empirical knowledge," in his specific sense, Kant calls his philosophy "transcendental." This is be-

6 Kant, *Critique of Pure Reason*, A 226/ B 273. Quotations of this work are from the familiar Norman Kemp Smith translation (London: Macmillan, 1929), with the first and second editions designated as A and B, respectively, followed by page numbers.

cause it speaks primarily not about objects as such but about our *a priori knowledge* of objects, that is, about the general principles that seem necessary if we are to have any empirical knowledge at all – and that are also claimed to be necessary for the new exact mathematical sciences that are taken to underlie all such knowledge. For example, transcendental philosophy does not itself supply a geometrical specification of objects, but it does argue for principles that are to "make intelligible"[7] an a priori link between geometrical science and the objects of experience. In this way Kant's philosophy is unique in focusing on a level "in between" the domains of ordinary empirical judgment and theoretical science. While it accepts both domains as legitimate, it takes neither as absolute by itself but rather aims to articulate the philosophical principles they need to share in order to be jointly understandable and acceptable. Elementary common knowledge, scientific theory, and philosophical reflection are thus all intertwined in a highly structured process of reflective equilibrium.

A. 3. The Problem of the Status of Kant's Option

Whatever the immediate attractions of this Kantian option, there is an obvious new problem that must be faced by all philosophies that take very seriously the precise theoretical perspective of modern science. The problem is that even if we were to go so far as to assume an easy fit between experience and one exact scientific framework of mathematics and physics – an assumption obviously much more questionable now than two centuries ago – there remains a cluster of prestigious disciplines that do not seem limited to that austere framework. There are, for example, the post-Newtonian disciplines of psychology, of chemistry and biology, of anthropology and history ("social science"), and also, somewhere along the line, the assertions of fields such as aesthetics and philosophy itself. In all these areas, highly respected authorities claim to have attained considerable knowledge, and yet the judgments that constitute their disciplines obviously cannot in any plausible way be translated or directly transformed into the terms of either actual physics or elementary common sense – or even the constitutive principles of Kant's mediating Transcendental Analytic.

For a long time the most influential philosophical way of reacting to this difficulty was dominated by the positivist presumption that there is no deep significance in holding onto the autonomy of domains less exact

---

7 Kant, *Critique of Pure Reason*, B 41; cf. A 11 / B 25. I am not presuming that Kant's argument here is persuasive.

than physics, or – in the case of the tradition from Hume to Mill and Mach – a psychological theory of sensations designed precisely to model the latest physics. To be sure, for various heuristic and practical purposes, disciplines other than physics (and its exact correlates) might be allowed to continue, but the common presumption was that they gained their ultimate theoretical value solely from their eventual foundation (whether or not it could ever be achieved in a "reduction") in a truly "hard" foundational science. When the laws of physics came to be taken in a less mechanistic and more dynamic manner, or for a time were even transposed into psychological laws, this only underscored rather than undercut the hegemony of the form of modern physics. Descartes's philosophical disinterest in manifest empirical qualities such as color (regarded as too "confused" to be a "true" idea in the ultimate science) was an indication of the attitude that was to be typical of most scientific philosophers throughout the modern period. In the end, the account of the domain of commonsense judgments, and of all disciplines that were not expressed with the exactness of physics, was little more than a matter of pragmatics and a theory of error. (This kind of attitude can still be seen in current approaches, e.g., in philosophies of mind that take explanations couched in commonsense language to have the status of nothing more than a scientifically immature and ultimately irrelevant "folk psychology.")

There are endless complications in this story, but for our purposes the first point to note is that initially *Kant's* own account can *seem* to fall right into this general dismissive pattern of modern philosophy. But the crucial second point to note here is that Kant's approach is actually quite distinctive and has aspects that make it appear both worse and much better than the typical modern system. On the one hand, there is the embarrassing fact that sometimes Kant is extreme about an allegiance to physics and physics alone. His textbook concerning natural science explicitly excludes all psychology (and intentionally ignores history) and even chemistry (because he did not see then that it had developed its own precise quantitative explanations)[8] from the domain of genuine science, and thus it appears to turn its back on the remarkable rise of two of the major cognitive developments of his time. On the other hand, and more importantly, it is clear that as Kant moved beyond the core principles of the understanding in the Transcendental Analytic even in his first *Critique*, he focused more and more on special nonmathematical "ideas of reason"

---

8 See Michael Friedman, *Kant and the Exact Sciences* (Cambridge, MA: Harvard University Press, 1992), esp. chap. 5, sec. III.

(and, at first, he invokes something like such ideas for systematic features even of physics). He argued we also need nonmathematical ideas in order to make intelligible the vast realm of common claims about our environment that we *cannot* hope to demonstrate from physics alone – since, as he puts it, there could *never* be "a Newton" for even "a blade of grass."[9]

Thus, at the same time that Kant criticized claims made on behalf of the rigor of fields such as psychology and chemistry, he still argued that they are governed by fundamental, and not merely empirical, "regulative" principles that we should never expect to be replaced by the claims of any physics that humans could actually develop. It is important to see that Kant always insisted on an *objective* place for such principles even for disciplines that he came to criticize strongly precisely with regard to their *exact* scientific status. (Matters are complicated here by the fact that Kant often tended to *call* such principles not "constitutive," and "subjective" rather than "objective," simply because no absolute *disproof* of their opposite is available to us. But surely there is an ordinary sense in which we can understand a claim to be objective in its *meaning* even if we cannot justify saying it is a certain or essential truth.) In Kant's schoolbook tradition, psychology, for example, was presented confidently as a science, in both empirical and rational forms, just as, in what appear to be older parts of the first *Critique*, Kant himself speaks of a distinct "physiological" science of mind fully parallel to that of body.[10] By the time of the *Metaphysical Foundations* (Introduction, 1786), however, he clearly denied that psychology was a genuine *science* – and yet he never took back his claim that its "idea" of "unity" provides a basic regulative principle that *we must* always use when *objectively* (i.e., for all public, rather than random individual, purposes) investigating the mind as such. He insisted that we reason in an entirely proper and inevitable fashion here, profitably organizing our common knowledge, as long as we do not inflate this idea of the mind's unity – even of the "necessary unity of apperception" – into a certain ontological claim at *either* the level of nature or beyond.

A similar perspective can be found in Kant's remarks on the other disciplines that fall "in between" elementary common sense and physics and also the constitutive transcendental principles underlying both domains. Psychology is hardly the only example here; the *Critique of Judgment*

---

9 Kant, *Critique of Judgment*, sec. 75. Prof. Joachim Waschkies has drawn my attention to the fact that Kant is intentionally choosing a very simple form of *Kraut* here, since it was a commonplace of the period to comment on the intricate structure of more complex plants, e.g., cabbage.

10 Kant, *Critique of Pure Reason*, A 846/ B 874.

is focused largely on the claim that biology is forever to be governed by a regulative idea of purposiveness. At the same time that Kant restricts all *constitutive* claims about organisms as purposive, he also insists that in "reflectively" judging about them, as we constantly must as the finite sensible beings that we are, we cannot progress otherwise than by thinking in purposive terms, by seeing them "as if" they have a unity that is a ground and not only an effect of their parts. For anthropology and history Kant introduces the similar – although only similar – idea of a "pragmatic" or moral purposiveness that provides for a distinctive unity in the study of human beings. Just as, for all that we "really know," blind mechanism and not genuine purposiveness might be the ultimate truth about living beings as such, so too an amoral structure and pointless end "might" be the ultimate truth about the history of the human race – and yet in neither case, supposedly, can a rational human judge "really think" in such terms. In the case of human history, we even realize that the purposive structures we are most interested in are generated not so much from heuristic *scientific* considerations as from hope in a destiny satisfying our own noblest ambitions – and yet for Kant this remains a common and thoroughly *rational* hope, a moral belief answering to a general interest that is even more compelling than that of scientific systematicity. Not surprisingly, notes from Kant's metaphysics lectures even contain a statement that such "moral belief is as unshakable as the greatest speculative certainty, indeed even firmer."[11]

Kantian aesthetic theory can be seen as one more development along this line, a line where pure ideas such as unity, purposiveness, and morality are presented as rationally inescapable in very specific contexts even while their "nonconstitutive" status is repeatedly noted. For Kant, a naturally beautiful object is to be thought of as "purposive *without* a purpose" (i.e., precisely as not designed beforehand, and yet as especially "fitting" our faculties), and as "disinterestedly" pleasing, that is, apart from merely sensuous or moral grounds – and yet[12] such an object is still to be taken as truly purposive *for all of us* and pleasing in a pure way. My main point here is that this claim – whatever its limitations and whatever the general difficulties in all talk of "merely regulative" principles – is clearly taken by Kant to have a universal standing, to be a claim on all humans as such, and to be about as solid in its own way as assertions in other "in-between" fields such as psychology or even biology, where one also proceeds in making

---

11 *Lectures on Metaphysics/ Immanuel Kant*, p. 134 (*AA*, vol. 29, p. 778).
12 See the discussion and references in K. Ameriks, "On Paul Guyer's 'Kant and the Experience of Freedom,'" *Philosophy and Phenomenological Research* 55 (1995): 361–7.

legitimate and nontrivial public claims about the sensible world that are not fully exact or clearly ontologically absolute.

If so much might be claimed in a highly disputed field such as aesthetics, it would seem only fair to preserve at least an equal dignity for the claims of philosophy itself. But on what basis? Kant denies that philosophy can model itself on quantitative disciplines, and he also draws attention to the fact that its central discipline, metaphysics, does not express even an informal "common knowledge" but rather has appeared as a "battlefield of endless controversies."[13]

In order to see in what sense Kant could still believe that philosophy, which itself is neither an exact science nor a mere part of "common knowledge" or a harmonious tradition, could nonetheless amount to knowledge and eventually "come forth" as a science, we must turn now, in the second part of these considerations, to consider in more detail how Kant thought that the Critical philosophy, and it alone, manages to satisfy in an exemplary fashion the key condition of science in a *general* sense, namely, *systematicity*. This will be a complicated story because Kantian systematicity, precisely when it is most charitably understood, can seem at first to be devastatingly modest – and yet, I will argue, this very modesty will turn out to be its saving grace and what allows Kant's work to remain uniquely relevant to this day, especially for the thematization of the relation of philosophy to other fields.

B. KANT'S ANSWER: PHILOSOPHY AS A MODEST SCIENCE

B. 1. Kant on Philosophy and System

Kant claimed that his philosophy was scientific, in a broad and crucial sense, because it was so truly systematic that it alone restored the rigor to philosophy that Wolff was to be praised for at least seeking.[14] This claim was quickly and energetically disputed, but to the very end Kant wrote with uncompromising insistence about the satisfactory systematic character of his own work. Against suggestions by Fichte and others that he had fallen short in any way in this regard, Kant protested vehemently:

the assumption that I have intended to publish only a *propaedeutic* to transcendental philosophy and not the actual system of this philosophy is in-

13 Kant, *Critique of Pure Reason*, A viii.
14 Kant, *Critique of Pure Reason*, B xxxvii.

comprehensible to me. Such an intention could never have occurred to me, since I took the completeness of pure philosophy within the *Critique of Pure Reason* to be the best indication of the truth of that work.[15]

Yet the clear fact is that by his own standards Kant never actually presented a "complete" philosophy. In a letter to Jakob of September 11, 1787, he explained in a brief outline what a "short system of metaphysics" might look like,[16] but he did not publish such a system himself. He often claimed[17] that the first *Critique* could be completed easily enough in an explicit system (in its "material part") that would take the two-part form of a metaphysics of nature and a metaphysics of morals, that is, a systematic theoretical philosophy and a systematic practical philosophy. But although toward the end of his career Kant did finish a volume called *The Metaphysics of Morals* (1797), that book always remained very much overshadowed by his interjection of the *Groundwork of the Metaphysics of Morals* (1785) and the second and third *Critiques*, works that approached moral issues in ways not foreseen in his first Critical remarks on a system (see below sec. D. 2). Moreover, Kant never even published a metaphysics of nature, and this failure goes much deeper than his not getting around to supplementing the *Metaphysical Foundations of Natural Science* (1786) – his theoretical parallel to the *Groundwork* – with a completed "transition" to a full philosophy of physics in his *opus postumum*. The most startling fact is that Kant himself never made it to writing out a theoretical metaphysical system, not even something in the short outline form that he recommended to Jakob. And yet he lectured year after year on this subject, clearly presenting it as his favorite and as the compendium of theoretical philosophy as such.[18]

    If Kant had published a general metaphysics textbook, the most basic systematic issue that one would hope to find resolved in it would be the

15 Kant, Aug. 7, 1799, "Public Declaration concerning Fichte's *Wissenschaftslehre*," in *Correspondence/ Immanuel Kant*, ed. and trans. A. Zweig (Cambridge: Cambridge University Press, 1999), p. 560n (*AA*, vol. 12, pp. 370–1). For a discussion of other portions of the letter, see above Introduction, n. 3. This aspect of the letter is a bit confusing. Generally Kant distinguished, within the Critical philosophy, between the transcendental portion of his work and the properly metaphysical, systematic part. The first portion he did call a "propaedeutic" to the rest, and he did not say that he had himself completed the second portion. It is unclear what a separate propaedeutic to transcendental philosophy itself would be, or why the principles of that part of the philosophy should be taken to be "the system" rather than the crucial foundation for it.

16 Kant, *Correspondence*, p. 125.

17 E.g., Kant, *Critique of Pure Reason* A 12/ B 26.

18 See the editors' Introduction to *Lectures on Metaphysics/ Immanuel Kant;* and the new Preface to my *Kant's Theory of Mind* (Oxford: Oxford University Press, 1982; rev. ed. 2000).

unity of his work, the problem of precisely how the metaphysics of nature and the metaphysics of morals are to be related. He repeatedly claims that what distinguishes science as such is that it is a study that has a unity of principles, rather than being a mere aggregate of claims. Philosophy is distinguished from natural science simply by its offering an explanation, and not merely an employment, of a priori principles as well as empirical ones. For Kant, both natural science and metaphysics are sciences, and they are also both said to be philosophical in a broad sense, since they systematically employ reason, in the one case merely for objects of experience, in the other case in such a way that this restriction is not a matter of definition.[19]

Does the lack of a fully unified and articulated Kantian system signify only an absence of incidental detail, or does it mean, as many readers have felt, that there are fundamental flaws in his whole approach to systematicity and his whole understanding of philosophy as a science? Kant himself remained extremely confident, and concluded his repudiation of Fichte by reiterating that the first *Critique* had accomplished basically all that is needed:

> the critical philosophy must remain confident of its irresistible propensity to satisfy the theoretical as well as the moral, practical purposes of reason, confident that no change of opinions, no touching up or reconstruction into some other form is in store for it; the system of the *Critique* rests on a fully secured foundation, established forever, it will be indispensable too for the noblest ends of mankind in all future ages.[20]

These are strong words, but the fact remains that the way that Kant's "foundation" grounds the two branches of his system is not worked out anywhere in detail; the *Critique of Pure Reason* says little about practical reason, and the second *Critique* says little about theoretical reason. The third *Critique* then makes matters more complicated by not providing a unification in retrospect but rather stressing a new threefold division of faculties: understanding, judgment, and reason. By multiplying faculties, Kant would seem to be only multiplying divisions and problems, rather

---

19 See, e.g., *Lectures on Metaphysics/ Immanuel Kant*, p. 113 (*AA*, vol. 29, p. 750). Kant also links systematicity closely to "ideas of reason": "By a system I understand the unity of the manifold modes of knowledge under one idea" (A 832/ B 860). This naturally generates the question of which idea, if any, is meant to tie all of the Critical philosophy together as a system. The best candidate here may be not an "idea" on Kant's basic list but simply the concept of the self-determination of reason itself, or autonomy at a metaphilosophical level.

20 Kant, *Correspondence*, p. 254.

than providing a straightforward account of what gives his philosophy a true unity. To understand Kant's most effective answer to this worry – and to avoid losing the forest for the trees – I propose that it is better not to get entangled in his complex terminological rearrangements, but rather to step back again to consider in more detail the broader context of his work in order to see how the basic issues in his era determine what lies behind all the special concern with a system.

B. 2. For Others, Why a System?

Quite apart from Kant, a natural beginning would be to think that systematicity is at best an ideal, not a requirement of knowledge in general or of philosophical knowledge in particular. If one starts with some relatively simple things that one obviously seems to know, it is natural to try to relate these to other cognitions that one may have. But one cannot be expected at once to know everything, or even what is most relevant, so one can hardly start with a full system or outline of knowledge, or even with a certainty that all will be able to be brought into such a system. And yet the major philosophers that Kant was most familiar with, the great modern thinkers, all clearly worked with the aim of erecting a system, and took this systematic orientation to be virtually self-evident. As was noted earlier, empiricists as well as rationalists all presumed that the human mind and its operations comprise a systematically connected whole. Whether the subjective basis be innate ideas or sensible impressions, whether the objective correlates be physical structures and metaphysical grounds or mere psychological propensities and reliable constructs, and whether the claimed results be phrased in terms of absolute certainty or probability, what classical modern philosophy produces, time and time again, is a confident reconstruction of a *new comprehensive system* that both common life and technical disciplines are taken to require and to be incapable of articulating themselves.

A major inspiration for this orientation is not difficult to find: the giants of the scientific revolution, figures such as Galileo, Descartes, and Newton, managed to discover what is a *real* system, the basic components of an exact and truly universal physics that provided a way of thinking that was to be a paradigm for all later research. The strong systematicity of their works was a striking feature from the start; the general laws that they contained, and the way that they were combined to explain many very different kinds of phenomena, were crucial to their initial formulation in precise mathematical "systems of the world." But if modern science already has a systematic explanation *in nuce* of the world, there would seem to be no basic need to duplicate things with special philosophical furniture. Hence one might well expect that the evident success of these scientific systems would have been a development encouraging the immediate demise of philosophy as a major discipline, or perhaps its return to something more in the form of rhetoric. What actually happened, however, is that philosophy experienced a remarkable expansion and flowering, with Descartes influencing everyone else by working out not only a new physics but also a "foundation" for it, with epistemological considerations and ontological components that are presented explicitly as not part of either "working" science or common knowledge.

This development was sketched earlier but without raising the crucial and often neglected question that can be put off no longer: What was the *point* of all this ingenuity?

One might regard the philosophical accounts as mere ideological ploys – desperate attempts to keep medieval interests alive by other means – or instead, and more purely, as just a legitimate scholarly addendum, as providing an abstract fine-tuning of basic terms, for example, of how "thing" and "action" might be understood now in their most general senses. This can be an interesting enterprise in its own right, and practices of this kind persist in our day. And yet there is a world of difference that is easy to recognize here: whereas current writers on subjects such as formal semantics or action theory almost always aim their clarifications only at other specialists, without expecting any dramatic influence on the world at large, or even the academy in general, the original moderns surely presumed that an awful lot was "hanging" on what they were doing.

This presumption was not a matter of an unrealistic sense of self-importance; it had an understandable explanation in a number of developments of the time, and in particular in the very success of the new science. The presence of this new paradigm of knowledge generated the acute question of what to do with the old views that were not part of it, that is, of what to make not only of religion, ethics, and scholastic philosophy, but also of elementary common sense and the whole range of notions developed in long-standing and prestigious disciplines that were not organized like the new fundamental and quantitative sciences. In addition to the plurality of respected but apparently mutually incompatible views that had to be sorted out here, there was, as noted earlier, also a dramatic rise in the stock of radical skepticism, abetted by the perplexing nature of the more abstract notions of the new science itself, and the constant desire to find for philosophy a certainty at least as persuasive as its fellow abstract discipline, the flourishing paradigm of mathematics.[21]

In this context there arose what was not merely a loose and general discussion about how to relate the "manifest" and the "scientific images"; rather, there arose one especially influential strategy, the dominant and so-called Cartesian move of isolating a privileged sphere, a set of foundational representations – be they clear and distinct ideas or sense impressions (or, later, noeses of primordial intentionality, or forms of language) – from which the claims of both prescientific and scientific experience could be evaluated and reconstructed. The key idea here, the main "point" behind the strong concern with systematicity in most classical modern philosophies, was the thought that only a special philosophical discourse about a *system of representations* could provide a coherent and fully responsible way of meeting skepticism while also incorporating the achievements of modern science. In this way, the third basic modern option discussed earlier can be understood as taking on a form – systematic representational metaphysics – that is designed precisely to meet at once the concerns of the first two options, skepticism and scientism. Unfortunately, this ambitious project led to a well-known dead end, because what really gave skepticism its greatest strength was the ironic fact that the very representational tools that modern philosophers turned to as a certain foundation (whether sense data, ideas, words, or associations) in order to find something immune from doubt, created an abyss of uncertainty between those tools and the separate objects that they were supposed to help us reach.[22]

Modern philosophy thus seemed condemned to two opposite but equally unappealing options. One option is to accept (or endlessly dispute) the challenge of skepticism and to try to save the claims of science only by integrating them within an internal system of representations – but then, unfortunately, to deny thereby their original meaning as claims that transcend what is already within the common knowledge of mere natural belief (hence the standard objections to Berkeley and positivism). The other option is to accept modern science all by itself as absolute, as scientistic naturalism has done with more and more popu-

---

21 See, e.g., work cited in n. 3 above, and J. B. Schneewind, *The Invention of Autonomy* (Cambridge: Cambridge University Press, 1997).

22 See Hegel's classic critique in the beginning of his Introduction to the *Phenomenology of Spirit*.

larity recently,[23] and not to worry that this leaves traditional philosophy as well as common sense, taken as special sources of truth, reduced rather to confusion, error, and irrelevance.

B. 3. Kant's System: Not against Skepticism but for Common Knowledge

If we try now to locate Kant in relation to these alternatives, it is all too tempting and common to see him, as, for example, Richard Rorty has at times, as but one more failed version of the representationalist option[24] – and in large part precisely because of Kant's strong interest in system. For many readers, the Kantian system, with its massive transcendental idealist architectonic, has appeared to be but one more desperate attempt to construct a modern pseudo-object, a literally fabricated philosopher's world, lying in an unneeded nowhere land between the informalities of common life and the strict claims of science itself. Even if one brackets the troublesome issue of Kant's metaphysical commitments, it remains hard from the start for most philosophers to accept any of Kant's complex

---

23 Quine has been most influential here, in denying a fundamental distinction between constitutive and nonconstitutive principles, and any in principle distinctive role for philosophy within the whole "web" of our knowledge. But see the fine Kantian counterattack by Michael Friedman in "Philosophical Naturalism," and his discussion of McDowell, "Exorcising the Philosophical Tradition," *Philosophical Review* 105 (1996): 427–67. Friedman has gone on to argue that, although Kantians should reject Quine's extreme philosophical naturalism, it is equally a mistake (both in reading the *Critique* and in constructing a contemporary flexible Kantianism) to try "to detach" transcendental principles from particular instantiations of exact science. My approach agrees with Friedman in seeing an essential and positive relation between a flexible Kantian position and natural science – in the distinctively philosophical project of "articulating and contextualizing" the most fundamental principles of particular scientific frameworks; but it does not involve limiting Kantian philosophy to that project alone or to espousing naturalism in a broad sense. A position closer to my own on this issue can be found in Graham Bird's response, in Michael Friedman and Graham Bird, "Kantian Themes in Contemporary Philosophy," *Proceedings of the Aristotelian Society*, supp. vol. 72 (1998): 111–29, 131–51. Although Bird and I are closer to Strawson than Friedman on this point, the three of us are all clearly in agreement, versus Strawson, on the independence of Kant's transcendental project from considerations of skepticism.

24 See Richard Rorty, "Strawson's Objectivity Argument," *Review of Metaphysics* 24 (1970): 207–44, and *Philosophy and the Mirror of Nature* (Princeton: Princeton University Press, 1979). An important recent interpretation, much more complicated but still accepting some of the same ideas against the adequacy of Kant's epistemology, can be found in John McDowell, *Mind and World* (Cambridge, MA: Harvard University Press, 1994), esp. pp. 42 and 102. See also below at n. 34, and Chapter 2, sec. A. 4.

apparatus because it still seems not even capable of responding to the challenge of skepticism without falling back into what is only a more complicated rearrangement of the old internal and inadequate tools of representationalism.

These are familiar complaints, and no doubt there are many aspects of Kant's own language that could lead to thinking of his system in terms of the problems that arise on the standard story. Nonetheless, as I have indicated, there is a quite different and more sensible way to understand his basic strategy, a modest transcendental approach that escapes these objections. This alternative interpretation can now be developed further by explaining how it contrasts directly with the original and still-common reaction to Kant.

Practically before the ink was dry on Kant's Critical work, the suspicion arose that for all his talk of a system, his own philosophy was not systematic in any satisfactory sense, and this for precisely the reasons that (1) it only exacerbated rather than alleviated the challenge of *skepticism,* and (2) it lacked basic *unity* because it divided the world, the self, and philosophy into untenable strict dualisms such as the phenomenal and the noumenal, the sensible and the rational, the theoretical and the practical. These issues dominate the worries not only of many current writers but also of Kant's first influential critics: G. E. Schulze, F. H. Jacobi, and J. G. Fichte – and even of his first major advocate, K. L. Reinhold, who soon insisted that Kant's system would have to be revised radically, so that it could be brought into an adequately "firm" and "broad" shape (see below Chapters 2 and 3).

Schulze and his successors in the late eighteenth century, just like Strawson and Stroud in our century, generated an atmosphere in which the measure of Kantian philosophy tends at first to be nothing other than how well it can defeat skepticism's challenge. It is as if Critical philosophy is all an obscure enterprise unless it can be formulated as a transcendental "objectivity argument" that ideally turns the very tools of Cartesianism against itself and shows that mere self-awareness absolutely requires physical objects.[25] This is an old issue in the Kant literature, and here I can do little more than refer to earlier work in which I and others have contended that, despite numerous complications, the intentions of the first *Critique,* and even of the legendary Refutation of Idealism, can be understood better by abstracting from any such claim to defeat radical skepti-

---

25 See P. F. Strawson's classic, *The Bounds of Sense* (London: Methuen, 1966), chap. 2, sec. II. Many interesting recent versions of the strategy can be found, e.g., Q. Cassam, *Self and World* (Oxford: Oxford University Press, 1996).

cism on its own terms.[26] This is not at all to say that there are no intriguing new responses to skepticism that can be teased out of suggestions in Kant's texts. The contention of the moment is only that seeking knockdown arguments on this issue need not be assumed to fit best with the literal intent or main value of the Critical philosophy, especially in the context of its relation to science. Behind this contention is also the ever-more-confirmed suspicion (which is of course still controversial) that radical skepticism is a position that no one is going to be able to defeat with a compelling theoretical argument,[27] and so it is not a significant failing if a specific philosopher such as Kant has no such argument either.

If we look back at the primary concern of modern skepticism, the problem of proving the existence of physical objects, it should be clear enough how this particular problem became acute in the era immediately preceding Kant. Not only did reflections on modern physics undermine naive presumptions of common sense (especially as infected by Aristotelianism or other outdated traditions) about the intrinsic nature of specific kinds of external objects (e.g., about their color or force); they also eventually undercut all assumptions about any insight into the form of causal connections – and without such insight there can be no clear, let alone certain, path from our perceptions to whatever external ground they may have, however systematically they might be organized. Kant was especially familiar with this problem from the lively disputes among his teachers concerning issues such as the doctrine of preestablished harmony,[28] and from early on he expressed a commonsense attitude toward it that I take to be a crucial and underappreciated indication of his general methodology. He remarked that on such issues even philosophers should simply accept what I have been calling "common knowledge," that is, what all normal people really do believe – in this case, a plurality of finite interacting things – and move on from there.[29] This might seem like

---

26 See K. Ameriks, "Recent Work on Kant's Theoretical Philosophy," *American Philosophical Quarterly* 19 (1982): 1–24; and *Kant's Theory of Mind*, chap. III, sec. C.

27 Here I have been influenced by the work of A. Brueckner and R. Fogelin.

28 See K. Ameriks, "The Critique of Metaphysics: Kant and Traditional Ontology," in *The Cambridge Companion to Kant*, ed. Paul Guyer (Cambridge: Cambridge University Press, 1992), pp. 249–79; Eric Watkins, "Kant's Theory of Physical Influx," *Archiv für Geschichte der Philosophie* 77 (1995): 285–324, and "The Development of Physical Influx in Early 18th Century Germany: Gottsched, Knutzen, and Crusius," *Review of Metaphysics* 49 (1995): 295–339.

29 I have been struck especially by the Moorean point made in the early Metaphysik Herder, *AA*, vol. 28, p. 6: "finden sich in der Folge Sätze die dem Sens commun widersprechen, so prüfe man alle vorhergegangene Beweise [if one finds propositions that contradict common sense, one should test all the prior arguments]." Little rests on this passage alone,

a horribly deflationary approach, one that would put him back in the ranks of the crude "popular philosophers" that he generally castigated. But such objections overlook other crucial differences or presuppose that Kant must be read as a representational foundationalist, as someone who takes private inner ideas as the absolute given and assumes that philosophy must rebuild a world from the start out of such components. I do not see Kant as ever committed to such a premise, but it is not necessary to try to prove that view here. There are countless exegetical complexities involved, and it is enough for immediate purposes if a nonrepresentationalist reading can be offered that at least seems to fit many aspects of Kant's texts here, and that opens a different and fruitful way to approach his basic philosophical project.

In favor of reading Kant as a representationalist, there are, to be sure, facts such as his very frequent use of the term "representation" and his general preoccupation with many problems that come straight out of the Descartes-to-Hume tradition. But there are harmless ways to explain these facts (see below Chapter 2, sec. B. 3), and it is at least equally obvious that Kant initiated a very striking departure from the common practice of beginning arguments from an elementary basis of mere "representations" in the typical modern (pre-Kantian) sense, for example, private images or sense data. While Kant did not deny the existence of such "data," he premised his arguments on a higher level of consciousness not adequately explored by his predecessors. In focusing on "experience" (*Erfahrung*) in the specific sense of putatively warranted empirical *judgment*, Kant made a decisive methodological break with all philosophies that insisted on beginning with simple ideas or impressions. Unlike impressions, judgments are not atomic entities that merely exist or fail to exist; they are already structured cognitive wholes, with essential semantic and normative features. In their paradigmatic form in Kant's texts, they are originally oriented toward external objects, as in the "judgment of experience," "bodies are heavy."[30]

A traditional representationalist might object that if Kant is starting with "common knowledge" judgments in this sense, then all the interesting questions are already being begged (but see below at n. 40). But the Kantian transcendental reply is that from this level on, there remain a

which is not part of Kant's own published work, since in any case the attitude it expresses clearly fits in with his whole view at the time on how to approach an issue like preestablished harmony.

30 Kant, *Critique of Pure Reason*, B 142. This interpretation of Kant owes much to Gerold Prauss, *Erscheinung bei Kant* (Berlin: de Gruyter, 1971). Cf. above Introduction, n. 21.

host of significant and genuine questions – for example, the questions at the heart of the *Critique:* supposing that there are legitimate empirical judgments, can we make sense of ordinary practices of justifying these without eventually invoking any formal limits, any a priori principles that would order them systematically? In the general spirit of the sciences of his time, Kant was sure that, with his doctrine of forms of judgment and its related table of the categories, he had discovered substantive and irrevocable answers here. Most philosophers now would prefer a more flexible and historical notion of "the a priori,"[31] but as long as it still appears worthwhile to explore some kind of answers here of a broadly Kantian type (helpful answers such as, e.g., those that Michael Friedman has shown that the Carnapian tradition produced in our own time),[32] some kind of formal constraints for knowledge at least as we can envisage it now, then the underlying idea of the Kantian system can maintain its value as a basic option. In place of leaving us with only radical subjectivism or radical naturalism – and all their limitations – and instead of resting content merely with common sense or technical disciplines alone, the Kantian hypothesis of a layer of structured formal principles can serve as a useful mediator between ordinary life and exact science. Principles such as causality (whose precise meaning needs to be refined over time, of course) can be argued, for example, to function both as necessary conditions for particular empirical judgments and as framework postulates for specific higher sciences, and in this way the whole fabric of our knowledge can take on a much more coherent sense for us as its major intertwining threads are revealed.

This general strategy can be filled out further by noting that Kant's own principles are hardly an accidental array but rather are linked to each other in a thoroughly systematic fashion in which the very structure of judgment itself provides a constant "clue."[33] Kant's approach is systematic in a multiple sense because it claims a necessary and tightly connected

---

31 See the works cited above at n. 23; and Philip Kitcher's "flexible" Kantian account, "The Unity of Science and the Unity of Nature," in *Kant and Contemporary Epistemology*, ed. P. Parrini (Dordrecht: Kluwer, 1994), pp. 331–47.

32 See again Friedman, "Philosophical Naturalism."

33 See Beatrice Longuenesse's work on Kant's table of judgments as a systematic clue to the whole structure of the *Critique*, in *Kant and the Capacity to Judge* (Princeton: Princeton University Press, 1998); and Reinhard Brandt, *The Table of Judgments: Critique of Pure Reason A 67–76/ B 92–101*, North American Kant Society Studies in Philosophy, vol. 4, trans. E. Watkins (Atascadero, CA: Ridgeview, 1995). The value of the main point here is not affected by the many incidental difficulties that must be acknowledged in Kant's claims about specific forms of judgment.

framework that provides philosophical principles that bridge the extremes of common and scientific judgments, while also implying similar although somewhat looser structures within each of the spheres of common and scientific judgments themselves, structures that parallel the architectonic of the philosophical principles. For example, the relations between Kant's specific principles of substance, cause, and interaction correspond in multiple ways to relations between both weaker "everyday" uses of these concepts, and also stronger, scientifically determined employment of them. This general notion of a nesting of types of systematicity can be worth exploring even if one allows that Kant himself went overboard in his confidence about the specific systematic structures that he thought he had established. Obviously, it is very hard for us now to accept the alleged unrevisability and extraordinary range of content of his particular transcendental claims. But such problems are common to modern philosophy and should not blind us to the heart of Kant's achievement, the opening up of a plausible role for philosophy as a systematic articulation of the sphere of conceptual frameworks that mediate between the extremely informal and the highly formal levels of judgment within our complex objective picture of the world. The crucial point about Kant's enthusiastic talk about a philosophical "system" is simply that he understood that more is possible – and desired by us now – than a simple reliance on a chaos of popular truths or an absolutized set of quantitative theories. Part and parcel of this stress on systematicity is Kant's rejection of foundationalism and naive representationalism: he understood, and argued more influentially than anyone else, that knowledge is anything but a "mirror of nature," a matter of isolated tokens magically picturing transcendent correlates;[34] it is a web of judgments, tied together by an order of conceptual "knots" that hold up over and over again in all kinds of arguments. It is no accident that concepts such as space, time, and causality, which structure everyday life systematically, also take on a fundamental role in the higher sciences. Practically any philosophical account that thematizes the relation between these concepts in an organized but nonreductionist manner – and thus contrasts

---

34 An appreciation for this side of Kant's work is one value of McDowell's *Mind and World*, the title and idea of which can be taken as a variation on C. I. Lewis's classic and Kantian *Mind and the World Order* (New York: Scribner, 1929). I am not claiming that Kant's talk of rules and synthesis fully explains the mysteries of intentionality, but it is a start that has at least made us sensitive to the limits of earlier and cruder theories. Cf. Prauss, *Erscheinung bei Kant*, and more recently, McDowell's Woodbridge Lectures, "Having the World in View: Sellars, Kant, and Intentionality," *Journal of Philosophy* 95 (1998): 431–91.

with prior modern systems – can qualify as Kantian in a flexible and most relevant sense.

Kant's own interest in philosophical systematicity goes far beyond a few analogies, and it is by no means limited to the well-known discussion of specific regulative principles near the end of the first *Critique* and developed throughout the third *Critique*. On a Critical view, philosophy itself, as a whole and in each of its major parts, has a fundamental systematicity in its basic transcendental structure, which contains three main steps. In the paradigmatic context of the *Critique of Pure Reason* these steps can be distinguished as: (1) an exposition of a commonly accepted basis, (2) a set of ordered immediate derivations from that basis, and then (3) a determination of the nature of the domain and boundary of these derivations.[35] More specifically, the first of these steps consists in explaining that we have experience, that is, episodes subject to a "principle" of judgment[36] and thus to a specifiable logical structure needed by any sensible beings who can make claims that aim to be true. The second step, the layer of particular deductions, takes the form in Kant's work of a sequence of ordered transcendental arguments, that is, deductions concerning space, time, categories, and principles – each of which already presumes some kind of objective knowledge, for which necessary epistemic conditions are then offered. In his third basic step, Kant tries to determine the full range of possible a priori knowledge, and to explain exactly where principles of reason become theoretically ungrounded when they lack an objective transcendental or "experience-constituting" role. A final aspect of this step (and a very important one, not to be conflated with the others), which can be abstracted from for now, is to give a metaphysical interpretation of the meaning of the whole domain of experience that has been transcendentally explored. For Kant this amounts to an endorsement of the specific doctrine of transcendental idealism as the only metaphysics that consistently helps "make intelligible"[37] all that we already know. At a somewhat different level there is a fourth step that usually follows in Kant's discussion, and that I also abstract from for now. It consists in the study of the full metaphysical implications of the prior

---

35 See, for example, the typical heading of *Critique*, Introduction, sec. III: "Philosophy stands in need of a science which shall determine [a] the possibility, [b] the principles, and [c] the extent of all a priori knowledge."

36 See already Kant's first Preface to the *Critique*, A xx, on "the common principle" by which "the inventory of all our possessions through pure reason is systematically arranged."

37 This expression comes from the Transcendental Aesthetic's first grounded assertion of transcendental idealism, at B 41.

steps, especially for topics that rest on our pure practical interests in the ideas of freedom, God, and immortality. This last step is ultimately dominated by a concern for autonomy, and this concern can be understood retrospectively as motivating all the other parts of the Critical philosophy as crucial means for the accomplishment of full human self-determination. (In later chapters I will argue that parallels to precisely these four steps – with a few significant variations – can be taken to define the structure of much post-Kantian philosophy, especially Reinhold's work and all that followed upon it.)

I have formulated this account primarily with an orientation toward the structure of the first *Critique,* and the "theoretical" common knowledge that starts from elementary empirical judgments about spatiotemporal objects. But the notion of common knowledge can be naturally expanded, and was expanded by Kant, to include what he took to be even more evident claims in other fields, especially ethics. There, too, one finds, for example in the three-part structure of the *Groundwork,* an initial exposition of what is taken to be the set of common or "popular" examples of moral judgment, followed by a regressive argument for underlying pure principles, and then a concluding reference to at least the outline of a unified metaphysics that would anchor these principles in Kant's general system. A parallel reconstruction could be given of Kant's discussion of aesthetic judgments, which also begins from a set of features presumed to be common in typical aesthetic judgments, then moves on to general principles about pure activities of the mind, and concludes with a discussion of relevant features of the metaphysical system in which these are to be understood as embedded.

While a system with all of these features may strike us as overly ambitious, what I want to draw attention to is how, in comparison to many other approaches, there still is a remarkable modesty that marks even the detailed Kantian notion of a philosophic system. Note, first, that there is no insistence on an absolute certainty for the basis. The "experience" that is the starting point is not metaphysically necessary, and it is not even claimed to be epistemically irresistible – skeptics could opt out of the discussion and not accept that there are any such warranted judgments. Note, secondly, that the derivations do not claim an absolute necessity, and Kant is perfectly willing to allow that various basic aspects of experience remain inexplicable primitives; we just *do* work with space, time, and forms of judgment, and there are no more basic entities – Leibnizian monads, Spinozistic substance, Humean impressions, and so forth – from which these commonsense notions are taken to be even in principle derivable. For Kant there is no discoverable single "root" faculty, nor is there a single top-down procedure for all truth, such as Leibnizian analysis. Thirdly, there are substantive limits that are stressed even in the account of the scope of Kant's system, both in its negative claims about what constitutive unifying principles of reason can be found and also in its general metaphysical thesis that our theoretical knowledge is restricted because of transcendental idealism. In the third *Critique* especially, Kant emphasizes that although there is a "regulative" injunction to seek to tie together all of our actual knowledge into an overarching natural science, in principle we can never expect to claim that this science will reach a point of absolute completeness. Similarly, whatever transcendental idealism exactly means, Kant stresses that it is not an account that even purports to give any positive "explanation" of how we come to have the basic powers of mind that we exhibit.

What all of this shows is that while, on the one hand, Kant departs from the level of mere common sense by constructing a complex philosophical system, on the other hand the system that he actually outlines, like the general idea of philosophical systematicity that he promotes, intentionally contains several clear limits, all linked back to a respect for common sense, and thus it still amounts to what can, after all, be called a position of "modest" systematicity. Unlike his predecessors, Kant does not set up a detailed ontology that conflicts with science itself, nor does he raise epistemological demands to unrealistic levels.

C. KANT'S IMMEDIATE SUCCESSORS: CONTRASTING REACTIONS TO MODESTY

The contrast between Kant and his successors, especially Reinhold and Fichte, also illustrates the importance of the issue of modest systematicity, and it will be filled out in detail in the chapters that follow. At this point I will merely indicate a few of the basic features of their response, features that define a very striking opposition to the structure of Kant's system as just outlined. This opposition derives from the fact that Reinhold and Fichte were still preoccupied with the problem of skepticism and were deeply disturbed by the limits of Kant's system. Thus, in contrast to Kant's hypothetical basis of experience, his conditional argument for the categories, and his notion of a "formal" idealism that still allowed meaningful claims about something beyond human sensibility, they repeatedly called for an absolutely certain basis, an absolutely necessary set of derivations, and a truly exhaustive (global and constitutive, rather than partial and regulative) interpretation of the scope of experience (see below Chapters 2 and 3).

In remarkable contrast to these relatively well-known figures, recent research has revealed that at the very time and place that Reinhold and Fichte developed their alternative to Kant, namely the late 1780s and early 1790s in Jena, there was a group of lesser-known thinkers who were acutely aware of the differences between Kant and his famous successors, and who pleaded desperately for a return to Kant's original modest conception of philosophy. It was at Jena that Kant's work first received intensive sympathetic study, not only in the reviews of the *Allgemeine Literatur Zeitung*, the efforts of C. C. Schmid and his *Kant Wörterbuch*, and the installments of Reinhold's extremely popular (in all senses) *Briefe über die Kantische Philosophie*, but also in the discussions that took place in the circle of Friedrich Niethammer. Niethammer is perhaps best known for his support of Hegel and Hölderlin, but in his first years in Jena he was connected with "early Romantic" geniuses such as Novalis, who delighted in undermining philosophical pretensions (and wrote detailed "Fichte-Studien" against the *Wissenschaftslehre*, even though his family estate had provided crucial financial support for Fichte). Niethammer was also especially close to two perceptive Kant enthusiasts, Johann Benjamin Erhard and Franz von Herbert, two thinkers who shared Novalis's appreciation for the limits of philosophy and who were intensely disturbed by the first attempts of Reinhold and Fichte to replace orthodox Kantianism with a radical foundational system that would supposedly be absolutely certain at its base and absolutely unified by reason in its extent.

In the lead article of his new *Philosophisches Journal*, entitled "On the Demands of Common Sense to Philosophy,"[38] Niethammer uses the dilemmas of foundationalism to argue for the view that "the claims of common sense have to be regarded as the supreme criterion of all truth in

---

38 Friedrich Niethammer, "Von den Ansprüchen des gemeinen Verstandes in die Philosophie," *Philosophisches Journal* (1) 1795: 1–45. See the compressed discussion of this and related issues by Manfred Frank, "Philosophical Foundations of Early Romanticism," in *The Modern Subject*, ed. K. Ameriks and D. Sturma (Albany: State University of New York Press, 1995), pp. 65–85, and his extended discussion (959 pages) in *Unendliche Annäherung: Die Anfänge der philosophischen Frühromantik* (Frankfurt: Suhrkamp, 1997), esp. pp. 439ff., which cites and discusses the letter of Herbert (with an afterword by Erhard) to Niethammer, May 4, 1794. Cf. also Marcelo Stamm, "Skepticism and Methodological Monism: Aenesidemus-Schulze Versus Arcesilaus-Erhard," in *The Skeptical Tradition around 1800*, ed. J. van der Zande and R. Popkin (Kluwer: Dordrecht, 1998), pp. 143–58; as well as special issues of *Revue Internationale de Philosophie*, no. 197 (1996), and of *Fichte-Studien* 9 (1995) and 12 (1998).

our knowledge."[39] He does not take this approach to be in conflict with all presentations of philosophy as a "science"; his point is simply, against the new foundationalist philosophers, that precisely for sensible scientific purposes, philosophy need not (and cannot successfully) try to start from any basis better than common-knowledge. Niethammer also notes explicitly that Kant's philosophy takes as its starting point the "general main fact, that there is experience."[40] Niethammer stresses that from such a point one can move "only" to hypothetical substantive claims, but he realizes that it would be a misunderstanding of both philosophy and science to take this fact as a devastating obstacle – since in fact the "hypothesis" that is started from is something that inevitably is commonly shared. It is important to keep in mind here again that for Kant "experience" corresponds to *Erfahrung*, which is precisely not a mere sense datum but an empirical judgment, a typical common knowledge claim. As Herbert explained in a letter to Erhard, October 7, 1794: "Kant's entire system can be expressed in the hypothetical proposition, 'If experience is, then. . . .' That experience is, is thereby presupposed, postulated, or however one calls it. Now if a skeptic were dumb and shameless enough to say, 'But is there experience?' there is really no answer for such a type other than a beating."[41]

This position indirectly had considerable influence in the "early Romantic" movement in Germany, but within most philosophical circles it was eclipsed by the huge wave of attention that was given to the rising stars, Reinhold and Fichte. But even though they failed to achieve anything like a similar fame, Herbert and his group had an uncanny eye for what was essential and also for what was coming. After hearing Fichte's own preview of the *Wissenschaftslehre* in Zürich, Herbert declared himself to Niethammer to be the "unreconcilable enemy of all so-called first principles in philosophy." He went on to stress that Kant himself based his

39 Niethammer, "Von den Ansprüchen," pp. 32–3.
40 Ibid., p. 23.
41 Cited in Frank, *Unendliche Annäherung*, p. 507. I am very indebted to Frank here, although I do not agree with a suggestion, mentioned in his discussion as coming from Niethammer, Henrich, and others, that Kant himself was still trying to ground experience on a supposedly "Cartesian" knowledge about the self. I would also dispute a common objection to Kant, noted by Frank in a striking formulation by Friedrich Schlegel (ibid., p. 508), which contends that if "experience" means empirical judgment and not mere sensation, then this already begs the task of the deduction, because it assumes the operation of the categories. The objection fails, I believe, because the categories are not taken to be part of any immediate commonsense definition of judgment (otherwise everyone would already be a Kantian), but are rather argued for in the course of the deduction as regressive conditions of a proper understanding of judgment.

philosophy on presumed commonsense judgments (especially concerning morality), and he bid Niethammer to use his special talent to give
Kant's philosophy a clear exposition and to remain "a simple teacher and
reader of the *Critique of Pure Reason.*"[42] Unfortunately, this path was not
taken by many, including Niethammer himself, who became a crucial
figure in the development of German idealism that eventually displaced
Kant with Hegel.[43] In the meantime the main effect that the genuine
Kantian students had on main currents in philosophy itself (in a narrow
sense, as opposed to the very significant aesthetic and Romantic movements of the age) was only to raise some specific objections to Reinhold
that were partially responsible for causing him to modify his system so that
it toned down its claims to certainty (see below Chapter 2, sec. C. 1).

The unfortunate immediate fate of Kantian philosophy at the hands of
his radical idealist readers will be traced in the next chapters. For now it is
important simply to record that *from the beginning* there definitely was
available an alternative reading which understood Kant much better in
his own modest terms, and which saw that both philosophy and science
can thrive even if the a priori principles that they introduce or use do not
need to be claimed to be connected with a system that has anything more
than a limited scope and a discursive, that is, nonintuitive and fallible,
certainty.

D. SYSTEMATIC MODESTY AND PRACTICAL PHILOSOPHY

D. 1. Philosophy as Apologetics

Underlying Kant's whole systematic approach is an important methodological feature that needs to be made explicit, namely the acceptance

42 Herbert to Niethammer, May 6, 1794, as cited in *Friedrich Immanuel Niethammer: Korrespondenz mit dem Herbert- und Erhard-Kreis*, ed. Wilhelm Baum (Vienna: Turia + Kant, 1995), pp.
76ff. Fichte's Zürich lectures, which have been only recently discovered and published,
give a fascinating first view of his system on the eve of his fateful departure for Jena: *Züricher
Vorlesungen über den Begriff der Wissenschaftslehre: Februar 1794*, ed. Erich Fuchs (Neuried: Ars
Una, 1996). For an analysis of Erhard's reaction to the lectures, see Marcelo Stamm,
"Prinzipien und System: Rezeptionsmodelle der Wissenschaftslehre Fichtes 1794," *Fichte-
Studien* 9 (1995): 215–40. On other early developments in Jena, see also below Chapter 2,
sec. C; Chapter 3, sec C; and Chapter 4, sec. C.
43 For extensive details on Niethammer and related matters, see Frank, *Unendliche An-
näherung*, esp. pp. 428ff.; and *Immanuel Carl Diez, Briefwechsel und Kantische Schriften.
Wissensbegründung in der Glaubenskrise Tübingen-Jena (1790–1792)*, ed. Dieter Henrich
(Stuttgart: Klett-Cotta, 1997).

of what can be called a fundamentally "apologetic" role for philosophy. One traditional way to develop a philosophy is, to use Strawson's words, to present a "revisionary" metaphysics,[44] that is, to introduce a philosophical construction that is meant to displace the commitments of ordinary people and ongoing disciplines. We know that this approach never appealed to Kant and that, after his early "Rousseau experience," he was especially reluctant to call into question, or demand some esoteric original ground for, the practical commitments of reason found implicitly in the simplest person, even a Savoyard vicar.[45] Yet he also knew that those commitments had been severely challenged by modern developments, scientific and philosophical, and that many philosophers had come to think that once modern people are reflective at all, it becomes very difficult for them to feel truly rational while holding onto ordinary beliefs such as common ethics and the core of popular religion. To meet this challenge, Kant came to realize that what he needed was not a theoretical explanation of how the metaphysics of ethics and religion work in detail; rather, he needed a good apology, a story of how the best examination of all the latest options of metaphysics and science – and a thorough exploration of all their own perplexities – shows that there is still room for (what he took to be) our most important common beliefs. Unfortunately, he sometimes also went on to suggest that he had proven there was no way that the core content of these beliefs could ever be shown to be impossible. This claim, like much of his talk about philosophical "certainty," was more than what was strictly needed, as was his extra belief that various alternative philosophies, such as materialism, were not only dubious or uncertain but definitely false. There was often some overconfident "overkill" in Kant's formulations, but we can bracket this again and still extract from his work an attractive apologetic strategy that gives philosophy the modest negative role of primarily defending modern agents simply against philosophy itself and its ever-growing alienating effects, including its challenges to the very notion of science as a crucial and distinctive form of knowing. This strategy nicely supplements the modest positive and systematic role for philosophy discussed earlier, its unique function of providing a struc-

---

44 P. F. Strawson, *Individuals: An Essay in Descriptive Metaphysics* (London: Methuen, 1959).

45 Kant, *AA*, vol. 20, p. 44. Kant developed a similar answer for other forms of presumed knowledge, such as mathematics, which seemed in the public mind to be at least not as vulnerable to philosophical undermining by problems at the foundation. He used this fact as a wedge against figures such as Hume, arguing that if a Humean would only admit the simple mathematical propositions that everyone else already concedes, then enough of an apparatus would ultimately have to be conceded to be able to underwrite other more contested a priori claims.

tured account of how all our different levels of knowledge hang together.[46]

At the heart of Kant's own understanding of the philosophical ideal of systematicity, as well as that of his idealist successors, there remained a deep interest in the unity of reason and a desire to establish some kind of clear link between theoretical and practical perspectives. Unfortunately, just as Kant remained long attached to dogmatism in theoretical philosophy before he came to his Critical perspective, it also took him some time, even after the first *Critique,* to settle on an approach to the concepts at the basis of his practical philosophy. One clear sign of this uneven development is the striking but often unappreciated fact that the discussion of Paralogisms in the first *Critique* makes only a partial attempt at unmasking dogmatic claims about the self and its spontaneity. Traditional arguments for the self's absolute freedom can be found to be even more prominent in Kant's pre-Critical notes than parallel arguments for similar claims about its substantiality and identity, and yet it is the spontaneity claim alone that is never made the object of a critique as a Paralogism in the Transcendental Dialectic. On the contrary, Kant continues to use strong, or at least strongly suggestive, language about how we "regard" ourselves as intellectual beings free from determination.[47] These statements have an ambiguity that is typical of his position in 1781, when he still has not gotten around to working out anything like a "groundwork" for his metaphysics of morals. He is evidently reluctant either to endorse a syllogism concluding in an assertion of our freedom, or to demonstrate that all such arguments must fail. It is therefore no accident that he hints at a unity of the fundamental concepts of theoretical and practical philosophy but he never details how that unity is to be conceived. He makes striking use of the concept of spontaneity as a form of intentionality in both its theoretical and practical meanings, but he is ambiguous about how absolute this spontaneity is to be understood.

Given this situation, it is not surprising that Kant's main successors – Reinhold, Fichte, Hegel – all tried to provide a new foundation for phi-

---

46 Is all this inherently "conservative"? No, there can be revolutionary scientific and social developments that seep into popular consciousness in such a way that theoreticians can mobilize them for the purpose of philosophically undermining repressive ideologies – as Kant did, for example, in his influential work as a liberating Enlightenment writer.

47 See K. Ameriks, "Kant's Deduction of Freedom and Morality," *Journal of the History of Philosophy* 19 (1981): 53–79 (reprinted as chap. VI of *Kant's Theory of Mind*); Ameriks, "The First Edition Paralogisms of Pure Reason," in *Immanuel Kant: Kritik der reinen Vernunft,* ed. Georg Mohr and Marcus Willaschek (Berlin: Akademie Verlag, 1998), pp. 369–88; and Ameriks, *Kant's Theory of Mind* (2d ed.), Preface.

losophy as a whole on a more detailed conception of spontaneity that is meant to correct Kant's account. This development is understandable, since it cannot be denied that there is an incompleteness in Kant's own discussions – but I believe it can also be shown that Kant eventually developed an attractive position that is relatively modest, and that, on the whole, still has much more to offer than the "improvements" of it that were immediately proposed by the idealists. This is a long story that depends largely on the details that will be supplied in the accounts of the idealist systems to follow. First, however, it is essential to set the stage for the contrasts to come by laying out some of the most basic features of Kant's own account of freedom.

As has been noted, Kant's first idealist critics repeatedly stressed two main objections to his Critical philosophy: that its theoretical component did not resolve the problem of *skepticism,* and that on the whole its system lacked a thorough *unity,* and especially a strong unity of theoretical and practical reason. Although it took him a while, and along the way he made statements that considerably exacerbated problems when taken out of context later, I believe that eventually Kant did appreciate these problems, and he developed a much-improved strategy in the programmatic reformulations of his important introductions to the second and third *Critiques.* The main idea of the new strategy fits naturally with Kant's response to the first main objection, the problem of skepticism: just as Kant can take a calm attitude toward skepticism by erecting a "modest" system that forgoes the extreme claims of representationalist foundationalism, so too he can take a calm attitude toward the second main objection and the calls for absolute unity by showing how we can do best with a philosophy whose unity remains modest and does not try to reduce theoretical considerations to practical ones or vice versa (or to some alleged "common root").

D. 2. The Systematic Significance of the "Fact of Reason" (1788)

Kant came to settle on the most important step in his final Critical strategy not right after the first edition of the first *Critique* (1781) but only in the second *Critique* (1788), when he finally made clear that he had in hand no ambitious unification of reason, and in particular nothing of the type suggested by his own arguments in the intervening *Groundwork* (1785).[48]

---

48 This development is discussed in detail in my "Kant's Deduction of Freedom and Morality."

The *Groundwork* culminates in a section that encourages taking the central experience of judgment as itself a demonstration of a kind of absolute theoretical as well as practical spontaneity. If such a demonstration could work, both the capacity for the absolute freedom of action needed for morality and the mind's independence from nature postulated by traditional metaphysics could be warranted in one magnificent step. But the second *Critique* gives up on any such demonstration, while it proposes that there is still a coherent way that theoretical reason and practical reason can support each other, even if they are not rooted in a ground that would defeat every kind of skepticism.

The main innovation in the *Critique of Practical Reason* is the introduction of the peculiar notion of a "fact of reason" (chap. I, part 7) as central to morality and to the idea of freedom, along with the continued insistence (on the first page of the second *Critique*'s Preface) that freedom constitutes the "keystone" of his system. The notion of a Kantian "keystone" that is called a "fact" may seem to be more than perplexing, but there is a fairly simple explanation that can be given of at least Kant's terminology here. The "fact of reason" is said to be a "fact" because it is *not derived* from something prior to it, that is, something meant as acceptable to a completely neutral audience, such as the bare notion of judgment. At the same time it is "of reason" because it is understood to be given to us not through contingencies of feeling but from part of our general and essential, albeit not merely theoretical, character as *rational agents.*

Kant took a long and winding route to come to the doctrine of a fact of reason. In the first *Critique* he had constructed an entire theoretical system, a global transcendental idealism (expanding the doctrine of the ideality of space and time in his *Inaugural Dissertation* to a doctrine of the ideality of all our determinate theoretical knowledge), just to make room for at least some crucial conditions of the *possibility* of asserting human freedom in an absolute rather than relative or compatibilistic sense. However, at that time he did not work out a positive argument for human freedom, and as has been noted (see above sec. D. 1), he even skipped over discussion of the issue at the natural place for it in his Paralogisms. The dense last part (III) of the *Groundwork of the Metaphysics of Morals* finally addresses the issue of freedom's *actuality* by directly confronting the worry that our belief in such freedom, which Kant took to be essential to our very notion of morality, might be a mere "figment of the brain," a *Hirngespinst.* The argument of part III of the *Groundwork,* for all its ambiguities and obscurities, then clearly presents itself as a deduction, as an argument that defends the assertion of human freedom from the starting point of general considerations such as the mere (supposedly always "spontaneous") nature of judgment, considerations that do not themselves already contain any practical and controversial moral presumptions in a "thick" Kantian sense. This is why it is such a striking shift when, in returning to the issue just a few years later in the second *Critique* (1788; some important clues were given in the second-edition Preface of the first *Critique*, 1787),[49] Kant entirely eschews reference to his earlier *Groundwork* argument, chooses to speak of a mere "confirmation" of freedom, and insists (Preface, n. 1) that the freedom which morality requires rather has its sole *ratio cognoscendi* in the "fact of reason," that is, in the authority of our *pure practical* reason itself.

Many different readings have been offered of these difficult texts, but my interpretation stresses that an understanding of the full context and development of Kant's thought allows us to take them at face value, and to see that Kant is openly retreating from a strategy that he knew quite well, that is to say, away from any argument that would give even the appearance of a "strong" or foundational deduction of freedom that could be meant to refute even skeptics about morality. He is explicitly falling back on a modest or "coherentist" argument that relies on the "fact" of what is already found in what is supposed to be our common moral reason. Against the worry that Kant could not have made such an important move so quickly without marking it out even more clearly, it is worth knowing that considerable evidence has now been assembled that shows that Kant went through *several* significant shifts in his treatment of major metaphysical issues, and especially freedom, from his early pre-Critical period through his lectures in the 1770s to the time of the first *Critique* itself.[50] It is striking, for example, that he starts as a compatibilist, shifts without explanation to a vigorous anticompatibilism, and then presents strong dogmatic arguments for freedom (in his lectures) which he later chooses totally to ignore rather than repeat, let alone criticize or modify, in the first *Critique*. Similar key shifts can be found also in later aspects of Kant's thought as well – for example, in the very idea of a separate second or third *Critique*. At one point such studies were said to be excluded or unnecessary for transcendental philosophy, and then in works very soon thereafter they were presented as essential to the Critical program.

49 The crucial passage is B xxviii: "If we grant that morality necessarily presupposes freedom . . . " For some problems, see below Chapter 2, sec. D.4.
50 See again my *Kant's Theory of Mind*, which is reinforced now by the materials available in *Lectures on Metaphysics/ Immanuel Kant*.

Many important contemporary philosophers would nonetheless dispute the sharp contrast drawn here between an early deduction that moves from broadly theoretical considerations *to* morality and a categorical assertion of freedom, as opposed to a later mere "confirmation" that moves *from* a moral fact of reason to simply an unpacking of freedom and other ideas supposedly implicit in the practical perspective that comes with that fact. One way to try to minimize this contrast would be to contend that the second *Critique* itself offers something that is still tantamount to a deduction of freedom,[51] but a more widespread strategy is to take the opposite approach and to contend that Kant in fact does not and need not ever claim to be giving an argument for the *actuality* of freedom. On this strategy, it is enough if Kant can be taken always to be reminding us merely that "from a practical point of view" we "must regard" ourselves as spontaneous and thus as ultimately subject to strict moral standards. Henry Allison, for example, has suggested that we should read Kant's ethics as not making any metaphysical claims about transcendent powers but as making only a "conceptual" point about how we regard ourselves as agents.[52] This is an especially appealing strategy for his popular type of Kant interpretation because (unlike some more traditional interpreters) Allison also takes many components of Kant's theoretical philosophy to express what is merely a "conceptual distinction" between points of view. Thus, "phenomena" and "noumena" do not stand for two possibly distinct realms of objects but rather indicate what are simply different ways, roughly epistemic and nonepistemic, of considering a realm of empirical objects in a manner that implies nothing about the existence of anything transcending experience. Christine Korsgaard and other Rawlsian neo-Kantians appear to endorse a similar strategy – for example, when Korsgaard argues that for a Kantian questions of personal identity are not a matter of absolute metaphysical status but rather merely depend on and

---

51 This line would be closer to the view of Lewis White Beck than to the opposite line of interpreters such as H. J. Paton and Dieter Henrich; see my analysis of these options in the works cited in n. 47 above.

52 See the essays collected in H. E. Allison, *Idealism and Freedom* (Cambridge: Cambridge University Press, 1996); and Christine Korsgaard, *The Sources of Normativity*, with G. A. Cohen et al. (Cambridge: Cambridge University Press, 1996), and *Creating the Kingdom of Ends* (Cambridge: Cambridge University Press, 1996), esp. chap. 12, "Personal Identity and the Unity of Agency: A Kantian Response to Parfit." Cf. my review of Allison in *Philosophy and Phenomenological Research* 49 (1999): 825–8, my critique of earlier work by Allison and Wood in "Kant and Hegel on Freedom: Two New Interpretations," *Inquiry* 35 (1992): 219–32, and my objections to "constructivist" readings of Kant's ethics in "On Schneewind and Kant's Method in Ethics," *Ideas y Valores* 102 (1996): 28–53.

reflect one's practical perspective.[53] For many readers it has thus seemed much easier, for both internal and external reasons, to defend Kant's notion of freedom when it is taken in a way that backs off from any traditional metaphysical and transcendent claims.[54]

Without claiming that Kant's own position can be entirely defended, I would argue that in this area metaphysical considerations are nevertheless inescapable, and for reasons both external and internal to Kant's work. Externally, it is hard to see how any philosopher today can flatly assert that "we must regard ourselves as free," even if only from "a practical perspective." If the "must" is meant to record a mere stipulative or accidental psychological fact, it goes against the seriousness of the commitment to spontaneity that is being implied. But if it is insisted that the "must" signals a deep and universal psychological standpoint, then this is directly contradicted by the army of nonlibertarian philosophers (growing ever larger since Hume's day, and certainly well known to Kant) who not only argue that their philosophies deny that we are free (in any noncompatibilist sense) but who also observe, accurately enough, that in daily life people in general seem to get along quite well without a belief in absolute freedom (cf. below Chapter 2, sec. D. 4). It can be conceded that people in general do use and need a belief in their own agency, but the thought that they can and do *act* does not entail that there is, or even that they must believe there is, no other sufficient cause acting on them. Of course, this does not settle the metaphysical issue of freedom, but it does show how in the end Kantian arguments become quite odd if they are taken to rest on mere conventional, pragmatic, or psychological presumptions. On the other hand, if it is said that we "must" believe in absolute freedom simply because this is a *normative* (rather than psychological) implication of a "genuine" moral perspective, then this still begs the issue with opponents of Kantian moral theory, and at most it points to where the real discussion has to begin.

There are not only external difficulties for the position that we must merely "regard ourselves as free"; it is hard to square this reading with central concerns internal to Kant's system. One can ask: What is the *point*

53 These interpretations obviously developed under the influence of John Rawls. See his "Themes in Kant's Moral Philosophy" in *Kant's Transcendental Deductions*, ed. Eckart Förster (Stanford: Stanford University Press, 1989), pp. 81–113.
54 A major source for this kind of interpretive strategy is no doubt Kant's talk about presupposing freedom "merely as an idea" at *Groundwork, AA*, vol. 4, p. 448n. This passage requires a long explanation; for a start, see above at n. 47.

of this belief that we supposedly must have in strict freedom, what exactly is it that cannot be captured by compatibilism, especially if (on such a Rawlsian neo-Kantian reading of Kant, in contrast to the "metaphysical" reading I propose) one refuses to assert that there literally are any "metaphysical powers," that is, sources of agency not determined solely by the rules we take to cover the empirical domain? In such a situation, talk of freedom becomes something like a wheel turning idly – whereas if one thinks that the idea of freedom is *not merely* part of our "conceptual standpoint" (presumably with only internal reference) but designates an actual and separate power, then it at least involves an ineliminable existential claim (going beyond what is merely within our thoughts, which is not to say that it must be certain or made on the basis of some claimed direct insight), and one can immediately see why Kant thought it was such a difficult issue. And not only is a literal notion of nonempirical agency something that would give talk of freedom a real reference and point, it appears to be clearly what Kant himself had in view. In the first *Critique* he talks explicitly of absolutely spontaneous and nontemporal sources of action, and the natural way to understand his argument in the third Antinomy is precisely as making room for some real causation that would transcend whatever action we can know empirically.[55] Confusions may arise here for readers who do not see that when Kant relies in the second *Critique* on a practical "fact of reason" as the ground for freedom, he is not denying a commitment to the *truth* that we have nontemporal agency, nor is he saying "we merely believe" we have such freedom. Rather, he holds explicitly that there *is a fact* here[56] and we can be certain about it; it is just that we should not suggest any longer that we might be in the epistemic position of being able to *derive* this fact from neutral theoretical considerations – for example, the general features of judgment cited in the *Groundwork*.

All this admittedly leaves Kant (after the *Groundwork*) in a position that makes him not only unable to defeat a moral skeptic but also still weighted

---

55 For an excellent account of the coherence of Kant's position here, even when Kant is interpreted in straightforward metaphysical terms, see Allen Wood, "Kant's Compatibilism," in *Self and Nature in Kant's Philosophy* (Ithaca: Cornell University Press, 1984), pp. 57–72.

56 I believe that the often invoked retreat here to a Fichtean notion of an "act" (*Tathandlung*) rather than a fact (*Tatsache*) is ultimately of no help here, since the relevant sense of fact at issue is simply that of a state of affairs that corresponds to a true proposition, a proposition asserting freedom exists. Acts are facts – even if they are free acts. Cf. below Chapters 3–5.

down by a literal belief in nonempirical agency that can embarrass many contemporaries who share an attachment to much of the content of his strict morality. There is a problem here, but I believe the difficulties his libertarianism presents *all by itself* are on the whole *not much* worse than those that other systems have when faced with the most fundamental philosophical questions. Nonetheless, I would admit that there remains a special and significant methodological problem concerning freedom (cf. below Chapter 2, sec. D. 4), whatever other apologies may be offered for Kant. The problem arises from the fact that in the *Groundwork* Kant himself appears to concede that a strong reply to skepticism, not merely a "confirmation" but a proof of the existence of our absolute freedom (or at least a *proof* that we "must" think we are free in this sense), is needed, *and* he seems to suggest that his system can provide such a reply even while satisfying not only the demands of global Newtonianism but also the perspective of neutral common sense. Kant's own abandonment in 1788 of even the suggestion of such a strong argument, that is, of his apparently "neutral" or categorical deduction of both freedom and morality in the *Groundwork,* naturally generated the suspicion that his final practical philosophy is inadequate on its own grounds. To start by calling for a deduction that any rational being as such could use to defeat moral skepticism, and to end by relying on something called a "fact," is to raise and to frustrate expectations that foundationalist philosophers especially would understandably want to see satisfied. I believe that these expectations, and the very keen interest in Kant's moral philosophy from the period of its first reception, go a long way in helping to explain the incredibly intense search, after Kant, for a philosophy with an absolute foundation – that is, the remarkable "Reinhold-to-Fichte" phase noted earlier, and its strong influence on all later phases of reaction to Kant. Note, however, that while Kant's own philosophy, on my reading of the *Groundwork,* naturally engenders this search for such a foundation, his general modest methodology and the *content* of his moral theory alone still do not require it. Kantians concerned merely with this content (and not irrevocably attached to incompatibilism; consider the work of, e.g., T. Nagel or T. Scanlon) could have rested with moral experience as simply a fact of commonsense like theoretical experience; in this way the projects of the first and second *Critiques* could have been accepted as having a parallel and relatively modest structure. But a peculiar combination of circumstances in the era of German idealism stood in the way of this more flexible commonsense approach. Three factors were especially important:

(1) Kant's own belief in metaphysical powers as not only actual but essential to the *common picture* of ourselves as agents (i.e., as free agents in a system that excludes compatibilism and yet takes nature to be governed by Newtonian laws) was responsible for keeping alive a drive for some kind of ambitious metaphysics, and this naturally led to a hope for a strongly unified system.

(2) The association of Kant's work with Hume, and a natural misunderstanding of the *Critique*'s basic structure, reinvigorated the disastrous thought that Kant's philosophy, like earlier modern philosophy, has to be evaluated primarily from the perspective of how well it can answer radical skepticism of all types.

(3) The tumultuous cultural circumstances of late eighteenth-century Germany, combined with Kant's own talk about instituting a new era of scientific philosophy and rational society, generated the thought that to lead and to preserve such an era, philosophy required an immediate certainty and exhaustive scope, a form that alone could give it the irreversible attachment not only of specialists but also of the whole public of the Enlightenment.

All these factors had as a consequence the fact that most readers were highly dissatisfied with the second *Critique*'s claim that it is enough if theoretical reason merely leaves room, that is, some certification of metaphysical permission, for the moral possibilities that our pure practical reason supposedly commits us to at the level of sound common sense. Nonetheless, in developing a third *Critique* and in expanding his account of a priori principles, Kant did not turn away from the doctrine of the fact of reason and a less than absolutely unified root for his philosophy. Rather, he showed in new ways how, in the areas of taste and natural science, reason and sense can cooperate with each other without principles that involve a strict demonstration, or even a strongly unified argument, against skepticism. This refusal earned him the disdain of his successors. Kant realized this, and yet, as is evident from his late letter on Fichte (see above at n. 15 and n. 20), he was not willing to retreat one inch from his estimate of his own system as completely adequate. Ironically, what makes that system most attractive today is the fact that, especially after 1788, it never insisted on being complete in the absolute way that a casual reading of his letter might suggest. On the contrary, the actual "complete" Kantian system is *meant* to remain something that must appear, at least from the perspective of many pre- and post-Kantians, as an incomplete work, characterized by mere "facts" at its base, and many "loose" and unfinished steps in its development. Fortunately, what others have regarded as weaknesses here, we can now accept, at least in large part, as strengths, as further signs of Kant's proper Critical appreciation of our limits. His general respect for these limits can be endorsed even if it is conceded that he went one step too far in his presumption about the commonsense status of his commitment to a libertarian metaphysics.

PART II

REINHOLD

2

REINHOLD'S CONTRIBUTION

A. THE GOSPELS REVISED: PRELIMINARY OVERVIEW OF FOUR CRITICAL DOCTRINES IN A NEW "IMPROVED" VERSION

A. 1. Kant and Reinhold: Influence and Difference

The work of Karl Leonhard Reinhold has come to receive growing attention recently from specialists, but I believe it has a much broader significance than has yet been realized. It can be argued that not only did this supposedly minor figure directly determine the main lines of the immediate reception of Kant's philosophy, but he also was at least indirectly responsible for determining some of the most influential preconceptions still current today about the basic alternatives within modern philosophy.

Reinhold presented his own system only after he had suddenly become famous through his exposition of Kant's *Critique of Pure Reason* (1781, A edition; 1787, B edition). It is often forgotten that the first responses to Kant's long and difficult main work were mixed at best,[1] and that even the

---

1 A typical very early response was Herder's letter to Hamann in March 1782: "Kant's *Critique* is hard for me swallow. It will remain nearly unread. It was thoroughly reviewed in the Göttingen papers and treated as idealism. I don't know what the point is of the whole heavy pie-in-the-sky [*Luftgewebe*]." Johann Gottfried Herder, *Briefe. Gesamtausgabe 1763–1803*, ed. W. Dobbek and G. Arnold, vol. 4, no. 209 (Weimar: Volksverlag, 1959), as cited in Marion

influential figures who did not attack the book, such as Mendelssohn and Goethe, made it known that the work was inordinately hard to understand, let alone appropriate. Here Reinhold played a crucial role, for he was not only very sympathetic to Kant's work but also unusually lucid and persuasive in his presentation of it. In setting forth to explain Kant, Reinhold conceded that the *Critique* had met considerable resistance.[2] While he contended that such resistance rested largely on misunderstandings, Reinhold also believed that the text needed to be reformulated so that its major points would not be obscured by its complex details. Kant had acknowledged as much himself in presenting a shorter and supposedly more accessible version of his thought in his *Prolegomena to Any Future Metaphysics Which Will Be Able to Come Forth as a Science* (1783), but what really turned the tide in his favor was not so much this work – which, to this day, never quite functions as the self-sufficient short introduction to the *Critique* that readers are always seeking – but rather Reinhold's *Letters on the Kantian Philosophy* (1786–7), published originally in a sequence of essays and then gathered in an expanded book version (vol. 1, 1790; a second volume was added later).

As D. J. Jenisch reported to Kant in a letter of May 14, 1787, Reinhold's *Letters* finally made the *Critique* the center of philosophical discussion throughout Germany. The *Letters* were also responsible for advancing Reinhold's career, for on their basis he was immediately made professor at Jena.[3] Reinhold was not bashful about soliciting Kant's support for his efforts, and Kant in turn was eager to cultivate a good connection with

Heinz, "Herders Metakritik," in *Herder und die Philosophie des Deutschen Idealismus*, ed. M. Heinz, *Fichte-Studien Supplementa*, 1998, p. 89. For other early reactions to Kant see also below at n. 64; Hermann Timm, *Gott und die Freiheit* (Frankfurt: Klostermann, 1974), p. 384; and the letters of L. W. Jacob to Kant, March 26, 1786, and July 17, 1786. Letters to and from Kant are cited in this chapter by date and recipient as published in Kant's *Briefwechsel*, ed. Otto Schöndörffer (Hamburg: Meiner, 1972). See also Reinhold's letter to C. G. Voigt, Nov. 1986, in Reinhold, *Korrespondenz 1773–1788*, ed. R. Lauth, E. Heller, and K. Hiller (Stuttgart: Frommann, 1983). Unless otherwise indicated, all translations are my own.

2 K. L. Reinhold, *Versuch einer neuen Theorie des menschlichen Vorstellungsvermögens* (Prague: Widtmann and Jauke, 1789), pp. 13, 49. Cf. his *Briefe über die Kantische Philosophie*, vol. 1 (Leipzig: Göschen, 1790), pp. 103, and vol. 2 (Leipzig: Göschen, 1792), p. 14. Hereafter vols. 1 and 2 of the *Briefe* will be cited as *Briefe* I and *Briefe* II. Detailed bibliographical data can be found in Alexander von Schönborn's invaluable *Karl Leonhard Reinhold: Eine annotierte Bibliographie* (Stuttgart: Frommann-Holzboog, 1991).

3 See Kurt Röttgers, "Die Kritik der reinen Vernunft und K. L. Reinhold: Fallstudie zur Theoriepragmatik in Schulbildungsprozessen," in *Akten des 4. Internationalen Kant-Kongresses*, vol. 2, pt. 2 (Berlin: de Gruyter, 1974), p. 801.

Weimar and Jena. It was there that Reinhold and Wieland – a famous literary figure and Reinhold's father-in-law – co-edited the important journal *Der Teutsche Merkur,* in which the *Letters* initially appeared.[4] Kant encouraged Reinhold in correspondence, offered work to his journal, and even gave an explicit endorsement to Reinhold in a short essay.[5] Meanwhile, Reinhold attracted unprecedented scores of students to Jena and to the Critical system, which at this point was occasionally referred to as the "Kantian-Reinholdian philosophy."[6] This was a rather misleading term, for initially Reinhold had not presented anything like a systematic philosophy, and when he did, departures from Kant became quickly apparent. Moreover, there is good evidence that from the start the positive relations between the two philosophers were often determined by ulterior motives rather than deep agreements on technical issues. There is no reason to think Kant studied the entirety of Reinhold's exposition. He was exceptionally busy at this time and may well have relied largely on hearsay (e.g., Jenisch) and Reinhold's own instructions about what parts of the *Letters* were to be stressed.[7] As for Reinhold, he has been charged with orchestrating the campaign for Kant primarily as a means to secure his own immediate preferment.[8] At the very least, it is clear that Reinhold had his most fundamental views set already in his pre-Kantian writings on

---

4 On the background of the *Teutscher Merkur,* see Leslie Bodi, *Tauwetter in Wien* (Frankfurt: S. Fischer, 1977), pp. 233–5; and Bruno Bauer, *Geschichte der Politik, Kultur, und Aufklärung des achtzehnten Jahrhunderts* (Berlin, 1843), pt. 2, chap. 3.

5 See Kant's letter to Reinhold, Dec. 28 and 31, 1788, and the end of Kant's "Über den Gebrauch teleologischer Prinzipien in der Philosophie," published originally in the *Teutscher Merkur,* 1788, *Kant's gesammelte Schriften* (Berlin: Preussische Akademie der Wissenschaften/ de Gruyter, 1900–), vol. 8, p. 183. Hereafter, the latter work will be cited as *AA.* It is significant that Kant ignored Reinhold's later bids for endorsement of his work.

6 See F. C. Schlosser, *History of the Eighteenth Century,* trans. D. Davison (London: Chapman and Hall, 1843), vol. 2, p. 184; and Theodore Ziolkowski, *German Romanticism and its Institutions* (Princeton: Princeton University Press, 1990), p. 236: "Reinhold's ardent Kantianism drew the students to his lecture rooms in ever larger numbers, with no fewer than six hundred of Jena's eight hundred students attending in 1793."

7 See Reinhold's letter to Kant, Oct. 12, 1787.

8 See Röttgers, "Die Kritik." But cf. the qualifications by Werner Sauer, *Österreichische Philosophie zwischen Aufklärung und Restauration* (Amsterdam: Rodolpi, 1982), p. 113, n. 114; and Wolfgang Schrader, "Introduction," in Reinhold, *Über das Fundament des philosophischen Wissens. Über die Möglichkeit der Philosophie als strenge Wissenschaft* (Jena: Mauke, 1791; and Jena: Mauke, 1790; reprint, Hamburg: Meiner, 1978), p. 20, n. 2. See also the fine overview of the age by Sabine Roehr, *A Primer on German Enlightenment, with a Translation of Karl Leonhard Reinhold's The Fundamental Concepts and Principles of Ethics* (Columbia: University of Missouri Press, 1995).

behalf of the Enlightenment.[9] What has not yet been appreciated enough is the fact that when Reinhold first discussed the *Critique*, he was also a selective reader and simply picked up on themes congenial to his earlier interests, while avoiding the harder epistemological and metaphysical discussions that occupy the Transcendental Analytic and thus the core of Kant's Critical philosophy (see below at n. 42).

In view of these considerations it should not be so surprising that I will argue that it is the differences between Kant and Reinhold that are fundamental. My ultimate concern, however, is not the mere existence or nature of these differences but rather their effect. On my reading, it was precisely Reinhold's revisions of the Critical philosophy that were primarily responsible for the direction that the mainstream of German philosophy took in the next generation and after – above all, for its extraordinarily ambitious, questionable, and still very influential conception of what philosophy as such needs to accomplish.

A. 2. The Strong Foundational Program

Perhaps the most remarkable thing about Reinhold's work is the fact that despite – or perhaps precisely because of – its audacity in "popularizing" Kant, it immediately received a huge echo and was enthusiastically perceived as capturing the essence of the Critical philosophy.[10] No matter how much this perception was affected by distorting factors, Reinhold was surely a genius in using his writing talents to exploit the overlap between his most basic concerns and a concise and appealing, even if not entirely accurate, reading of Kant. Any fair outline of Reinhold's Kant presentation must therefore acknowledge ideas that are close to a straightforward recapitulation of the Critical doctrines, even while emphasizing how much a significant revision of these ideas defines the special claims Reinhold added to the Critical philosophy.

9 See Wolfgang Schrader, "Systemphilosophie als Aufklärung: Zum Philosophiebegriff K. L. Reinholds," *Studia Leibnitiana* 15 (1983): 72–81. Cf. Reinhold, "What Is Enlightenment?" trans. Kevin Geiman, in *What is Enlightenment? Eighteenth Century Answers and Twentieth Century Questions*, ed. James Schmidt (Berkeley: University of California Press, 1996), pp. 63–77; Reinhold, *Schriften zur Religionskritik und Aufklärung, 1782–1784*, ed. Zwi Batsha (Bremen and Wolffenbüttel: Jacobi, 1977); Sauer, *Österreichische Philosophie*, p. 75; and Wilhelm Teichner, *Rekonstruktion oder Reproduktion des Grundes* (Bonn: Bouvier, 1976), pp. 238, 432–3.

10 See e.g., Frederick Beiser's account, *The Fate of Reason: German Philosophy from Kant to Fichte* (Cambridge, MA: Harvard University Press, 1987), pp. 228–9.

This pattern is found throughout the *four main claims,* each with a number of key subclaims, that I will contend dominate Reinhold's Kant presentation, as well as his own philosophy and all that it influenced. In shorthand terms, the main claims are that the Critical philosophy is uniquely and simultaneously: (1) *public,* (2) *professional,* (3) *bounded,* and (4) *autonomous.* These claims define, in turn, the starting point, development, completion, and ultimate aim of Reinhold's philosophy. For each of these claims, a parallel and relatively innocuous meaning can be found easily enough in Kant's philosophy (they correspond roughly to a four-part structure set out at the beginning of Chapter 1 above and Chapters 3 and 6 below), but the terms are each given a radical new definition in Reinhold's discussion. The first three claims are listed explicitly, in various formulations, in a number of Reinhold's summaries of the *Critique,* whereas the fourth, concerning autonomy, is so central, complex, and seemingly so close to Kant's own view that it is often missing in Reinhold's summaries simply because it "goes without saying" and appears too basic to be treated as but one of a number of aspects of Kant's work. After a preliminary overview of these main claims, the remaining sections of this chapter will go over each of the claims in more detail.

Throughout this analysis I will employ the general label "strong foundationalism" to stand specifically for the formal pattern of any philosophy that shares Reinhold's insistence on incorporating this whole fourfold set of claims in his strict meaning. This label is intentionally chosen to suggest a similarity to many aspects of the general notion of "foundationalism" that is widely used in current epistemology and accounts of the history of modern philosophy.[11] The term "strong foundationalism" is also meant to be a reminder of Reinhold's original contribution on the topic, the influential essays that inaugurated the systematic turn in his work: "On the Foundation [*Fundament*] of Philosophical Knowledge" and "On the Possibility of Philosophy as a Rigorous Science."[12] Reinhold's title equally suggests the term "fundamentalist," but that word is freighted with too many connotations from American religious life to be most appropriate here. All the same, it is good to keep in mind that there are many analogies between his thought and typical "back to the basics"

11 For some concise accounts of foundationalism, see the essays in *Faith and Rationality,* ed. Alvin Plantinga and Nicholas Wolterstorff (Notre Dame: University of Notre Dame Press, 1983). See also below at n. 20.
12 See above at n. 8. An excerpt from the "Fundament" has been translated in *Between Kant and Hegel,* ed. G. di Giovanni and H. S. Harris (Albany: State University of New York Press, 1985), pp. 53–96.

movements – especially when religious concerns play a key role, as they do here. But it must also be kept in mind that Reinhold is very much an advocate of the Enlightenment rather than a reactionary, and it is explicitly a return to the "spirit" rather than the "letter" that is paramount.[13] Like the Reformers, he seeks a foundation that is new and modern – and also a kind of return to something that has always been with us, as close as our own selves.

A. 3. Popular Science? A Fateful Tension in Reinhold's Doctrines

The first main claim that Reinhold found attractive in the spirit of Kant's philosophy has to do with its anti-elitist, public nature. The *Critique* is said to offer *immediately certain* premises that *can* gain *actual* and *universal approval*. This means that they have the crucial virtue of being what Reinhold calls *allgemeingeltend*, that is, *taken* as valid by all, and not merely *allgemeingültig*, that is, intrinsically valid for all. In contrast to traditional metaphysical speculation, the aim here is to insist on continuing Rousseau's project of bringing philosophy away from mere abstractions and into a direct relation, at least in principle, with what the public in general already believes, at least implicitly, and in just this sense to make it *popular*. The Reinholdian demand for a public philosophy is thus defined by a complex of subclaims having to do with a specific strong type of certainty, universality, and corresponding popularity.

Secondly, in stressing the "professional" nature of the Critical enterprise, I take Reinhold to be pointing to what he sees as its paradigmatic *scientific* nature (hence, despite the first point, he is to be aligned against, rather than with, the completely antisystematic so-called popular philosophers of his time, such as Feder or Nicolai).[14] He understands this nature as enabling the *deduction* of a whole realm of significant consequences from a foundation that is not only popular but *absolutely solid*, and thus the construction of a whole system that can account for itself in a special *reflexive* way that makes it the most "fundamental" of all types of "science." Although the term "science" is (and will be) used here in its broad Ger-

---

13 These terms and their role in the whole era are discussed by Rolf-Peter Horstmann, *Die Grenzen der Vernunft* (Frankfurt: Anton Hain, 1991), pp. 78–81.

14 See Reinhold, *Versuch*, p. 11, and *Fundament*, p. 12. This is still compatible with the important point, put well by Paul Franks, that Reinhold's "heart lay less in system construction than in the construction of a consensus whose foundations the right system would provide." "Review of S. Roehr, *A Primer on German Enlightenment*," *Philosophical Review* 106 (1997): 142.

man meaning, and not, as is common in current English, in a sense that is restricted basically to exact or quantitative science, it clearly is intended to have a meaning that involves a discipline that is actually much stricter than what is often found in the natural sciences. Reinhold's initial call for a professional philosophy is thus defined by a complex of subclaims that challenge philosophy to be a scientific discipline in the specific strong sense of having a fully rigorous basis, a strict deductive development, and a demonstrated closure in its principles.

I will be arguing that Reinhold's first two main claims are in a fateful tension with one another, a tension inherited to some degree from Kant (see above Chapter 1, sec. D. 2, and below Chapter 2, sec. D. 4) but clearly exacerbated by his own strong reading of the Critical project.[15] The claim of being public is supposed to save Critical philosophy from the shortcomings of esoteric writing (just as, not coincidentally, Protestantism was to save Christianity from the elitism of clerics), whereas the implications of the claim of being professional threaten to make philosophy a mere sport of experts after all. Although there are deep differences between these claims that have far-reaching consequences – and that forced Reinhold to loosen the meaning of both claims fairly quickly – one can also see the claims as forming a natural pair and as being understandable variations of a path to a common end. The end that encompasses them, and the entirety of Reinhold's writing for that matter, is the objective of replacing methodological, ethical, religious, and political authoritarianism by a philosophy that can bring about and *secure* enlightened and universal self-determination. It is obviously because he assumes that philosophy must play the crucial role in gaining this ultimate goal of full *autonomy* (claim 4) – grounded in a *bounded* system (claim 3) that blocks traditional metaphysics – that Reinhold calls for it to have a basis that is immediately accessible and evident to all (hence claim 1). Similarly, it is clearly this ultimate goal that dictates for Reinhold that philosophy must not be

15 Reinhold's overly strong sense of "public" and "professional" causes special difficulties here, but for Kant as well the difficulty goes to the heart of his philosophy. This is especially obvious in works such as his *Groundwork*, and in the relation between the categorical imperative as a principle of common life and as a principle for philosophers. Recognition of this point as a general problem is not as common as might be expected, although it was already addressed explicitly in Schleiermacher's review of Kant's *Anthropology*, which criticizes Kant sharply for aiming to be "systematic and also popular at the same time." Friedrich Schleiermacher, *Schriften aus der Berliner Zeit 1796–1799*, ed. Günter Meckenstock, *Kritische Gesamtausgabe* I/2, ed. Hans-Joachim Birkner et al. (Berlin: de Gruyter, 1984), p. 368. Cf. the discussion of the quotation in the editors' introduction (1997) to *Kant's Vorlesungen über Anthropologie*, ed. Reinhard Brandt and Werner Stark, in *AA*, vol. 25, pt. 2, p. xxii, n. 3.

allowed to relapse into a chaos of conflicting and ineffective intuitions. Hence, Reinhold insists that philosophy requires a strict method, indeed, that it must be the most rigorous of all scientific disciplines (claim 2), so that it can build out from its basis in such a way that it need not ever fear being outdone or undermined.

Although their common end gives Reinhold's first two claims an obvious connection to Kant's well-known emphasis on the general idea of self-determination, the fact is that the claims themselves, taken in their original full sense, are extremely ambitious, hardly self-evident, and not even clearly required by Kant's texts (see above Chapter 1, sec. B). Hence it is only appropriate to pause over a question that is too often neglected, namely, why were Reinhold and his many followers so committed to these very strong claims? For now, I will merely indicate my own hypothesis that the fatal step here is a curious presumption, a momentous and highly questionable "argument" from desperation: Reinhold repeatedly stresses that unless *philosophy* can take on the character required by all four of these main doctrines taken together, we will be left with no adequate basis at all for claiming *any* fundamental natural rights or duties – and not merely without a proper answer for our ultimate personal concerns, such as the existence of God, freedom, and immortality (Kant's "postulates of pure practical reason").[16] This is a remarkable presumption, springing no doubt from various historical factors in the intense self-assertive struggles of German scholars at that time (see below sec. C. 5). Note that Reinhold's presumption demands much more than just that philosophy itself be autonomous, or that it be somewhat instrumental in the general achievement of autonomy. It amounts to nothing less than the radical demand that there be an extremely strict form of *philosophical* autonomy that is itself the crucial condition for *any* genuine autonomy at the level of ordinary life. Here the requirement of strong foundationalism within philosophy passes over into a demand that philosophy play a foundational role even with respect to all that is of basic value outside of it. This insistence is tantamount to a metaphilosophy that goes beyond "mere" strong foundationalism to what might be called (in part with an eye to Reinhold's original ruler, the similarly well-intentioned and overreaching Habsburg emperor, Joseph II) "imperialist foundationalism." That is,

16 See below Chapter 2, secs. C. 5 and C. 8; and Reinhold, *Briefe* II, p. 24, *Philosophie als strenge Wissenschaft*, p. 367, and letter to Baggesen, March 18, 1793, in *Aus Jens Baggesens Briefwechsel mit Karl Leonhard Reinhold und Friedrich Jacobi* (Leipzig, 1831), p. 258, as quoted in Zwi Batscha, "Reinhold und die französische Revolution," in *Studien zur politischen Theorien des Frühliberalismus* (Frankfurt: Suhrkamp, 1981), p. 109.

Reinhold often works with nothing less than the presumption that if *any philosophy – and ultimately, any society –* is to maintain legitimacy and meaningful existence, it must provide for an "imperial" discipline that is public and professional in his strong sense. Only such a discipline can provide the ground that is needed for responding to the basic and inescapable questions of value that Reinhold emphasizes. Reinhold also believes, *a fortiori,* that if *Kant's* work is to be of value, it had better be seen as providing such a ground. Hence it is only proper that as soon as Reinhold encounters difficulties in finding what he wants in Kant himself, he is consistent enough immediately to develop a system of his own that is designed specifically for yielding such a ground, that is, for being public and professional in the strictest sense.

A. 4. Contemporary Reactions

The remarkable reception that Reinhold immediately received proves that he was hardly the only one in his time to think in these extreme terms. Even in our own time, the pathos behind this development remains vivid in the title and dramatic spirit of Frederick Beiser's recent grand narrative of this period, *The Fate of Reason.*[17] Beiser provides an expert, and at least rhetorically sympathetic, documentation of the widespread presumption of the age (1781–93) that unless philosophy after Kant could be given a genuine foundation in an absolutely certain and scientific form, reason itself would be undermined, and thus nihilism – a term introduced at this very time by Jacobi – would become a pressing danger. A treatment of some aspects of this very same presumption, but from a quite negative and more thematic than historical perspective, can be found in Richard Rorty's earlier and highly influential account of the main path of philosophy since Descartes and Kant.[18] Rorty sketches an engaging analytic version of the old story of how the Kantian era, and everything in its long shadow, was marked by a confused obsession with representationalism and the project of securing for philosophy a strict scientific status of its own (through the invention of a pure and transcendental *Fach*), so that it could provide a ground or adequate substitute for

17 See my "Review of F. C. Beiser, *The Fate of Reason*," *Philosophical Review* 98 (1989): 398–401.
18 Richard Rorty, *Philosophy and the Mirror of Nature* (Princeton: Princeton University Press, 1979). For stimulation on the need to address these issues, I am very much indebted to Gary Gutting; see his *Pragmatic Liberalism and the Critique of Modernity* (Cambridge: Cambridge University Press, 1999).

the old moral and theological ideals that seemed undermined with the rise of modern science.

Without endorsing Rorty's dismissive attitude toward some of these ideals, one can still grant his point that it has been a deep and long-lasting mistake for so many Western intellectuals to believe that the fate of the basic values of our ordinary life is essentially tied to the success of the complex pseudoscientific systems of the major modern philosophers – as if "everything is permitted" once these systems run aground. In this regard, there is much to agree with in Rorty's late-Heideggerian and late-Wittgensteinian suspicion that the pretensions of philosophy itself and its main traditions are themselves a significant problem and require some form of deconstruction. But even if this much is conceded, it still does not follow that we must turn away *completely* from all of modern philosophy, especially as presented in the *Critique* itself, that is, *before* philosophy was dominated by generations of epigones and "all or nothing" foundationalists and representationalists (from Reinhold through to twentieth-century positivism).

My own treatment of this period will aim to combine something of Rorty's critical attitude with something of Beiser's historical detail, while also trying to move beyond some presumptions common to their work. In particular, instead of going so far as to follow Rorty's own proposal that we now take a pragmatist turn beyond traditional philosophy altogether, I will be arguing that the popular view of our history that Rorty expresses makes a fundamental mistake. This mistake is similar, ironically, to the very error that it is trying to diagnose that of overvaluing the significance of representationalism and foundationalism. That is, Rorty, like Beiser and many other important interpreters of modernity (e.g., Rawlsian neo-Kantians, who insist on an "ethics that leaves ontology behind"), appears to presume that traditional modern philosophy is altogether a futile enterprise simply because of its heritage of metaphysical projects, projects that are supposedly all doomed because they rest on nothing more (aside from wholly arbitrary intuitions) than a variety of extreme and outdated epistemologies. This presumption seems to me to involve taking a precipitous step that can be avoided with a little systematic and historical patience. Just as Rorty's pragmatism is correct in reminding us that in general there is considerable "life" (e.g., art and democracy without "foundations") outside of the foundationalist forms of modern philosophy, so too it can be correct to stress, *against* pragmatism, that there is still considerable life within much of traditional philosophy itself, even of a basically metaphysical and, I would contend, fairly orthodox Kantian variety – once that philosophy is distinguished from its foundationalist distortions and the overreactions to them.

The work of analytic "Reformed" epistemologists and metaphysicians such as Alvin Plantinga and Nicholas Wolterstorff has recently given a very impressive exhibition of many ways in which contemporary philosophy of a traditional kind (e.g., metaphysics without "the linguistic turn") can remain quite fruitful by moving beyond foundationalism in all its forms.[19] This movement, however, has tended to distance itself very much from the mainstream German tradition, largely because it shares the representationalist misinterpretation of the Critical philosophy. Hence it unfortunately misses the fact that there is much of value in Kant's work that deserves to be separated from the fate of the foundationalisms that surrounded it – and especially from the "imperialist" foundationalism that happened to become influential after him primarily because of hasty desperation in some of his readers rather than essential weaknesses in the Critical philosophy. This situation is easily overlooked because leading analytic epistemologists and metaphysicians tend to be non-Kantian, while most contemporary writers who have expressed an interest in Kant tend to ignore or look down on metaphysics. Because of caricatures and misinterpretations, Kant's own metaphysical system, which was clearly at the very heart of his work, is often neglected on all sides. As a first step toward understanding and reversing this peculiar development, I propose to take a closer and more critical look at history by focusing on the pivotal role that Reinhold played in the crucial early moments of the Kantian era, and on the moments at which Kant's relatively modest but fatally ambiguous systematic ideas became transformed into philosophies that took on the form of a self-undermining imperialist fantasy.[20]

19 See, e.g., Nicholas Wolterstorff, *John Locke and the Ethics of Belief* (Cambridge: Cambridge University Press, 1996); and Alvin Plantinga, *Warrant: The Current Debate* (Oxford: Oxford University Press, 1993).
20 A more optimistic view of developments in this era has been given by Dieter Henrich, who has characterized it in terms of a "supernova" of philosophical brilliance, complicated by the dominance of various long-obscured "constellations" of intense conceptual interaction. See his voluminous *Konstellationen: Probleme und Debatte am Ursprung der idealistischen Philosophie (1789–1795)* (Stuttgart: Klett-Cotta, 1991), and *Der Grund im Bewusstsein: Untersuchungen zu Hölderlins Denken (1794–1795)* (Stuttgart: Klett-Cotta, 1992), and, for a very concise statement, the section "The Rapid Development of Thought after Kant," in "Hölderlin in Jena," in *The Course of Remembrance*, ed. E. Förster (Stanford: Stanford University Press, 1997), pp. 90–4.

A. 5. Reinhold's Third Doctrine: An Insistence on Bounds

The first two main claims of Reinhold's work, his stress on a thoroughly public and professional discipline, are closely connected with his ultimate project of trying to secure the fate of reason and its ideals through pure reason itself. This aim is meant to be supported in a crucial way by the *third* main claim in Reinhold's picture of Critical philosophy, its "bounded" nature. By this I mean its taking on such a *thoroughly* systematic and *all-inclusive* form that it *restricts* all our knowledge claims to ones that can be enclosed within a realm defined a priori by what follows from a certain foundation in our most basic representations *and* their evident conditions. For Reinhold, these basic representations need not be sensory, and the "and" here allows for his version of Kant's crucial "moral argument," according to which pure reflection on our self and its duties ultimately reveals conditions that demonstrate the existence of God. The *object* that is asserted in this case is admittedly meant as transcendent, but the *basis* for asserting it is still one that supposedly is entirely within our ordinary experience and does not involve an intuition of a "beyond"; it remains, as Kant was to say, "within the bounds of reason alone." All traditional and *wholly theoretical* transcendent claims to knowledge are thus ruled out, and in this way finally ruled out *in principle,* so that the fundamental objective of antiauthoritarianism can be made absolutely secure. Reinhold argues that if (and only if) all dogmatic claims to know what lies beyond experience can be totally dismissed in this way, there need be no fear any more of modern philosophy lapsing back into the uncertain state that undermined any lasting claim to a "public" and "professional" character in previous metaphysics. He was especially worried about this point because he feared (somewhat like Locke, but with less patience and more of a taste for strong medicine) that, unless philosophy could put its own house in order and show how everything worthwhile belongs within its domain, nonrational theology and other "enthusiastic" movements might regain the mantle of authority and thus, with their reactionary allies, manage to reverse the Enlightenment.

   I have labeled Reinhold's third main claim the assertion of the "bounded" nature of philosophy primarily because it corresponds in many ways to what has been called Kant's idea of the "bounds of sense," or the "restriction principle." The claim has obvious connections to the limitations on human pretensions that are stressed in Kant's central theoretical doctrine of transcendental idealism as well as in his more popular writings on the Enlightenment. This does not yet decide, however, whether the specific subclaims that define Reinhold's understanding of this familiar doctrine amount to a genuine parallel with Kant's views or, on the contrary, a very significant departure, as was indicated with the first two points. Rather than getting entangled already in the complicated details of that discussion (see below sec. C. 2), it is more useful here to complete the preliminary outline of Reinhold's version of Critical philosophy by moving on to the most relevant aspects of his fourth and final main claim, the doctrine of autonomy.

A. 6. Reinhold's Fourth Doctrine: Autonomy

The doctrine of autonomy, that human beings can be, are, and should be fundamentally determined by their own legislation, is known best because of its central significance as a normative principle in Kantian ethics, but it also has a meaning for philosophical methodology in general. What is striking about Reinhold's understanding of the doctrine, aside from the radical autonomy that he demands from philosophy itself, is the way that he remains remarkably attached to Kant's belief that autonomous morality needs to culminate in an account of how we can rationally maintain hope for the "highest good," a universal state of both virtue and appropriate happiness. According to this account, it is only by accepting the "postulates of pure practical reason," namely the existence of God and immortality, that we can coherently maintain a rational commitment to the pure ends that our pure practical reason legislates for itself, and to the hope for a human community where persons are fulfilled as well as dutiful. These postulates amount to a "liberal" compromise between traditional faith and modern unbelief; the core commitments of rational religion are maintained while the traditional theoretical grounds for them are all rejected. Reinhold's full understanding of the claim of autonomy follows closely on the residual orthodox strands in Kant's thought here, and his stress on the postulates is what allows him to add a significant spiritual *content* to balance the highly formal and this-worldly orientation of his first three main claims. Unlike the more radical generation that immediately succeeded him, Reinhold begins by arguing that a philosophy of self-determination can still ground the *literal* core of the traditional belief in providence that previous philosophy, in the mainline Christian and modern tradition, was committed to but was now supposedly unable to demonstrate. The key condition for establishing this goal rests in the twofold strategy of a purely moral approach to religion that limits theological claims to (a) the hopes supported by our autonomous ethical experience and the "need of reason" to have our highest practical ends fulfilled, and (b) a metaphysics that alone prevents these hopes from seeming impossible by grounding them in a doctrine of transcendental idealism that guarantees that there exists something ultimate, even if for us not theoretically determinable, underlying the realm of spatiotemporal appearances.

Reinhold begins by accepting the Critical doctrine that if there were nothing more than these appearances, then our hopes would have to be taken as illusory. As Kant stresses in the *Critique of Practical Reason*, without the transcendental ideality of space and time, we are left with a futile Spinozism.[21] Because of this second, highly metaphysical component, Kant's own version of the strategy for defending the self-satisfaction of autonomous reason was criticized from the start by all the later idealists and other radicals as a relapse to dogmatism or worse. I will argue that the difficulties alleged here in Kant's own approach were to a large extent exaggerated, and that when Reinhold developed a variation of it, the strong foundationalism that he added led to a version of the strategy that actually made it even more open to objections and multiple misunderstandings than Kant's original argument. This weakness had enormous consequences precisely because the unfortunate presumption of most readers of the time was that it was Reinhold who had provided the most promising version of the Critical philosophy – and so it was concluded all the more hastily that if Reinhold's "improvement" was manifestly unsatisfactory, then the whole Critical approach had to be drastically revised or left behind. More generally, ever since Reinhold, philosophy has lived in the shadow of the thought that if it cannot succeed as a foundational project that autonomously grounds all knowledge, then there is no significant autonomy in it, or anywhere else, that can be defended in a specifically philosophical way. Nietzsche, Rorty, and others have reveled in this suicide of pure philosophy, but theirs may be a premature and unnecessary celebration, especially if it can be shown that it was only the projects of strong foundationalism, and not the Critical philosophy as such, that suffered shipwreck.

A. 7. Preliminary Summary

A typical summary expression of Reinhold's commitment to the four main claims that have been introduced in this overview can be found in

---

21 Kant, *AA*, vol. 5, pp. 101–2; *Critique of Judgment, AA*, vol. 5, pp. 393, 452.

the *Letters,* which defends the *Critique* at a crucial point as "natural," "subjective," and "affirmative."[22] The term "natural" here corresponds to the first two claims discussed earlier: Kant's principles are said to be "natural" primarily because they are supposedly both (1) fully public, that is, *allgemeingeltend,* and (2) professional, that is, rational and absolutely "scientific," rather than arbitrary and speculative.[23] The term "subjective" here maps on to what has just been called (3) the "bounded" nature of Critical philosophy, its ruling out theoretical knowledge about what is objective in any sense that wholly transcends experience. Finally, the "affirmative" claim expresses the key point – which Reinhold most wants to stress against the famous Mendelssohnian image of Kant as all-destroying (*allzermalmend*)[24] – that (4) Kant's practical philosophy contains not only a set of autonomous basic principles for ethics but also a legitimation of traditional interests in a "kingdom of ends," complete with personal immortality and a personal God. It is significant that a similar commitment to precisely these points can also be found in Reinhold's characterization of the principle he introduces later as the basis of his own philosophy, the "principle of consciousness." This principle is characterized as (1) "clear, accessible, certain, basic," (2) "scientific," and (3) "thorough," that is, not transcendent but providing a complete, idealistic, and "bounded" system capable of accounting for itself in a reflexive way.[25] The principle also

22 Reinhold, *Briefe* I, p. 131. For an interpretation with similar points, cf. Wilhelm Teichner, *Rekonstruktion,* p. 219, which summarizes Reinhold's philosophy as resting on (1) absolute evidence, (2) scientific character, and (3) consistency with the Enlightenment. Cf. Timm, *Gott,* pp. 412–13; and Reinhard Lauth, "Fichtes und Reinholds Verhältnis von Anfang ihrer Bekanntschaften bis zu Reinholds Beitritt zu Standpunkt der Wissenschaftslehre Anfang 1797," in *Philosophie aus einem Prinzip,* ed. R. Lauth (Bonn: Bouvier, 1974), p. 150. These points also coincide with much in Beiser, *Fate of Reason* (1987), chap. 8, although we worked without reference to each other. The early papers in which I worked out my first ideas on Reinhold happened to experience a delay of four years before publication: "Reinhold and the Short Argument to Idealism," in *Proceedings: Sixth International Kant Congress (1985),* ed. G. Funke and T. Seebohm (Washington: Center for Advanced Research in Phenomenology and University Press of America: 1989), vol. 2, pt. 2, pp. 441–53; and "Kant, Fichte, and Short Arguments to Idealism," *Archiv für Geschichte der Philosophie* 72 (1990): 63–85 (Chapter 3 below).
23 Cf. Reinhold, *Briefe* II, p. 25, where the Critical philosophy is called natural in a somewhat different sense because it rests "on the mere decomposition of the necessary and universal laws of the power of representation, which it knows through reflection (without special effort) on the facts of consciousness belonging to inner experience." See also ibid., p. 350, for an instance where the stress on "natural" is meant in yet another way as a contrast to the supernatural.
24 Reinhold, *Briefe* I, p. 170.
25 Reinhold, *Fundament,* p. 100.

reveals and expresses our freedom and in a manner that is fundamental to (4) the doctrine of autonomy as well.

I will argue eventually that a parallel quartet of commitments, with problems similar to Reinhold's, can also be found (with distinctive variations in subclaims) at the heart of the systems of his major successors, Fichte and Hegel (see below Chapters 3 and 6). For this chapter, the initial characterization of Reinhold's philosophy is meant merely to set the stage for the sections that follow, which will be devoted to investigating the four main doctrines in detail by explaining their particular meaning in Reinhold's work, indicating their connections with his ultimate motives, and preparing the study of their more general ramifications for the later reception of Kant in the major German idealists.

B. REINHOLD'S FIRST DOCTRINE: PHILOSOPHY AS PUBLIC AND CERTAIN

B. 1. The Background of the Quest for Certainty

In elaborating on this first aspect of Reinhold's treatment of Kant, it is necessary to determine more precisely what the insistence on certainty consists in and how Reinhold arrived at it. Philosophers have often insisted on certainty, but this demand has rarely been understandable to outsiders, and usually it has been tied up with some kind of obscure and complex epistemological project. It is significant that originally Reinhold's concern with certainty developed independently of any deep epistemological investigations and had precisely the main aim of giving philosophy a form that could make it immediately effective with nonspecialists. What Reinhold initially demands is not the mere certainty that an expert might claim relative to his colleagues, as in the case of the mathematically self-evident, but rather a kind of immediate certainty, a certainty that can be shared by layman and professional alike.

The background of Reinhold's concern here can be easily understood from his involvement in the controversies that arose during the period of enlightened despotism. At the time of Joseph II and Frederick the Great, theological views in German-speaking lands took on an extremely liberal character at the level of the academic and governmental establishment, a tendency that was not shared by the population at large.[26] The contrast

---

26 See Wilhelm Lütgert, *Die Religion des deutschen Idealismus und ihr Ende* (Gütersloh: Bertelsmann, 1923), vol. 1; Karl Aner, *Die Theologie der Lessingzeit* (Halle: Neimeyer, 1924); and Werner Schneiders, *Die wahre Aufklärung* (Freiburg: Alber, 1974).

between a loose deism at the top and a resurgent pietism at the broad base of society was enough to force academies to pose questions such as how proper it is to "deceive one's own people" by leading them by various indirect means toward liberal views that they would never accept directly on first sight. Reinhold had experienced this contrast in a very personal manner in Austria when his youthful commitment to an advanced intellectual life in the priesthood was shattered by threats to reform movements and a decree suspending the Jesuits. After a period of disorientation (1774–82), he found a home with the leading radical group of Viennese intellectuals, the famous lodge Zur Wahren Eintracht.[27] He wrote numerous pseudonymous articles for them against reactionaries in the church hierarchy,[28] but the restrictions of his vows and the growing power of conservatives in Vienna forced him to flee to Germany. When he eventually gained refuge in Weimar (1784), his underground connections and literary talents allowed him to use Wieland's influential *Teutscher Merkur* as the vehicle for similar but more theoretical pieces in behalf of the Enlightenment.[29] Reinhold was a zealous convert to Protestantism, which he took to be responsible for the fortunate "secularization of the sciences" and their deliverance from scholastic superstition, as illustrated by a frequently invoked contrast between political as well as scientific developments in modern England and authoritarian Spain. In aiming to reinvigorate the "spirit of the Reformation," he naturally focused on Catholicism as a scapegoat and attacked all political and moral domination of common people by authorities.

At this time Reinhold had not developed a very detailed or original philosophical program, and yet the fundamentals of his later thought were already in evidence. He campaigned for *Aufklärung* – literally, a

27 For more on this lodge period, see H. Gliwitzky, "C. L. Reinholds erster Standpunktwechsel," in *Philosophie aus einem Prinzip*, pp. 63ff.; Charles H. O'Brien, "Ideas of Religious Toleration at the Time of Joseph II," in *Transactions of the American Philosophical Society* (Philadelphia) 59 (1967): 59ff.; Helmut Reinalter, "Josephinismus, Geheimgesellschaften und Jakobinismus," in *Ungarn und Österreich unter Maria Theresa und Joseph II*, ed. A. Drabek, A. Plascka, and A. Wondruszka (Vienna: Verlag der österreichischen Akademie der Wissenschaften, 1982), p. 66; Lodi, *Tauwetter*, p. 228; Gerhard W. Fuchs, *Karl Leonhard Reinhold: Illuminat und Philosoph* (Frankfurt: Peter Lang, 1994).

28 Later Reinhold spoke of the "allgemeiner Autorwut" that broke out in Vienna, when "in a space of less than three years, thousands of authors arose, each an apostle of Enlightenment" (*Schriften*, p. 11). On this "Broschürenflut," see Lodi, *Tauwetter*, pp. 217ff. Reinhold's flight is understandable because, despite the liberalism of Joseph II, especially harsh measures were taken against violations of vows by clerics. See O'Brien, "Ideas," p. 28.

29 The titles of some of Reinhold's essays in the *Schriften* are revealing: "Thoughts on Enlightenment," "The Sciences Before and After their Secularization," and "Vindication of the Reformation."

"clearing up" of concepts[30] – and for popular education, Erastianism, and a more natural structure of social life. Not surprisingly, he condemned monastic vows, especially celibacy, which was perhaps the sore point of his own turn from the Roman church.[31] The main claims that would be the pillars of his system were already present in these popular essays. The enemy was esoteric and unscientific monkishness; the weapons against it were the secular thoughts that human satisfaction could be gained through understanding this world alone,[32] and that the power of the idea of *Selbstdenken,* self-determination, was ultimately irresistible.[33] Reinhold effectively promulgated the textbook notion that the scientific revolution rested on turning to "graspable things" and expressing their principles in a way that the common crowd (*Pöbel*) could appreciate,[34] and he argued that similar methods could lead to a realization of universal rights independent of special authorities. Reinhold repeatedly conjoined the two themes of the autonomy of morals (especially its independence from dogmatic religion) and the emptiness of esoteric "scholastic logic."[35] At one point he practically defined the "revolution" of the Enlightenment in terms of an appreciation of these points, but he added that this growing appreciation tended to get stuck in disappointing generalizations, so it had not yet really penetrated the masses.[36] It was because of this basically practical purpose of thoroughly and irreversibly changing the ideology of the common people that Reinhold was already at this time looking for a philosophy that could ground his Enlightenment doctrines in immediate certainty.

At first Reinhold unfortunately did not have much of a method for attaining such certainty. The best he could do was to stress the idea of clear "mediating" or "overlapping" concepts ("communication bridges between science [*Wissenschaft*] and ignorance [*Unwissenheit*]")[37] such as the image of God as a loving father, which were supposedly not too high for the layman and not too low for the philosopher, and thus could help to lead ordinary people from authoritarian to critical attitudes – for exam-

---

30 Reinhold, *Schriften*, p. 12.

31 Ibid., p. 38; cf. his *Versuch*, p. 52.

32 Reinhold, *Schriften*, p. 37.

33 Ibid., p. 39.

34 Ibid., p. 40. Cf. Reinhold's *Briefe* I, p. iv–v.

35 The enemy here was not merely the old stalking horse of scholastic syllogisms. Pre-Critical metaphysics in general was under fire. Thus the whole "spiritualist" (dualist) tradition is treated by Reinhold as "neo-Platonic esoterica" (*Briefe* I, p. 178).

36 Reinhold, *Schriften*, p. 13. The underdeveloped structure of Austrian society was also a cause of Joseph II's failure. Cf. Reinhold's concern for the social conditions for moral development at *Briefe* I, p. 336.

37 Reinhold, *Schriften*, p. 130; cf. *Briefe* I, p. 369.

ple, from thoughts of God as tyrant to God as designer. This example illustrates the basic rationalist approach that Reinhold took to certainty: he always stressed the uncertainty that arises from ambiguity rather than mere ignorance or distance, and so, despite his great familiarity with the empiricists, skeptical representationalism was never his own main worry. What he desperately sought was some means for securing premises that would avoid the problem of ambiguity, premises that would carry, as his example suggests, substantive metaphysical implications while somehow remaining free from the entangling complexities of the dogmatic philosophical tradition. In general, his methodological faith, here and to the very end of his career, rested in the power of analysis. He believed that if philosophers could only break down their concepts – or, as he would later say, the pure phenomena, or the terms of their language – simple components would be revealed about which no one could disagree. In fact, though, he did not get very far with such analysis, and it seems all too obvious that the more he moved in this direction, the more he was heading into the very intricacies of academic philosophy that he wanted to avoid. Reinhold thus has an uncanny resemblance to the philosophers who succeeded him more than a century later in Vienna, and who temporarily swept the field with their own enthusiastic foundational programs, such as phenomenology or the "linguistic turn," only to flounder on the dogmas of their own revolutions.

It was only after Reinhold struck out on his own, when he had a chance to search for a method among the latest philosophical movements in Germany (in 1785), that he began to appreciate Kant. Reinhold's struggle for a politically effective philosophy coincided with his search for a firm philosophical ground for the ethical and theological version of the doctrine of autonomy to which he was *antecedently* committed. This explains how he so suddenly believed that Kant's Critical system alone provided the practical effectiveness and theoretical firmness that was simultaneously required. He immediately focused on the end point of Kant's system, the moral proof of God, and he even claimed that this new proof was as immediately certain as our own self-consciousness: "The cognitive ground practical reason provides for the existence and attributes of God is thus not only as *firm and unchangeable* as the essence of reason itself, but it is as intuitive and illuminating as the self-consciousness which one has of one's rational essence."[38]

It is amazing that such a strong claim could have been made prior even

---

38 Reinhold, *Briefe* I, p. 174; cf. ibid., p. 214. Anticipations of this view can be found in Rousseau's well-known account of the faith of the Savoyard Vicar in *Émile* (book 4).

to the publication of Kant's second *Critique* (1788), in which the moral proof was first properly set out in detail (and in a way that tried to avoid talk of "intuition" of one's "essence"), and yet it is really not surprising that Reinhold located the philosophical foundation he was seeking in the slim nontheoretical component of Kant's first Critical work. Reinhold had always been a man of action, and, as Fichte fairly observed, above all he "always wanted to improve people through philosophy."[39] Time and again he claimed, like most thinkers of his era, that the "real" philosophical issues were "the ground of our duties" and "the basis for an afterlife."[40] When he first wrote to Kant, Reinhold admitted that it was the moral proof of God that had initially attracted him to the Critical philosophy, and even that it was all he really understood.[41] Later he explained that the prime purpose of the *Letters* was to "draw attention to those results of the *Critique of Pure Reason* which bear on the basic truths of religion and morality,"[42] for these are the ones to which "we cannot be indifferent."[43]

Contemporary philosophy students, who are taught to focus almost entirely on the first three hundred pages of the *Critique,* and all its complicated arguments about space, time, and the categories and principles of theoretical understanding, would be astounded to see how these sections are neglected by Reinhold. The volume that succeeded in supposedly delivering the main content of the *Critique* to its immediate German audience simply passed over the key theoretical discussions and jumped to the relatively slim sections on practical issues, as is immediately evident from the surprising individual titles of Reinhold's *Letters:*

1. The spirit of the age and the present situation of the sciences gives notice of a general reformation of philosophy.
2. The need for a highest rule of taste; guiding principles for positive theology and jurisprudence, but above all for a first principle of natural law and morals.

---

39 See the letter of Fichte to Reinhold, April 22, 1799. Cf. Fichte to Reinhold, July 2, 1795. Correspondence with Fichte will be cited by date as published in *J. G. Fichte-Gesamtausgabe der Bayerischen Akademie der Wissenschaften* (*GA*), ed. R. Lauth and Hans Jacob (Stuttgart: Frommann, 1964–).
40 Reinhold, *Briefe* I, p. iv; *Briefe* II, p. 24; *Versuch,* p. 74; *Philosophie als strenge Wissenschaft,* p. 359.
41 See the letter of Reinhold to Kant, Oct. 12, 1787. Cf. *Versuch,* p. 54; and below at n. 211.
42 Reinhold, *Versuch,* p. 57.
43 Reinhold, *Briefe* I, p. 92. This volume includes the twelve letters that I list in the text; for a list of the similar titles of the shorter set of eight letters in the earlier *Teutscher Merkur* version, see von Schönborn, *Bibliographie,* pp. 69–70.

3. Agitation in the field of philosophy of religion gives notice of a reformation. My judgment on the Kantian philosophy in general.

4. The result of Kantian philosophy on the question of the existence of God, compared with general as well as specific results of previous philosophy on this.

5. The results of the critique of reason on the necessary relation between morality and religion.

6. Kantian rational faith compared with metaphysical and hyperphysical grounds of conviction.

7. On the elements and previous manner of conviction of the basic verities of religion.

8. The result of the critique of reason for the afterlife.

9. Exposition of the metaphysical grounds for knowing the immortality of the soul, in respect to their origin as well as their consequences.

10. Outlines of the history of the idea of mind.

11. Key to the rational psychology of the Greeks.

12. Points on the influence on civil and moral culture of undeveloped and misunderstood basic verities of religion.

The main feature of the remarkable – and at first very widely accepted – reformulation of the Critical philosophy in Reinhold's *Letters* is the implication that the *Critique* concerns almost nothing other than considerations about the conditions of morality and freedom, and is designed to give a definitive resolution of these issues in a way that can at once satisfy both "the schools" and "the world." Methodologically, the key point here is that Reinhold obviously believes that by shifting the discussion wholly to topics of practical concern, such as freedom, the philosophy of the *Critique*, and it alone, can address fundamental issues in a way that connects with what is truly popular. Only in this way can it be actually received as universally acceptable, or *allgemeingeltend*, and not only valid in principle.

Kant himself often emphasized that his Critical approach to the old metaphysical issues of rational theology and psychology was meant as not just one more scaffolding of subtle arguments. Rather it was rooted, in a typical Enlightenment and Rousseauian manner, in something that is already part of common belief. This view was held not only with an eye to finding beliefs that could continue to hold out under all rational investigation, so that they could be part of a truly solid system; it was also held because Kant regarded any other approach *inappropriate*, no matter what hidden theoretical validity it might have. This is because, on account of his strong notion of fairness, it was crucial to Kant that one's ultimate fate could not be determined by complex theoretical methods to which one could not expect all mature people to have adequate access.[44] Reinhold's background shows that he was, if anything, even more devoted to this egalitarian ideal of the Enlightenment. It may well be that it was primarily because of what he took to be the centrality of this ideal that Reinhold even went so far as to call the *Critique* the "Evangel of Pure Reason," and to speak freely of Kant as the new Immanuel who would eventually be at least as honored as Jesus.[45]

B. 2. Tensions in "an Easier, More Popular Approach"

In explaining the results of the *Critique,* Reinhold had to admit that he was connecting them not with Kant's actual premises, which were too complex for a work aimed at a broad public, but with "the present convictions of the time," "its essential scientific and moral needs."[46] There is an obvious problem here, a tension that was noted above (sec. A. 2). On the one hand, Reinhold is turning to Kant because he promises a unification of the "commonest and the most enlightened faith,"[47] a "strict" proof that rests on "ever-present motives"[48] and avoids the "unholy distinction between esoteric and exoteric religion."[49] On the other hand, Reinhold's

---

44 J. B. Schneewind traces the significant theological presuppositions at work here in his *The Invention of Autonomy* (Cambridge: Cambridge University Press, 1997).

45 Reinhold, *Briefe* I, p. 104. At one point, thinking it was written by Kant, Reinhold also called Fichte's *Critique of All Revelation* the "Evangel." See Reinhold's letter to Baggesen, June 22, 1792, in *Fichte im Gespräch*, vol. I, ed. Erich Fuchs (Stuttgart: Frommann, 1978), p. 35; and Schiller's letter to Körner, Aug. 29, 1787, in Friedrich Schiller, *Werke. Nationalausgabe*, vol. 24, p. 143, which is discussed in Sabine Roehr, "Zum Einfluss K. L. Reinholds auf Schillers Kant-Rezeption" (forthcoming). A major leader of this "evangelical" movement was Friedrich Niethammer. See above Chapter 1, n. 38, and Hans-Peter Nowitzki, "'Geh hin und predige das Neue Evangelium': Friedrich Phillip Immanuel Niethammers Weg von der Nostrifikation zur Renuntiation als ausserordentlicher Professor der Philosophie in Jena," in *Evolution des Geistes: Jena um 1800*, ed. F. Strack (Stuttgart: Klett-Cotta, 1994), pp. 94–123.

46 Reinhold, *Versuch*, p. 57. This led to a general tendency to read the *Critique* "backward," i.e., beginning with the religious themes at the end of the Dialectic. See Timm, *Gott*, p. 387.

47 Reinhold, *Briefe* I, p. 147.

48 Ibid., p. 139.

49 Ibid., p. 136. H. Timm argues that throughout his work Reinhold was dominated by the idea of a "philosophy of reconciliation" that presupposes that the fundamental problem of philosophy is a basic cultural division caused by the faith-versus-reason controversy raised by the "Pantheismusstreit" of 1785 (*Gott*, pp. 397ff.; cf. Beiser, *Fate of Reason*, p. 235). This interpretation has to be balanced by the evidence noted above that Reinhold's basic attitudes were already formed in his Vienna years, when he was stressing political and religious issues well before this specific controversy. Nonetheless, the later controversy can

reluctance to present a full version of the proof itself implies that there is more than what can be handled with truly immediate certainty.[50] The best he can say is that while the "results" of the *Critique* satisfy "the most common understanding," its "grounds" satisfy the "sharpest thinker."[51] Here he is conceding that Kant's own premises may after all lack certainty in the immediate, popular fashion he had originally demanded.[52]

In trying to resolve this difficulty, Reinhold had to embark on a new stage in his thought wherein he became much more a reviser than an expositor of Kant.[53] Even with his sympathetic preconceptions, he could hold on only so long to the idea that one of the last – and, for most readers, one of the most debatable – aspects of the Critical system, the moral proof of God, was a matter of Cartesian certainty. Rather than move away from insisting on absolute certainty at the foundation of philosophy,[54] Reinhold's first move was to give up on adhering absolutely to Kant, and instead to stress all the more heavily the demand for an *allgemeingeltend*[55] ultimate premise, a premise that "is not simply found true by all who understand it but rather also actually understood by every sound and philosophical mind."[56] The concession that such a premise was not to be found anywhere in Kant himself, let alone in the moral argument, came most directly in the preface (also published in a separate version) to Rein-

certainly help us to understand many of Reinhold's works, and esp. his *Herzenserleichterungen zweier Menschenfreunde in Vertraulichen Briefen über Johann Caspar Lavaters Glaubenserkenntnis* (Frankfurt: Weidmann, 1785).

50 In a letter of Jan. 12, 1788, Reinhold admits to Kant that he hasn't given an "actual exposition" of the argument.

51 Reinhold, *Briefe* I, p. 139. Cf. below at n. 99. The project of finding better "grounds" for Kant's "results" was taken over later not only by Fichte but also Schelling, and, through him, Hegel.

52 I mean this implicit concession to be distinguishable from Reinhold's much later and more general Jacobian view that all philosophy lacks certainty and must leave room for faith and a basic gulf between speculation and life. See below at n. 87; Lauth, "Fichtes und Reinholds Verhältnis," p. 197; and A. Klemmt, "Die philosophische Entwicklung K. L. Reinholds nach 1800," *Zeitschrift für philosophische Forschung* 15 (1961): 275.

53 This change is marked by Reinhold's decision not to call his next work, as he had once intended, an "Introduction to the Critique of Pure Reason." See his letter to Kant, March 1, 1788, and cf. Teichner, *Rekonstruktion*, pp. 220, 238. Ironically, Kant's own objection to Reinhold was that Reinhold had become too abstract and hence failed to make the details of Critical philosophy truly popular. See Kant's letters to Reinhold, Sept. 21, 1791, and to Beck, Nov. 2, 1791.

54 This path was espoused at the time by J. F. Fries. See, e.g., his *Reinhold, Fichte, und Schelling* (Jena, 1803), p. 8.

55 See Reinhold, *Versuch*, p. 66; and *Beyträge zur Berichtigung bisheriger Missverständnisse der Philosophen* (Jena: Mauke, 1790), vol. 1, chap. 2; and the discussion in Daniel Breazeale, "Reinhold's Elementary Philosophy," *Review of Metaphysics* 35 (1982): 790–4.

56 Reinhold, *Versuch*, p. 72.

hold's first major systematic work, entitled "On the Previous Fate of the Kantian Philosophy" (in *Versuch einer neuen Theorie des menschlichen Vorstellungsvermögens*, 1789). The "previous fate" consisted precisely in the first *Critique's* failing to find the kind of immediate acceptance – even after the *Letters* – that Reinhold had anticipated. As a consequence, Reinhold set about charting his own all too influential "easier way"[57] – eventually employing what I will call the "short argument" – for presenting the heart of the Critical metaphysics (see below sec. C. 6). True to his long-standing convictions, he suggested that the main problem here rested in a failure of analysis: Kant had "simply assumed" the basic concept of representation (*Vorstellung*).[58] By focusing on and breaking down this central concept into its components, one could supposedly gain "that which in its nature [would] thoroughly insure against the previous misunderstandings and [which] when put at the base of the Kantian theory of cognition would provide certainty for it."[59] Such an approach, which entirely bypassed the *Critique's* own focus on the transcendental structure of judgment as the source of the categories, went directly against Kant's own view, as expressed most vividly in a letter to the reviewer Garve:

> It is of the highest importance to give a deduction of the pure concepts of the understanding, the categories, that is, to show the possibility of wholly a priori concepts of things in general; for, without this deduction, pure a priori knowledge can have no certainty. Well then I should like someone to try to do this in an easier, more popular fashion [NB]; he will then experience the great difficulties that are to be found in this field of speculation. But he will never deduce the categories from any other source than that which I have indicated, of that I am certain.[60]

Although Kant had no way of knowing of Reinhold's work at the time, the "popular fashion" he warned about in this remark from 1783 applies perfectly to Reinhold's new approach, which substituted, for Kant's complex treatment of judgmental experience, an "easier" approach from the mere notion of representation as such. It appears that Reinhold simply could not escape the lure of a strong foundationalist program once he thought he had found in representation an Archimedean point for constructing a whole system with an immediately accessible, absolutely cer-

---

57 Ibid., p. 62.
58 Ibid., p. 63.
59 Ibid.
60 Kant, letter to Garve, Aug. 7, 1783, translation from *Correspondence/ Immanuel Kant*, ed. and trans. A. Zweig (Cambridge: Cambridge University Press, 1999), p. 197.

tain, and endlessly fertile basis. This was a fateful shift, for when later idealists placed slightly different notions at the base of their own systems, they still took over the main features of the questionable key changes in the form and content of Critical philosophy that Reinhold introduced (see below Chapter 3).

B. 3. The New Basis: Representation

Although it is well known that the notion of representation is central to the whole tradition growing out of Locke's "new way of ideas," and that later developments in a wide range of traditions into our own time have continued to give it a central role, it is still remarkable that Reinhold came to focus so strongly on the notion. "Representation" does function as the most general term in one list that Kant provides,[61] but there is no indication that the term is meant to have any privilege. Rather – and this is precisely what is unsatisfactory to Reinhold – Kant tends to begin his arguments with the much more limited notion of experience *(Erfahrung)* or cognition *(Erkenntnis)* (see above Chapter 1, sec. B. 3). This notion signifies not a simple impression but rather a complex of concepts and intuitions that is organized by a logical structure of judgment, and that is examined on the presumption of our having some kind of warranted objectivity (without which there is no point in even asking, as Kant does from the beginning, e.g., *how* our geometrical representations of space and time might "always" fit the objects of our experience). Reinhold felt such a beginning point was simply too hypothetical. Presumably it left the *Critique* without an absolute ground that all must affirm, even the ignorant and the skeptical.[62]

There are a variety of incidental factors that may well have influenced Reinhold here. We know that just before this period Reinhold had worked as an instructor teaching about Leibniz. Representation is, of course, a basic notion of the Leibnizian system that dominated Germany

---

61 See Kant, *Critique of Pure Reason*, A 320/ B 336. This passage was noted in a review by C. G. Schütz that Reinhold read in the *Jena Allgemeine Literatur Zeitung* (1785). See below at n. 68; and Angelica Nuzzo, "Metamorphosen der Freiheit in der Jenenser Kant-Rezeption (1785–1804)," in *Evolution des Geistes*, p. 489.

62 See Reinhold, *Fundament*, pp. 91, 129; and his *Beyträge zur Berichtigung bisheriger Missverständnisse der Philosophen*, vol. 2 (Jena: Mauke, 1794), p. 419. Cf. J. E. Erdmann, *A History of Philosophy*, vol. 2, trans. W. S. Hough (London: Sonnenschein, 1897), p. 475. I believe Erdmann errs here, however, in implying that Kant read and approved all of the essay that was published as the "Vorrede" of the *Versuch*.

at the time, and it was emphasized by Reinhold's first teacher in Germany, Ernst Platner of Leipzig.[63] It is also clear that Reinhold knew of reactions to the first *Critique* that took Kant's talk of representation (as in the phrase "space and time are mere forms of representation") in the doctrine of transcendental idealism to imply a mysterious and entirely subjective position.[64] It was an obvious task, then, for any defender of Kant to attempt to clarify the notion of representation. Unfortunately, in picking up on this notion, Reinhold tended to exacerbate rather than to set to rest the main problem of Kant's readers, namely, their tendency, like that of many interpreters to this day, to project back on to the Critical system what is a crude conflation of empirical and transcendental uses of the term – a distinction that Kant himself introduced and would have been the last to confuse. On an "empirical" understanding of the term, which tends to be the focus for Reinhold as well as Kant's first reviewers and the whole empiricist tradition, "representation" signifies an inner, psychological episode, typically involving mere private "sense data." Beginning with such episodes, especially from a standard empiricist perspective, naturally leads into all sorts of thorny skeptical problems as soon as one tries to move from this slender basis, by whatever psychological mechanisms, to rational claims about an external world with physical objects, other minds, or, for that matter, anything with genuine semantic content. What Kant himself emphasizes, however, is not the empirical notion of representation but a "transcendental" understanding of the term, one that stands, first of all, simply for a methodological reminder that, for epistemic purposes, a formal distinction can be made between any view of things (whatever way they are cognitively represented, be it in theories, maps, sensibility, language, etc.) and the things themselves (so that we can *begin* to ask questions such as how good is a particular view, what is it like, etc.). He goes on to add, of course, that he believes that we can find specific a priori features governing our perceptual experience (i.e., empirical knowledge). The crucial point to realize is that the eventual discovery and deduction of these features, and the further metaphysical interpretation of them as requiring a doctrine of transcendental idealism, is something that obviously *follows* upon, and cannot precede or be reduced to, the mere taking of an initial and general transcendental, or nonem-

---

63 See Fuchs, *Reinhold*, pp. 34, 51. Platner criticized Kant and had a considerable following of his own.

64 Reinhold, *Versuch*, p. 31. The Feder-Garve Göttingen review (see below n. 69) and Jacobi's work were most influential in generating this subjective reading.

pirical, perspective on experience.[65] Nowhere in Kant's methodological *or* eventual metaphysical distinction between representations and things in themselves does he give any reason to give priority to isolated minds and private impressions as such, or to presume that there is some barrier in principle to knowing objects at all, and so it is no wonder that Kant himself never focuses on the notion of a bare particular representation, as if he would have to work his way "out" from there.

B. 4. Reinhold's Principle of Consciousness and Kant's Transcendental Deduction

All this leaves it unclear why the notion of representation was not merely treated by Reinhold but given priority in the manner it was, especially since at first sight it hardly seems a fertile enough notion to be able to function as the keystone for a whole system. There is, however, one well-known way that one might *try* to use it as such a keystone while also connecting it to themes that *seem* Kantian. This would be to take the bare notion of representation, or perhaps a minimal notion of one's own representation,[66] as the starting point for a transcendental deduction which would prove, and not "simply assume," that there is objective experience. This is in fact the way that Kant's deduction of the categories has often been read[67] – especially in the Strawsonian antiskeptical reconstructions of our own time – and it explains one reason why later interpreters, such as Rorty, have interpreted Kant as starting from a foundation of representation in the empirical sense. But although this approach fits much of the spirit and effect of *Reinhold's* work, there are great intrinsic and textual difficulties with ascribing this strategy to Kant. There is also

65 A fine account of such a "nonempirical" methodological perspective is given in Gerold Prauss, *Einführung in die Erkenntnistheorie* (Darmstadt: Wissenschaftliche Buchgesellschaft, 1980).

66 As P. F. Strawson's interpretation (*Bounds of Sense* [London: Methuen, 1966]) stresses, in understanding a representation as itself something in contrast to what it is about, one is naturally led to the thought of oneself as having representations. This approach, along with the fact that Kant uses the phrase "I think" so often, can easily suggest a basis for the deduction that focuses on beginning from the "self-ascribability" of representations. Some exegetical as well as systematic problems with this tempting and still-influential line of interpretation are pointed out in my "Kant's Transcendental Deduction as a Regressive Argument," *Kant-Studien* 69 (1978): 273–85.

67 See criticisms in my "Recent Work on Kant's Theoretical Philosophy," *American Philosophical Quarterly* 19 (1982): 11–12, and "Kant and Guyer on Apperception," *Archiv für Geschichte der Philosophie* 65 (1983): 174–86.

the remarkable fact that the details of the deduction do not figure much at all in Reinhold's discussion, so it is unlikely that whatever interest he had in representation was dependent on this or any other particular reconstruction of the deduction. One explanation for this may be his predominantly practical orientation; another is perhaps the fact that even Johann Schultz's straightforward summary of the *Critique,* on which Reinhold, like many others, relied heavily from the start, played down the deduction.[68] This is not untypical for the times, for the famous Feder-Garve review did the same.[69]

What may make it especially difficult to believe that Reinhold could have so ignored Kant's deduction is the fact that, in distinguishing Kant from Leibniz, Reinhold shows he is quite aware of the importance of the notion of the *synthetic* unification of representations, a notion that does of course play a key role in the deduction. That is, Reinhold's own basic principle might understandably be thought to be an analog to the notion of the synthetic unity of apperception in Kant's deduction. The "principle of consciousness," which Reinhold introduced as fundamental imme-diately after the *Letters,* also makes a basic claim about consciousness as synthetic, for it states that with every representing there must be a repre-sented (object) and a representer (subject) that are distinguished and related. Nonetheless, the *Letters* reveals that Reinhold's idea of a general principle of synthesis in consciousness has its source not in the Transcen-dental Analytic's account of synthesis as judgment (at B 129), which is the account directly relevant to Kant's deduction, but rather in his study of the Transcendental Dialectic, and, in particular, in Kant's discussion in the Paralogisms of the metaphysical rather than epistemological nature of the notion of the "I."[70] The main idea of Reinhold's own systematic book, *Essay on a New Theory of the Human Power of Representation* (*Versuch einer neuen Theorie des menschlichen Vorstellungsvermögens*) can thus be under-

---

68 See Reinhold's letter to Kant, Oct. 12, 1787. Reinhold read the review in the *Allgemeine Literatur-Zeitung* (Jena, 1785) of Johann Schultz's *Erläuterungen über den Herrn Professor Kants Critik der reinen Vernunft* (Königsberg, 1784); cf. the helpful apparatus of the English edi-tion, *Exposition of Kant's Critique of Pure Reason,* trans. James Morrison (Ottawa: University of Ottawa, 1995). On Reinhold's bypassing of the deduction, see below Chapter 2, sec. C. 8; and Richard Kroner, *Von Kant bis Hegel* (Tübingen: Mohr, 1977, 3d ed.), vol. 1, p. 325. For similar reactions by Reinhold's contemporaries, see Benno Erdmann, *Kants Kriticismus in der ersten und der zweiten Auflage der Kritik der reinen Vernunft* (Leipzig: Voss, 1878), p. 127. I do not agree with the idea that Reinhold can be seen as directly completing Kant's deduc-tion, as suggested by Gunther Baum, in "K. L. Reinholds Elementarphilosophie und die Idee des transzendentalen Idealismus," in *Philosophie aus einem Prinzip,* p. 93.
69 The review is translated in Morrison's edition of Schultz, *Exposition.*
70 See Reinhold, *Briefe* I, letter 9.

stood as coming simply from his consideration of what the first Paralogism indicates is left of our mind once all dogmatic fallacies are pared away: "If one separates the part that the representing subject has in the power of representation [*Vorstellungsvermögen*], then one obtains the pure faculty [*Vermögen*] of representation [*Vorstellung*] and the theory of what the representing subject can accomplish [*vermag*] in representing."[71]

While this passage discloses the main explicit source of Reinhold's approach, an incidental occasioning ground of Reinhold's sudden emphasis on representative faculties could also have been Kant's first letter to him, where Kant explained that whenever he had difficulties, his strategy was always to "refer back to the general outline of the elements of cognition and the relevant powers of the mind."[72] It is understandable that Reinhold may have picked up on this passage in terms of his own interest in tracing everything back to the power of representation. If he did read the letter this way, however, he was not following Kant's own intentions. It was a much disputed question of the time whether the various powers of mind could be deduced from some one basic power, as Leibnizians had suggested, and Kant was in fact quite insistent about doubting that possibility.[73] In passages like his remark to Reinhold, what Kant probably meant to stress was that the "outline" of faculties, like all else in his philosophy, could be approached through his table of categories (which he also calls his basic "clue" or "principle"),[74] which is based on judgmental and not merely representative powers. Kant would also have been especially loath to follow the details of Reinhold's understanding of representation, because in the principle of consciousness Reinhold took representation to be coextensive with consciousness, whereas Kant (like Reinhold's immediate opponents, Maimon and G. E. Schulze) sharply distinguished the two and allowed nonconscious representations.[75]

---

71 Ibid., p. 249.

72 Kant, letter to Reinhold, Dec. 28, 1787. Kant goes on to detail how the Critical system is arranged in terms of a treatment of the faculties of cognition, pleasure/pain, and desire. This discussion seems to have influenced the *Versuch*, but it is notable that, at *Briefe* I, p. 49, Reinhold had already called for a systematic investigation of our faculties.

73 See Dieter Henrich, "Über die Einheit der Subjektivität," *Philosophische Rundschau* 3 (1955): 29–69; and Vladimir Satura, *Kants Erkenntnispsychologie* (Bonn: Bouvier, 1971), pp. 40ff. For relevant details on the Leibnizian tradition, see Udo Thiel, "Leibniz and the Concept of Apperception," *Archiv für Geschichte der Philosophie* 76 (1994): 195–209.

74 See, e.g., the first Preface to Kant's *Critique*, A xx, which speaks of "the common principle" by which "the inventory of all our possessions through pure reason is systematically arranged." Cf. Beatrice Longuenesse, *Kant and the Capacity to Judge* (Princeton: Princeton University Press, 1998).

75 See Satura, *Kants Erkenntnispsychologie*, pp. 53ff.

B. 5. The Significance of the Problem of Representation

Although there is no single reason for emphasizing the notion of representation, there are many obvious factors that taken together should
make it not so surprising now that Reinhold would have focused so much
on the notion, despite its secondary role in Kant's work. Above all, one
should keep in mind Reinhold's ultimate practical objectives and the way
that the notion of representation could appear to meet his strong desire
to find some popular and Archimedean point from which to get hold of
the broadest possible audience to meet those objectives. It was never the
standard, purely epistemological reasons for this focus that most concerned Reinhold, although these reasons are what remained central to
the mainline representationalist tradition in philosophy, from the early
empiricists to Russell's era.[76] This tradition never became directly dependent on Reinhold, but its general approach was in a significant relation of
mutual reinforcement with the way that Reinhold's focus on the notion of
representation (especially when combined with the impact of his strong
foundationalist model for philosophy) affected the reading of Kant in
Reinhold's immediate audience. This reading became so widespread that
it could not help but determine general presuppositions about German
philosophy elsewhere. Within idealist circles, Reinhold's focus had a very
significant responsibility for the surprising fact that Fichte and Hegel
read Kant as a Berkeleyan or Lockean (see below Chapters 4 and 6). This
development also had important implications much later, even in empiricist circles, because no major barrier was set up against very influential
writers, such as Moore, who took Kant to be just one more philosopher
bedeviled primarily by the problems of skepticism and the external world.
The representationalist reading continues to be widespread to this day,
and, ironically enough, it dominates precisely in traditions such as the
English-language literature of our own time, from Broad, Bennett, and
Strawson through Rorty, where Reinhold's own name and influence are
never even recognized.

Aside from the specific complications it has led to for appreciating the
true structure and value of Kant's philosophy, the Reinholdian focus on
representation and its intractable problems can also be understood as a
key source of the development of the perplexing general character of our
contemporary philosophical situation. Here, once again, it is helpful to

---

76 See, e.g., the standard account in David Pears, *Bertrand Russell and the British Tradition in
Philosophy* (London: Fontana, 1967).

keep in mind how, originally for Reinhold, the focus on the mere notion of representation, and even its role in his basic principle of consciousness, was never designed for purely epistemological purposes. It was essentially tied to the very concrete and practical Enlightenment project that he shared with his readers, and that from the very beginning was the major impetus behind his urgent insistence on a universally effective and professional, scientific philosophy. This insistence had effects that went far beyond the short-lived popularity of Reinhold's own ambitious systems. These systems stalled at about the same time that, contrary to expectations, the Enlightenment project became commonplace rather than remaining a radical movement that believed it had to exploit the authority of an academic pedigree. The idea of "pure philosophy," especially of a rigorous foundational type, then began to float free and to lose a clear motivation and point. One gets the image of a magnificent eighteenth-century sailing ship out on a voyage where the crew has become fascinated simply by the rigging and has lost all sight, interest, and hope of reaching the original goal of being the philosopher kings of the modern era.

By the time that Reinhold's own elaborate notion of philosophy as a "rigorous science" had become an historical curiosity, the general foundationalist ideal that it expresses had so permeated philosophical culture that its formal model was still being employed without being recognized as such. The ideal was pursued without any clear memory that the enterprise had once attracted intense devotion because it appeared to be essential for an evidently valuable and general end. The pure analysis of representation changed from being an instrument, however confused, for a vital public project, to becoming a game that it was assumed it made sense to play for its own sake (albeit with less and less confidence). A major result of this loss of bearings in our own time has been a deep and long-lasting split ("analytic"/"continental") among philosophers, many of whom have retreated to a pursuit of rigor at all costs, while forswearing anything like an attempt at a general "system," while others have been tempted more and more to abdicate traditional philosophical writing for the sake of literature or similar pursuits – on the hasty presumption that if philosophy on the grandest scale has become questionable, something else altogether should be done. Tracing some of the early steps toward this situation as they developed in Reinhold's own lifetime may help us to see its contingency, and to liberate us to some degree from the narrow models of philosophy that it, and the extreme reactions to its grand failure, encouraged. But before tracing those steps, it is necessary first to lay out some of the remarkable details of the heart of Reinhold's own theoretical work: the second and third of his four main claims, which are best represented in the landmark essays "On the Possibility of Philosophy as a Rigorous Science" (1790) and "On the Foundation of Philosophical Knowledge" (1791).

C. REINHOLD'S SECOND AND THIRD DOCTRINES: PHILOSOPHY AS RIGOROUS AND BOUNDED

C. 1. Different Notions of Science

Reinhold's concern with a rigorously scientific character for philosophy goes back, as has been noted, to his earliest writings. Two related demands dominate Reinhold's early picture of philosophy as science. The first demand involves merely the general idea of a scientific discipline that would exclude the "chaos" of arguments and counterarguments that has characterized the history of metaphysics.[77] The second demand involves the specific hypothesis that, to prevent this chaos, science must achieve a thorough unity, that is, a strong unity of principle covering the entire domain of knowledge. Reinhold came to believe that this requires more than just a modest unity coordinating different kinds of evidence (as in Kant); it requires working out a whole system of the world by derivations from an absolute first principle (*Grundsatz*),[78] a substantive base that must be much more than a mere formal rule such as the principle of contradiction.

In his first system Reinhold insisted that the basic principle be not only evident in itself but also in fact universally *held* to be valid; in other words, it must be an "*allgemeingeltendes* Prinzip allgemeiner Evidenz."[79] Originally, Reinhold justified the demand for such a principle by arguing that, in its absence, disagreement about metaphysical arguments concerning objects of essential concern such as God would persist and then develop – as in his time they already had developed – into a general threat to the credentials of reason.[80] This worry led him to make explicit what I have called the key "imperialist" presumption of his era, namely the claim that "An actually valid universal [*allgemeingeltender*] principle must be possible as a first principle, or [NB] philosophy as science is impossible, and the

---

77 Reinhold, *Briefe* I, pp. 22, 161, 170.
78 Ibid., p. 24; and Reinhold, *Philosophie als strenge Wissenschaft*, p. 367. The influence of Wolff seems strongest here, but Timm (*Gott*, p. 399) argues that Reinhold is trying to bring together Kant and Spinoza, since the principle is also an *Alleinheitsidee*.
79 Reinhold, *Briefe* I, p. 25; cf. his *Philosophie als strenge Wissenschaft*, p. 367.
80 Reinhold, *Briefe* I, letter 3.

basis of our moral duties and thus [NB] of all duties and rights must remain ethically undecided."[81] In the *Letters,* Reinhold made the remarkable, and unjustifiable, claim that Kant's *Critique* should be read as if it were responding directly to this complex problem in laying out the general structure of human knowledge (determining in principle what reason can and cannot know),[82] and in replacing the multitude of traditional proofs of God by a single compelling practical proof and a unified moral system: "previous metaphysics . . . was nothing more than an aggregate of indefinite and disconnected propositions, which lacked the essential condition of a system, a unity of principles and a single basic principle . . . [whereas] the moral cognitive ground, which the critique of reason posits as the sole ground [NB], really has in itself the character of being the first principle of a system."[83]

Despite these confident remarks, the alleged unifying character of the moral argument soon proved even for Reinhold to be no more persuasive than its ostensible Cartesian certainty.[84] After the *Letters,* Reinhold realized that his ultimate interests were not to be met by having at the base of his system a principle that was so controversial, specific, and practical in content. He shifted away from a direct focus on Kant's beleaguered postulates of pure practical reason and attempted to achieve his aims by finding a new and much more general foundation in a fundamental science that focused simply on representation and what he called the basic principle of consciousness (*Satz des Bewusstseins*). His original conviction was that, since the starting point of his own theory of representation is so elementary that it is not merely certain in itself but also universally present, *allgemeingeltend,* it would also be a relatively elementary task to develop a full range of rigorous consequences from its basic principle. It soon became obvious, however, that this theory was itself highly controversial, and that it generated complications that could not be claimed to be resolvable at a popular level. In a very important methodological shift right before Fichte's taking over at Jena, Reinhold came to concede, "the genuine premises of a science can be found only [NB] after science itself."[85] Within a very short time, Reinhold's conception of philosophy as rigorous

81 Reinhold, *Versuch,* p. 367.
82 Reinhold, *Briefe* I, pp. 100, 114, 161–3.
83 Ibid., p. 170; cf. ibid., p. 146.
84 Cf. Reinhold, *Versuch,* pp. 71, 76, which, as Timm (*Gott,* p. 420) notes, concedes that the moral proof fails to be *allgemeingeltend.* The proof was, in any case, obviously much too specific to be the "basic principle" of Kant's first *Critique.*
85 Reinhold, *Versuch,* p. 67.

science had thus moved from (a) an explicit reliance on a moral argument as foundational, to (b) a new, theoretical and, supposedly, immediately self-sufficient foundation, and then to (c) a revised conception of science itself as a process that can approach its "genuine" foundations only as it develops (perhaps, as the Romantics would say, as at best a matter of only "infinite approximation," *unendliche Annäherung*).

Many interpreters recently have remarked on the general form of this shift and its explicit "concession," which takes Reinhold away from his original and linear, deductive program to a much more hypothetical, self-correcting and "coherentist" model of philosophy.[86] The explanation of the grounds and effect of this shift amounts to an extremely complex story in its own right, with significant ramifications for many very important figures, including Novalis and Hölderlin. I will pass over these intriguing complications here, however, since it is not clear that Reinhold's *main* successors were *fundamentally* affected by them, or much interested in the details of Reinhold's later systems, and there is more than enough to explain in the present context without going into all of Reinhold's many phases. Before attending to the details of Reinhold's main system, however, there is one peculiar and unappreciated aspect of his shift that

---

86 Henrich links this concession to what he calls the shift from "Reinhold I" to "Reinhold II," a shift much discussed in the German literature, and the topic of a forthcoming work by Marcelo Stamm on Reinhold's *Systemkrise*. My own view is that this was a very important event for the Jena community but not so crucial for the specific purpose of Kant interpretation. In switching from an axiomatic to something like an a priori hypothetico-deductive method, Reinhold did not fundamentally alter his emphasis on certainty and science, although he "reorganized" his conceptions significantly from the strict version of his original strong foundationalist program – and he had to suffer ever after by being mocked, especially by Hegelians, as the advocate of a "merely hypothetical" philosophy. See the letter of Reinhold to Erhard (explaining his recognition of relevant criticisms by Diez), June 18, 1792, in *Immanuel Carl Diez, Briefwechsel und Kantische Schriften. Wissensbegründung in der Glaubenskrise Tübingen-Jena (1790–1792)*, ed. D. Henrich (Stuttgart: Klett Cotta, 1997), pp. 911–14; Dieter Henrich, *Konstellationen*, and *Der Grund im Bewusstsein*, pp. 114–25; Manfred Frank, *Unendliche Annäherung* (Frankfurt: Suhrkamp, 1997), pp. 151–661; Marcelo Stamm, "Das Programm des methodologischen Monismus: Subjekttheoretische und methodologische Aspekte der Elementarphilosophie K. L. Reinholds," *Neue Hefte Für Philosophie* 35 (1995): 18–31; T. Rockmore, "Epistemology in Fichte and Hegel, a Confrontation," in *Erneuerung der Transzendentalphilosophie*, ed. Klaus Hammacher (Stuttgart: Frommann, 1979), p. 103. In fact there are more than two phases of the early Reinhold. Even in this limited period, it helps to keep in mind differences between (a) Reinhold before he heard of Kant, (b) after he heard of Kant but before he read him sympathetically, (c) after he studied the *Critique* and wrote the *Briefe*, (d) after he set up his own *Elementarphilosophie*, and (e) after he revised his position and backed off from his original foundational system in his last days in Jena. Henrich's "Reinhold I" and "Reinhold II" correspond to (d) and (e) here.

deserves attention because of its general implications for my reading of Reinhold's main goals and methods.

Reinhold's concession implies that the discovery and use of his basic doctrines, whatever they happen to be, must be left up to professionals, people already acquainted with a variety of propositions within a relatively advanced, even if not complete, philosophical science. He thus came to emphasize that his science called for the construction of a professional class of "first philosophers," "scientific" specialists who would replace the traditional priestly caste and would work out derivations from the theory of representation to help ground and inculcate a full range of liberal programs.[87] Once it was accepted that "genuine" certainty is to be had only in this way, *after* working through a complex philosophical process, it became obvious that Reinhold's new strategy required giving up any claim to possess certainty of a completely immediate and popular kind – and this implied giving up the advantage not only of presuming a technically purer form of evidence but also of starting with a much broader audience, in effect the whole public. As a compensation for this loss, Reinhold was forced to a new "elitist" strategy that involved appealing more explicitly to a particular professional class, something very much like a revolutionary cadre, that would supposedly be more reliable than traditional scholars or the public as a whole, and that would remain "popular" only in an ex-tended sense, in the basic components and eventual "results" of its work. It is not surprising that considerable evidence has now surfaced which proves that Reinhold's writing efforts were very much intertwined with activities connected with the far-flung political cells of the secret society (or "invisible church") of the Bavarian Illuminati.[88] The influence of this radical movement, which was remarkably strong for at least a short time, gives a much more concrete meaning to Reinhold's frequent and other-wise mysterious references to an imminent alliance of academic, moral,

---

87 It is no wonder there arose at this time a genre of essays on the "vocation of the scholar" (Fichte, Schelling, etc.). This is anticipated by the appeal to "Selbstdenker" in Reinhold, *Fundament*, p. v. Reinhold's strategy was no doubt related to the problem of the "overstaffed clerical profession" in Germany at this time. See Henri Brunschvig, *Enlightenment and Romanticism in Eighteenth Century Prussia*, trans. F. Jellinek (Chicago: University of Chicago Press, 1974), pp. 123–4; and Anthony La Vopa, *Grace, Talent, and Merit: Poor Students, Clerical Careers, and Professional Ideology in Eighteenth-Century Germany* (Cambridge: Cambridge University Press, 1988).

88 See Fuchs, *Reinhold*, p. 37. Cf. below at n. 164. There is an obvious parallel, in form and content, between Reinhold's involvement with radicals and later philosophical programs (from Schlick to Chomsky) that were also concretely involved with repressed "progressive" movements.

and political leaders. He obviously believed this alliance fit right into his philosophical program. The main idea was that although only a few people may know exactly what to do with a theory of representation, and perhaps no one has yet found its ultimate principles, it is still a theory that can be expected to be conceded even by skeptics, and that in principle can eventually be made accessible to everyone by experts.

This program was seriously flawed from the beginning. Even if one grants the idea that everyone could have access to at least the basic terms of the *Elementarphilosophie,* the actual "foundation" for the science of knowledge was now conceded to be under construction at a level that definitely exceeded the grasp of the common public, and that for all practical purposes was being put off for an indefinite future. A similar difficulty, of course, infects not only whatever are the foundational claims of the pure epistemology of our own time, but also most of its presumptions of being anything like a rigorous science at all. By the late twentieth century, however, the prestige and ambition of philosophy has receded to the point where this difficulty is no longer considered to be a major issue. But this difficulty is not at all a minor problem if one believes, as Reinhold and many of his associates certainly did, that the true Enlightenment is a project that cannot be achieved without the *clear* success of something like his *Elementarphilosophie.*

C. 2. Reflexivity and the Problem of Determining Bounds

Despite the complexities forced upon him, Reinhold himself remained confident about the project of philosophy as rigorous science, and he believed it required merely a few "simplifying" modifications of Kant's system. For Reinhold, the ultimate benchmark of science, the quality that lies behind his concern with universal agreement, strict unity, and deductive fertility, and that he especially came to emphasize was *not* met by Kant, is full *reflexivity.*[89] Reinhold's favorite way of putting his objection to Kant is to say that the *Critique* is neither "firm nor broad enough."[90] In one sense these points simply repeat the previously noted criticisms involving Reinhold's first two main claims, that philosophy must be certain and fully scientific. That is, in turning from expositor to critic, Reinhold was saying that Kant's philosophy lacked an appreciation of the notion of representation, which alone was supposedly firm enough to be accessible

---

89 It is in emphasizing this point that I may be departing most from D. Breazeale, "Reinhold's Elementary Philosophy," p. 791.

90 Reinhold, *Fundament,* p. 129; *Briefe* II, p. 416.

even to all doubters, and general enough to serve as a source for all philosophy. But the point about breadth also anticipates Reinhold's third main claim, that philosophy must be properly "bounded." Here too, what was originally said to be a virtue of Kant's approach became an object of criticism. Kant had claimed to draw the bounds of knowledge, but since he supposedly did so in a crude way, he lacked a *thoroughly* systematic theory, one that could derive everything needed in a self-sufficient manner, including an account of its own knowledge of bounds. A truly complete system must be reflexive, it must include an account of itself and of how it can assert the general limits to knowledge that it claims, in order to provide a guarantee in principle for its results against dogmatic backsliders. In this situation, all three of Reinhold's first main claims about what philosophy requires come together: As soon as Reinhold believed that the *Critique* did not include a reflexive account of its own mode of argument, he also believed it was lacking in breadth (i.e., its claim about bounds) in a way that would put its very basis and development in jeopardy (i.e., its claim to be certain and scientific). These shortcomings obviously imperil its chance for meeting Reinhold's fourth main requirement as well, since the weakness of reflexivity in Kant's philosophy must diminish its autonomy, its ability to govern itself and thus to ground other forms of human self-governance.

Reinhold's concern here involves a classic foundationalist quandary: if a philosopher such as Kant claims to be able to set the bounds of knowledge, what is the warrant for the principle that sets those bounds? If the source of the restriction is not explained, or does not cohere with the knowledge it is supposed to legitimate, the system lacks self-accountability, and thus, Reinhold would say, it forfeits its scientific character. Kant can *seem* to be caught in this dilemma. If we suppose, as Reinhold does,[91] that the basic principle of much of the *Critique* is something like "the conditions of the objects of experience lie in the conditions of the synthesis of the manifold in intuition," then there is both (a) the *ungroundedness objection,* that Kant does not explain the basis for this principle itself, and (b) the *inconsistency objection,* that the principle itself appears to constitute a type of knowledge with an absolute status that contradicts the Critical claim of transcendental idealism that we can know only appearances, not things in themselves.

The inconsistency objection, broached by Herder, Jacobi, and Hegel and all their followers, continues to arise frequently in the literature

91 Reinhold, *Fundament,* pp. 68, 71.

concerning the problem of a "metacritique."[92] Reinhold, however, unlike
his immediate successors, prefers to press the charge of ungroundedness.
I am inclined to follow Reinhold in deemphasizing the charge of inconsistency, since, taken strictly, it appears to rest on a conflation of "applicable
to things in themselves" and "unconditionally true." That is, the objection
ignores the point that unconditional truths need not be only about things
in themselves but can also be merely formal, or necessary relational claims
about what is by definition not a *thing* in itself. Thus, in simply asserting
the transcendental truth about our epistemic situation, that we cannot
(theoretically) know things in themselves, we are not thereby absurdly
claiming to know the nature of any such things. In addition, it is possible
to avoid inconsistency by taking Kant's arguments to exclude only certain
specific kinds of claims to theoretical knowledge of things in themselves,
namely, claims about their spatiotemporality. (I will argue that this is a
crucial consideration, but not one available to Reinhold; see below secs.
C. 6–7.)

While Reinhold pressed the ungroundedness objection, he did so in a
strong way that is close to making another kind of charge of inconsistency,
for he contended that Kant not only does not, but also *cannot*, prove his
basic principle. That is, Reinhold insists (a) that Kant needs a basic principle, and (b) that Kant himself cannot have such a principle. Thus: (a) "As
a propaedeutic of metaphysics, the *Critique of Pure Reason* has grounded
the sense of its basic principle in so far as it has developed the concept of
the possibility of experience . . . the newly discovered (Critical) metaphysics cannot be actually valid until that which lies at the base of its
foundation stands firm in basic, doctrinal, and derivative principles, that
is to say, until the propaedeutic of metaphysics has itself been raised to a
science of the faculty of cognition."[93] However: (b) "the basic principle of
the metaphysics of experience [i.e., the Kantian presumption about
synthesis of intuition noted above] is unprovable in and through this
science."[94]

It is not at all obvious that Reinhold has a fair charge against Kant's
system here, since the *Critique*'s whole first half is usually read as precisely
an attempt to ground, or at least to explain, and not simply presume, the

92 See, e.g., Heinz, "Herders Metakritik"; and L. W. Beck, "Towards a Meta-Critique of Pure
    Reason," in *Proceedings of the Ottawa Congress on Kant in the Anglo-American and Continental
    Traditions*, ed. P. Laberge, F. Duchesneau, and B. Morrissey (Ottawa: University of Ottawa
    Press, 1976), pp. 182–96. Cf. below at n. 175.
93 Reinhold, *Fundament*, pp. 69–70. Cf. ibid., p. 77; and Teichner, *Rekonstruktion*, p. 398.
94 Reinhold, *Fundament*, p. 69. Cf. Fichte's similar statement, cited in R. Lauth, "Reinholds
    Vorwurf des Subjektivismus gegen die Wissenschaftslehre," in *Philosophie aus einem Prinzip*,
    p. 253.

"principle" of experience stated here. Moreover, there is no reason to think Kant has to, or ever thought that he had to, present this principle as a foundational proposition in Reinhold's very strict sense. In addition, the foundationalist's call for a foundation is itself notoriously hard to hold on to consistently – must it or must it not have a foundation? Neither option is appealing. This dilemma need not be a major issue here, however, since it does not come up explicitly as a dispute between Reinhold and Kant. This may be because, as was noted earlier, Reinhold had very strong ulterior motives for presuming that strict foundations were needed, and he simply assumed that apparent allies like Kant would agree. And even if Kant might not agree on the necessity of foundationalism, Reinhold assumed that any Critical philosopher would accept a basic principle that is clearly consistent and self-explanatory, and this is what Reinhold believed distinguished his principle.

C. 3. Reinhold's Solution: The Principle of Consciousness

Whether or not it can be shown that Kant is in trouble on his own grounds, Reinhold believed he had the clear advantage that he could at least show that his own philosophy had an easy solution for the reflexive problem he raised. However much Reinhold may have come to back off from claims about the immediate certainty of the basic principle of his system, he always held that it could still be warranted as scientific because of the system of rigorous inferences that it supposedly generated. That is, he thought that from the mere conception of representation one could deduce the notion of an object, and enough consequences about the structure of the world, to provide a systematic and satisfying account of unique breadth, including a transparent account of itself. (Fichte was to employ a similar argument; see below Chapter 4, sec. C.) Reinhold saw himself as going far beyond Kant in providing results not only in the form of principles for objects of experience but also in the form of certain implications that could be drawn concerning the subjective faculties responsible for such principles. A completely scientific and self-authenticating metaphysics of experience and its sources could supposedly be developed simply from the underlying ground or "fundament" of a reflexive study of the self-analyzing act of representation itself.[95] This science Reinhold calls the *Elementarphilosophie*, which Kant failed to provide, and which, Reinhold promised, would give the common ground for both

95 Reinhold, *Fundament*, p. 71.

theoretical and practical philosophy: "through it and it alone is the ultimate and genuine foundation of philosophy revealed."[96]

In this way Reinhold can present his own system as no incidental
supplement to Kant but rather as that which first makes Critical philosophy a science and so guarantees its effectiveness.[97] Furthermore, in introducing the principle of consciousness, Reinhold originally wanted to
show that he had not only met the general demand for a reflexive component for whatever is to count as science but also that he had found a
foundational proposition that itself meets the very highest requirements
of reflexivity. It is supposedly known and determined solely through itself:
"the principle of consciousness is a proposition thoroughly determined
through itself and indeed the only possible such proposition. All other
propositions can only present concepts that are determined through
other propositions, and the properties of these necessarily must be ultimately referred back to the ones which are determined originally in the
principle of consciousness."[98]

C. 4. Problems for Reinhold's Principle

It is precisely this unique self-determinability[99] that encouraged Reinhold
to believe that his principle could still meet the core demand for a public

96 Ibid., p. 72. Reinhold calls it an "elementary philosophy" to indicate that it can serve as a
    common base for the theoretical and the practical, but in fact it never developed as a
    sufficient common base, and its basic principle of consciousness is really a piece of theoreti-
    cal philosophy, in the relevant Kantian sense, since it is initially characterizable indepen-
    dent of any moral considerations. For Kant, the propositions of the key postulates of God
    and immortality have a mixed status because although they are theoretical in their basic
    content and meaning, they are practical in their foundation, since supposedly they can be
    proven only by the addition of moral considerations. See, e.g., AA, vol. 20, p. 297: "Such a
    faith is a holding true by practical reason of a theoretical proposition, e.g., God exists"
    ("Ein solcher Glaube ist das Fürwahrhalten eines theoretischen Satzes, z. B., es ist ein Gott,
    durch praktische Vernunft"), a passage from Kant's "Progress in Metaphysics," cited by W.
    Martin, Idealism and Objectivity: Understanding Fichte's Jena Project (Stanford: Stanford Univer-
    sity Press, 1997), p. 163, n. 7. Fichte develops the even more radical view that not only the
    epistemic ground but also the very meaning of the propositions in the postulates can be
    only practical and immanent. See below Chapters 3 and 4.
97 Reinhold, Philosophie als strenge Wissenschaft, p. 366. Kant himself spoke often about the
    scientific and systematic character of philosophy (Critique of Pure Reason, A 10/B 24, B vii, B
    xii, B xv, B xxxvi; A 840/B 868), but without going so far as to ever write a system as such.
    See his letter to A. G. Kästner, Aug. 5, 1790, and cf. above Chapter 1.
98 Reinhold, Philosophie als strenge Wissenschaft, p. 354. Cf. ibid.: "the concepts of subject, object,
    and representation, which are presented by it [the principle of consciousness] are deter-
    mined by itself, that is by the distinguishing and relating which it expresses."
99 For a review of some of the difficulties, see D. Henrich, "The Origins of the Theory of the
    Subject," in Philosophical Interventions in the Unfinished Project of Enlightenment, ed. A. Hon-

foundation of philosophy. He claims that "since the properties it contains are thoroughly determined in the action of judging itself, it must be either correctly thought or not thought at all; in this way it does not allow of being either affirmed or denied through a misunderstanding."[100] Note, however, that even if it is granted that this point meets the fundamental concern for reflexivity, it does not meet Reinhold's initial requirement for "public" certainty, which is not merely that a principle be accepted *whenever* it is understood – whenever, if ever, that may be – but is rather that it also be *allgemeingeltend,* that is, *actually* thought as valid, or immediately so thinkable by anyone at any time. To address this concern, Reinhold at first adds that his principle is to be taken not as the result of difficult inference or "raisonnément" but rather as a matter of "mere reflection on the meanings of words (which are determined by the principle itself for the fact which it expresses)."[101] Later, Reinhold expresses the idea somewhat differently: "It is not through any inference of reason but rather through mere reflection on the fact of consciousness, that is, the comparison of what passes in consciousness, that we know: *the representation in consciousness is distinguished by the subject from the subject and the object and related to them both.*"[102]

The introductory comment made here by Reinhold before the statement of his basic "principle of consciousness" involves an important concession that the highest part of science is not itself to be proved directly but rests on an ultimate given "fact." Reinhold remains confident about his system, nonetheless, because he believes that once this "fact" is presented, it can easily analyzed and developed into a "scientific conception"[103] that makes all its components explicit and that derives enough consequences to warrant it. In particular, it can be supposedly be used to derive a whole system of basic objective principles from an exhaustive set of basic subjective faculties. Unfortunately, Reinhold's method becomes more mysterious with every attempted derivation from this "fact," and the debate about his alleged "fact of consciousness" itself became as lively in its time as the similar debate about Kant's alleged "fact of reason" has remained to this day. To characterize the peculiar kind of knowledge

---

neth et al. (Cambridge, MA: MIT Press, 1992), pp. 29–97; Breazeale, "Reinhold's Elementary Philosophy," pp. 790–4; and F. Beiser, *The Fate of Reason,* p. 246.

100 Reinhold, *Philosophie als strenge Wissenschaft,* p. 356.

101 Ibid.

102 Reinhold, *Fundament,* p. 78 (my emphasis, added to highlight Reinhold's basic principle). Cf. his *Beyträge* I, p. 144; and Teichner, *Rekonstruktion,* pp. 163, 226, 233, 416.

103 Reinhold, *Fundament,* pp. 77–8.

involved with his "fact," Reinhold was ultimately driven to speak of an "intellectual" as opposed to empirical intuition.[104] Later idealists, of course, picked up on and broadened this conception – despite the fact that, understandably, it was sheer dogma to Kant. Other philosophers (G. E. Schulze, J. F. Fries) plausibly insisted that here Reinhold was introducing what had to be a mere empirical and uncertain claim.

Reinhold's heavy emphasis on the principle of consciousness can be explained as a natural but desperate attempt to meet at one stroke the conflicting demands that a philosophy be at once popular and professional in a strict sense. The principle of consciousness itself was quickly and severely attacked by Schulze and Maimon,[105] and it did not convince even a reader as sympathetic as the early Fichte.[106] As soon as it is taken to have anything more than an analytic form, it loses the special certainty it is supposed to have; and if it is instead taken to be a matter of definition, it can hardly warrant the substantive deductive claims that are needed to develop a full science – as can be seen from Reinhold's poor attempts at "deducing" the results of Kant's system from his principle.[107] Reinhold tries, for example, to map the distinction between the representer and the represented onto a general distinction between form and matter and to conclude from this that the form of knowledge must be due to the representing subject and it alone – a weak argument that he gave up on himself as soon as the first objections were raised against it. A priori efforts to show that representation must be spatial and temporal fared no better. No wonder that Reinhold soon sought another basis in the next version of foundationalist philosophy – Fichte's philosophy, which promised an even stronger foundation, one beyond all disputed "facts."

C. 5. Motives for Reinhold's Principle

Rather than try to justify Reinhold's specific principle, the best one can do is to attempt to make its general idea seem understandable given his

104 Teichner, *Rekonstruktion*, p. 412.
105 See Maimon's (unanswered) letter to Kant, Sept. 20, 1791; and R. P. Horstmann, "Maimon's Critique of Reinhold's 'Satz des Bewusstseins,'" in *Proceedings of the Third International Kant Congress*, ed. L. W. Beck (Dordrecht: Reidel, 1972), p. 337, n. 16. See also Bernhard Mensen, "Reinhold zur Frage des ersten Grundsatzes der Philosophie," in *Philosophie aus einem Prinzip*, p. 126.
106 See Fichte, "Review of *Aenesidemus*," in *Fichte: Early Philosophical Writings*, trans. and ed. D. Breazeale (Ithaca: Cornell University Press, 1988), pp. 53–77.
107 See Reinhold, *Versuch*, pp. 319ff and pp. 441ff; and cf. A. P. König, *Denkformen in die Erkenntnis* (Bonn: Bouvier, 1980), pp. 110–27; and Kuno Fischer, *Geschichte der neueren Philosophie* (Heidelberg, 1877), vol. 6, pp. 42–3. How these points were made in Reinhold's own time is well documented in Frank, *Unendliche Annäherung*, pp. 207–8.

situation and ultimate intentions, and to note again how enormously influential his general project remained, despite the difficulties in his own formulations. The remarks cited earlier[108] about the defense of human rights as resting on a scientific philosophy are no aberration or peculiarity of Reinhold's. Even his emperor, the "enlightened despot" Joseph II, tried to put philosophy at the basis of his reforms. Reinhold repeatedly stresses that "rights can be recognized by states only when philosophers are clear about them,"[109] and he ties this idea directly to contemporary disputes about slavery. He clearly expects Critical philosophers to play a major role in the campaign against such abuses of freedom, as he had tried to do from his earliest days in Vienna, and he argues that their effectiveness is in doubt as long as philosophers have not reached clarity about the concept of right at the basis of their normative doctrines. Similarly, he argues at length that correctness in applied or practical philosophy requires correctness at the more basic level of pure or elementary philosophy.[110] This in turn, he believes, is not possible in a piecemeal fashion, that is, there cannot be separate autonomous areas of philosophy, each directed simply by its own crew of specialists.[111] Rather, philosophy is a tight systematic whole, and just as there is one science of sciences (philosophy) to ground and unify the rest, so there must be within philosophy no ultimate divisions but rather one underlying first philosophy, and one general principle within it to ground all the subparts.[112] The application of this principle requires a special scientific language, and this requires a class of "professional" philosophers whose competence and results are to be judged not by the standards of the other particular disciplines but by its own principles. Here Reinhold anticipates a position that might look something like what Kant articulated in the late treatise on *The Conflict of the Faculties* (which was published only after the revocation of censorship). In fact, however, Reinhold goes significantly further in holding explicitly that genuine knowledge and goodness are

---

108 See above at n. 17 and n. 81.

109 Reinhold, *Fundament,* p. vii; cf. his *Briefe* II, p. 337.

110 Reinhold, *Briefe* II, p. 37; cf. his *Fundament,* pp. x–xi.

111 Reinhold, *Philosophie als strenge Wissenschaft,* pp. xii, 369 (note the reference to "Selbstdenker von Profession"). Cf. his *Versuch,* p. 32, which discusses various philosophers' rejections of Kant, and reveals that Reinhold does not think that the mere existence of a philosophical community is sufficient for change. What is specifically required is a reorganized community of philosophers qua *Selbstdenker,* i.e., strong advocates of Critical philosophy. The spirit here is very much like what one finds in the later grandiose programs of positivism.

112 See above Introduction at n. 1. For one well-known exception to this tendency of the epoch, see Fries, *Reinhold, Fichte, and Schelling.*

impossible for anyone short of the apparatus of a supreme and autonomous philosophical science. Kant attacked excessive claims to authority made by lawyers, theologians, and physicians, but he did not claim to start from something more basic than the unquestioned theoretical and practical experience already present in the life of common citizens.

The many steps from the mere notion of representation to the whole program of strong foundationalism are hardly clear and convincing, but it should be evident at least that Reinhold hit upon an extraordinarily straightforward means for trying to realize his project, a project that reflected the implicit ideals of a whole era. Any strong divisions within philosophy, any ceding of authority to other disciplines, would raise questions about the very special status Reinhold wanted to give the new class of philosophers that he was calling upon – and that to a large degree he actually generated. Without such a new class, Reinhold thought he would be forced back to a crude popular philosophy; there would be no established philosophical method to guarantee results or to give even the appearance of a guarantee. For the purposes of everyday life and knowledge, this consequence may seem quite bearable, but if one is, like Reinhold, devoted to bringing about an immediate, deep, and lasting "revolution,"[113] then the desire becomes intelligible for some kind of drastic remedy along the lines of the radical new science he proposes. In addition to an obvious methodological attachment to the formal purity of strong foundationalism, the basic assumption behind this approach appears to be a strong traditional rationalism tempered by an acute sense of historical frustration, a frustration evidenced by Reinhold's frequent expressions about how ongoing disagreements show there is as yet no scientific philosophy whatsoever.[114] Taken together, these points lead to the belief that previous methods have not and never will provide the kind of broad and firm agreement that the project of the Enlightenment supposedly requires. The eschatological impatience behind this project is understandable in the era of the French Revolution, but it is unsettling how much this fantastic ideal of philosophy as a fully rigorous and even imperial science would continue to determine German thought and beyond – through the schools of Fichte, Hegel, and even Husserl and the positivists[115] – long after the abatement of the special concerns that gave it at

113 Reinhold, *Fundament,* p. xiii.
114 Reinhold, *Beyträge* I, p. 344.
115 For a documentation of the parallels between Husserl and Kant on the need for a systematic, scientific philosophy, see G. Funke, "The Primacy of Practical Reason in Kant and Husserl," in *Kant and Phenomenology,* ed. T. Seebohm and J. Kockelmans (Washington:

least an understandable point as a rallying theme in Reinhold's time. Once introduced, the idea of modeling philosophy on the strictest conception of science remained a steady, self-perpetuating fashion, and despite its repeated failures, each new attempt confidently offered, just as Reinhold had done, its own story of the "previous fate" of its naive predecessors.

Fortunately, there are several alternatives to the Reinholdian project of a completely autonomous pure philosophy that claims to be the essential foundation of an autonomous life and society. The fascinating failure of his project should not keep us locked in the presumption that the only option is its radical opposite, the common doctrine of the latest naturalist and continental philosophy, that all traditional philosophy is regressive and dead. There are several other options, and one alternative is Kant's basic idea of a critical philosophy that serves the enhancement of our moral and scientific self-determination by developing merely a distinctive and maximally inclusive account linking principles in all domains, an account that is not offended by accepting some propositions as innocent general features of experience given to us before and outside of anything that philosophy can "ground" on its own (see above Chapter 1).

C. 6. The "Short Argument" for the Unknowability of Things in Themselves

The focus so far has been largely on *why* Reinhold introduced a basic principle of consciousness as supposedly an "easier" ground for establishing a reflexive and complete account of knowledge. At this point it is appropriate to look more closely at *how* Reinhold specifically employs the principle to try to establish the bounds of knowledge through a new and "short" proof of idealism.

The idea of a bounded system has an obvious source in Kant's "Copernican revolution," and in his many claims to have found a philosophy that is in principle complete and all-inclusive. It was typical of Kant to write: "To no one has it even occurred [before him, Kant] that this faculty [of a priori judging reason] is the object of a formal and necessary, yes, an extremely broad science . . . [capable of] deducing out of its own nature all the objects within its scope, enumerating them, and proving their completeness by means of their coherence in a single, complete cognitive

University Press of America, 1984), pp. 1–24. Husserl was also directly influenced by acquaintance with Fichte's programmatic ideals.

faculty."[116] Reinhold very much agreed that philosophical systematicity is requisite,[117] but he soon complained that Kant had not actually accomplished it.[118] For Reinhold the problem is not a matter of the simple failure, which Kant freely admitted, to work out all the incidental details of the Critical system (or even the fundamentals of all its subparts, such as the definitions of the categories). Rather, there are at least two major difficulties: a failure (i) to find a common ground for unifying the theoretical and practical aspects of Critical philosophy,[119] and (ii) to show in principle that the realm covered by Kant's a priori laws exhausts all we can ever know (theoretically). The former problem concerns the elusive "keystone" doctrine of freedom, and it will be discussed in the next section, which deals with autonomy. The latter problem concerns the doctrine of transcendental idealism and Reinhold's desire to find a "short argument" to ground the fundamental Kantian distinction between appearances and things in themselves. This is an important development, because in constructing his own argument to save Kant's distinction, Reinhold managed to distort the basic meaning of Kant's original doctrine. This generated misunderstandings that led to its improper dismissal by all the later idealists. At the same time, Reinhold's own "short argument" became a prototype for not only the major systems of his own day but also, indirectly, for many of the leading conceptions of idealism in our own time, conceptions that have much less to do with Kant than they suppose. Here it is important to distinguish Kant's own route to idealism from other possible routes.

For Kant, the distinction between appearances and things in themselves is ultimately a specific distinction between what we can know *theoretically*, which happens to be spatiotemporal phenomenal determinations, and what cannot be known that way, nonspatiotemporal things in themselves. This distinction expresses substantive bounds that are meant to be established at the *end* of a long course of argument, and it is not to be conflated with the mere formal distinction between empirical and transcendental, or epistemic, perspectives that the Critical philosophy employs at the *outset* of its investigations.

---

116 From Kant's letter to Garve, Aug. 7, 1783, as translated in *Correspondence*, p. 198. See, however, the qualifications in Chapter 1, sec. A. above.

117 Reinhold, *Fundament*, p. 166. Timm suggests part of the motive for this interest in systematicity was to counter Mendelssohn's suggestion that Kantian philosophy undermines all metaphysics (*Gott*, p. 412).

118 Reinhold, *Briefe* I, p. 163.

119 Reinhold, *Philosophie als strenge Wissenschaft*, p. 344.

If we abstract from Kant's own theory, we can express the general idealist problem of the bounds of our knowledge as the problem of *why* it is that we are blocked in principle from knowing things in themselves. Let us call this the problem of the Unknowability Thesis. Some major kinds of response to this problem, starting with the most radical, are: (a) the *concept* of such things is internally incoherent; (b) the *knowledge* of such things in any form is in principle incoherent; (c) the specific nature of *our theoretical* way of knowing is such that we are left with the capacity for knowing only certain kinds of features, so that there may be (or are, or must be) other features, features of things in themselves, unknown in this way but perhaps available for other kinds of knowing.

Whereas Kant offers a response of type (c), and stresses the fundamental limits brought specifically by the spatiotemporality of our theoretical way of knowing, it is a modification of a response of type (b) that Reinhold adopts in his distinctive explanation of transcendental idealism. He argues: "The concept of a representation in general contradicts [that of] the representation of an object in its distinctive form independent of the form of representation, or the so-called thing in itself; that is, no thing in itself is representable."[120] Reinhold's position is a modification of type (b) rather than (a) because what he is saying is not that a thing in itself is absolutely incoherent, but rather that it is unknowable because it is unrepresentable: "Thus one can begin to understand in a shorter way [NB] the impossibility that Kant established of knowing the thing in itself. The thing in itself is not *representable,* so how could it be *knowable?*"[121]

The now-familiar and questionable focus on representation is not as important here as the mere fact that Reinhold is proposing what he calls a "short" route to grounding the Unknowability Thesis. The route involves a "short argument"[122] simply in the sense that it abstracts entirely from any treatment of the "lengthy" peculiarities involved in our specific way of knowing, and, in particular, from any reference to our having to use certain forms of intuition. On this route there is no need for considering any of the claims that figure in the *Critique*'s familiar and complex arguments to transcendental idealism, such as the mathematical or orientational knowledge these forms make possible, the schematic conditions of

120 Reinhold, *Versuch,* p. 244. Cf. his *Beyträge* I, pp. 180–7.
121 Reinhold, *Versuch,* p. 255. Cf. his *Fundament,* pp. 76–7.
122 My designation of the argument as "short" is meant as a reference to what Reinhold called the "shorter way" of his argument (*Versuch,* p. 255). This is quite compatible with the fact that various versions of the argument developed later by Reinhold or others might take up a large number of pages of text. Cf. below at n. 150 and also Chapter 4, n. 31.

application they provide for the categories, or the contradictions about the world's dimensions they lead to when employed dogmatically. Instead, mere reflection on the notion of a form of representation is taken to be sufficient for the Unknowability Thesis. This is not because Reinhold means to reduce everything in some crude way to representations in the sense of images. On the contrary, he rejects the relevance of talk of images, and he systematically distinguishes the represented, the representation, and the representing.[123] Unfortunately, this only makes it harder to see how we are to understand the ground for his contention that "the object distinguished from the representation . . . can only be represented under the form of representation and so in no way as a thing in itself."[124]

One might naturally try to understand Reinhold's strategy by comparing it with Kant's own. This has been done in a discussion by Henry Allison, who contends, "Reinhold's chosen expression, 'form of representation,' has precisely the same logic as Kant's 'form of sensibility' . . . such a form . . . pertains only to what is represented in virtue of a specific mode or manner of representing."[125] On this account, the transcendental ideality of what is perceived is said to follow immediately just because a "form of sensibility" is something "that only pertains to objects in virtue of our peculiar mode" of representing them.[126] There is, however, a problem with applying this interpretation to capture the logic of Reinhold's argument. It may be understandable why Kant's "form of sensibility" brings ideality immediately along with it, because it involves what is said to be "only" a "specific" or "peculiar" mode of representing, namely space and time, but Reinhold's "form of representation" is clearly not "peculiar" in this way, precisely because his argument abstracts from any reference to a specific form of representation.[127] Reinhold is quite insistent that the ideality of a content is to follow from its being part of a representation at all; the kind of representation does not matter. He explicitly contrasts his

123 Reinhold, Versuch, p. 237.
124 Ibid., p. 246.
125 H. E. Allison, Kant's Transcendental Idealism (New Haven: Yale University Press, 1983), pp. 112–13.
126 Ibid., p. 114.
127 Perhaps these specific terms are not essential to Allison's own intentions, for he says, "a reference to mind and its concepts is, therefore, built into the very notion of such a form, just as a reference to a sensibly affected or receptive mind is built into the Kantian conception" (ibid., p. 113). If all that matters is that there be "some reference to a mind," this would be very close to Reinhold. On the relation of Allison's interpretation to Kant, see my review of his earlier work, "Kant's Transcendental Idealism," Topoi 3 (1984): 181–5; and K. Ameriks, "Kantian Idealism Today," History of Philosophical Quarterly 9 (1992): 329–42.

approach with one that would, for example, show "inductively" that representations of sense, and then those of understanding and reason, are limited to appearances, for his whole point is that it is the mere representability of something that keeps it from being a thing in itself.[128] He even explicitly stresses that it is not the spatiotemporality of (the content of) our representations that is the ground for their ideality, but, on the contrary, it is the ideality of representation as such that explains the ideality of space and time.[129] (Here one should not be distracted by the fact that for Reinhold there turns out in the end to be not much to be distinguished between the *actual* limits of space and time and those of sensibility, since, unlike Kant, he does not regard space and time as merely what happen to be our specific modes of sense, but as the essential forms of sensible representation as such.)[130]

All this indicates that, rather than seeking comparisons, we must approach Reinhold's "form of representation" in its own terms. In his initial account, Reinhold takes the form of representation to be simply that general feature of it which allows it to be referred to a subject. He says every representation has such form, as it also must have "matter" *(Stoff)* that allows it to be referred to an object.[131] Reinhold concedes that the form of an individual representation can depend on the form of its particular object, but he insists that representation as such, that is, the fact that something is actually being represented, cannot be due to the object but only to the representing subject, what Reinhold calls the *Gemüt* (mind) or *Vorstellungsvermögen* (faculty of representation).[132] His main point is that, whatever form a particular object has "objectively" as "mere matter," it is only under the form of representation, only under the "subjective" form that it takes on as determined matter (content) in the mind,[133] that it can be *present to* consciousness: "What is represented, as object, can come to consciousness and become represented only as modified through the form of representation, and not in a form independent of representation, as it is in itself."[134]

---

128 See esp. Reinhold, *Fundament*, p. 75; and *Beyträge* I, p. 269.

129 Reinhold, *Versuch*, p. 41.

130 Ibid., p. 419.

131 Ibid., pp. 244–5. Cf. *Beyträge* I, p. 185. Here there are several striking anticipations of modern phenomenology.

132 Reinhold, *Versuch*, p. 239.

133 Ibid., pp. 239–40.

134 Ibid., p. 240. Cf. ibid., p. 235: "that which can correspond to no matter in a representation is absolutely unrepresentable."

C. 7. Problems for the Short Argument

This exposition should make clear what Reinhold means, but it also appears to trivialize the Unknowability Thesis. In a fair recapitulation of
Reinhold's discussion here, Daniel Breazeale has taken the argument to
be based on "the unrepresentability of matter apart from form."[135] But
once we recall that here "form" just means represented form, or the bare
quality of "coming to consciousness," then it becomes evident that, with
these definitions, to claim knowledge of things in themselves would be to
claim [a1] to represent something (since we are claiming to know it)
while [b1] not representing it (because the object of the putative knowing is, by the stipulation of meaning of "thing in itself," not to have the
"form," i.e., not to be represented). The components of this trivial absurdity correspond to those of Reinhold's later and most systematic expression
of the argument: "The great chief result of Kant's *Critique of Pure Reason*,
that things in themselves are unknowable, depends on the proof of these
two propositions [a2] 'that a priori all that is knowable is the form of mere
representation and what it makes possible,' and [b2] 'the form of mere
representation cannot be the form of things in themselves.'"[136] I take
what I have labeled as [a1] and [a2] each to be saying that the knowable
must be representable, and [b1] and [b2] to be saying (or to be based on
the idea) that what is *meant* by "in itself" is simply "not as representable."
On this account, things in themselves turn out to be immediately unknowable as a matter of implicit definition.

　　If there is any hope for an escape from triviality it must come from
Reinhold's earlier remark about things being represented only as "modified" by the form of representation.[137] This hope can be maintained only
as long as the modification involves something *more* than the bare fact of
something's becoming conscious. Yet we also know it cannot mean *as
much* as the fact of something's becoming conscious in a *specific* kind of
way, such as through sense or reason, or space and time.

　　There is some middle ground here, at least hinted at by Reinhold,[138]
when he goes on to argue that there are "distinctive" marks of form and
matter, namely that the first is "produced" and the second is "given."[139]
Form reflects the "spontaneity" of our faculty of representation, and mat-

---

135 Breazeale, "Reinhold's Elementary Philosophy," p. 801.
136 Reinhold, *Fundament*, p. 73.
137 Reinhold, *Versuch*, p. 240. See above at n. 125.
138 And perhaps Allison. See above at n. 127.
139 Reinhold, *Versuch*, pp. 255–6.

ter its "receptivity"; the former is responsible for the unity in representation, and the latter for multiplicity.[140] There are, of course, different degrees of spontaneity and different types of unity involved in the different faculties of sense, understanding, and reason, but in each case there does seem to be some kind of common and nontrivial "modification" by consciousness. Unfortunately, the relation between these distinctive marks and ideality is still not at all clear, especially since Reinhold clouds the issue (i) by equating representation and consciousness,[141] and (ii) by allowing "connections" in "mere matter" that are independent of the form of representation.[142] The first point forces him to insist on a mysterious kind of spontaneity even at levels simpler than those of explicit synthesis, let alone judgmental or cognitive activity,[143] and this makes it even more unclear what kind of relevant "modifying" always has to be taking place. (Note how the thesis of the omnipresence of "productive unity" is much easier to accept at the level of cognitive experience that Kant stressed.)[144] Reinhold's second point calls into question the original thesis that all unity must be mind-generated, and so, if the mind is not responsible for unity, it again becomes unclear why it has to be responsible for ideality. In addition to these difficulties, the equation of givenness and multiplicity remains dubious,[145] especially for an analysis like Reinhold's that focuses on the lowest levels of consciousness. One naturally asks, *why* can't something be given without any multiplicity (or spontaneity on our part), and be presented – that is, represented, even if not known – just as it is in itself? Above all, there is still no account of why, for any multiplicity that is united, our unifying activity must amount to a modification that gives the representation a *different character* than the object itself. One might hold, for example, that although we act as we unify what is given to our mind, we do so because the thing in itself appropriately lends itself to such treatment. For example, the most natural explanation for why we unify a multiplicity of three things as a triad is that they are a triad. Reinhold does not have much to say about this

---

140 Ibid., p. 283; cf. ibid., p. 432.
141 Ibid., p. 256: "A representation without consciousness would have to be one that represented nothing and [so] did not represent."
142 Ibid., p. 430.
143 Here Reinhold was attacked by Schulze and Maimon. See again R. P. Horstmann, "Maimon's Critique," p. 337, n. 16.
144 Reinhold rejects arguments starting at this level because he wants a certain starting point for philosophy, an insistence largely explained by the concerns discussed above at Chapter 2, sec. B.1.
145 See Kiesewetter's letter to Kant, Dec. 15, 1789, and Kant's reply, Feb. 9, 1790.

problem, and it seems there is little that he could concede without giving up what is distinctive to his whole approach to the problem of the bounds of knowledge.

The main point here is that it still seems *possible* that the forms through which we represent things *correspond* precisely to the forms of things in themselves, where "in itself" can mean (as it should, if it is not to become a trivial notion) "in its intrinsic character" and not simply *by definition* "not representable." This objection is one Reinhold considers and even emphasizes, for he thinks it a deficiency of Kant's own exposition that in it "all that is displayed is only the *baselessness* and not the *impossibility* of applying the form of ideas to things in themselves."[146] Reinhold's initial response is that talk of a possible correspondence with such things cannot be cashed in and involves an absurd misconception of representations as images or pictures, which can bear a similarity relation to things and can be judged to be correct precisely in view of such a relation.[147] Reinhold stresses that we must not confuse visual impressions, which can be compared in a literal way with their sources for similarity, and mental representations, which we cannot compare with an "original" at all but only with other representations.[148] This Berkeleyan point (which may well come from Reinhold's considerable familiarity with English philosophy) is well taken, but on the matter at issue it still shows at most only that one cannot literally bring the correspondence to consciousness, not that there could not be one, or that it couldn't be indirectly affirmed – just as we might not be able to bring our own nonexistence to consciousness but still can affirm that it can, and some day will, occur. Perhaps aware of this difficulty, Reinhold repeats the objection of a possible content common to representation and object (in itself), but he responds merely that "this

---

146 Reinhold, *Beyträge* II, p. 431. The full passage reads: "But if it is not shown that a thing in itself as such cannot merely (as the *Critique* proves) never be *actually* represented through an Idea but also (as can be shown *only* from the nature of an Idea *insofar as it is mere representation*) that it *never* could be represented through it – then clearly all that is displayed is only the *baselessness* and not the impossibility of applying the form of ideas to things in themselves." Cf. *Fundament*, p. 66; and Breazeale, "Reinhold's Elementary Philosophy," p. 801, n. 31. This objection to Kant, famous through the Trendelenberg-Fischer debate, is reviewed in Hans Vaihinger, *Commentar zu Kants Kritik der reinen Vernunft*, vol. 2 (Stuttgart: W. Spaemann, 1892), pp. 290–326. Reinhold's inattention to the Antinomies and even the Aesthetic made him discount Kant's major treatment of the problem.

147 Reinhold, *Versuch*, p. 240.

148 Ibid., pp. 242–3. Cf. Reinhold, "Preisschrift" in *Preisschriften über die Frage: Welche Fortschritte hat die Metaphysik seit Leibnitzens und Wolffs Zeiten in Deutschland gemacht?* (Berlin, 1796; reprint, Darmstadt: Wissenschaftliche Buchgesellschaft, 1971), p. 246.

content loses its similarity with the object in itself [as soon] as it takes on the form of representation."[149] This response takes us back to the point that something represented is as such, that is, *only* in *this* respect, not similar to something not represented, a point whose only virtue is that it is so trivial that now it could at least explain Reinhold's special *confidence* that he can show how knowing things in themselves – just in his sense – is in *principle* excluded. In sum, Reinhold's "shorter argument" to idealism either warrants only an unknowability of things in themselves in principle that is too stipulative to be of significance, or it is to be reconstructed (as above) as resting on a substantive but not warranted claim that things are modified in character by us simply because we are involved in some action with them.

C. 8. Motives for the Short Argument

This clarification and evaluation of Reinhold's argument forces one to return again to trying to explain why he felt led into promoting such a questionable position. One very relevant consideration, emphasized above, is that for all of Reinhold's extensive writing on and association with Kant's work, he, like many of his famous colleagues, scarcely bothered to go into the theoretical details of the first *Critique* – and so it is no wonder that similar arguments, with similar backgrounds, recur to this day.[150] His famous *Letters* turns out to focus almost exclusively on the cultural conditions and the appropriateness of the Critical philosophy, its relation to various ethical and religious traditions.[151] Very little is ever said about how the key specific arguments of the transcendental deduction or the Antinomies proceed, and so it is really no wonder that Reinhold would desire a "shorter" way around Kant's longer and more complicated arguments for transcendental idealism.[152] But even more significant than how Reinhold's desire fits in with his *knowledge* and acknowledged *capabilities* is the fact that it fits in perfectly with his overriding *goal* in appropriating the Critical philosophy. We have seen how much Reinhold hoped

---

149 Reinhold, *Versuch*, p. 243.

150 For references to recent short arguments, e.g. in Putnam and Wolterstorff, see my "Hegel's Idealism," *Monist* 74 (1991): 386–402; and my "Kant and Short Arguments to Humility," in *Kant's Legacy: Essays in Honor of L. W. Beck*, ed. P. Cicovacki (Rochester: Rochester University Press, 2000); and see above at n. 127.

151 See above at n. 42; and the account of Reinhold's "theoriepragmatischer Verzerrung" of the *Critique* in Röttgers, "Die Kritik," p. 801.

152 There are some specific worries about the Transcendental Aesthetic raised by Reinhold later in *Beyträge* II, p. 424.

this philosophy offered an immediately certain, or at least easily convey-
able, philosophical perspective that could have not only a scholarly validity (*Allgemeingültigkeit*) but also a popular acceptability (and so be *allgemeingeltend*) that would allow it to be a prime vehicle for bringing about
the general moral, democratic, and anticlerical goals of the Enlightenment.[153] It should now be quite obvious why he would be so attracted to
the short argument, for in one quick stroke the argument would exclude
forever, if only it were successful, the whole sense of traditional theoretical
speculation about what transcends our experience. Since practical philosophy was of supreme importance for Reinhold, it is not surprising that
what most appealed to him was the practical benefit of completely blocking mystical and authoritarian references to a spiritual realm by establishing the sheer impossibility of cognitive access to things in themselves.

In some of his last reflections on Kant during this period, Reinhold
makes his practical concerns most explicit. He stresses that as long as the
"non-impossibility of the representation of things in themselves is left
open," philosophers posing as Critical will seek some way in which to
determine such things.[154] All the pre-Critical traditions that were to be
overcome could then return to the scene. Thus Reinhold warns of "dogmatic theists" (rationalists who claim to know God theoretically), of
"Kantian-Spinozistic atheists" (who transform the formal ideas of an absolute subject, cause, and community into predicates of an all-encompassing substance in itself – an uncanny premonition of Hegel), of "super-
naturalists" (who use revelation to determine the noumenal), and of
"dogmatic-critical skeptics" (who use difficulties with the thing in itself to
undercut all knowledge claims).[155] The very chaos engendered by this
quartet of options is part of Reinhold's worry, but ultimately these alternatives are not regarded as on a par. Like others of his circle, Reinhold is
influenced by Jacobi and presumes that the Spinozist clearly has "the
most consistent of all possible systems" for things in themselves.[156] Rein-

<hr/>

153 See above at n. 14, and Wolfgang Schrader, "Systemphilosophie als Aufklärung." Over
   time Reinhold seemed to give more and more priority to the claim of boundedness rather
   than certainty. The crucial matter for him was an attractive philosophy that would rule out
   traditional transcendent claims and dogmatic attitudes. If that philosophy could be certain, it would be all the better, but the exclusionary effect was the main goal.
154 Reinhold, *Beyträge* II, p. 431 (from "Über das Fundament der K. d. r. V.").
155 Ibid., pp. 432–3.
156 Ibid., pp. 433–4. See F. J. Jacobi, *Über die Lehre des Spinoza in Briefen an den Herrn Moses
   Mendelssohn*, 2d ed. (Breslau: Löwe, 1789); and Manfred Frank, "Philosophical Foundations of Early Romanticism," in *The Modern Subject: Conceptions of the Self in Classical German
   Philosophy*, ed. Karl Ameriks and Dieter Sturma (Albany: State University of New York
   Press, 1995), pp. 66–7.

hold argues that if *any* aspect of the form of our theoretical ideas is allowed to apply to things in themselves, then the basis of this form can also be sought there, in which case the arguments of Spinoza will force us to regard even the activity of unifying in our mind as only "an action of the thing in itself, and in particular of the single infinite substance."[157] Remarkably, Reinhold objects merely that this would imply a fatalism that would leave no practical (i.e., absolutely free) side to human beings as such. Given his earlier views[158] he should have also concluded that there would be no genuine theoretical side left to human beings either, no activity of mind and no form really imposed by us at all.

C. 9. An Alternative

There is an alternative to these Reinholdian options. One could hold that, just as some partial influence of things on us – and even of things in themselves – need not destroy our whole capacity for theoretical activity (for why can't we, as a dependent cause, still be a cause?), so too it should not exclude our being regarded as having some sphere of genuine practical agency. Reinhold's reason for resisting this alternative lay in heavy and dubious presuppositions of his own subculture about the immediate untenability of compatibilism, and about Spinozism as "the most consistent" view in its field. That is, it appears Reinhold believed the only philosophically responsible way that we might picture a thing in itself would be as an all-encompassing and deterministic Spinozistic substance, and since this would be too horrendous a possibility to allow ourselves as practical beings, it must be said that there is no genuine thought of a thing in itself possible at all.

Here it seems that it is the respect for Spinoza that has gone beyond the bounds of sense. As soon as one considers that there could be *non-*Spinozistic things in themselves, then there should be no fear, even for Kantians, of allowing some representation, even if not any theoretical

---

157 Reinhold, *Beyträge* II, p. 434. Perhaps these remarks were directed against Pistorius's suggestion that Kant's theoretical agnosticism about our substantiality left open the Spinozistic conclusion that there is a single thing in itself. See Timm, *Gott*, p. 464; and B. Tuschling, "Widersprüche in transzendentalen Idealismus," in *Probleme der Kritik der reinen Vernunft*, ed. B. Tuschling (Berlin: de Gruyter 1983), p. 234. Unlike Kant, Mendelssohn was very clear in rejecting this Spinozistic conclusion: "Subjectively considered, all thoughts are of undeniable truth. Hence the power to think them is truly a primitive power that cannot be grounded in a higher original power." "Erinnerung an Herrn Jacobi," in *Jacobis Spinoza Büchlein*, ed. F. Mauthner (Munich: G. Müller, 1912), p. 105.
158 See the points about the spontaneity of judgment above at n. 143.

knowledge, of such things. This does not disprove fatalism, but it does leave room for not assuming that it is the only alternative to consider seriously. Perhaps if Reinhold had never fallen prey to an unnecessary fear of the strength of Spinozism he would not have committed himself to the extreme and fallacious strategy of trying to establishing the bounds of knowledge through his desperate "short argument." This would have complicated his interest in strong foundationalism, but at least it would have allowed him to fall back more easily on his earlier clear belief in the postulates, and on the general position of common sense – and Kant – that there is much beyond the realm of our speculative knowledge that can be coherently represented, and perhaps even true of things in themselves, even if it cannot be known through theoretical demonstration.

D. REINHOLD'S FOURTH DOCTRINE: ALL FOR THE SAKE OF SELF-DETERMINATION

D. 1. Reinhold's Metaphysical Interest in Autonomy

The previous components of Reinhold's version of Critical philosophy had to do primarily with his effort to make it as easy as possible to accept the claim that the rules of the spatiotemporal world give us all we can ever expect to know (theoretically). As was just noted, this claim about the epistemic priority of the bounded and "secular" domain was attractive to Reinhold only as long as room was still left for our freedom, and thus his whole emphasis on the claim needs to be understood in terms of his master strategy for the realization of human self-determination. This strategy culminates in his complex doctrine of autonomy, a notion that must be broken down into two closely connected Kantian components, metaphysical ("transcendental freedom") and moral ("practical freedom"). The metaphysical component rests essentially on the general thought, made possible by transcendental idealism, that there is a realm of things in themselves that, for all we know, need not be governed by principles of absolute necessity. The moral component rests on a notion of categorical obligations that supposedly require a specifically practical form of absolute freedom, a power to act properly as an uncaused cause (obviously, the notion of cause is being used here in a more general sense than its schematized spatiotemporal meaning) through one's intentions. By putting these components together, the Critical philosophy aims to meet the deterministic threats of modern philosophy and science by construing freedom as originally a power of the self in itself, and in particular as a power of a will whose transcendence leaves it independent from any conflict with phenomenal laws, even if it has phenomenal "effects" that follow the order of natural causes.[159]

According to Kant's settled view in the second *Critique* (Preface, n. 1), the most basic connection between these components is that transcendental freedom is the *ratio essendi*, or necessary *metaphysical* condition, for the existence of practical freedom, while our recognition of the moral law is the *ratio cognoscendi*, or necessary *cognitive* condition (and, once transcendental idealism is accepted, also the sufficient cognitive condition), for properly asserting this freedom in our own case.

It is also natural to think of these components of autonomy as connected through the image of the Copernican revolution. Just as the metaphysics of transcendental idealism means that the ontic principles of our sensible world are in some sense due to us, and not wholly imposed from the outside, so too the structure of Kant's moral theory is supposed to imply that our deontic principles are in some sense also due to us, and not simply imposed from the outside. Although the thought of this kind of connection has certainly been very influential, I will not pursue it much. It involves a dangerous analogy that is easily misunderstood in absurdly subjective terms, and it is all too easily forgotten that different contexts give quite different senses to the common phrase "due to us."[160] Even in theoretical contexts, Kantian *principles* are "due to us" not in any sense that is dependent on individual exercises of reason but rather just in the sense that they are in general relative to our spatiotemporal form of sensibility. Kantian practical principles are even less subjective in any ordinary sense since, unlike the physical laws of nature, the basic laws of value are not relative to human sensibility at all, even if their taking on an imperative "pressure" on us presupposes a context of sensibility. What makes practical self-determination literally "auto*nomy*" for Kant is the fact that it involves strict laws, laws of value that must be necessary – and so cannot be products of actual individual or social legislation but are rather the determinations of practical reason as such. And it is only because he sees reason as our "true self" that he can speak of the laws as "due to us,"

---

159 For a fine defense of the internal coherence of this view, see Allen Wood, "Kant's Compatibilism," in *Self and Nature in Kant's Philosophy*, ed. A. Wood (Ithaca, NY: Cornell University Press, 1984), pp. 73–101.

160 Reinhold is alive to the problem insofar as he explains that the individual is responsible for the *Wollen* but not the *Sollen* of moral action. See *Briefe* II, p. 292, and cf. above Introduction, sec. A.2, and my "On Schneewind and Kant's Method in Ethics," *Ideas y Valores* 102 (1996): 28–53.

meaning precisely not that they come from particular constructions but that they come from a general essence beyond all particular action and any caprice of physics or a supreme being. But although the *content* of freedom's law is determined by reason, the *actuality* of freedom cannot be shown from reason alone in any mere intellectual sense. This is why, for purposes of the *ratio cognoscendi*, Kant comes to put an emphasis on what can be revealed to us solely through a practical perspective.

This point has been somewhat obscured by the circumstance that for a while Kant himself suggested that the very fact that we have a general theoretical power of judgment (involving a "spontaneity" of the intellect that contrasts with the passivity of sensibility) responsible for the principles of what *is* (theoretically knowable), might be enough to demonstrate that we actually have, or cannot help but assume that we have, the absolute power of transcendental freedom required for responding to the principles of what *ought to be*. It was only later that Kant explicitly backed off from this highly controversial suggestion by emphasizing in the second *Critique* that the actuality of such freedom can be revealed only through a "fact of reason" that is cognized *only* in moral contexts and not through merely theoretical considerations.[161] Kant's temporary unclarity was to have enormous consequences, and it forced Reinhold and then Fichte and others[162] to focus intensively on the nature of the will and the relation between theoretical and practical reason. To move toward a proper investigation of that development, however, it is essential to come first to an understanding of what is unique about Reinhold's most remarkable modification of Kant, namely, his unusual metaphysical perspective on things in themselves.

Despite his "short argument," Reinhold continued to allow the *existence* of things in themselves,[163] and this left him in a unique position, closer to Kant than any of his other major successors. Reinhold's metaphysical allowance for things in themselves was tied to his master strategy, his desire to make the *Critique* immediately "popular" and to save it from being dismissed as a complete rejection of the core of traditional re-

---

161 See above Chapter 1, sec. D. 2, and my *Kant's Theory of Mind* (Oxford: Clarendon Press, 1982), chap. VI.

162 See below Chapter 4. For a discussion of a typical example of the confusion this caused for Kant's important first readers, see Jacqueline Mariña, "A Critical-Interpretive Analysis of some Early Writings by Schleiermacher on Kant's Early Views of Human Nature and Freedom (1789–1799), with Translated Texts," in *Schleiermacher on the Workings of the Mind*, ed. Ruth Drucilla Richardson (Lewiston, NY: Edwin Mellin Press, 1998), pp. 12–31.

163 See, e.g., Reinhold, *Versuch*, pp. 240, 244, 250, 255, 294, 297, 299, 420.

ligion.[164] He realized that as long as his philosophy allowed things in themselves separate from experience, God and providence could still exist in a literal transcendent sense. In this way the reforms Reinhold espoused could appear to maintain a "moderate" or nonthreatening character, and so he could eventually be all the more effective in his efforts to accomplish far-reaching reformist changes with a reluctant public. This careful strategy was in large part responsible for Reinhold's considerable initial success, and it saved him from the debacle that Fichte was to suffer in the *Atheismusstreit*. Still, it could not outrun problems in the theoretical intelligibility of the ground of his position, problems that arose immediately from Reinhold's very attempt to recast Kant's work in a more attractive manner.

D. 2. Special Problems for Reinhold

The most general philosophical reason for Reinhold's allowance of the things in themselves was to provide a realistic counter to the many readers who believed the Critical philosophy had no room at all for objects separate from the self.[165] Unfortunately, the reasons Reinhold offered for realism brought about more harm than help for the Critical cause. In introducing his principle of consciousness and in insisting that there had to be outer objects or else there would be nothing responsible for the "matter" of representation, Reinhold relied on the crucial and unconvincing assumption that the subject is to be *defined* as that which is responsible for *only the form* of representation.[166] Even if one puts aside basic questions about the ground and scope of the principle of consciousness, it can be countered that even for the events that the principle is conceded to cover, all that is clearly needed by consciousness is an object-directed content, not a genuine transcendent referent or cause. In other words, Reinhold does not really prove what he wants against skeptics, namely

---

164 Reinhold, *Briefe* I, p. 170. The point was also stressed by J. Schulze. Cf. J. Erdmann, *A History*, p. 429; and Kiesewetter's letter to Kant, Dec. 15, 1789. Reinhold's tactics here were intertwined with his complex involvement with the Illuminationist movement, which he believed could be used to help solidify the Enlightenment in a radical way "from above" once the proper philosophical movements had infiltrated public opinion. See Fuchs, *Reinhold*, p. 138.

165 This reaction is documented in Benno Erdmann, *Kants Kriticismus*. It should again be kept in mind that Reinhold's *Letters* (in the initial version) appeared before the second edition of the first *Critique* (1787).

166 See above at n. 131 and n. 139. All this shows, as Henrich and his students have emphasized, that Reinhold's general theory of consciousness appealed to but did not adequately develop the notion of subjectivity, and thus a task was set for the next generation.

that matter could not also be due to the subject. With this weak kind of
basis for realism, it is not surprising that under pressure Reinhold retreated from his position at a later point (his "Fichtean period") and
suggested that the "given" is not a matter of passive reception but rather a
mere correlate of our intentional but preconscious positing.[167] Eventually he spoke of the "paradox" that philosophical speculation leads to
subjectivism, while only immediate and irresistible faith holds one to
realism.[168] Such a desperate position understandably led to the more
ambitious philosophies of Fichte and Hegel and their scorn for the notion of a thing in itself.

What made the idea of the thing in itself especially troublesome for
Reinhold was the fact that he had gone out of his way to argue for the
epistemic irrelevance of reference to whatever transcends representation.
Precisely because philosophers prior to Kant assumed that knowledge
must involve a discoverable agreement with something wholly independent of representation, Reinhold had argued that they were unable to
ward off skepticism.[169] Yet Reinhold also showed an unwillingness to let
truth become a matter of the mere coherence of our representations.[170]
Similarly, Kant's own "formal idealism"[171] had *appeared* to become inconsistent when it insisted on supplementing whatever "internal realism" its
cognitive principles provided by also claiming a need for the existence of
something external to all our representations as an unknown "ground" of
phenomena. Difficulties with this insistence, and especially its apparent
conflict with the Critical restrictions on the use of the concept of causality,
were stressed immediately by Jacobi, Maimon, G. E. Schulze, and Fichte.
Unfortunately, rather than considering that these difficulties may have
been exaggerated (for a response, see below Chapter 4, n. 4) and only

---

167 See Magnus Selling, *Studien zur Geschichte der Transzendental Philosophie I. Karl Leonhard
   Reinholds Elementarphilosophie in ihrem philosophiegeschichtlichen Zusammenhang, mit Beilagen
   Fichtes Entwicklung betreffend* (Lund, 1982), p. 92; R. Lauth, "Fichtes und Reinholds Verhältnis," p. 153; A. Klemmt, *Reinholds Elementarphilosophie,* pp. 537–8; and Reinhold's
   letter to Erhard, Feb. 22, 1797, in *Fichte im Gespräch,* p. 407.
168 Lauth, "Fichtes und Reinholds Verhältnis," p. 157.
169 Reinhold, *Fundament,* p. 66; "Über den gegenwärtigen Zustand der Metaphysik und der
   transzendentalen Philosophie überhaupt," in *Auswahl vermischter Schriften* (Jena: Mauke,
   1797), vol. 2, p. 320; and his "Preisschrift," p. 243. Cf. Manfred Zahn, "K. L. Reinholds
   Position in der Phase seiner grössten Annäherung an die Wissenschaftslehre," in *Philosophie aus einem Prinzip,* pp. 167–9. Cf. Kant, R 5642, *AA,* vol. 18, p. 281.
170 See, e.g., Reinhold's letter to F. C. zu Schleswig-Holstein-Augustenberg, Feb. 1795, in
   Fichte im Gespräch, p. 238. On Reinhold's later attack on the correspondence theory of
   truth see Klemmt, "Die philosophische Entwicklung," p. 265.
171 See esp. Kant, *Prolegomena,* Part I, Remark II.

warranted closer attention to Kant's arguments, the idealists tended to focus more and more on Reinhold's especially absurd version of things in themselves. Reinhold's "shorter argument" to the Unknowability Thesis not only had the argumentative weaknesses that have just been noted, it also had the enormous burden that arose from replacing the Kantian idea of things in themselves that still could be thought even if not known (theoretically) by us with a very strange new idea of things in themselves that must be posited but are not even representable.[172] In other words, Reinhold was left in the extremely awkward position of insisting on things in themselves at the same time that he completely undercut their mere comprehensibility.

Reinhold tempered his approach somewhat by distinguishing an allowable *general* concept of things in themselves[173] – by means of which they could be discussed indirectly at a metalevel – from an impossible particular representation of specific things in themselves as such. This distinction was helpful, but it still left an unsuccessful compromise, for while a pre-Reinholdian could at least allow some sense to things in themselves (because of the general meaning of the categories of pure thought and their possible determination by intuition that we happen to lack), and a post-Reinholdian could simply dismiss such things altogether, Reinhold was left with insisting on something that exists and yet, precisely because it is in principle indeterminable, has to be absolutely indeterminate. His last formulations express the absurdity of his own invention, for he calls the thing in itself "the thinkable in so far as it is not thinkable," and he even suggests that the principle of contradiction is not relevant to it.[174] The exceptionally counterintuitive construal Reinhold gave to things in themselves was to be a major factor in the later reception of Critical philosophy, where it appears that the difficulties that were noted in Reinhold's view were often falsely assumed to hold for Kant's philosophy as well (see below Chapters 3 and 4).

D. 3. Freedom and the Problem of Reflexivity

A further problem with Reinhold's position here arises when it is combined with the strict scientific and reflexive aspect of his philosophy. Earlier it was noted that Kant was criticized for claiming not to be able to know things in themselves while simultaneously claiming to know what

172 Reinhold, *Beyträge* I, p. 269.
173 Reinhold, *Versuch*, p. 422.
174 Ibid., p. 32.

our cognitive apparatus is really like.[175] It was also argued that Kant has a response here, but for Reinhold there remains a much more severe problem. This is because Reinhold makes stronger claims about what we can know, namely, the sources of a full a priori system covering all representation, while also making stronger claims about what we cannot know, namely, anything that transcends mere representation.

There are two ways to go on from here to try to defend Reinhold's claims. The first way is to argue that while in one sense Reinhold's transcendental knowledge about our subjective faculties is more than "mere representation," it is still meant to be only a very indeterminate and general kind of knowledge, and so it at least does not make inappropriate determinate claims directly about a concrete thing in itself. The other route, which Fichte was to pursue,[176] is to argue that transcendental knowledge itself is "only" knowledge of mere representation, that is, knowledge of how the self represents its own nature to itself, and yet it is none the worse for that, since supposedly no other kind of knowledge ever makes sense. Accepting the strong claim of this latter argument involves (see below Chapters 3 and 4) giving up the whole notion of the thing in itself, and any chance of the traditional transcendent entities of Kant's postulates – something that Reinhold was unwilling to do. This would seem to leave only the first route, a merely indirect and general acknowledgment of things in themselves. In fact, however, Reinhold becomes inconsistent here by originally claiming to know what he does of the "in itself" not in mere general terms but rather by means of an "intellectual intuition," something that clearly seems to be an illegitimate

175 See above at n. 92. The charge is that to assert transcendental idealism is to violate its own principles, for if it is true (as it supposedly says) that what we know is "merely" due to us, then even that assertion must be merely due to us, and so, absolutely speaking, not true. The problem was indicated in 1792 by G. E. Schulze in *Aenesidemus oder über die Fundamenta der von den Herrn Professor Reinhold in Jena gelieferten Elementarphilosophie*, reprint ed. A. Liebert (Berlin: Kant-Gesellschaft, 1991), p. 140; and by many others later, e.g., the early Schelling, *On the Possibility of a Form of All Philosophy* (1794), trans. Fritz Marti, in *The Unconditional in Human Knowledge* (Lewisburg, PA: Bucknell University Press, 1980), p. 48n; Kuno Fischer, *A Critique of Kant*, trans. W. S. Hough (London: Sonnenschein, 1888), p. 134; Lorenz Puntel, "Transzendentaler und absoluter Idealismus," in *Kant oder Hegel?*, ed. D. Henrich (Stuttgart: Klett-Cotta, 1983, p. 215); and R. Walker, "Empirical Realism and Transcendental Anti-Realism," *Proceedings of the Aristotelian Society*, supp. vol. 57 (1983): 155–77.
176 See Fichte, *GA*, I, 2, p. 57; and Reinhold's anticipation in *Versuch*, p. 544. At one point Reinhold uses the general and strange expression that whatever reason proves is valid "only for how we see things," *Briefe* I, p. 242. G. E. Schulze exploited this formulation against him frequently, and this charge passed over into a complaint Hegel raised against Kant. See below Chapters 3 and 6.

claim of dogmatic insight into the *particular* nature of a self in itself after all.[177]

Before attending further to Reinhold's special problems here, it is only fair to note that there are conceptual difficulties that have to be faced by *anyone* working in the Kantian tradition with something like the notion of a thing in itself, especially when one tries to combine this with a Critical account of freedom and the unity of our faculties. As critics often point out, saying that there is Kantian freedom, on a traditional reading, does seem, after all, to involve more than merely allowing that there *could* be something beyond the empirical domain; it appears to involve *asserting* the existence of something external to representation that functions in a *specific* and mysterious way as an intentional ground of phenomena.

It is crucial to distinguish different kinds of objection here. In contrast to the unintelligible notions that arise in Reinhold's strictest system, Kant's own system does not imply things in themselves operating in ways that would not even be "representable." The *Critique* does and can say easily enough that such things can be "thought," even if not "known," for example, through our general concepts of what is a ground, what is ungrounded, and so forth. The mere *meaning* of such terms need not be completely limited to the spatiotemporal contexts that according to the *Critique* determine our actual sphere of theoretical *knowledge*. In his orthodox Kantian moments, especially in the early period of the *Letters*, Reinhold himself could still fall back on such a view, and so his basic commitment to freedom need not be dismissed immediately, despite the special difficulties that he created for himself in his own system, and despite whatever problems he may have had in finding positive grounds for it.

Nonetheless, it can still be objected that even if the notion of metaphysical freedom in its original *Kantian* meaning is not completely *unintelligible*, it does not seem to be a clear part of what *ordinary* people understand, at least not at the same time that they are committed to a thoroughly law-governed structure for experience of the sort insisted upon by Kant and early modern science (see above Chapter 1, sec. D. 2). This is an important issue because it raises what would be an *immediate* objection to any hope of reconciling the thought of such freedom with the general demand for a philosophy that is popular. Because of this difficulty of reconciling the law-governed system of the *Critique* and the practical interests of common sense, later "Kantians" have sometimes suggested that Kant

---

177 See Reinhold, *Beyträge* I, pp. 245, 395; and Teichner, *Rekonstruktion*, p. 412. Later Reinhold attacked the term "intellectual intuition" (as too intellectual), replacing it by the notion of a "feeling" of an individual. See Lauth, "Reinhold's Vorwurf," p. 230.

leaves room for "gaps" *within* nature, that is, within the spatiotemporal framework circumscribed by our theories and possible knowledge. But I see no ground for holding that Kant's system allows such internal gaps,[178] or that he supposed that ordinarily people do or should believe in them. A major point of the *Critique,* and especially of the Antinomies, is to stress the all-encompassing "closed" character of physical laws within nature, whatever the incidental problems in our actually identifying particular laws – and also to note the "external" metaphysical point that physical nature cannot be assumed to exhaust what there is.

All this implies that there is an inescapable *nonpopular* aspect to Kant's own metaphysical belief that, in addition to the nature we know, there exists some nonmaterial feature of reality.[179] For theoretical reason alone this is admittedly an obscure thought. But although any such nonpopular metaphysical idea about things in themselves cannot tell us very much, Kant can immediately add that it is not supposed to; he introduces the idea merely to defend the point that there is no clear *immediate philosophical* absurdity in the metaphysical component of the contested strong notion of freedom that the Critical philosophy affirms. Nonetheless, even if it is conceded that there is no definite theoretical absurdity in the metaphysical idea of freedom, there remain serious issues about how its use fits in with a proper Critical method (see below sec. D. 4). There is also the issue of whether the practical notion that Kant and Reinhold build on their idea of freedom can be developed in a concrete way that can maintain an adequate positive relation to common sense and support the program of a philosophy aimed at being acceptable to all.

With these background problems in view, we can consider more closely how Reinhold presents his own basis for asserting human freedom. Although he puts off discussion of the issue for a surprisingly long time, his basic view emerges clearly enough in the important eighth letter of the second volume of his *Letters* (1792). Here he asserts that the self does have a privileged insight into its own freedom, its absolute power of choice, and he maintains that this insight is introduced not in terms of a moral or

178 For support, see, e.g., Michael Friedman, "Causal Laws and the Foundations of Science," in *The Cambridge Companion to Kant,* ed. Paul Guyer (Cambridge: Cambridge University Press, 1992), pp. 249–79.

179 See my "Kant and Mind: Mere Immaterialism," *Proceedings of the Eighth International Kant Congress 1995,* ed. H. Robinson (Milwaukee: Marquette University Press, 1995), vol. 1, pp. 675–90. A position somewhat like Kant's need not be outdated as long as contemporary work in cosmology and philosophy of mind considers possible reference to underlying connections and grounds that could be real and yet go beyond anything that human beings can *in principle* comprehend.

practical perspective but a general theoretical one: "But reason has *a very significant ground* for thinking freedom as an absolute cause, namely self-consciousness, through which all the action of this faculty announces itself as a fact, *and common and sound understanding is justified* to infer from its actuality to its possibility."[180]

This passage betrays a serious weakness in Reinhold's approach, a weakness with many consequences for his successors. Whereas by this time Kant had moved away from his earlier ambiguities toward a fairly clear claim that the assertion of our freedom rests on what can be seen *only* from a *practical* perspective,[181] Reinhold appears caught in an especially dogmatic position in making a very substantive claim, on mere *theoretical* grounds, about a specific nonphenomenal feature of a particular individual. Both Kant and Reinhold allow a *theoretical meaning* to freedom that involves the general metaphysical notion of some kind of ungrounded grounding, but Reinhold alone *asserts a particular instantiation* of this notion on the basis of considerations that are themselves strictly theoretical in that they do not have to involve any direct reference to morality.

The obvious weak point here is the lack of a strong basis for concluding that one's self-consciousness is an "absolute cause." It is true that even the "common understanding" could "infer from the actuality" of such causation to its possibility, but this does not say how it can properly get to assert the actuality of such causation in the first place. It is one thing to say that there is a common conception of the self as active, and even that there is no immediate proof that it is determined from outside; it is quite another thing to claim flatly that the self is an "absolute cause" and has nothing outside of it ultimately determining it. Reinhold suggests that popular and philosophical perspectives coincide in affirming absolute freedom,[182] but it turns out that his philosophical scrutiny of alternative explanations of the appearance of freedom is very limited.[183] After the

---

180 Reinhold, *Briefe* II, p. 283 (my emphasis); cf. *Beyträge* II, p. 220. Cf. E. G. Schulz, *Rehbergs Opposition gegen Kants Ethik* (Cologne: Bohlau, 1975), p. 170.

181 See again Kant's Preface to the *Critique of Practical Reason,* and *Critique of Pure Reason,* B xxxii–xxxiii. See above at n. 85, which documents that Kant is not saying that the *truths* asserted by the postulates are not about what exists (e.g. God); his point is simply that the *grounds* for asserting them are in part essentially practical, i.e., involve a claim about what ought to be.

182 See Reinhold, *Beyträge* II, p. 229, and *Briefe* II, pp. 308–9.

183 Reinhold ignores, for example, the compatibilism of Rehberg. See E. G. Schulz, *Rehbergs Opposition,* pp. 22–3. See also his quick attack on Ulrich's determinism at *Briefe* II, p. 303, and cf. Kant's letter to Reinhold, March 7, 1788.

broad impact of Luther, Leibniz, Wolff, and the *Spinozastreit*, it can hardly be presumed that deterministic positions were unknown at the popular level either. Later, but only considerably later (when, ironically, he had moved away from Kant), Reinhold conceded that an "optical illusion" might be responsible for our believing the assertion of freedom has a basis in something theoretical rather than merely in our practical demands.[184]

It is important again to be clear about the relative merits of the Reinholdian and Kantian varieties of the Critical position. They each have their limitations, but they are not the same kind of limitations. The absolute claim that Reinhold asserted, the assertion of transcendental freedom based on the mere phenomenon of self-consciousness, had long held an appeal for Kant as well[185] – but Kant did manage to liberate himself from this kind of dogmatism at a purely *philosophical* level, and it is striking and unfortunate that Reinhold did not immediately pick up on this point. This does not entirely settle the matter, however, of how the two philosophers are to be evaluated with respect to the crucial question of how assertions of freedom relate to the popular aspect of their program. One might argue that Reinhold was not worrying so much about traditional philosophical doubts about freedom because he was preoccupied with finding an argument to freedom that could work at the level of common sense.

D. 4. The Tension of the Metaphysical and the Popular as a Problem for Kantian Freedom

When one moves on to consider the issue of freedom at the level of common sense, it turns out that a fundamental problem remains here as well. This problem, however – unlike the purely philosophical issue of freedom – is one that affects Kant's own system almost as much as Reinhold's. The problem is simply that, just as there are traditional *philosophical* alternatives to concluding freedom from the theoretical experience of self-consciousness, there are also *more than a few* alternatives to this conclusion *already within common sense*. The notion of absolute freedom is in an important respect unlike the notion of the basic validity of empirical judgment, which can be understood to be such that only a fool or a radical

---

184 Reinhold, letter to Fichte, Dec. 1795, in *GA*, III, 2, p. 439.
185 On the appeal of the claim of freedom in contemporary interpreters of Kant, see below Chapter 5. See also the references to freedom in my *Kant's Theory of Mind*, and *Lectures on Metaphysics/ Immanuel Kant*, ed. and trans. Karl Ameriks and Steve Naragon (Cambridge: Cambridge University Press, 1997).

skeptic would actually question it. That is, there are *not* only purely logical or scholarly alternatives to the assertion of absolute freedom; there are also several elementary alternatives to its assertion – and, what is even more important, common sense itself appreciates this fact. Even if Hume overstated the case by saying the "doctrine of necessity" in human experience is something to which we all do and must subscribe, he gave good enough reasons to remind us that it is a very common view, and that philosophers might miss this (in their picture of common sense) because of their own confusions about what human liberty and absolute freedom involve. In particular, there is a tendency to forget that even if in everyday life we may all believe – and may be unable to act without the idea – that our thoughts in fact play a *crucial causal role* in our action, this is not yet at all to believe, let alone to know, that they are thereby "absolute" causes.

To this day, some Kantians will still insist, "but *practically*, we all just do act on the idea of freedom, we always head into projects with the thought that we are the ones ultimately responsible for them."[186] Here all one can do is to counter again that such a claim about what is "ultimately" going on can hardly be *presumed* to be showing its face in common life to everyone the same way. If Hume's (or Schopenhauer's, or Mill's, or Aristotle's, etc. – just to mention figures within our own culture) phenomenology of everyday life is even plausible – and its positive reception by many readers should be enough by itself to settle *this* kind of issue – then, at the very least, it certainly appears that many agents can and do get along in a lot of action without indulging in a commitment to any strong presumption of absolute freedom – both when they proceed without reflection and even after considerable reflection (which is not to say that this decides the ultimate metaphysical issue of freedom).

On the other hand, if the claim here about being "ultimately responsible" is not taken from questionable presumptions about universal commonsense views of *action in general*, then it would seem that the only other way it can be understood at this point is in terms of a specific and fairly reflective kind of *moral* view, one involving a strong notion of "responsibility" tied to something like the Kantian idea of categorical obligation. But in that case, even if it is granted (and this is hardly uncontroversial) that, for most people *accepting* such a moral view, an absolute notion of freedom is required, it is most significant that the argument has now shifted to a very different area. At this point it has become a matter of specific and

---

186 See Kant's *Groundwork of the Metaphysics of Morals*, p. 448n; and, e.g., recent work by Henry Allison and Christine Korsgaard. Cf. above Chapter 1, n. 52.

controversial practical, rather than theoretical, considerations that are being appealed to, and while the just-mentioned difficulties concerning claims about action in general do not apply, there remains a very serious problem here, one that is generated by proper methodological demands of the Critical philosophy itself. The problem comes from the fact that, although there is an important distinction to be made between the theoretical and practical perspectives, this distinction still does not mean these perspectives can be completely separated from each other. In particular, Kant properly indicates that *even positive unanimity from a practical perspective at a commonsense level could not save the claim of our freedom if it comes into conflict with what can be established about nature,* either by science or by metaphysics. This is to allow, quite properly, that there is one respect in which it is the theoretical perspective that prevails, and to this extent there is precisely not a total "primacy of practical reason."[187]

Kant himself seems not even to want to leave matters at a point where the moral perspective is allowed its way as long as no *actual* conflict arises with theoretical knowledge. He rather wants an argument that the *main* theoretical objections (i.e., those that seem to derive from modern science) to the belief in our absolute freedom can be shown to be *completely* groundless. He believes that it is in this way and this way alone that he can lay claim to a solid system that will always be of popular value. The doctrine of transcendental idealism is especially significant for him here because it can show not only that there might be some "nonnatural room" for uncaused causing but also that there always *must* be some such "room," given the antinomies that arise from taking determined spatio-temporal nature to exhaust reality. This is not yet, in his technical sense, to say that the "room" is actually filled, nor is it even to give a positive *theoretical* grounding of the "real possibility" of absolute freedom, but it is to offer a specific consideration that goes beyond noting that such freedom is merely a verbal possibility. Kant acknowledges that there might be, beyond all our possible theoretical knowledge, other metaphysical factors (e.g., God's powers) that would make our freedom nonactual and even metaphysically impossible. Yet because (and only because) he believes he has made it clear that we can have no foreseeable ground at all for theoretically determining such factors, it follows that we have a "defeater" against skeptics here that always allows us to listen to the voice of practical reason and to go on to assert in our own case the absolute power that its

---

187 See Kant, *Critique of Pure Reason*, B xxviii–xxix, and *Critique of Practical Reason*, AA, vol. 5, pp. 100–1. Cf. above Chapter 1, sec. D.2, and below Chapter 4, sec. B.

categorical demands appear to presuppose. In this way, Kant's first *Critique* can be seen as fundamentally a piece of apologetics (see above Chapter 1, sec. D) for our moral intentions and all that (he believes) depends on them. Against those who say they are irrational, it aims to shows how we have something more than mere words and bare logical possibility underlying our commitment to these intentions – even if in fact we cannot hope ever to demonstrate theoretically the actuality (or even the full metaphysical conditions of "real possibility") of much that these commitments presuppose.

Reinhold's theory is close to Kant's here, but it has an extra difficulty – in addition to the serious problem of its dogmatic argument from self-consciousness – as well as a special virtue. The extra difficulty comes from the fact, noted earlier, that while Reinhold makes some room for the orthodox Kantian account by holding onto things in themselves, the peculiar way that he was forced to speak of such things as "unthinkable" makes them seem much more mysterious than they are on Kant's theory, and this destroys the crucial intelligibility of the speculative "room" that absolute freedom requires. Despite these very serious epistemological and metaphysical weaknesses, there does remain an appealing general virtue in Reinhold's approach, and this is simply his much more constant sensitivity to the *problem* of reconciling philosophy and common sense. Kant's position on freedom, whatever its complications and advantages, still has the difficulty that it appears to presume that an absolute notion of freedom is an inescapable part of commonsense morality. In other words, even when all the rest of Kant's system is accepted, all we know is that transcendental idealism best combines a libertarian notion of freedom with the conjunction of commonsense experience of empirical judgments and the *presumption* of a certain strong conception of the conditions of morality. But we do not know that Kant's presumption about the nature of these moral conditions matches common sense to anything like the same degree that his premise about the notion of empirical judgment does. The theoretical skeptic who actually presses his case, and who wonders if any empirical judgments are true, is quite an oddity, whereas there are many normal and admirable people in common life as well as philosophy who do not subscribe either to the substantive details of Kant's notion of morality or even to the presumption that such a morality can be held onto only from a libertarian position. In his *Groundwork*, Kant does appear to start out by trying to handle precisely this problem by devoting a section to arguing that his view about morality and its presuppositions transparently underlies our most common practical judgments. But his argument is complex, and his very effort draws attention to, rather than solves, the problem of the asymmetry of theoretical and practical "common sense": while the former is quite broadly shared, the specific Kantian version of the latter is broadly disputed. It is no wonder then that in later works Kant ultimately must engage in all sorts of quasi-religious consider- ations about radical evil and techniques of self-delusion to try to explain how so many people manage to hide from themselves the basic claims of morality that he believes are as clear in themselves as are the basic claims of our theoretical common sense.

None of this proves that Kantians have to give up on or rethink the validity of their moral position, but it does indicate that, after centuries of efforts to promote Kant's view, it is unrealistic to assume that without some modification this philosophy can clearly meet the specific demand of popularity.[188] Reinhold's even more determined effort at bringing Kant's philosophy "down" to the popular level makes the severity of this common problem more vivid than anything Kant himself did – and this is its special virtue, that it keeps the issue in view and makes it so hard to pass over the problem. Reinhold's version of Critical philosophy turns out to be most valuable, then, not for showing how philosophy can actually achieve the ideal of being at once strict and popular, but rather for being a reminder of how devotion to this ideal can engender enormous difficulties. The obvious next step for contemporary (mildly revisionist) Kantians is to construct a more appropriate version of this ideal for phi- losophy without giving up entirely on the appealing components involved in the original ambitious program that did not work. Just as theoretical Kantians have had to give up on claims to a "strictly scientific" Critical theoretical philosophy but can retrench to a looser notion of systematicity that still maintains considerable distinctiveness and plausibility, so practi- cal Kantians need to explore looser but still distinctively Critical models of popularity. In particular, just as, with respect to claims of validity, it clearly seems appropriate to move far away from the theoretical idea of an *Ele- mentarphilosophie* and to go back to a much looser notion of system, so also, with respect to claims of popularity in the practical realm, it seems best

188 It should be kept in mind that this notion of the "popular" is tied to Kant's concept of "public" reason, a concept that brings strong demands with it. See, e.g., Onora O'Neill, "Political Liberalism and Public Reason: A Critical Notice of John Rawls' *Political Liberal- ism*," *Philosophical Review* 106 (1997): 424–5: "On Kant's account, communications that can reach only some socially defined and restricted audience will not count as fully public . . . In requiring the most general and basic uses of reason to be public in this demanding sense, Kant requires that they be based on principles which any, hence all, others, what- ever their political and social identities may be, can follow."

now to consider a looser version of a broadly conceived Critical position on freedom.[189] Such a position would be clear about not presuming or insisting on absolute freedom, and yet it would remain distinctive by still placing special emphasis on the notion of universal rational self-determination, albeit in a broad sense that is open to compatibilism (without foreclosing the possibility of absolute freedom), for this is the sense that alone can be expected to have any chance to be truly popular or *allgemeingeltend*.

D.5. Reinhold's Grounds for Freedom: The Fact of Consciousness

In addition to these fundamental problems of Critical philosophy, there are a number of more specific shortcomings in Reinhold's detailed treatment of freedom. This treatment is complicated throughout by his unclear merging of various types of considerations, some having to do more with considerations about thought, and others with considerations about action.

On the approach that was noted above, Reinhold's claim is that our freedom is presented as simply a "fact of consciousness,"[190] a fact that, at one level, is immediately accessible to all and so has a full popular warrant.

---

189 See above Chapter 1. On the practical issue of freedom one natural strategy here would be to try to combine the "discourse philosophy" of our own time with Reinhold's and Kant's ultimate concerns so as to construct a new "Critical theory" of consensus that would employ the best of the eighteenth- and twentieth-century understandings of the term. While such efforts may not have exactly the same problems that Kant and Reinhold had in combining the metaphysical issue of absolute freedom with the methodological problem of popularity, they could learn from these problems. Rawls's arguments, for example, seem originally to have made a mistake like the one Kant committed, in presuming at a popular level to appeal to only noncontroversial principles while drawing conclusions that actually depend on hidden and controversial substantive presumptions. In the case of Kant and Reinhold, what seems to have gone wrong is a similar mistake about the audience involved. They were claiming an argument that would appeal to the public, or at least the Enlightenment public, at large, whereas in fact they employed philosophical assumptions that belonged to the ideology of what was merely a subset of even the liberal public, the particular strand of the intelligentsia in the areas in and between Königsberg and Jena, from which they arose and received their main support. Neo-Kantians have perpetuated this mistake in our own day, and although it can be regarded as something of a purification in methodology when (as in Rawls's *Political Liberalism* [New York: Columbia University Press, 1996]) they now mark many of their claims as expressly meant to appeal to only certain kinds of liberal societies, the task remains of extending their method so that it really can be expected to reach a universal audience.

190 See, e.g., Reinhold, *Briefe* II, p. 283. The "principle of consciousness" was similarly introduced as a "Faktum" at *Beyträge* I, p. 143.

But Reinhold sees that the perspective of another level needs to be considered, for the question is about an ultimate ground, that is, about whether we ever act as an absolutely uncaused cause, so it must be decided by more than just an appeal to immediate appearances.[191] When Reinhold tries to move up a level, from popular to philosophic certainty about freedom, he employs two kinds of strategies, analytic and historical. The first strategy begins by noting that a proper assertion of freedom requires at least a clear concept of what constitutes freedom.[192] Here Reinhold shifts to an approach that emphasizes action, and he claims that a mere analysis of our faculties reveals as a *Grundvermögen*, or basic capacity, a faculty of will not reducible to knowledge or feeling: "I know that I have a will and it is free as well as I know that I have sensibility, understanding and reason."[193] Unfortunately, this claim itself appears to be either another mere dogmatic intuition or a limited stipulative result that can at most disclose the independence of a certain concept of the will, and cannot yet prove that there really is such a distinct will, especially with the special capacity of absolute freedom.

Rather than directly shoring up this argument, Reinhold shifts to a focus on precisely the historical problem noted earlier, the lack of any commonsense consensus on freedom. He recognizes that if our freedom is considered to be as clear as he says, then it is mysterious that agreement about it has not been established long ago. Reinhold's response is a secular historical explanation of the blindness to what should be so obvious to all of us. The explanation is that the dominant metaphysical schools, precisely because of their pre-Critical nature, have stood in the way of common clarity on freedom. The good side of this response is that it allows Reinhold to make clear that his Critical approach does not by any means intend to sidestep metaphysics altogether. In contrast to later thinkers, and to the popular writers of his day who would try to settle the matter by a mere appeal to commonsense beliefs, Reinhold sees that it is incumbent on the philosopher to show that the common evidence offered for freedom truly has weight by showing that the metaphysical objections to its very possibility can be handled. What Reinhold says after this is not so convincing, but it is significant that he at least recognizes the

191 Reinhold, *Briefe* II, p. 307.
192 Ibid., p. 310; cf. ibid., pp. 263. Later Reinhold conceded defeat here, saying "we have no determinate concept of freedom," in "Die Drei Stände" (1792), reprinted in *Von der ständischen zur bürgerlichen Gesellschaft*, ed. Zwi Batscha and J. Garber (Frankfurt: Suhrkamp, 1981), p. 144.
193 Reinhold, *Briefe* II, pp. 283, 345.

need to work to keep a metaphysical space open for the assertion of our freedom.[194] In this regard he remains genuinely Kantian because, despite all his orientation toward the domain of the practical, he does reserve a methodological place of relative primacy for theoretical philosophy to meet claims about what is absolutely impossible (in contrast to Fichte; see below Chapter 4).

In clearing the space for freedom, Reinhold relies on two moves. The first is a drawn-out negative treatment of four old metaphysical schools that are said to work against a proper ground for freedom. These schools are divided into (a) supernaturalist and (b) naturalist forms; then the naturalist option is divided into (b. 1) skeptical and (b. 2) dogmatic forms; and the dogmatic option in turn is divided into (b. 2. 1) materialist and (b. 2. 2) spiritualist forms. Reinhold's second strategy is a quick positive appeal to transcendental idealism. The positive argument is especially weak, since its main claim, that the self is free from complete determination by spatial features of the world,[195] is insufficient for excluding all kinds of determinism, and it can be helpful only as long as Reinhold either fleshes out and improves on Kant's own argument for idealism – which he does not do – or develops a better one of his own. Reinhold did put forth an argument of his own in the *Elementarphilosophie*, but, as has been noted (see above sec. C. 7), this "shorter" argument only creates new problems.

This leaves only the details of Reinhold's first move, his negative argument concerning different schools of thought on freedom. Since Reinhold says little about skepticism, and he takes supernaturalism to be aligned with spiritualism[196] (the first believes on faith what the second claims to know), the question comes down to one of the treatment of freedom in spiritualism and materialism. Reinhold's aim is to show how within their own frameworks neither of these schools can affirm freedom, and then how these frameworks are not themselves compelling and thus leave open a Critical alternative. Against materialism, Reinhold typically, and all too quickly, assumes that it is incompatible with freedom, and his main objection is simply that no one has *yet* been able to explain the

194 See ibid., p. 358–61. Here I see a need for a "middle ground" in interpreting Reinhold, between those like Nicolai Hartmann, who claim Reinhold introduced "the determination of the theoretical faculty by the practical," *Die Philosophie des deutschen Idealismus*, vol. 1 (Berlin: de Gruyter, 1923), p. 15; and the opposite view, reviewed by Zwi Batscha, in "Reinhold und die französische Revolution," pp. 91–2, that Reinhold remained a theoretician, aloof from dealing with practical affairs.
195 Reinhold, *Briefe* II, p. 347, and *Versuch*, p. 544.
196 Reinhold, *Briefe* II, pp. 320–8.

action of anything organic by the mechanical laws of matter.[197] Obviously
this objection uses an unfair definition that excludes dynamic and
"emergent" forms of materialism. It remains unclear why materialists have
to be determinists, and, even if they are, why they would have to try to
express the exclusion of absolute freedom by modern science in dubious,
strictly mechanistic terms.

Reinhold's attack on the only other possibility he considers, namely
spiritualism, culminates in a critique of Leibniz that argues quickly that
the Leibnizian system requires the Principle of Preestablished Harmony
and that this ultimately contradicts any absolute human freedom.[198] Even
if this claim is granted (here Reinhold is at least in harmony with many
interpreters), this response still does not undercut traditional non-
Leibnizian libertarianism (Reinhold notes simply that such views are vulnerable because of difficulties dualists have in explaining interaction –
but then, so are many other views),[199] and it leaves the status of Reinhold's own position unclear. Leibniz is taken to be vulnerable because he
makes dogmatic assertions about things in themselves, but as long as
Reinhold also wants to insist on our absolute freedom, it is hard to see
what his position can come to if it does not imply a very similar assertion,
namely, that we know the self as an absolute agent, a free thing in itself.[200]
The only reason Reinhold may feel that he is saved from saying this would
be because of a relapse to the weak idea – noted earlier and to be invoked
also by Fichte – that the self is not to be said to be a thing "in" itself at all
because it is essentially something "for" itself (see below Chapters 4 and
5).

D. 6. Freedom, Morality, and Will

It was noted above that, when Kant faced the problem of establishing
freedom, he eventually saved himself from at least some traditional dogmatic claims by stressing (in the second *Critique*) that only moral-practical
considerations could supply a basis for the assertion of freedom. For all
too long, Reinhold is not clear in making the same move, as when, for
example, he says that it is only in the moral context that we are aware of a

197 Ibid., pp. 332–3.
198 Ibid., p. 342. Note that "spiritualism" is a Kantian term that signifies much more than
    idealism or immaterialism, since it entails that there are eternal higher mental beings.
199 Reinhold, *Briefe* II, p. 336.
200 Reinhold, *Versuch*, p. 544.

freedom that is "absolute."[201] It turns out that with this statement he is not really saying that moral action, as opposed to thought, is the sole sure *ground* for asserting freedom. The lack of "absoluteness" Reinhold notes in the freedom of mere thought has to do simply with its having to rely on some *given* material. This does not weaken the suspicious boldness of the claim that mere thought reveals a being that is free in the causal sense essential to the determinism issue.

Later, when Reinhold does connect knowledge of freedom to considerations of action and morality, he makes their relationship too close. His system ultimately defines the will in terms of a power to choose between alternatives that satisfy or do not satisfy the self's desires,[202] and he takes this to mean that to be aware of one's freedom one must be aware of morality as one of the alternatives of choice.[203] But it seems quite unfair to define the alternatives this way. Reinhold can understandably argue that unless there were more than one path one could take, one would not be free, but this does not show what the paths are. There might be some situations where agents face what appear to be free choices that have nothing to do with morality. Reinhold seems trapped here by his terminology and his love of simple dichotomies. He assumes one path always open to us is the selfish path, the path of doing what is most *eigennützig*, and that the alternative to this is the *uneigennützig*, the unselfish, which is immediately equated with the moral.[204] Here Reinhold has left out the thought that what is not selfish could be simply nonselfish rather than unselfish in the moral sense.[205]

There is another embarrassing difficulty for Reinhold that comes from his own development of the definition of freedom. In arguing that freedom requires the presence of *both* moral and nonmoral options, he claims that they are each to be pictured as a drive (*Trieb*) that would automatically direct the agent if it were not for the force of the other.[206] (This talk of the moral as a kind of "drive" is especially questionable, but it is not the

---

201 Ibid., pp. 559, 572. Later Reinhold distinguishes between the theoretical independence ("Selbstätigkeit") or "conditional absoluteness" of the "I" and the genuine freedom ("Freiheit") or "unconditional absoluteness" of the moral self. See Reinhold's letter to Fichte, Dec. 1795, in *GA*, III, 2, pp. 438–9, and also his letter to Erhard, Aug. 2, 1790, in *Fichte im Gespräch*, p. 368.
202 Reinhold, *Beyträge* II, pp. 219, 270; *Briefe* II, p. 263.
203 Reinhold, *Briefe* II, p. 306.
204 Ibid., p. 289.
205 Ibid., p. 307.
206 Reinhold, *Versuch*, p. 573. This language has parallels in Schiller.

only problem here.)[207] This implies that, if a being never has the possibility of being automatically subject to the absolute rule of natural desire, it could not be a free being. But this entails that God (or whatever essentially good beings), as traditionally pictured, could not be called free, a highly nonorthodox conclusion. In a later writing Reinhold faces up to this consequence by saying that God is to be allowed to have only an "analog" to our freedom,[208] and so God does not have a "genuine" will. This is quite a significant retreat from Reinhold's earlier position that the very virtue of the Critical approach was that it would save us from having to treat the nature of God as a transcendent mystery, beyond philosophical science or common belief; our own moral consciousness was to provide a natural and traditional model for all that ordinary people supposedly know and need to know about God.[209] This difficulty about God is especially embarrassing since it is clear that Reinhold turned to Kant's philosophy largely because he thought it would help him to meet his own religious concerns scientifically, to save him from both nonbelief and superstition, *Unglauben* and *Aberglauben*.[210]

This may be one reason why Reinhold did not come out very *clearly* about having a nonpractical way of trying to prove freedom even when he did seem to accept such an argument from mere thought, that is, the "fact of consciousness." He was no doubt sensitive to the point that if freedom were presented as established essentially by reference to morality, and if, as Kant indicated, morality was inextricably related to religion, then our inevitable concern with freedom would bring us fairly directly to enlightened religion and the satisfaction of our deepest interests. Reinhold must have also realized that, if, on the other hand, there did seem to be a clear and independent theoretical route to freedom (especially one that makes the self absolute), then this could work against interest in morality and any argument for God and immortality. As he explained in a letter to Fichte: "I have believed up to now that the pure I, in so far as it is not merely thought problematically, is to be deduced from the *moral law*, not vice versa. For I always still feared that otherwise the true sense of the

---

207 See G. Prauss, *Kant über Freiheit als Autonomie* (Frankfurt: Klostermann, 1983), pp. 87–90. For a more detailed analysis of the development of Reinhold's views here, see the excellent study by Alessandro Lazzari, "K. L. Reinholds Behandlung der Willens- und Freiheitsthematik zwischen 1789 und 1792" (forthcoming).

208 Quoted from an excerpt from Reinhold, *Auswahl Vermischter Schriften*, vol. 2, in *Materialen zu Kants 'Kritik der praktischen Vernunft,'* ed. R. Bittner and K. Cramer (Frankfurt: Suhrkamp, 1975), p. 312.

209 Reinhold, *Briefe* II, pp. 373, 377.

210 See Reinhold's letter to Baggesen, June 22, 1792, in *Fichte im Gespräch*, pp. 35–6.

moral law could be put in danger if one derives it from an *absolutely posited* I. Not to mention that I have no idea about what would happen with *God* and *immortality* (and, similarly, religion). . . ."[211] Nonetheless, for all too long Reinhold was willing to live with making dogmatic claims about the self while not indicating precisely how these claims were related to his practical considerations about freedom. This problem was never resolved, and although Reinhold began with the promise of a nondogmatic approach, in his late work he was able to save freedom and the connection between it and morality and religion only by a dubious appeal to what he called a sheer feeling of "the infinite."[212]

Despite all these difficulties, Reinhold's treatment of freedom also contains some of the more valuable aspects of his work. In particular, it involves an important correction to some of Kant's early formulations,[213] and especially to the express doctrines of supposedly orthodox followers such as Schmid,[214] which can leave the unfortunate impression that the actuality of freedom is to be found only in obedience to the moral. Many readers have mistakenly thought that the Kantian position leaves only the options of necessitation by reason (which is tantamount to moral action) or necessitation by empirical (and thus immoral) motives. Reinhold brings out that on the Critical view human freedom must instead involve the ability to reject or accept one's given desires.[215] On Schmid's view,

211 Reinhold, letter to Fichte, Dec. 1795, *GA*, III, 2, pp. 438–9. Reinhold goes on to say, "In Schelling's work [*On the Ego*] there are expressions [from which I must shrink back]." Cf. his letter of Jan. 12, 1794, ibid., p. 37.

212 Thus Reinhold approached a Jacobian position: "I find freedom in this feeling only in so far as I also find next to it God . . . the infinite . . . the supernatural . . . the absolutely incomprehensible." *Sendschreiben*, Reinhold to Fichte, March 27, 1799, in *GA*, III, 3, pp. 315–16. Cf. Zahn, "Reinholds Position," p. 197; and Fuchs, *Reinhold*, p. 141. On the postulates, Reinhold's change was slower but followed the course that was typical for most of the leading thinkers of the era. Niethammer, for example, was only one of several famous people who came to Jena after resisting an orthodox reading of Kant's postulates by Storr in Tübingen – although, unlike his close friend Hegel, Niethammer seems to have come back to a more orthodox view in later life. See Wilhelm Baum, "Vorwort," *Friedrich Immanuel Niethammer: Korrespondenz mit dem Herbert- und Erhard-Kreis* (Vienna: Turia + Kant, 1995), p. 13.

213 See *Briefe* II, p. 285, where Reinhold excuses Kant from really intending such an error. Cf. also Reinhold's letter to Kant, Jan. 21, 1793, where Reinhold specifically requests (unsuccessfully) that Kant attend to the discussions of freedom in *Briefe* II, letters 8 and 9.

214 Against C. C. Schmid, see Reinhold, *Beytrage* II, pp. 210, 230ff., 266–7, 303; *Briefe* II, pp. 267, 296.

215 Reinhold, *Beyträge* II, p. 219: "The will is the capacity of the person to determine itself to satisfy or not to satisfy its desire." Cf. ibid., p. 270, and *Briefe* II, p. 263. There are special difficulties with taking this as a definition of freedom, but when Reinhold attacks Kant's definition in the *Metaphysics of Morals*, I think his (sharp) objections are largely ver-

freedom occurs when we simply happen not to be determined by empirical motives, and this, as Reinhold argues, makes the occurrence of freedom itself something quite out of our control. Even more troubling, on
this view when "freedom" does occur it is nothing but an automatic consequence of our seeing certain intellectual relations. Thus, Reinhold can
argue, it becomes a matter of our being determined by things in themselves after all, which would seem to be the very opposite of Kantian
morality.[216]

It is also to Reinhold's credit that he insists on clearly distinguishing
the formal and moral "independence" of practical reason itself, which is a
matter of the general rationality of its basic principle (as a principle free
from contingent "material" determination in its content), from the efficient and particular independence of the free will of an agent who happens to choose that principle or choose to reject it.[217] Both the principle
and the choice can be said to involve a kind of self-determination, but a
self-determination at very different, although related, levels. In addition,
Reinhold was able to sketch some ways in which the concept of freedom
might serve as a bridge between our theoretical and practical faculties, so
that it might have a chance of providing the Critical system with a true
unity. He argues, for example, that the different cognitive faculties of
sense, understanding, and reason can each be represented as manifesta-
tions of different degrees of freedom (sensibility is "forced" and "bound,"
understanding is only "bound," reason is neither), and that pure practical
reason can then be regarded as freedom taken one step further because,
in contrast to theoretical reason, it (supposedly) legislates in full independence of what is given.[218] In the end, however, such ideas were not ade-

bal. (See *Materialen zur Kants 'Kritik der praktischen Vernunft,'* pp. 310–11.) Reinhold insists
that *Willkür* should be treated as an aspect of *Wille*, where the latter means a general
capacity to do right *or* wrong, and the former is the actualization of this in a particular
case. When Kant instead treats *Wille* as in effect an aspect of *Willkür*, i.e., as the principle of
pro-moral choice alone, he may be going (as Reinhold notes) against common usage, but
he can be understood easily enough as introducing a technical term. For a defense of
Kant's definition, see Wood, "Kant's Compatibilism," pp. 80–2.

216 Reinhold, *Briefe* I, p. 266.
217 Reinhold, *Briefe* II, p. 288. Reinhold's argument immediately influenced figures such as
Schiller. See Jeffrey Barnouw, "Freiheit zu geben durch Freiheit," in *Friedrich Schiller,* ed.
W. Wittkowski (Tübingen: Niemeyer, 1982), p. 176; S. Roehr, "Zum Einfluss K. L. Rein-
holds auf Schillers Kant-Rezeption"; and Reinhold, letter to Baggesen, Jan. 15, 1795, in
Fichte im Gespräch.
218 Reinhold, *Versuch,* pp. 535, 558–9, 569. Cf. H. J. Engfer, "Handlen, Erkennen, und
Selbstbewusstsein bei Kant und Fichte," in *Probleme der Handlungstheorie,* ed. Hans Poser
(Freiburg: Alber, 1982), p. 108.

quately developed, and Reinhold wound up with a philosophy that had as little real unity as the Kantian system that he wanted to overcome.

E. THE END OF REINHOLD'S PROJECT: SHIPWRECK WITH SPECTATORS

In retrospect, it is fairly easy to trace a common pattern through Reinhold's treatment of the four main aspects of Critical philosophy that have just been covered. From the beginning there were strong practical (cultural as well as moral) reasons, quite independent of Kant, for Reinhold's seeking a philosophy that is (a) thoroughly public, (b) professional, (c) bounded, and (d) oriented to complete autonomy. The acquaintance with Kant's philosophy then provided Reinhold with a system that seemed beautifully designed to stress precisely these points, although eventually Reinhold decided his program could be carried out only with revisions in each doctrine. Thus: (a) the popular and immediately certain foundation of philosophy must be not Kant's own moral argument or transcendental deduction but rather the mere notion of representation; (b) the professional and scientific character of philosophy must depend not on Kant's complex arguments but on a self-determining "principle of consciousness"; (c) the bounds of the system, and the limitation of theoretical knowledge to the spatiotemporal realm, must lie not in the first *Critique*'s detailed, specific grounds for transcendental idealism but in a "short argument" that immediately restricts all representation to mere ideality. Unfortunately, the promised practical advantage of turning from the "letter" of the *Critique* to the notion of representation, the principle of consciousness, and the short argument, is undercut by the fact that all these turns bring with them very ambitious doctrines that are much more dubious than the ones they were meant to replace.

The situation with (d) the doctrine of autonomy is more complex. There Reinhold stays closest to Kant himself by ultimately stressing, even if often very unclearly, the practical argument to freedom and by allowing the existence of things in themselves. Nonetheless, the other components of Reinhold's philosophy undermine these attachments to orthodoxy. Things in themselves, as the "thought of the unthinkable," take on a much more mysterious role than in Kant himself, and the ground that Reinhold himself offers for freedom is frequently obscured by dogmatic appeals to special intuitions or "facts" of consciousness. Later idealists were deeply affected by these Reinholdian transformations. Fichte, for example, can be understood as taking over, with minor modifications, the first three points while seeking to overcome Reinhold's unclarities on the fourth point and to move completely beyond arguments from mere thought, or facts (*Tatsachen*), to arguments only from morality or action (*Tathandlungen*). It turns out, however, that these modifications themselves remained entangled in serious ambiguities about thought and action, and thus there is a need to explain in some detail precisely how the Reinholdian image of Critical philosophy was initially received by Fichte and his contemporaries (see below Chapter 3). Only then can one finally begin to make sense of the most important and difficult aspect of the reception of Kant's philosophy, namely its near-total eclipse by later German idealism and especially Hegelianism (see below Chapter 6).

PART III

FICHTE

3

KANT, FICHTE, AND SHORT
ARGUMENTS TO IDEALISM

From Fichte on, reactions to Kant have been dominated by the notion, first emphasized by K. L. Reinhold, that there is a "short argument" to idealism. The key idea of what I mean by a "short argument" is, very roughly, that reflection on the mere notion of representation, or on such very general features as the passivity or activity involved in representation, is what is meant to show that knowledge is restricted from any determination of things in themselves. Such a general starting point allows one not only to depart from lengthy and controversial aspects of the *Critique;* it also means that the resultant restriction to phenomenal knowledge is to cover just about any kind of finite knowers, and not simply those who happen to have our specific forms of intuition.

Although there has been considerable recent use of the short argument,[1] my aim here will be just to show how the early attachment of the short argument to Kant's philosophy, combined with the underlying motives for that attachment, was of the greatest significance for the remarkable nature of the initial reception of Kant's idealism, namely its almost immediate supercession by Fichte and then the wave of absolute idealism. More specifically, after a brief account (in sec. A) of aspects of Kant's writing that bear on both the temptingness and the ultimate illegitimacy

1 See K. Ameriks, "Recent Work on Kant's Theoretical Philosophy," *American Philosophical Quarterly* 19 (1982): 1–24.

of the Reinholdian short argument interpretation, I will explain (in secs. B and C) how this line of interpretation heavily influenced Fichte and thus determined the peculiar picture of Critical philosophy that came to dominate German idealism. This picture still dominates current views of Kantianism, as it is often shared by its advocates (e.g., Putnam) as well as its critics, but exploring those views is a task for another occasion.

For Kant himself, I believe, there is no such short argument, for his transcendental idealism rests, first, on a series of complex considerations entailing the ideality of space and time, and, secondly, on an equally complex series of considerations requiring that all our theoretical knowledge is limited to spatiotemporal determinations (and hence is limited to their ideality). The two sets of considerations are to be combined, but they can be and were developed independently. The first goes back to Kant's *Dissertation,* while the second distinguishes the *Critique of Pure Reason.* The first involves a variety of arguments; the so-called argument from geometry is probably the central one, but Kant does offer other epistemological considerations, as well as metaphysical objections to realist theories of space and time, and, in addition, the indirect argument of the Antinomies chapter. The second set of considerations is intertwined with Kant's transcendental deduction, in which he tries to show that our theoretical knowledge depends on pure concepts and yet that these concepts (and all they cover), despite their pure nature, are of cognitive significance to us only when organizing spatiotemporal manifolds.

The repeated use of the phrase "cognitive" or "theoretical" significance to "us" is important, for it is to signal that at the end of Kant's own long route to an idealistic conclusion, the conclusion that is obtained is meant to have a relatively moderate sense. That is, it is to be compatible not only with some kind of empirical realism, but also with the assertion that there are ultimate nonspatiotemporal features of objects, features that are even determinable by us, though strictly on practical grounds (by "practical" I will always mean, as Kant generally did, something that requires moral grounds in the Kantian sense). In contrast, those who follow Reinhold in advocating or claiming to find a short argument in Kant usually combine it with a more radical conclusion, namely the necessary phenomenality of all knowledge. And the common reason for this is that they start from a more elementary premise, viz., the general features of representation noted earlier.

A. KANT'S PROGRAM REVIEWED

A. 1. Kant's Premise

For purposes of comparison with the later idealists, it is helpful to break Kant's philosophy down into four components. *First,* there is the starting point of Kant's theory, which is the notion of experience; thus transcendental investigations are studies of the necessary conditions of experience. *Second,* there is the *system* built from this starting point, in particular the pure concepts that are argued to be required by experience and that are involved in principles such as the law of causality. *Third,* there is the general *metaphysical account* of the possibility of this system, namely the doctrine of transcendental idealism, as explained by the long argument sketched earlier. *Fourth,* there are the *metaphysical implications* of this idealism, the most important for Kant being that it leaves it possible for us to assert, on moral grounds, our absolute freedom, and to postulate our appropriate treatment by God. In this way the existence of things in themselves, and of nonspatiotemporal agencies, which can appear to be a mere relic of older dogmatic metaphysics, is meant rather to serve the new Critical purpose of providing a ground and field for the operation of the antidogmatic doctrine of autonomy.

While none of these four components justifies the short argument view, each of them is at times treated by Kant in ways that can *seem* to invite it. With the first component, for example, the use of the notion of "experience" can make it appear as if Kant is asking about what is required for the mere having of representations in one's mind, a having that need not by definition involve any epistemic factors or specific forms. The word is used in this way on occasion in the *Critique* (B 1, B 219), and of course this is its common English meaning, and the favored meaning for those who would see the *Critique* as a direct attack on skepticism. Clearly, if Kant's principles are required for experience in this minimal sense, then their ideality would mean that every representation would be ideal, and so there would not even be any sense to items beyond their realm.

The term "consciousness," which is sometimes interchanged with "experience," presents similar problems. In basing the transcendental deduction on what is requisite for the "identity" or "unity" of consciousness or apperception, Kant might appear to be using the minimal sense of experience, the only difference being that here he may be focusing on a reflexive representation of representation, rather than on the mere having of a simple representation. Fortunately, Kant really doesn't leave this

ambiguity unresolved, for he says repeatedly (e.g., B 147, and even elsewhere at B 219) that his arguments use "experience" and "consciousness"
in a so-called thick sense, that is, as tantamount to empirical knowledge,
or at least to what we would call warranted judgment.[2] Thus, apperception and consciousness are relevant to him, in the B edition at least, only
as involving such judgment. Hence representations that might in some
metaphysical, or merely subconscious or animal sense, belong to one's
self (as to a Lockean soul-substance) but are nothing "to one" (B 132) for
purposes of cognitive synthesis, are not argued to be directly subject to
the categories.[3] Yet however strong these qualifications are, they did not,
as we will see, stop Kant's successors from preferring a version of the
deduction that would begin with a minimal premise and that would, as
Reinhold put it, not rely on any given "facts" such as the fact of experience
in the thick sense.[4]

A. 2. Kant's Deductive System

Secondly, it is also possible to object to the "given" nature of the categories derived in the *Critique*. Their apparently dogmatic dependence on a
given table of forms of judgment can be contrasted with Kant's own
frequent talk of how transcendental philosophy uses the "unconditioned"
(B xx) and is to "flow" from "a single principle" (e.g. A 10/ B 24, A 67/ B
92).[5] And, just as Kant objected to Aristotle's "haphazard" list, Kant's
successors objected that the specific categories needed to be derived
more rigorously. Rather than being found, somehow, all at once on a
single level, one could attempt to regiment them so that from the first the
last would follow. In addition, one could also object to the tension be-

---

2 See K. Ameriks, "Kant's Transcendental Deduction as a Regressive Argument," *Kant-Studien*
   69 (1978): 273–85. Cf. above Chapter 1, sec. B. 3.
3 See K. Ameriks, "Kant and Guyer on Apperception," *Archiv für Geschichte der Philosophie* 65
   (1982): 174–86. Cf. below Chapter 5.
4 See citations from Reinhold's review of Fichte (*Allgemeine Literatur Anzeiger,* 1798), in Magnus Selling, *Studien zur Geschichte der Transzendental Philosophie I. Karl Leonhard Reinholds
   Elementarphilosophie in ihrem philosophiegeschichtlichen Zusammenhang, mit Beilagen Fichtes Entwicklung betreffend* (Lund, 1938), p. 321. There was considerable discussion at this time about
   "facts of consciousness" or "facts of reason." See above Chapter 1, sec. D. 2, and Chapter 2,
   sec. C.
5 Cf. Kant, *Critique of Practical Reason,* p. 91, and *Prolegomena to any Future Metaphysics,* p. 263. All
   citations of Kant in this chapter refer to the original editions. The first and second editions
   of the *Critique of Pure Reason* are designated as A and B, respectively, followed by page
   numbers. For evidence of the influence on Fichte of Kant's remark on the "unconditioned,"
   see Manfred Zahn, "Fichtes Kant-Bild," in *Erneuerung der Transzendentalphilosophie,* ed. Klaus
   Hammacher (Stuttgart: Frommann, 1979), p. 87n.

tween the Kantian insistence on unity in reason (B xviii) and the apparent independence of the various faculties of mind that he analyzes. Here one could follow up on Kant's mention of the idea of a "common root" (A 15/ B 29) of understanding and intuition, and of a common ground to the theoretical and practical faculties, faculties that are, as he says, just different aspects of one and the same reason.[6] This tactic is not essential to the short argument view, but obviously it would facilitate it, for *if* the various basic concepts and operations of mind were interconnected in this way, then the ideality of the elementary ones would automatically transfer to the others. This would rule out noumenal worlds of understanding with different forms of intuition than ours, and moral worlds determined in ways that escape our theoretical philosophy.

However, against such exclusions Kant himself has some explicit warnings (B 72), and he clearly stops short of ever tracing a common root or single principle or faculty from which all other kinds of representation are to be derivable.[7] He is ultimately willing to allow, as a brute fact, that we have different and not reducible ways of representing, just as the fact that we intuit through space and time is, for him, not something that is to be derived from anything else (B 146).

A. 3. Kant's Idealism

Thirdly, if one looks even at passages that fill out what I have called Kant's long route to idealism, one can find some expressions that suggest the short argument view. This is especially the case in the complex discussions where Kant explains and defends his view of the ideality of self-knowledge, for here most of his other considerations, which focus on spatial knowledge, are not directly relevant. In the tortuous passage from B 67 to B 69, for example, the concluding claim that the subject knows itself only "as it appears to itself, not as it is" is explained primarily in terms of various general ways in which the mind is "affected." What is stressed initially is that, unlike a fully active, intuitive intellect, our self needs (i) to receive data, then (ii) to focus on and gather them, and finally (iii) to determine them conceptually. In this way the mind is both passive and active, and it might seem that it is this general threefold "affectability"

6 Kant, *Groundwork of the Metaphysics of Morals*, p. 391; cf. *Critique of Practical Reason*, p. 121. A closer examination of the problem of systematically justifying the list of categories would have to take into account the study of Klaus Reich, *The Completeness of Kant's Table of Judgments*, trans. Jane Kneller and Michael Losonsky (Stanford: Stanford University Press, 1992).
7 See Dieter Henrich, "Über die Einheit der Subjektivität," *Philosophische Rundschau* 3 (1955): 29–69; and Vladimir Satura, *Kants Erkenntnispsychologie* (Bonn: Bouvier, 1971), pp. 40ff.

which explains the claim of the phenomenality of self-knowledge. Indeed, this is just about all that is said about it in Kant's brief discussion of the topic in the *Groundwork*.[8]

Fortunately, though, a closer look at the *Critique* shows that Kant's argument rests on a reference to our having to make use of temporal intuition in our self-determination, and it is the ideality of this intuition that is to entail our ideality (and, for those who wonder whether time's ideality is itself sufficiently established, Kant eventually argues that here its ideality is a function of the ideality of spatial knowledge), just as we would expect according to the "long" argument view.[9] Similarly, in the equally tortuous discussion of this point in the B deduction, Kant at first hints of a short argument by saying "we appear to ourselves, not as we are in ourselves. For we intuit ourselves only as we are inwardly affected" (B 153). Only later (at B 159) does Kant again reveal the true linchpin of the ideality claim by saying that "the combination of our representations can be made intuitable only according to relations of time," and so our intelligence "can know itself only as it appears to itself." The problem here is that in contrasting the self with an active intelligence that would know itself as it is in itself, Kant misleadingly leaves open the suggestion that he has proved *any* nonactive intelligence must know itself not as it is in itself (i.e., whether or not it has our "forms" of sensibility). And all too often Kant abbreviates his position by speaking simply of the ideality of sensible knowledge, when all he has really argued for is the ideality of certain species of such knowledge (those involving synthetic a priori cognitions).

A. 4. Kantian Freedom

Fourthly, Kant is not innocent of inviting the short argument view even when discussing the consequences of his idealism. Its main consequence is, to be sure, in direct conflict with that view, for it is to limit our knowledge so as to make room for faith, or, more specifically, to limit our theoretical determinations so as to admit things in themselves that can be and are determined by our practical reason. Given Kant's view of the exceptionless rule of causality within our intuitive and phenomenal realm, the absolute freedom presupposed by his moral theory requires a noumenal realm that contrasts not with mere representation (or sensibility in general) but with spatiotemporal determination specifically. Yet even on this cardinal point Kant carelessly left in passages in the *Critique*,

8 Kant, *Groundwork*, p. 451.
9 See K. Ameriks, *Kant's Theory of Mind* (Oxford: Oxford University Press, 1982), pp. 252–79.

namely in the "Canon" (which was probably written relatively early), that understandably have been taken to imply that transcendental freedom, and thus a limited form of idealism, is not required by the Critical philosophy (A 803/ B 831). This suggestion was corrected forcefully in the *Groundwork* and later works (such as the second-edition preface to the *Critique*, but not the "Canon" itself, which, like the rest of the end of the book, was something Kant did not get around to revising), but not before it had misled even such close followers as Johann Schultz of Königsberg. The *Critique*'s very first sympathetic readers (Schultz and Reinhold) were in fact simply at a loss when trying to explain Kant's position on freedom.[10]

Elsewhere I have analyzed Kant's complex treatment of freedom during this period;[11] here I will simply draw attention to a few previously unstressed texts that indicate his general attitude. The issue was an especially important one for Kant because of two developments in the late 1780s, namely the rebirth of sympathy for Spinoza's philosophy and the suggestion by Jacobi[12] that Kant's system need not be thought of as entirely contrary to Spinoza's. In reaction to these developments, in a short essay on Mendelssohn in 1786 Kant clarified two major points. The first is that discussions of freedom are not mere scholastic or verbal matters. Thus, despite what an apologist for Spinoza might imply, Kant insists the determinist position is in no way to be reconciled with the Kantian view.[13] Secondly, Kant directly met Mendelssohn's challenge to explain what the concept of a thing in itself (which is the prerequisite for his notion of freedom) might mean by saying that one needs simply to abstract from the sensible qualities with which we are familiar and to form a concept such as the traditional notion of God as an intelligible being, with purely intelligible properties of will, power, and so forth.[14] In other words, Kant aligned himself with an orthodox idea of God, even while holding we have no theoretical proof for the existence of such a being. This view is confirmed in another short essay of the period (on "Orientation in Thinking") which opposes Jacobi and directly challenges the presumption that the Spinozistic nonpersonal, nontranscendent notion of God is the only

---

10 See Eberhard Günter Schulz, *Rehbergs Opposition gegen Kants Ethik* (Cologne: Bohlau, 1975), pp. 80–7, 166. See above Chapter 2, sec. D.

11 See *Kant's Theory of Mind*, pp. 189–227.

12 See F. H. Jacobi, *Über die Lehre des Spinoza in Briefen an den Herrn Moses Mendelssohn* (Breslau: Löwe, 2d. ed., 1789).

13 Kant, "Einige Bemerkungen von Herrn Prof. Kant (aus *Ludwig Heinrich Jakobs Prüfung der Mendelssohnschen Morgenstunden oder aller spekulativen Beweise für das Dasein Gottes*)," p. liv.

14 Kant, "Einige Bemerkungen," p. lix. Cf. *Critique of Practical Reason*, pp. 101–2.

one available (qua meaning, not justification) for theoretical philosophy.[15] All this is consistent with Kant's later attack (in 1796) on the pretension of being able philosophically to determine the nature of such a being through a supposed "intellectual intuition."[16] Indeed, this attack on it is of a piece with his aversion to the monistic metaphysics that tends to accompany the advocacy of a short argument.

B. REINHOLD'S MODIFICATIONS OF KANT REVIEWED

Given the ambiguity of Kant's own work and yet the strong indications of his overriding commitment to the long argument for idealism, how are we to explain his successors' overwhelming commitment to the short argument? The answer lies in the two-phase nature of the initial reception of Kant's work. First, there had to be someone who was close enough to Kant to inspire confidence as an interpreter, and who was such that he introduced the short view, but in a tentative way and in combination with enough of an unappealing presentation of the long view that the stage was set for the second phase of the reception, the pure advocacy of the short argument. This is what happened, I believe, when Reinhold presented the Critical system in his extremely influential *Letters on the Kantian Philosophy* and then his own *Elementary Philosophy,* and when Reinhold was in turn succeeded by Fichte (who also worked under the influence of Jacobi and G. E. Schulze) and then by Hegel (who worked under their influence and that of Schelling).

If this hypothesis is worth pursuing, it provokes a prior question, which is why and how Reinhold was himself so attracted to the short view. Elsewhere I have traced the specifics of Reinhold's reconstruction of the argument to idealism;[17] here I will only review the overall organization and background of Reinhold's thought insofar as is absolutely necessary for understanding the later "pure" modification of Critical philosophy by Fichte. That background is dominated by a split of attitudes with regard to the four main components of Kant's philosophy listed earlier.

On the one hand, it is Reinhold who first proposes beginning philosophy with the general notion of representation rather than our specific

15 Kant, "Was heisst: sich im Denken orientieren?" p. 324.
16 Kant, "Von einem neuerdings erhabenen vornehmen Ton in der Philosophie," pp. 387ff.
17 See K. Ameriks, "Reinhold and the Short Argument to Idealism," *Proceedings of the Sixth International Kant Congress (1985),* ed. G. Funke and T. Seebohm (Washington: Center for Advanced Research in Phenomenology and University Press of America: 1989), vol. 2, pt. 2, pp. 441–53. Cf. above Chapter 2, sec. C.

kind of experience, and who then insists on deriving all from a single "principle of consciousness," rather than allowing an irreducible plurality of concepts and faculties of mind. Thus he develops a paradigmatic form of the short argument to idealism and modifies Kant's first three points accordingly. On the other hand, though, Reinhold initially accepts Kant's fourth component in Kant's own terms, that is, he accepts transcendental freedom, a personal God, a realm of transcendent things in themselves. It turns out that these two attitudes have an understandable origin. Reinhold was initially attracted to Kant precisely because of his practical philosophy, and he was responsible for making Kant's philosophy so well known precisely because he was able to make it appear as if the theoretical components of the Critical system (on his reconstruction) were simply a means for advancing the relatively unthreatening (though to some quite enlightening and liberating) moral and religious philosophy contained in what I have called the fourth component. These goals can explain why Reinhold was attracted to a short argument for idealism, for he believed that route would have an especially attractive and simple starting point and would carry the prestige of a genuinely "scientific," that is, thoroughly unified and systematized, philosophy. Furthermore, Reinhold was strongly drawn to such a short argument because of its elimination of any *possible* representative connection to things in themselves. As long as the "non-impossibility of the representation of things in themselves is left open,"[18] as it is by other than short arguments to idealism, Spinozism seemed unavoidable to him. For Reinhold, as for many others at the time, Spinozism was just the most consistent theory that allowed the form of our ideas to apply to things in themselves. Unfortunately, it also implied for Reinhold that even the activity of unifying in our mind is a mere determination of "an action of the thing in itself, and in particular of the single infinite substance."[19]

Kant's own position on this issue was much more complex. On the one hand, he ridiculed the Spinozistic notion of "thoughts that think themselves," implying apparently that Spinoza would absurdly have to say that particular thoughts are without an ordinary empirical subject, since supposedly there is only one true subject and substance, nature.[20] But unlike Reinhold, Kant did *not* assume that *if* we allow *some* of our representations and concepts to overlap with the structure of noumenal reality (albeit in

18 K. Reinhold, *Beiträge zur Berichtigung bisheriger Missverständnisse der Philosophen II* (Jena: Mauke, 1794), p. 431.
19 Ibid., p. 434.
20 Kant, "Was heisst: sich im Denken orientieren?" p. 324n.

ways that we cannot assert with theoretical justification), then we have to
go on to say that our thinking must have its substantial or causal ground in
sources beyond our individual control. On the other hand, Kant stopped
short of the tendency of his contemporaries – including both pre-
Kantians such as Mendelssohn and post-Kantians such as Jakob and
Abicht[21] – who did not worry about theoretically determining things in
themselves, and who insisted that the mere existence of thought and
judgment in us proves we are ultimately spontaneous agents. It is true that
some passages in the original *Critique* lean toward this claim, and Kant's
work during the *Groundwork* period, especially in the notorious third part
of that book, appears to try to develop a backing for such a claim, but soon
enough (by 1786) Kant retreated to a clearly agnostic position on this
issue from a theoretical perspective.[22] No strictly theoretical premises can
lead either to the conclusion that we are ultimately free or to the conclusion that we are ultimately determined. This position did not go un-
noticed, for Kant's similar theoretical agnosticism about our individual
substantiality provoked the suggestion by Reinhold's fellow interpreter
Pistorius that the Critical philosophy is compatible with the Spinozistic
conclusion that there is a single (and determined) thing in itself.[23] Kant
would have rejected this suggestion, but not with the extreme methods
that Reinhold employed.

C. FICHTE'S RADICALIZATION OF REINHOLD'S MODIFICATIONS

C. 1. Fichte's Premise

If we turn now to Fichte and his objections to Reinhold's version of
Critical philosophy, it can be shown that the Spinozistic threat to the
Kantian claim of freedom dominates all four main areas listed earlier,
namely, (i) the starting point (the notion of representation in place of
experience), (ii) the resultant system (the implications of the principle of

21 See M. Mendelssohn, "Erinnerungen an Herrn Jacobi," in *Jacobis Spinoza Büchlein*, ed. F.
   Mauthner (Munich: G. Müller, 1912), p. 105. On J. H. Jakob, see Schulz, *Rehbergs Opposition*, pp. 91ff.; and J. H. Abicht, "Über die Freiheit des Willens" (1789), in *Materialen zu
   Kants 'Kritik der praktischen Vernunft,'* ed. R. Bittner and K. Cramer (Frankfurt: Suhrkamp,
   1975), pp. 229–40. See also Kant's remark in a newly found lecture note, *Kant's gesammelte
   Schriften* (Berlin: Preussische Akademie der Wissenschaften/ de Gruyter, 1900–), vol. 29, p.
   1022. Hereafter, the latter work will be cited as *AA*.
22 See again *Kant's Theory of Mind*, pp. 189–227.
23 Hermann Timm, *Gott und die Freiheit* (Frankfurt: Klostermann, 1974), p. 464. See again
   Schulz, *Rehbergs Opposition*, pp. 110–12.

consciousness in place of Kant's transcendental deduction), (iii) its meta-physical interpretation (the "short" and "radical" construal of transcendental idealism), and (iv) its practical consequences (with respect to religion and morality).

On the first point, namely, objections to Reinhold's initial emphasis on representation, the concern with freedom initially may not seem as important as the heavy influence on Fichte of G. E. Schulze's *Aenesidemus,* which pointed out that neither Kant nor Reinhold had an adequate reply to the diehard skeptic. The Kantian notion of experience would obviously be an unsatisfactory starting point for Schulze, since it involves a presumption of (phenomenal) objectivity (although in fact Schulze objected not so much to this as to Kant's hints of an *Einwirkung* of things in themselves upon us).[24] Reinhold's notion of representation can at first seem more promising for meeting skepticism since it is meant to indicate a more basic level of awareness. Unfortunately, as Schulze noted and Fichte reiterated, Reinhold in fact merely assumed the influence of objects, or else he conflated the intentional character of representation with the accomplishment of genuine reference.

For these reasons, and perhaps also because of the influence of Jacobi, then, Fichte frequently pictured prior transcendental philosophy as if it were tantamount to skepticism, that is, as if it gives us nothing more than representations in the sense of a series of connected individual images.[25] This reading involves a peculiar mix of Kant and Hume. Fichte sees that the transcendentalist, unlike the empiricist, is claiming genuinely necessary (and even a priori) connections, but, like Hume, Fichte takes it that what is connected is nothing more than a set of private impressions. Like other interpreters of this stripe, Fichte never shows that Kant truly is committed to this picture; he (Fichte) just appears to have his own antecedent bias toward it, and he implies that since Kant did not directly show its impossibility, it must be what he (the pre-Fichtean transcendentalist) is stuck with. (All this is obviously easier to maintain as long as Fichte, like Schulze, focuses not on Kant but on Reinhold and his individualistic orientation.) Yet it is clear that what really bothers Fichte about such

---

24 Gottlob Ernst Schulze, *Aenesidemus oder über die Fundamente der von Herrn Prof. Reinhold in Jena gelieferten Elementarphilosophie* (1792), p. 374.

25 See Fichte's *Vocation of Man,* ed. Roderick Chisholm (Indianapolis: Bobbs-Merrill, 1969), Book 3. Cf. F. H. Jacobi, *David Hume über den Glauben* (Breslau, 1787), p. 225: "So ist unsere ganze Erkenntnis nichts als ein Besitz von verknüpften Bestimmungen" (Thus our entire knowledge is nothing but a possession of connected determinations). Cf. below Chapter 4, sec. C, with several citations where Fichte makes use of similar Jacobian formulations.

"representationism"[26] is not the pure theoretical scandal of solipsism, the lack of a sure reply to radical skepticism, but rather the moral emptiness that he sees attached to the position, the lack of meaning that taints images as mere images (no matter how connected) within us.[27] Hence it should be no surprise that, connected with the charge of theoretical inadequacy in beginning with representation, there is for Fichte the deeper charge against Reinhold that his "representationism" leaves no room for our absolute freedom.

In one respect this is a remarkable charge, given that Reinhold, like Fichte, was first drawn to Critical philosophy precisely because of what it seemed to promise about how such freedom could be established. But as was just noted, and as Fichte saw better than Reinhold, Kant did not provide a theoretical proof of freedom in his system. It was, as Fichte remarked when he was first studying the *Critique of Pure Reason,* something Kant "can't justify or explain."[28] Moreover, in Fichte's view Reinhold's modification of the Critical system here only made things worse: the focus on representation left determinism not only unchecked, it supposedly entailed the very "fatalism" it was meant to escape.[29] This strong claim arose from Fichte's charge that when Reinhold went on to distinguish between the general *Wille* of pure moral reason and the actual *Willkür* in each individual choice (in order to avoid the suggestion that free action, just because it must be intelligibly grounded, must be pro-moral), he simply pulled "the intelligible down into the chain of natural causes."[30]

Fichte appears to have two related grounds for this objection. One idea is that since the power of choice is supposedly revealed in an empirical way, the will itself is taken to be just one more phenomenon among others

26 I use "representationism" at this point rather than "representationalism" because in English the latter term (in contrast to phenomenalism) can sometimes connote the view that there is something external to the representer, whereas this is not to be implied by the position Fichte is discussing. "Imagism" might be a better term, but it is somewhat misleading here since Reinhold explicitly contrasted images and representations.

27 Thus, at the beginning of the *Vocation of Man,* Book 3, Fichte says, "I demand something beyond a mere presentation . . . my presentations must have a meaning beneath them, and if my entire knowledge revealed to me nothing but knowledge [i.e., mere connected representations], I would be defrauded of my whole life." Cf. above at n. 25.

28 See Fichte, "Aphorismen," in *J. G. Fichte Gesamtausgabe der Bayerischen Akademie der Wissenschaften* (hereafter *GA*), ed. Reinhard Lauth and Hans Jacob (Stuttgart: Frommann, 1969–), II, 1, p. 290. Cf. Schulz, *Rehbergs Opposition,* pp. 22, 78ff. Similar charges of fatalism had been made against Kantian rationalism by Jacobi. See P. Kondylis, *Die Entstehung der Dialektik* (Stuttgart: Klett-Cotta, 1979), p. 157.

29 See Fichte's letter to Heinrich Stephani, Dec. 1793, *GA*, III, 2, p. 28.

30 Fichte, "Rezension Creuzer," in *GA*, I, 2, p. 10. Cf. Reinhold, *Briefe über die kantische Philosophie,* vol. 2 (Leipzig: Göschen, 1792), p. 282; and see below at n. 42.

and so should be determined after all. The second idea is that if the free will is conceived as something that has an empirical effect, then its being in such a causal relation to the natural world makes it something natural as well. There are weaknesses to each objection. On the first point, Reinhold eventually allows that it is not an ordinary or theoretical experience of selection that reveals an absolute power of choice, but rather it is only experience as seen from a moral perspective that gives us the idea that we can choose to act morally or counter-morally. So Fichte's claim that the focus on representation as such makes Reinhold's philosophy "theoretical" in the sense that it precludes freedom is unfair or at least misleading. On the second point, Fichte presumes something that neither Reinhold nor Kant need concede, namely that a generic notion of causality (which spans temporal and nontemporal contexts) cannot apply to the intelligible and the sensible domains in such a way that an intelligible ground can have a sensible effect. Here Fichte has too quickly accepted the view of Schulze and Jacobi that such causality is self-contradictory or in conflict with Critical restrictions on our knowledge.[31] In reality there is no conflict here as long as the ground of asserting such a relation here is a moral-practical one, which is just what it is for Reinhold and Kant (eventually).

Instead of pursuing this orthodox Kantian point, Fichte rather contended that the very meaning of the relation of freedom to our action should be reconstructed so that all Kantian talk about "effects" here must be "charitably" reinterpreted as "provisional."[32] Autonomous reason is to be taken as the explanation for action simply in that it is its goal or rationale rather than its efficient cause. This tactic has a contemporary ring but it also has a current rebuttal, namely that there need be no contradiction in the idea of one and the same item serving as a reason and as a cause of an action.

A last and related objection Fichte frequently offered to the "representationist" starting point is that this position allows a causal effect of things on perceptions that directly undermines freedom. This idea by itself (i.e., if it is not reinterpreted as just a pointer to the other arguments) surely rests on a conflation of what is needed for freedom with what is needed for omnipotence. That is, unless more is said, there is no reason why the mere fact that we are sometimes constrained – as on the realist view we are in perception – should at all count against the claim that we are some-

31 See Fichte, *Science of Knowledge*, trans. Peter Heath and John Lachs (New York: Appleton Century Crofts, 1970), pp. 54ff.
32 Fichte, "Rezension Creuzer," *GA*, I, 2, p. 11; cf. "Über den Begriff der Wissenschaftslehre," *GA*, I, 2, p. 151; and *Versuch einer Kritik aller Offenbarung*, *GA*, I, 1, p. 152.

times free. The latter is all that the traditional advocate of freedom needs. This confusion may play some role in Fichte's insistence – which again shows the secondary role for him of mere theoretical skepticism – that an adequate ("scientific") philosophy must say not only that there is a source of representation but also what this source is like, that is, it must provide an explanation of why there is consciousness at all, presumably an explanation that secures our freedom.[33]

C. 2. Fichte's Deductive System

This reluctance to accept a "given" is related to Fichte's second main line of attack on previous transcendentalisms: that these involve an improperly developed (and hence not truly "scientific") system. It is obviously from Reinhold that Fichte got the main idea here, namely that Kant's transcendental deduction, with its mysterious dependence on the metaphysical deduction and its "given" list of categories, should be replaced by a "fundamental thesis" from which all further basic concepts would be derived in order and in such a way that the possibility of such a deduction would itself be reflexively explained. Fichte did accept criticisms of Reinhold's thesis by Schulze, but his counter was not to give up on a strict system but rather to find a substitute for the specific thesis that Reinhold thought was first and then to show that even more could be derived from it.[34] In place of Reinhold's basic "principle of consciousness" (that each representation distinguishes itself from its subject and object), which expresses a fundamental fact (*Tatsache*), Fichte insists there is a most fundamental act of consciousness (*Tathandlung*) that, by opposing subject to object, first makes representation possible.[35] As others have pointed out,[36] here Fichte is again following Schulze's lead, for

---

33 See e.g., Fichte, *Science of Knowledge*, p. 13, and Fichte's letter to Reinhold, July 2, 1795, *GA*, II, 2, p. 345. Cf. F. W. J. Schelling, "Of the I as the Principle of Philosophy," trans. Fritz Marti, in *The Unconditional in Human Knowledge* (Lewisberg, PA: Bucknell University Press, 1980), p. 79: "If the principle of the fact is to be a thing in itself, then every I is done away with, there is no longer any pure I, any freedom . . . "

34 I think this point is undervalued in Tom Rockmore, *Hegel's Circular Epistemology* (Bloomington: Indiana University Press, 1986). Rockmore provides a fine documentation of the role of systematicity in Kant and post-Kantians (pp. 18–45), but he goes too far in saying Fichte's system is "circular" whereas Reinhold's is "linear" (p. 43). The more radically idealistic position that Fichte adopts in wholly rejecting things in themselves does not amount to a change in method. Fichte always saw himself as continuing with Reinhold's idea that philosophy must deduce all from one principle. See *GA*, III, 2, pp. 18, 315, 345.

35 See Fichte's "*Aenesidemus* Rezension," *GA*, I, 2, pp. 46–8.

36 Daniel Breazeale, "Fichte's 'Aenesidemus' Review and the Transformation of German Idealism," *Review of Metaphysics* 34 (1981): 545–68.

Schulze had argued precisely that Reinhold's "fact" could not be absolutely fundamental since its complexity presumed simpler components such as the processes of opposition and synthesis. Furthermore, it is only in dissecting the necessary components of these processes that Fichte believes a genuinely systematic justification of categories can be provided.

In Fichte's development of this criticism of Reinhold we can see once again how he slides toward an emphasis on a practical moral perspective that passes over crucial theoretical issues. Basically, what Fichte does is insist that for philosophy to be true to what he calls the "spirit" of the Critical turn, the "I" must be taken as its sufficient basis, and then he slowly shifts from hinting that a theoretical notion of the I can be such a basis to relying on a pure practical construal of the notion.

Thus, in his first notes on Kant's own deduction, Fichte spoke simply of the "essence of Critical philosophy" as a "deduction from the I."[37] Like other philosophers later, Fichte understood this I not in terms of the logical forms of apperception, but rather (as Jacobi had hinted) in terms of the idea that the I stands for the principle of a "thoroughgoing unity" of the self. This ambitious strategy was not developed, as it has been by others today, into a clear theoretical argument that the categories are necessary conditions for a priori knowledge of personal identity.[38] Fichte typically was not oriented toward such speculative issues that focus so narrowly on the individual. His arguments soon had a more practical form:

> it must be proved that reason is practical. Such a proof, which could also easily be the foundation for all [!] philosophical knowledge, would have to be carried out roughly as follows. Consciousness is given to man (the I) as a unity. This fact is only to be explained on the presupposition of something absolutely unconditional in him, thus something absolutely unconditional must be presumed in man. But practical reason simply is something unconditional.[39]

Fichte applied this practical reorientation in picking up Reinhold's idea that the fundamental thesis of philosophy is revealed via an "intellectual intuition" of the I.[40] While Fichte accepted the notion of such intuition,

---

37 Fichte, "Transcendentale Elementarlehre," *GA*, II, 1, p. 312; and *GA*, I, 2, p. 335. Jacobi may have been influential here. See H. Timm, *Gott und die Freiheit*, p. 388.

38 See D. Henrich, *Identität und Objektivität* (Heidelberg: Carl Winter, 1970); and Fichte, *Science of Knowledge*, p. 51.

39 Fichte "Rezension Creuzer," *GA*, I, 2, p. 28.

40 See Fichte, *Science of Knowledge*, pp. 38ff.; and Breazeale, "Fichte's *Aenesidemus*," p. 565.

he claimed that Reinhold's "intuition" expressed a mere theoretical proposition, a proposition about a fact of consciousness, namely the existence of representation, and he went on to argue that this fact presupposed a prior practical power to generate representation.

Even if one grants Fichte the notion of such a prerepresentative power (i.e., the notion, which even Reinhold came to accept, that something which can't be explained through representation itself is responsible for the actuality of representation), the question remains of how it is to be correlated, as Fichte insists it is, with the concept of the I. Where Spinozists had argued that the power could be divorced entirely from reference to an ultimate personal self, Fichte wanted to maintain reference to a self, but without falling back into dogmatic theoretical claims about special intuitive insight into either our phenomenal or our noumenal nature.[41] Fichte's answer was precisely to reinterpret the I involved with this power in nonpsychological and nonconscious terms, that is, as standing for a general principle of practical reason. This is why Fichte argued, in criticizing Reinhold's treatment of the will, that freedom is fundamentally to be attributed to the general autonomy of moral reason, and not the selective choice of individual agency: "without this absolutely first expression of freedom (the moral law), the second (freedom of choice) merely empirical expression couldn't be saved, it would be mere illusion."[42]

I believe this idea rests on an unfortunate confusion of logical and epistemic conditions (since even if the law is a condition of our knowledge of freedom, it is not a condition of the existence of freedom), but it does help explain why Fichte's discussions of intellectual intuition in the *Wissenschaftslehre*, and his claim of being able to "deduce the whole system of necessary presentations from it," must always be interpreted in view of his prior proviso that his procedure "calls upon the listener or reader to think a certain concept freely."[43] Given Fichte's critique of Reinhold's (apparent) appeal to nonmoral evidence of freedom, it should be expected that Fichte understands the "freedom" in the listener that he appeals to as derivative from the moral law. Indeed, Fichte states, "consciousness of this law . . . forms the basis for the intuition of self-activity and freedom,"[44] and intellectual intuition "comes about solely by exhibi-

---

41 See the materials cited in Schelling, *The Unconditional*, p. 133, n. 25, and p. 135, n. 34.

42 Fichte, *Versuch*, GA, I, 1, p. 47. Cf. Reinhold's reply to Fichte, Dec. 1795, GA, III, 2, pp. 437–9, and to Erhard, Aug. 2, 1796, in *J. G. Fichte im Gespräch* (Stuttgart: Frommann, 1978), p. 368; and see above at n. 30.

43 Fichte, *Science of Knowledge*, p. 25.

44 Ibid., p. 41.

tion of the moral law in us,"[45] and signifies that "I *ought* in my thinking to set out from the *pure* self."[46]

Unfortunately, what complicates matters is the fact that Fichte also inserts – just before and after these clear statements – remarks that could be taken (out of context) to suggest a nonmoral basis for his system, as when he says intellectual intuition is simply "that whereby I know something because I do it,"[47] or when he refers to Kant's transcendental deduction as if its reference to pure apperception as an "act of spontaneity" is by itself an independent proof of freedom.[48] What he really means, I propose, is not that the mere appearance of action or judgment proves freedom, but that once we take on the free perspective opened by the moral law (and it alone), we can see these nonexplicitly moral contexts as involving absolute spontaneity as well, since they are to be seen as dependent (in Fichte's system) on the absolute freedom of our moral being. Thus, Fichte's second corrective to Reinhold's approach, like his first, rests on a standpoint that is fundamentally, although not always clearly, determined by moral-practical considerations.

C. 3. Fichte's Idealism

A similar pattern can be found in Fichte's third revision of transcendental philosophy, his reinterpretation of transcendental idealism. Fichte's treatment of this issue is closely connected with his ultimate interest in freedom (his fourth point) as well as with specific features of his first two objections. Thus, one aspect of his objection to the lack of systematicity in prior philosophy (his second point) also becomes a crucial aspect of his construal of the meaning of any acceptable idealism, namely that all basic (theoretical) "facts" of our consciousness, and thus even the very forms of space and time that Kant had taken to be inexplicable, are to be derived as absolutely necessary conditions for the possibility of any consciousness. Reinhold had hinted at such a view, but Fichte charged him with not going far enough, with merely coordinating and not fully subordinating the various faculties of man.[49] This means that in place of Kant's long deduction of specific categories demonstrably necessary only for beings with forms of intuition like ours, Fichte picks up and develops Reinhold's

45 Ibid., p. 40.
46 Ibid., p. 41; cf. ibid., p. 46.
47 Ibid., p. 38; cf. "*Aenesidemus* Rezension," *GA*, I, 2, p. 57. On these ambiguities in Fichte's approach, see below Chapter 4, sec. D.
48 Fichte, *Science of Knowledge*, p. 49.
49 See Fichte's letter to Reinhold, April 28, 1795, *GA*, III, 2, p. 309.

espousal of a deduction that bypasses the details of Kant's own and ends with conditions held to be required for any form of consciousness at all.[50]

Fichte's radicality here is motivated by more than just his pure moral orientation, which allows him, unlike Reinhold, to accept the full consequences of such idealism, namely the incoherence of the very idea of a traditional transcendent and personal concept of God and our moral destiny.[51] In addition, Fichte is encouraged in two further ways, first by a desire to meet his initial interest in not leaving anything significant beyond our reach that a skeptic might worry about, and second by a striking incidental peculiarity of Reinhold's system. This peculiarity is that although Reinhold had completely dismissed the representation of particular things in themselves, he had allowed the general concept of such a thing, and he even encouraged the assertion that it exists, for he thought that otherwise there would be no ground for the matter of representation.[52] All Reinhold could say about the thing in itself is that it is "the thinkable in so far as it is not thinkable."[53] Fichte picks up on this absurdity while remaining clearly dependent on the essentials of Reinhold's approach when he argues:

> But now how is the Critical system distinguished from what we have presented as the Humean one? Simply in that Hume still leaves open the possibility of somehow going beyond the limitation of the human mind, whereas the Critical [i.e., Fichte's] system shows the absolute impossibility of such a move, and shows that the thought that a thing, as it is in itself and independent of any faculty of representation [*Vorstellungsvermögen* – Reinhold's main term] has existence and certain characteristics is a freak, a dream, a non-thought.[54]

Thus, having been convinced by Jacobi and Schulze's claim that things in themselves cannot consistently function as sources of the matter of expe-

---

50 See below at n. 57, and Fichte, *Science of Knowledge*, sec. 48, which argues that intuition as such is subject to the "I." For more on Fichte's neglect of Kant's theoretical philosophy, see M. J. Siemek, "Fichtes Wissenschaftslehre und die kantische Transzendentalphilosophie," in *Der Transzendentale Gedanke*, ed. K. Hammacher (Hamburg: Meiner, 1981), p. 527.

51 See Fichte, "On the Foundation of Our Belief in a Divine Government of the Universe," trans. Paul Edwards, in *Nineteenth Century Philosophy*, ed. Patrick Gardiner (New York: Free Press, 1969), pp. 25–6. Reinhold had attacked Rehberg for holding precisely this position. The common source of the view is of course Spinoza. See Schulz, *Rehbergs Opposition*, pp. 82, n. 7, 88, 160, 177–87, and the excerpt from Rehberg, pp. 261–8.

52 Reinhold, *Versuch einer neuen Theorie des menschlichen Vorstellungsvermögens* (Prague: Widtmann and Jauke, 1789), p. 422.

53 Reinhold, *Über das Fundament des philosophischen Wissens* (Jena: Mauke, 1791), p. 32.

54 Fichte, "*Aenesidemus* Rezension," *GA*, I, 2, p. 57.

rience, Fichte modifies the Reinholdian line in just the way we would now expect, namely by rejecting the existence, where Reinhold had rejected only the representation, of things independent of a faculty of representation. Fichte even says that no one would ever naturally claim to have the thought of something independent of all representation, though of course that is exactly what Reinhold's peculiar notion of the thing in itself required.[55] Thus we can understand how, in his later introduction to the *Wissenschaftslehre*, Fichte rejects the thing in itself as something that is "pure invention and has no reality whatever."[56] He is simply rejecting the sheerly unrepresentable, while avoiding coming to grips with the grounds for the Kantian possibility of something beyond the spatiotemporal realm. Fichte explicitly rejects Kant's own long argument to idealism by saying, "Kant demonstrates the ideality of objects from the presupposed ideality of space and time: we, on the contrary, shall prove the ideality of space and time from the demonstrated ideality of objects."[57] Thus he favors a short but ambitious argument that would entirely do away with things in themselves:

> In terms of its own chosen route, the Kantian system may have need in this fashion [namely, by excluding us from intellectual intuition] to shut out the thing in itself; the Science of Knowledge has disposed of it by other means. We recognize it to be the uttermost perversion of reason, for we must derive the entire concept of existence only from the form of sensibility and are thus protected against the claim to any connection with the thing in itself.[58]

The questionable theory of concept formation behind this strong conclusion should be distinguished from another more general line of argument that Fichte also employs, namely that all must be "for" consciousness because we do not and cannot use reference to anything absolutely transcendent as a criterion for comparison in testing our knowledge claims (since in any test we cannot abstract from our own self-consciousness).[59] While this line is distinct, it is equally inadequate because it would show at most only that there is nothing fully independent of us that we can directly consider, not that there is not and cannot be any such thing.

55 Ibid., pp. 58, 61.
56 Fichte, *Science of Knowledge*, p. 10.
57 Ibid., p. 171, n. 3. Cf. Reinhold, *Beyträge* I (Jena: Mauke, 1790), p. 297.
58 Fichte, *Science of Knowledge*, p. 45. Cf. ibid., p. 224; and the "empiricist" citations in R. Adamson, *Fichte* (London: Blackwood, 1881), p. 108; and F. Bergmann, "The Purpose of Hegel's System," *Journal of the History of Philosophy* 2 (1966): 91, n. 7.
59 Fichte, *Science of Knowledge*, p. 82. Cf. ibid., sec. 8; Fichte, "*Aenesidemus* Rezension," *GA*, I, 2, p. 61; and Kant, *AA*, vol. 18, p. 281.

Also very influential on Fichte was a similarly insufficient notion that things cannot explain consciousness whereas consciousness can explain things. This holds only in the sense that a sheerly mechanical explanation of consciousness seems futile (like Kant, Fichte tended to suppose this was the only relevant "objective" explanation), whereas an "explanation by consciousness" is always available for all things we can know just in so far as any explanation of things that can be offered by us must be constituted in terms of evidence we have.[60]

Minimizing these limited arguments, we can say that so far, in addition to (i) Fichte's moral and (ii) antiskeptical interests, and (iii) his willingness to exploit special difficulties in Reinhold's formulations, we have found but two major grounds for his rejection of Kant's own transcendental idealism, namely that it supposedly violates the empirical meanings of the notions of (iv) causality and (v) existence. These grounds fail because of a lack of appreciation for Kant's distinction between pure and schematized categories, and so they still leave us with no decisive reasons for abandoning Kant's own position. But there is a last major consideration that Fichte advances more directly in favor of his own brand of idealism. The main original idea that he repeatedly employs is that all must be taken to be "for" the I because even the I itself is only for the I.[61] He expressed this position originally in terms of Reinhold's proposal that all (we can know) is relative to our "faculty of representation" by saying that the faculty of representation itself is only for the faculty of representation. This argument appears to be very close in effect to one in which Fichte says that the I is because it "posits" itself, and it is not "before" this act,[62] although it is "before" any act of perception.

To have any hope of understanding such difficult claims it is crucial both that one take the term "I" as not being meant to designate the conscious self, for then it could not "precede" perception; and that one take the term "positing" as not being meant to designate an ordinary causal relation, for then the I would (absurdly) have to bring itself into

---

60 Fichte, *Science of Knowledge*, pp. 16–19, 31, n. 1, and his "*Aenesidemus* Rezension," *GA*, 1, 2, p. 55, where critical philosophy is defined as the idea that "alles, was in unserem Gemüt vorkommt, aus ihm selbst vollständig zu erklären und zu begreifen ist" (everything that takes place in our mind is to be completely explained and comprehended through it). Cf. Reinhold's remark, cited in Selling, *Studien*, p. 345, that representation cannot be a thing in itself because it cannot be explained as a mechanical effect of things. For more detail see below Chapter 4, sec. C.

61 Fichte, *Science of Knowledge*, sec. 3; cf. "*Aenesidemus* Rezension," *GA*, I, 2, p. 66. For more detail, see below Chapter 5, sec. C. 2.

62 Fichte, "*Aenesidemus* Rezension," *GA*, I, 2, p. 51; cf. *Science of Knowledge*, sec. 48.

being temporally from a situation in which it is not yet temporal. The "positing" relation of the basic *Tathandlung* is also not meant to be a perceptual relation, for it is to designate precisely what is to be presupposed if representation is to be possible at all.[63] At the very least, to say that the I posits itself "before" it perceives itself is to say that a reflective apprehension of the self cannot be what originally constitutes it. That seems sensible enough, if one is to avoid obvious problems of circularity – but can anything more positive be said about what Fichte means by "I" and "positing" here? A natural proposal, and one immediately suggested by work that clearly influenced Fichte, is to construe these notions in terms of the Kantian idea of the inner nature of the moral self and its self-legislative character. There we also do not have a natural ego that naturally causes anything, but we we do have a subjective entity (a "pure" I) that "posits" something by itself. The moral law is egolike in that it reveals something that has an inner relation to the moral agent, yet without being dependent on an actual individual; and, it is like a self-positing in that it provides something binding and yet does so on the basis of what the individual himself would will to do.

Even if all this can give some sense to Fichte's notion that the (individual, reflected) I is inescapably "for" the (prereflective, pure) I, clarifying the thesis of the ideality of the I still does not amount to making comprehensible the ideality of the non-I. At this point I believe Fichte's only recourse is to retreat again to his practical perspective, and to say simply that the claim that the non-I depends on the I just means that there is no other ground for any assertion of external existence than one which the moral law implies, since (on his view) all theoretical refutations of skepticism fall short.[64] This interpretation fits Fichte's mature view in the *Vocation of Man*, and it is the way to make the best sense of his conviction that any admission of a thing in itself, that is, a theoretically allowed absolute non-I, destroys freedom and entails skepticism.

C. 4. Fichtean Freedom

This last line of thought takes us to the essence, and the essential weakness, of Fichte's position, his fourth and major objection, the critique of the Kantian notion of freedom. Expanding on the concept of idealism

---

63 Fichte, "*Aenesidemus* Rezension," *GA*, I, 2, p. 47. Cf. Breazeale, "Fichte's Review," p. 562, and D. Henrich, *Fichtes ursprüngliche Einsicht* (Frankfurt: Klostermann, 1967).

64 See Fichte, "*Aenesidemus* Rezension," *GA*, I, 2, pp. 55–6; and Fichte, *Vocation of Man*, Book 3, pp. 83–91.

just noted, Fichte proclaimed, "to the idealist, the only positive thing is
freedom; existence, for him, is a mere negation of the latter."[65] Taken
literally, this suggests that we could affirm freedom without first affirming
something that would be free. This is a peculiar thought because the very
idea of actual freedom is the idea of uncaused or self-caused action, and
this seems to require something that can so act. At the very least, the claim
that such freedom is possible would seem to need the prior idea that
there *can* be items that would be able to act freely. But the key to Fichte's
radicality is precisely his rejection of this need. In this way he goes against
Kant's central belief that transcendental idealism, and hence the possibility of a realm (or aspect) of items not naturally determined (B xxix), is
required before anything (such as morality) that seems to require freedom can be affirmed as more than a mere "phantom of the brain."

Fichte was aware of this belief and he directly rejected it. He argues:
"Our contention is not: I ought since I can; it is rather: I can since I ought.
The I ought and what I ought to do comes first and is most evident. It
requires no further explanation, justification, or authorization."[66] One
defensible element of this claim is the thought that *if* there is no known
threat to the possibility of a being who "can," that is, who has absolute
freedom, then morality, even if it is presumed to require such freedom,
may require no prior explanation of its possibility (at least if it is just to be
considered permissible and sensible, if not clearly mandatory). But the
fact is that after Kant there is such a known threat. As Kant emphasized,
his own transcendental philosophy and its proof of the causal law seems at
first to leave no room for absolute freedom. Unless a philosopher has first
defused that threat – and Fichte has not – he cannot proceed within
transcendental philosophy. More harshly, it can be said that Fichte wants
to assert Kantian morality and freedom (in an absolute, noncompatibilist
sense) without appreciating the conditions for such assertion. Moreover,
he cannot plead he was unaware of this difficulty, for it was stressed clearly
in a book he reviewed closely, Schulze's *Aenesidemus*.[67]

My suspicion as to how Fichte could have proceeded nonetheless is
that he was overinfluenced by a response he had to the question of the
relation of morality to actuality. Against those who said it was unclear that
a truly moral agent could really be effective, Fichte replied that Kant has
taught us that morality requires only proper intentions, that is, a purity of

65 Fichte, *Science of Knowledge*, p. 69.
66 Fichte, "Divine Government," p. 23.
67 Schulze, *Aenesidemus*, pp. 430–1. Cf. Alfred Klemmt, *Karl Leonhard Reinholds Elementar-
    philosophie* (Hamburg: Meiner, 1958), pp. 500, 521, n. 2.

striving,[68] and so even if the ends of morality seem thwarted by nature, its essential possibility remains beyond doubt, since surely we can strive properly. But this consideration forgets that the Kantian thesis of determination applies to both the outer and the inner realms. Hence, unless one knows something about the ultimate origin of one's experienced inner "strivings" toward the good, one does not really know that there can be free acts that have the possibility of moral value. Thus the freedom that Fichte originally saw as "unjustified" in Kant is more unjustified in his own system, and with even greater consequences, since it is even more crucial to that system. Later idealists would not fundamentally improve on this position.

D. HEGEL'S REACTION PREVIEWED

Reinhold is typical of this development when in a late work he pleads that freedom must somehow be in accord with the overwhelming appearance of necessity in our life, since both are (supposedly) crucial to reason, and reason must be in harmony with itself.[69] Earlier in the era, Lessing had encouraged this compatibilist view; Hegel was to purify it at the end of the idealist line, pausing only to make fun of Fichte's emphasis on mere striving. While Kant never fully resolved the problem himself, his idealist followers never got back to addressing the problem clearly and directly.

There are also other respects in which one can look forward to Hegel as merely completing the process of Kant's reception initiated by Reinhold and Fichte. I discuss some of these points in detail elsewhere; in conclusion here I will end with a bare outline of the main aspects of this process. Although it is true that Hegel abhorred talk of intellectual intuition, or *Tathandlungen,* or any explicit basis for philosophy in doctrines of pure moral freedom, he did develop a monistic system that mirrored Fichte's modifications of Kant's four main points. First, he rejected a beginning with the merely "hypothetical" Kantian notion of experience.[70] Second, he also opposed the haphazard Kantian list of categories by insisting the transcendental deduction can begin with the general concept of the I and can proceed to derive the categories in order, and can even show the

---

68 Fichte, *"Aenesidemus* Rezension," *GA,* I, 2, p. 64. The criticism of Fichte made below was partially anticipated by Rehberg; see Schulz, *Rehbergs Opposition,* p. 74. Cf. also H. J. Engfer, "Handlen, Erkennen, und Selbstbewusstsein bei Kant und Fichte," in *Probleme der Handlungstheorie,* ed. Hans Poser (Freiberg: Alber, 1982), p. 610.

69 See M. Selling, *Studien,* p. 335.

70 On these points, see my "Hegel's Critique of Kant's Theoretical Philosophy," *Philosophy and Phenomenological Research* 46 (1985): 2–15 (Chapter 6 below).

necessity of space and time. Third, Hegel agrees with the essence of Fichte's idealism, the statement that "the thing is itself and actually so constituted as it must be in thought . . . by any thinkable intelligent I."[71] That is, since the short argument so totally excludes the sense of any thing in itself outside of what we could know, the only sensible way left to speak of things is to speak of them as that which is representable by us, that is, by finite subjects. (Hence Fichte could say that since even his ultimate being, the absolute I, is only "for itself" too, there is nothing significant left that could be "merely in itself.") Thus Hegel mocks the thing in itself as the "unthinkable,"[72] in an obvious reference to the absurdity that Reinhold had landed in, even while he holds on to Reinhold's main idea of reconstructing Kant without relying on the intricacies of the transcendental deduction and the notion of our specific forms of intuition. Finally, and fourth once again, the exclusion of noumena was made all the easier for Hegel since, after having been influenced by the radicalism of the early Schelling (who also agreed on the four modifications of transcendentalism that have been stressed here), he was even more ready than Fichte to dispense with traditional transcendent notions of freedom, divinity, and moral fulfillment. In this way it turns out that the very issues of moral and religious philosophy that had led Reinhold to try to make Kant's practical views more effective, by means of a reformulation of the theoretical aspects of the Critical philosophy via the short argument, are what led Reinhold's successors, most notably Fichte, to adapt the short argument in such a way that that practical philosophy (in its original meaning) was no longer even possible.

71 Fichte, "*Aenesidemus* Rezension," *GA*, I, 2, p. 62.
72 G. W. F. Hegel, *Science of Logic*, trans. W. H. Johnston and L. G. Struthers (London: George Allen and Unwin, 1929), vol. I, p. 55.

4

KANT, FICHTE, AND THE RADICAL
PRIMACY OF THE PRACTICAL

4. THE MANY MEANINGS OF "IN THE BEGINNING
WAS THE ACT"

Fichte's philosophy made an epoch-defining impression on its first students and readers in Jena. In our own time, after almost two centuries of considerable neglect, it has experienced a remarkable return in popularity that has reached even to the distant circles of analytic philosophy in America.[1] This resurgence has been tied closely to Fichte's claim to im-

---

[1] Here is a preliminary list of relevant literature: Dieter Henrich, *Fichtes ursprüngliche Einsicht* (Frankfurt: Klostermann, 1967), *Identität und Objektivität* (Heidelberg: Carl Winter, 1976), and "The Identity of the Subject in the Transcendental Deduction," in *Reading Kant*, ed. E. Schaper and W. Vossenkuhl (Oxford: Blackwell, 1989), pp. 250–80; Frederick Neuhouser, *Fichte's Theory of Subjectivity* (Cambridge: Cambridge University Press, 1990); Manfred Frank, *Selbstbewusstsein und Selbsterkenntnis* (Stuttgart: Reclam, 1991) and *Selbstbewusstseinstheorien von Fichte bis Sartre* (Frankfurt: Suhrkamp, 1991); Robert Pippin, *Hegel's Idealism: The Satisfactions of Self-Consciousness* (Cambridge: Cambridge University Press, 1989); and (for a powerful Kantian and non-Fichtean theory of radical self-activity) Gerold Prauss, *Die Welt und wir*, 2 vols. (Stuttgart: Metzler, 1990, 1993, and 1999). I have discussed Henrich in "Kant and Guyer on Apperception," *Archiv für Geschichte der Philosophie* 65 (1983): 174–86, and "Kant and the Self: A Retrospective," in *Figuring the Self: Subject, Absolute, and Others in Classical German Philosophy*, ed. D. Klemm and G. Zöller (Albany: State University of New York, 1997), pp. 55–72; Neuhouser in "Kant and the Self"; Frank in "The Ineliminable Subject: From Kant to Frank," in *The Modern Subject: Conceptions of the Self in Classical German Philosophy*, ed. K. Ameriks and D. Sturma (Albany: State University of New York, 1995), pp. 217–30; Pippin in "Hegel and Idealism," *Monist* 74 (1991): 386–402; and Prauss in "Contemporary German

187

prove upon the Critical philosophy by turning Kant's well-known concern
with the self into a more focused and radical emphasis on the self's
activity, what Fichte called its primordial *Tathandlung*. This is clearly an
idea whose time had come; it is no accident that Goethe called Fichte to
take Reinhold's place in Jena, and that his Faust rewrote Scripture for
modernity by declaring, "Am Anfang war die Tat," that is, in the beginning was the *act*, and not the mere *word* of speculative theology or "gray"
theory. More recently, "moral constructivism" (an ethics that "leaves ontology behind") is just one striking example of important contemporary
trends that, indirectly at least, owe much more than is realized to Fichte
rather than Kant. Even within the field of theory itself, contemporary
philosophers have proposed a myriad of new ways to follow Fichte's call
for a stress on activity under the heading of the many-sided doctrine of
the "primacy of the practical." Both the popular and the academic appeal
of Fichte's philosophy can be understood easily enough in terms of its
being the first important radicalization of this doctrine. The implications
of Fichte's doctrine for classical *theoretical* issues of philosophy have been
recently discussed primarily in terms of his appropriation of Kant's notion
of the "act" of apperception for the purposes of developing a theory of
self-consciousness as "self-positing." In the next chapter I will focus on
aspects of that difficult discussion, but in this chapter I will concentrate
first on the more *explicitly practical* aspects of Fichte's treatment of the
self's activity.

   Fichte's direct concern with the practical is expressed at two different
levels: the *concrete* dimension of actual sociohistorical praxis and the *philosophical* dimension of the doctrine of practical reason as the primary form
of reason in general. With respect to the first dimension, it is sufficient
simply to recall some of the highlights of Fichte's sensational career, his
meteoric rise from poverty to a life of activism and a leadership role in the
renovation of German academic institutions. Among Fichte's earliest
tracts are passionate defenses of the French Revolution: "A Discourse on

Epistemology," *Inquiry* 25 (1982): 125–38. The initial presentation of my general perspective on the Fichtean era is in "Kant, Fichte, and Short Arguments to Idealism," *Archiv für
Geschichte der Philosophie* 72 (1990): 63–85 (reprinted above as Chapter 3). An impressive
recent indication of the "analytic" trend I have in mind is Susan Hurley's aptly titled *Consciousness in Action* (Oxford: Oxford University Press, 1998), a work that does not directly
invoke Fichte but provides an extensive discussion of "action-oriented" readings of Kantian
apperception, with an insightful critique of "the myth of the giving." For an original analysis
of "self-synthesis" that directly invokes Fichte, see Robert Nozick, *Philosophical Explanations*
(Cambridge: Harvard University Press, 1981), pp. 87–110.

the Reclamation of the Freedom of Thought from the Princes of Europe, Who Have Hitherto Suppressed It" (1793) and "A Contribution Toward Correcting the Public's Judgment of the French Revolution" (1793–4). His first academic treatise, *Attempt at a Critique of All Revelation* (1792), was a bold anticipation of Kant's liberal views on church and religion, and led eventually to the famous *Atheismusstreit* (1798–9), a political dispute over the teaching of doctrines perceived as atheistic. Throughout his time in Jena (1794–9) his "philosophy of freedom" was the main philosophical provocation (as a model, but also as a catalyst for alternatives; see above Chapter 1, sec. C) for the revolutionary cultural movement of German Romanticism. In timing, content, and radicality he also outdid Kant in setting out the details of a Critical social philosophy in his *Foundations of Natural Right* (*Naturrecht*) (1796) and *System of Ethical Theory* (*Sittenlehre*) (1798). These books laid down the cornerstones of later Hegelian and socialist programs that had massive effects on world history. After his highly influential *Addresses to the German Nation* (1808–9), Fichte's later career was capped by his call (1810) to be the first philosopher to head the faculty of the new university at Berlin.[2]

Despite the unquestionable historical significance of Fichte's specific social *commitments,* it is important not to let one's attitude toward them interfere with a careful evaluation of the second and quite distinct (though, of course, not unrelated) dimension of his explicitly practical orientation, namely his doctrine of a general primacy of practical *reason.* It is this second, purely philosophical, dimension that I will focus on, and in this chapter I will study it under a further crucial restriction, following the terminology of both Fichte and Kant, who usually used the term "practical" in a "pure" sense equivalent to what is determined by *moral duty* – and this, in turn, in not just any traditional sense, but one defined by freedom and autonomy. Despite the differences that arose with Kant, Fichte always held onto the basic twofold Critical idea that, in signifying freedom and autonomy, "the practical" implies an executive power to determine oneself absolutely, in absolute spontaneity as an uncaused cause of intentional acts, as well as a legislative capacity to do so morally in line with laws of one's own general essence, that is, one's rationality. The philosophical doctrine of the primacy of the practical thus has to be understood in

2 For brief overviews, see Allen Wood, "Fichte's Philosophical Revolution," *Philosophical Topics* 19 (1991): 1–28; and Daniel Breazeale, "Fichte and Schelling: The Jena Period," in *The Routledge History of Philosophy,* vol. 6, *The Age of German Idealism,* ed. R. Solomon and K. Higgins (London: Routledge, 1993), pp. 138–60.

terms of a preeminence of deontological moral reason that requires acts of both pure execution and pure legislation. This preeminence, however, can be and was taken in different ways by Kant and Fichte.

B. THREE SENSES OF THE PRIMACY OF PURE PRACTICAL REASON

It will be central to my interpretation that although for Kant there is also a kind of primacy of pure practical reason, this primacy concerns (1) the special *significance* and (2) unique *detail* that comes with our duties, and the doctrine is *not* to be taken as implying any absolute priority of practical reason at the level of (3) philosophical *method*. In contrast to what happens in Fichte's "practical foundationalist" system, practical reason in Kant's philosophy has a kind of preeminence because it discloses the basic sources and goals of what is valuable, but not because it can set the fundamental conditions of philosophical argument; that remains the prerogative of theoretical reason, in both its strictly logical and metaphysical forms. The first two points about primacy are presumably familiar enough to require no more than a brief sketch, but the third point requires considerable elaboration and a close reading of Fichte's texts.

Kant spoke of our awareness of duty as revealing a fundamental "fact of reason," the irreducible (and hence "factual," because not derivable from anything more basic) fact that through the categorical imperative we recognize that we are called by our own reason to follow the moral law. As categorical, this law is (1) the *most significant* object of our attention in the sense that it alone reveals what is of unconditional interest and value, the moral will. Although Kant recognizes that mere theoretical and prudential activities also have considerable positive value, he insists that by themselves they are rooted in secondary interests that have nothing like the incomparable worth of morality. Kant also argues that the moral law is what alone makes it possible, through the postulates of pure practical reason and the idea of the highest good (a highest happiness justly apportioned to a dutiful character), for us to "determine" what we can rationally hope regarding (2) the *basic details* of our own final reality (as moral beings) including the general end of human history. Mere speculative reason and mere natural philosophy can at most reveal some basic parameters, some broad features that our moral perspective must be consistent with, but they alone cannot provide anything like the positive and relatively "filled in" version of our ultimate destiny given by the postulates of practical reason.

Despite the importance of these first two kinds of primacy, which Fichte takes over in broadly Kantian terms (if one minimizes Fichte's secularization of the postulates), the most striking fact here is that in the crucial third, or *methodological* sense, it turns out that Fichte does not follow Kant in relegating practical reason to a secondary rather than primary status. Kant's view is reflected in the fact that practical reason as such is treated only in his second *Critique*, since he holds that the crucial assurance that we *can* have the absolute freedom needed to be able to heed the call of morality presupposes the first *Critique*'s theoretical doctrines and, in particular, its metaphysics of transcendental idealism (see above Chapter 1, sec. D. 2). For Kant, this metaphysics is crucial because he believes *only* it can prove that the spatiotemporal laws covering all the ordinary appearances of our life need not constrain our inner or noumenal reality, and so, rather than having to give up morality in the face of a law-governed nature, we can and should accept morality as the guide to a nonspatiotemporal realm that exists and is more fundamental than nature. His most basic claim is this: "If we grant that morality necessarily presupposes freedom in the strictest sense . . . and if at the same time we grant that speculative reason has proved that such freedom does not allow of being thought, then . . . morality would have to yield to the mechanism of nature."[3] Only because he believes that his transcendental idealism has provided for the sole escape from "nature" and the metaphysical contradictions that would keep our freedom from being able to be thought consistently, can Kant hold onto the rigorous demands that he believes define our practical reason.

Fichte could not accept Kant's crucial metaphysical claim because he believed that Kant's first critics (especially Jacobi) had already shown the metaphysics of transcendental idealism to be inconsistent.[4] Here we need

---

3 Kant, B xxix. All quotations of Kant's *Critique of Pure Reason* are from the Norman Kemp Smith translation (London: Macmillan, 1929), with the first and second editions designated as A and B, respectively, followed by page numbers.

4 Fichte made a vehement denial of "things in themselves existing outside us" after invoking Jacobi's influential note, "On Transcendental Idealism," a supplement to *David Hume on Faith, or Idealism and Realism, a Dialogue* (1787), in *The Main Philosophical Writings and the Novel Allwill, Friedrich Heinrich Jacobi,* ed. and trans. George di Giovanni (Montreal: McGill University Press, 1994), pp. 331–8. See Fichte's "Second Introduction to the Science of Knowledge," in *Fichte: Science of Knowledge (Wissenschaftslehre), with the First and Second Introductions,* trans. and ed. P. Heath and J. Lachs (Cambridge: Cambridge University Press, 1982), p. 54; *Johann Gottlieb Fichtes sämmtliche Werke,* 8 vols., ed. I. H. Fichte (Berlin: Veit, 1845–6), I, p. 482; hereafter cited as *SW.* Unlike Reinhold's most radical view, Fichte allows the thought of a thing in itself, but he denies that a "mere thought" can have "efficacy." However, this does not show that what the thought is *about could not* have efficacy. Fichte appears to take

not go into the details of this disagreement (see above Chapter 3, sec. C), but it is important always to bear in mind that from the outset of his philosophical career Fichte assumed that Kant's philosophy, as it stood, was no more capable than any other metaphysics or theoretical philosophy of saving (what he took to be) our commonsense belief in absolute freedom and the claim of the moral law upon us. The only options remaining for him were either to renounce morality as a "phantom" or to question the methodological preeminence of theoretical philosophy. Fichte himself could never imagine questioning morality, and he was keen on downgrading theoretical philosophy for a number of reasons. Influenced again by Kant's first critics (especially his own teacher, G. E. Schulze, an expert on skepticism), Fichte thought that, in addition to the specific metaphysical complications of transcendental idealism, there was the general epistemological problem that supposedly no purely theoretical philosophy could be reconciled with the basic commonsense belief in an external world, a world beyond our mere representations.[5] For Fichte, the solution was not to become a skeptic but rather to downgrade theoretical philosophy by saying that the call of pure practical reason, and all its implications, could be endorsed without any prior consideration of its theoretical possibility. If one accepts morality as absolute, one already makes a commitment to freedom; one can then argue, as Fichte does, that it is this commitment in turn that properly leads one to "posit" (i.e., seriously intend as actual) the world beyond representations that theoretical philosophy cannot in any case deliver. In this way practical reason gains methodological primacy; it gives us not only the details for responding to the questions we take to be most significant (our *Bestimmung*, or

---

from Jacobi the objection that if Kant's view invokes nonspatiotemporal causality, then supposedly this is immediately contradicted by the very meaning of causality on Kant's own theory of transcendental idealism. This often-repeated objection overlooks the fact that, as Kant stresses, the categories have a source in the understanding, not sensibility, and hence they must have some kind of meaning independent of their specific spatiotemporal schematization; causality in the broadest sense is not defined by space and time. A failure to appreciate this point leaves dogmatists trapped in the Third Antinomy, and with no way to explain Kant's postulates or his bothering with his criticisms of specific arguments in speculative theology and other dogmatic disciplines. For some recent useful acknowledgments of Kant's reliance on the meaningfulness of concepts for which we do not have an empirical warrant, see Robert Merrihew Adams, "Things in Themselves," *Philosophy and Phenomenological Research* 57 (1997): 801–25; and John E. Hare, *The Moral Gap: Kantian Ethics, Human Limits, and God's Assistance* (Oxford: Oxford University Press, 1996). See also below Chapter 5, n. 52.

5 See Fichte's 1794 "Review of *Aenesidemus*," in *Fichte: Early Philosophical Writings*, ed. Daniel Breazeale (Ithaca: Cornell University Press, 1988), pp. 59–77.

"determination," "destiny," "vocation") but also the first substantive truths of philosophy in general. Theoretical philosophy has its first condition in practical philosophy, rather than vice versa, as with Kant. It cannot be emphasized enough that Fichte was very explicit about his procedure: "observe the logical sequence of the ideas here presented. Our contention is not: I ought since I can [i.e., since I do have prior theoretical arguments to meet the main claims against the very possibility of transcendental freedom]; it is rather: I can since I ought. That I ought and what I ought to do comes first and is most immediately evident."[6] The primacy of practical reason thus becomes a primacy in not merely one or two respects, but a radical primacy that includes the third and systematically most basic respect.

It should be noted that what is meant here by the methodological primacy of pure practical reason, that is, the "radical" primacy of the practical, does not entail having to go so far as to claim a fully "global" primacy of the practical, since it need not require distinctively practical considerations to be an internal part of all substantive assertions.[7] All that the claim of methodological practical primacy asserts is that to get to the first step of properly asserting any nontrivial existential assertions, one has to rely on at least one premise that is irreducibly moral and has no significant precondition in prior "neutral" ontological investigations. Once the existence of the "world," and thereby the reliability of a range of relevant representations, is established by practical reason, there can be a use of many purely theoretical characterizations concerning the different kinds of things within that world. The procedure at this point roughly parallels Descartes's system after the demonstration of the existence of God, a demonstration that also involves essential value considerations, though not of a Kantian type.

---

6 Fichte, "On the Foundation of Our Belief in a Divine Government of the Universe," trans. Paul Edwards, in *Nineteenth Century Philosophy*, ed. Patrick Gardiner (New York: Free Press, 1969), p. 23. Cf. above Chapter 3, n. 64. This is not a casual remark of Fichte's, for he had long focused directly on the relation of "ought" and "can," e.g., in his "Review of *Aenesidemus.*" My interpretation in no way denies that, even more than Kant, Fichte tried to work out a unified and balanced system with both practical and theoretical components. The crucial question still always remains whether the ultimate basis of the system requires *from the beginning* an ineliminable reference to a moral "ought."

7 My interpretation contrasts with those who find in Kant a "global" primacy of practical reason, one that applies even to logic or the employment of theoretical principles such as the Analogies. Cf. Richard Velkley, *Freedom and the End of Reason* (Chicago: University of Chicago Press, 1989); and Onora O'Neill, *Constructions of Reason* (Cambridge: Cambridge University Press, 1989).

C. THE PRACTICAL FOUNDATION OF PHILOSOPHY
IN FICHTE'S TEXTS

C. 1. The *Vocation of Man*

In his *Vocation of Man* (1800), Fichte gave the classic statement of this strategy by dividing the work into three sections: Doubt, Knowledge, and Faith (*Glaube*). "Doubt" is his term for the blind alleys of modern pre-Kantian theoretical philosophy, the familiar conundrums that arise after Cartesian dualism, and, in particular, the conflict between a deterministic nature and a privileged sphere of inner appearances. "Knowledge" is here Fichte's ironic term for his understanding of what we are left with when we move beyond "doubt" to a theoretical strategy like Kant's. He concludes that this strategy is a futile attempt to get to objects by building an empirical realism upon a transcendental idealism. The attempt is futile because it supposedly leads only to contradictions and "empty knowing," that is, to mere rules for connecting representations and not for consistently determining the ultimate nature of what is outside or within us. (This account turns Kant's epistemology back into a version of representationalism, a common but very unfortunate misreading; see above Chapter 1, sec. B. 3.) "Faith" is the term Fichte introduces for describing what is left when we abandon all the empty theoretical approaches of what has been called "knowledge" and recognize that our only foundation is belief, specifically belief in the moral law and what it requires. One might be led by this kind of terminology, and the fact of Fichte's training as a Protestant minister, to suppose that here he means to employ Kant's own notion of "moral faith," but Fichte is clear that he cannot accept even the meaningfulness, let alone the truth, of the transcendent ideas (especially a separate God) that Kant's moral religion originally postulates. Fichte is rather picking up on, and channeling in an entirely moralistic direction, Jacobi's broad use of the term "faith" to stand for whatever first gives us access to any significant existential claims, an access that Fichte and Jacobi, like Hume, believe is blocked (on typical representationalist grounds) for all our merely theoretical faculties.[8] All this fits Fichte's explicit claim that we are to take only the "ought" of morality to be the essential condition of our belief in the "can," that is, the possibility of absolute freedom, rather than vice versa, as would happen if one started with Kant's concern with metaphysics and transcendental idealism.

8 See F. H. Jacobi, *David Hume on Faith, or Idealism and Realism, a Dialogue* (1787), in *The Main Philosophical Writings*, pp. 253–333.

Fichte is very careful and explicit about his procedure here. He notes at the beginning of Book 3 that one might try to get to a foundation, a disclosure of our absolute nature (i.e., of how we ultimately exist – as first subjects or substances, or rather as mere determined accidents), by focusing on the fact that some of our ideas seem to be archetypes (*Vorbilder*) rather than images (*Nachbilder*), that is, they seem to function as guides to our activity rather than merely reflect our receptivity. Fichte observes the strong *temptation* to think that this impression of ourselves as agents rather than spectators affords proof enough of the existence of our freedom and its intended objects. But he resolutely refuses to accept evidence of such a broadly "practical" nature as his foundation. Rather, he insists that it is only with specifically moral intentions that one regards oneself with certainty as free. For any nonmoral practical intention, just as with any purely theoretical intention (e.g., an alleged perception of an external object), Fichte says we could always take it to be the case that things are not at all as we suppose them to be: "Do I then indeed *feel* that real power of free action? By no means . . . I cannot *will* to act, for according to that [nonmoral] system, I cannot *know* whether I can really act."[9] It is supposedly only with moral thoughts and their implications that one can no longer take seriously the possibility that freedom is an illusion – which is not to deny that it remains a theoretical possibility, ever present to be exploited, as Fichte notes, by skeptics and moral scoundrels.

The ultimate foundation of all of Fichte's thought lies in this fundamental moralistic strategy, a strategy that claims to see devastating limits in all arguments from any general, nonmoral notion – be it a merely passive speculative notion or even the common impression of planning and activity itself. Whatever the virtues that may be found in the details of this remarkable system, its radical basic structure leaves it open to serious objections, especially from a Kantian perspective. Against Fichte, one can hold, as Kant did, that even if one regards practical reason as preeminent in some very important respects, it is not clear that all theoretical philoso-

---

9 From selections from Fichte's *Vocation of Man*, in *Nineteenth Century Philosophy*, trans. W. Smith, pp. 29, 30. This very well-known work is often dismissed by Fichteans as a mere "popular" writing. I agree that it is popular, but not that it should be dismissed. It is very hard to believe that such a conscientious writer as Fichte would provide an extensive version of his own philosophy that needlessly distorts its foundations. This work was not perceived in its own time as an anomaly, and it clearly fit in with what became the general image of Fichte's work. Whatever scholars may say about his more "technical" works or his unpublished lectures, they cannot displace works like the *Vocation* until a lot more is done to show that there is truly a clear, attractive, and historically relevant alternative version of Fichte's philosophy within them. See below at n. 11 and n. 14.

phy is so limited and methodologically secondary in the way Fichte presumed – especially since it need not be understood, even in Kant, as defined by the flawed representationalist theories that Fichte always begins with and then lampoons (see above Chapter 1, sec. B. 3, and Chapter 2, sec. B. 3). Moreover, even if theoretical philosophy were to appear to entail a metaphysics that blocks our pure practical presumptions, one would think that our first course should be, like Kant, to reconsider these presumptions and their alleged preconditions and consequences rather than to jump immediately to insisting on a radical primacy of the practical. Of course, since Kant believed that in the end the only solution for preserving these moral presumptions involves the complex construction of a transcendental idealist metaphysics, his route has difficulties as well. But one can easily enough accept Kant's general denial of the methodological primacy of practical reason while pursuing other alternatives besides the extremes of orthodox Kantian metaphysics or anything like Fichte's radical practical option. For example, one could reconsider compatibilism, or deny that our current theoretical knowledge any longer makes determinism within the spatiotemporal realm a compelling doctrine; or one could even tinker just a bit with some of Kant's presumptions about the entirely nonnatural and overriding character of morality.[10] Hence, regardless of whether one is fully Kantian, there is good reason to wait before leaping to build everything on a "practical foundationalism" – especially if, as with Fichte, that practical foundation makes very strong and controversial claims, and if the prospects for theoretical philosophy are not nearly as limited and dim as they are at first assumed to be.

C. 2. Ambiguities in the Practical Foundation

The difficulties with this kind of direct and radical advocacy of the primacy of the practical may help to explain why many of Fichte's followers today have been tempted by a much more indirect strategy that exploits a broader notion of the "practical." This strategy attempts to found an idealist philosophy of freedom on an active but not directly "practical" phenomenon that appears to escape both the controversial claim of an absolute primacy of moral considerations and the limitations of a typical "objectivist" theoretical philosophy. The obvious phenomenon in Fichte

10 See my "Kant and Hegel on Freedom: Two New Interpretations," *Inquiry* 35 (1992): 219–32. See also above Chapter 2, sec. D. 4, and, on one interesting way of trying to integrate many of Kant's insights into a more naturalistic perspective, Samuel Scheffler, *Human Morality* (Oxford: Oxford University Press, 1992).

that offers itself for this purpose is the basic act of apperception, which can be expanded from a single *cogito* to an activity of self-conscious reflection of the most general form. This act has the marvelous quality of occupying a central place in many key passages in both Kant's and Fichte's work, and of seeming to undergo a careful appropriation under Fichte's care. In recent discussions this appropriation has been taken to reveal an alternative and less contentious way of making sense of Fichte's work as a genuine improvement on Kant while still maintaining some kind of emphasis on the feature of activity and, perhaps, even freedom. In the next chapter (sec. C. 5) I will directly examine and criticize several of these Fichtean discussions of apperception. The strong appeal of this general strategy of focusing on apperception has some effect on almost all discussions of Fichte, so it is important to be warned about it ahead of time, but rather than at this point anticipating the specific criticisms that can made of it, I will first devote the rest of this chapter to offering some further textual documentation for my basic contention that it is instead a purely moral perspective that underlies Fichte's ultimate commitment to the primacy of the practical (Chapter 4, sec. C. 3). I will then use this evidence to indicate how my interpretation differs from four important recent accounts that also closely examine Fichte's explicitly practical considerations (Chapter 4, secs. D–F).

There is a historical complication that should be noted before going on to further Fichtean texts. Many interpreters (e.g., Neuhouser) make a distinction between works of the early and the later Fichte, and so the appeal that has been made to what I take to be the clear and decisive text of the *Vocation of Man* of 1800 might seem irrelevant to the issue of determining whether there is a strong "nonmoralistic" strand in Fichte's best-known systematic work, his *pre*-1800 writings. The issue is further complicated by the fact that undoubtedly in Fichte's *very* early private reflections in the 1790s ("Eignen Meditationen über Elementarphilosophie," 1793/4)[11] there are considerations that do fairly clearly (though in an undeveloped way) appear to go from the *non*moral feature of apperception to the general claim that subjectivity is an absolutely spontaneous ground of philosophy. On my view the natural way to understand these matters is, first, to concede that for at least a short period Fichte – like Kant – did have an initial fascination with the idea of a unifying nonpractical ground for philosophy (or a "neutral" ground un-

---

11 See the careful analysis of these private notes by Jürgen Stolzenberg, *Fichtes Begriff der intellektuellen Anschauung* (Stuttgart: Klett-Cotta, 1986), chap. 1.

derlying both practical and theoretical reason), and then, second, to stress that nonetheless Fichte's own direct commentary on the first official version of his system, namely, the two famous "Introductions" (1797) that he added after the initial presentation of his *Wissenschaftslehre,* show clearly enough that there is a systematic *pre-*1800 commitment to a radical primacy of the practical. Furthermore, this commitment can be found reiterated explicitly in the *System of Ethics* of 1798, and thus already earlier than the *Vocation of Man,* and in a systematic work that can in no way be dismissed as "merely popular."

C. 3. The Introductions to the *Wissenchaftslehre*

Here is how Fichte explains the foundation of his philosophy in the so-called First Introduction to the *Wissenschaftslehre.* Fichte begins (sec. 1) by noting as basic in our experience the distinction between representations that seem free and those that seem necessary (*SW,* I, 423). He then (sec. 2) defines philosophy as the explanation of the ground of this distinction, or, as he puts it, as a search for the "ground of experience" (*SW,* I, 425). Fichte goes on (sec. 3) to distinguish the fundamental options in philosophy in terms of identifying this ground either "dogmatically" with a transcendent thing in itself – which he strangely presumes could *not* operate freely – or "idealistically" with an "I" – which he strangely presumes *must* operate freely. The only promising procedure is (sec. 4) to explore the "I," since the "thing in itself" is *defined* by Fichte here as a mere figment of imagination. (Note that the "thing in itself" is clearly not understood here in the manner of the *Critique of Pure Reason* – where its cognitive status has rather to be established; Kant hardly begins by simply *defining* things in themselves as totally beyond us, for otherwise he could have saved himself all the work of *arguing* that space, time, and so on, are not transcendentally real.) This I is what Fichte says comes into view whenever we focus on the thinking I, irrespective of the content of what is thought. Fichte claims two immediate advantages for this approach: the I, unlike the "thing in itself," is at least something that comes directly into view; and it is something that we believe "each person can freely create in himself" [*SW,* I, 428, 429]. This is not to say that our reflecting literally generates the "existence" of the self; rather, it is said to be responsible simply for "determining" the self, for making it what it is on a particular occasion (*SW,* I, 427). Fichte adds that this is still not to give an "explanation" of how the I is a "ground" of experience (*SW,* I, 428). He also goes on (sec. 5) to concede that idealism has not yet refuted dogmatism, and thus (I take it) he has already reached the conclusion that also structures the later *Vocation of Man*, the conclusion that "from the speculative point of view" alone dogmatism can still appear to be valid. Fichte stresses that while it may be true that we *believe* our reflection on the self is a manifestation of a "free activity" (since it has "free range," i.e., it supposedly can find the thinking self whatever the content that happens to be thought), this very belief in "freedom," and thus the initial activity of the I that is the precondition and focus of the belief, might still, for all we "know," be rooted in a hidden and unfree ground (*SW,* I, 430).

It is at this point that Fichte states that one's standpoint on the conflict between idealism and dogmatism is solely a reflection of one's "interest" (*SW,* I, 433). "Interest," of course, is Kant's technical term for the basic orientations of our reason, and here Fichte is surely playing on Kant's idea that it is practical, that is, moral concerns, that determine a highest and inescapable interest for us. In the final two sections of this Introduction Fichte reviews (sec. 6) the inability of dogmatism to provide an explanatory ground of experience (for we can know nothing of how a thing defined as beyond experience can act on experience; and, supposedly, within experience we "understand only mechanical action" [*SW,* I, 438]), and he introduces (sec. 7) a way in which idealism can at least offer some kind of explanation. This explanation also comes from a use of Kantian ideas, and, in particular, from the idea that the mind can be conceived as legislative, as determining in a lawlike manner.[12] Its manner of determination is unfortunately not spelled out explicitly here; Fichte simply invokes the notion that the I, precisely since it is being *contrasted* with a "thing," should be considered as an "activity." Given his reference to "interest," it is natural to suppose that Fichte wants us to think of this activity as rooted in a moral standpoint, but he complicates matters by merely referring back to earlier works in which he had called upon his readers "to think a certain concept freely," that is, to think of their very thinking, abstracting from whatever their object of thought is (*SW,* I, 445). Obviously what Fichte needs to do is to spell out that *this* reference to "free" thinking is not, like his discussion at the beginning of the Introduction, something that can be neutralized simply because "from a speculative point of view" the counterassertion of an underlying necessity is still possible. That is, I believe the only way in which the last part of the Introduction can make sense as an intended *advance* in argument is if the reference to "free" thinking is meant to be understood not as an arbitrary

12 Cf. Kant, *Critique of Pure Reason,* B 430–1.

claim but as *backed up* by an implicit connection with a significant "non-speculative" perspective, one that has a direct relation to freedom. This perspective is provided by the practical view of ourselves as moral legislators, a view that Fichte apparently presumes can be given primacy since it seems internally coherent and the alternative of a foundational theoretical philosophy allegedly suffers from the defect of not being able to deliver even the minimal basis needed to defeat skepticism concerning the external world.

Fichte's strategy is spelled out in more detail in the Second Introduction, published some months later in August and November 1797. After a review of the familiar options of idealism and dogmatism (sec. 1), Fichte states (sec. 2) quite clearly that the idealist position rests "on the highest law of reason, that of autonomy (*practical* legislation), to which *all* other rational laws are subject" (my emphases), and it cannot be put forth on "objective" grounds (*SW*, I, 456). Matters become complicated, however, because Fichte goes on (secs. 3–5) to discuss idealism for a while merely in terms of the idea that the possibility of self-consciousness ("reverting" into itself [*in sich zurück gehen*]), of existing "for oneself," is the "condition" of "all other acts of consciousness" (*SW*, I, 462). (This sounds like a radical idea, but it could be taken as the fairly innocuous claim that our consciousness cannot be structured such that it immediately makes self-consciousness *impossible*.) Here he also characterizes this self-consciousness as a kind of activity, indeed a "free" activity (*SW*, I, 460), so it might again look as though there is a nonpractical argument, an argument from mere thinking, to absolute freedom and the ultimate ground of experience. But Fichte goes on to make it clear once more that this appearance is but a phase in his real line of argument. He insists that as soon as we want to "explain" the "possibility" of this activity, as soon as we need to "confirm" and "vindicate" that it is truly a matter of genuine freedom, we can do so "*solely* by exhibition of the moral law" (*SW*, I, 466, my emphasis): "The consciousness of this law, which is itself doubtless an immediate consciousness derived from no other, forms the basis for the intuition of self-activity and freedom . . . only through this medium of a moral law do I behold *myself*" (*SW*, I, 466).

At this point Fichte borrows Schelling's positive use of the term "intellectual intuition" to designate the "immediate consciousness" at the base of his system, but he contrasts his procedure explicitly with some non-moral Schellingian accounts that would try to base an idealistic philosophy on theoretical representations such as space and time rather than simply on concepts of right and virtue (*SW*, I, 467–8). Fichte even defends his use of the term "intellectual intuition" as Kantian, for he claims that Kant rejects intellectual intuition only if it is understood in terms of theoretical access to *a transcendent thing* in itself. As long as we understand this intuition merely in terms of consciousness of the "categorical imperative," Fichte claims it is clearly something that must be accepted and not rejected by Kant (*SW*, I, 472). Kant himself, of course, vigorously rejected this proposal, and for good reason, given the basic methodological differences that have been uncovered now, and the fact that Fichte is using "intuition" *directly* to ground absolute and nonsensory existential assertions.[13]

Much of the remainder of Fichte's lengthy Second Introduction includes digressions about the structure of apperception that, read in isolation, can easily generate again the mistaken impression that a merely theoretical phenomenon is the basis of his philosophy. Fortunately, Fichte continues to insert reminders of his real strategy, by saying, for example, that it is not "consciousness of individuality" but rather the "concept of the pure self" (*SW*, I, 476, 505) that is fundamental. Each time this reminder is made, the reader should recall that the purity of this self is tied to its "free activity" – and that Fichte has by now made clear enough that "solely" moral grounds allow us to "explain" and "confirm" that there is genuine freedom here, and not a mere appearance (cf. below sec. E.1).

C. 4. The *Foundation of Natural Right* and the *System of Ethics*

This perspective on Fichte as a "practical foundationalist" also fits the great systematic ethical works of this period: The *Foundation of Natural Right (Grundlage des Naturrechts nach Prinzipien der Wissenschaftslehre)* of 1796 and the *System of Ethics (Das System der Sittenlehre nach den Prinzipien der Wissenschaftslehre)* of 1798.

13 One might still wonder why Kant never characterizes his moral philosophy as basically a matter of pure intuition, especially since it appears to involve synthetic a priori claims. One answer is that he sees that its claims are not entirely *immediate* because – unlike, e.g., geometry – they have controversial metaphysical presumptions that have to be clarified before philosophers can proceed with them at all. This is, of course, the *opposite* of popular Rawlsian readings according to which Kant is not a moral intuitionist largely because of an alleged desire to *avoid* metaphysics. This is not to deny that for Kant there are, in addition to the differences, also many analogies between mathematics and philosophy; see Alison Laywine, "Problems and Postulates: Kant on Reason and Understanding," *Journal of the History of Philosophy* 36 (1998): 279–309.

These are the main works flanking the so-called Introductions that give
Fichte's own immediate and most direct reflections about the ultimate
basis of his published *Wissenschaftslehre*.[14] Fichte's position is not so easy to
see in the argument of the *Foundation of Natural Right* simply because, like
most writers in this area, he employs a basically relative and political
notion of freedom that is not directly concerned with the question of
one's absolute metaphysical freedom. Moreover, the focus on the topic of
rights involves a notion of the practical that is explicitly not restricted by
moral considerations. Even if people are not assumed to be interested in
moral ends as such, or to be the ultimate source of any of their ends, one
can still compare how much legal "freedom," in a loose and popular
sense, is provided by various systems of rights. Nonetheless, when Fichte
says that the "innermost root of the I is practical" (*SW*, III, 6), he has sworn
off any purely theoretical ground for his philosophy, even if here he does
not elaborate his full view about what the primacy of the practical must
consist in.

All this is clearer in the *System of Ethics*, where there is not only a familiar
stress on "rational nature" in general as ultimate (*SW*, IV, 14), and a
reminder of the primacy of practical reason (*SW*, IV, 53–4, 165), but also
an explicit insistence on understanding the practical in terms of the
moral "ought" (*SW*, IV, 61, 169–70). Once more, the bottom line is that
the "primacy of practical reason" means that "the ultimate foundation of
all my knowledge is my duty. This is the intelligible 'in itself'" (*SW*, IV,
169). Here again Fichte is invoking Kant while going beyond him in the
controversial methodological way indicated earlier; he is making moral
knowledge the ground of *all* knowledge, and not something that relies on
any prior theoretical conditions, as it does with Kant. At the same time,
Fichte is making a memorable play on the term "intelligible," for he is
obviously using it in this passage not only to remind us that morality
contrasts with sensibility but also to suggest that, unlike the supposedly
"unintelligible" metaphysical notion of the thing in itself in orthodox
Kantianism, his moral I is fully intelligible, for it is clearly determinable
and is nothing other than what it can be determined to be.

14 For the sake of simplicity I bracket discussion of notes taken from lectures by Fichte in
   1796–7 and 1798–9, now published in *Fichte: Foundations of Transcendental Philosophy
   (Wissenschaftslehre) nova methodo (1796/99)*, trans. and ed. D. Breazeale (Ithaca: Cornell
   University Press, 1992). These notes are important but they were unpublished until very
   recently, obviously had a limited effect on the era, and do not (I believe) show any sustained dramatic change of course. They are discussed in Günter Zöller, *Fichte's Transcendental Philosophy: The Original Duplicity of Intelligence and Will* (Cambridge: Cambridge University Press, 1998).

D. AMBIGUITIES IN INTERPRETING FICHTE AS A PRACTICAL FOUNDATIONALIST

D. 1. Fichte's Idealism as Practical but Not Subjective

I have been stressing that the kind of foundation Fichte insists on is practical, but this is also to say that Fichte holds that philosophy, and our belief in an external world, do have a certain foundation. To this extent my interpretation contrasts with familiar subjectivist caricatures of him, especially those long dominant in English, as a fanatical egoist or metaphysical idealist who must believe that the physical world itself literally does not exist, or that it is nothing more, in being or in knowledge, than a construction by a human being or a humanlike supermind. On the other hand, my interpretation does not limit itself to noting Fichte's epistemological concerns with the sources of our knowledge and especially the structure of our experience of "objectivity."[15] Precisely because he follows in Reinhold's wake, it can hardly be denied that Fichte is very concerned with knowledge, especially knowledge in a most rigorous "scientific" sense, a true *Wissenschaftslehre*. But it also cannot be denied that he has strong metaphysical concerns, and that he repeatedly characterizes himself as an "idealist" because of his interest in freedom and focus on thought and representation, rather than nature, as a starting point. All this is consistent with taking Fichte to have a robust belief in physical reality, very much as most of us ordinarily think of it, with beings and powers that are not literally contained in or completely under the control of human or superhuman personal agents. This interpretation is also consistent with taking Fichte to have a view that in many ways is closer to empiricism than traditional rationalism, insofar as he stresses that things in themselves are to be dismissed not merely as an affront (supposedly) to

---

15 See Wayne Martin, *Idealism and Objectivity: Understanding Fichte's Jena Project* (Stanford: Stanford University Press, 1997), chap. 1. My interpretation of Fichte as leaving room for an ontological "realism," despite his exclusion of things in themselves and his advocacy of "idealism," is compatible with Martin's claim that "idealism" is largely a methodological term in Fichte. That is to say, it involves a commitment to ideals and a critique of various crude naturalist modes of "explanation," and it intends not to contradict or undermine ordinary realism but to expose bad "dogmatic" conceptions and defenses of realism – which is not to deny that it makes some controversial ontological claims of its own. However, I believe the most crucial question here has to do with what Fichte's ultimate grounds are for affirming ordinary real things, and since these grounds turn out to be irreducibly practical, it seems appropriate to characterize Fichte as above all a "practical" foundationalist. Cf. Peter Baumanns, *Fichtes Wissenschaftslehre: Probleme ihres Anfangs* (Bonn: Bouvier, 1974).

any philosophy of freedom but already on the ground that nothing meaningful can even exist beyond what humanity has some kind of access to
through common experience. Fichte explains his position in precisely
these terms in his very typical and revealingly entitled "A Crystal Clear
Report to the General Public Concerning the Actual Essence of the Newest Philosophy: An Attempt to Force the Reader to Understand" (1801):

> I hereby declare what is the innermost spirit and soul of my philosophy:
> Man has nothing at all other than experience, and all that he arrives at, he
> arrives at only through experience, through life itself. All of his thinking –
> whether unrestrained or scientific, common or transcendental – proceeds
> from experience, and, in return, intends experience. Nothing has uncondi-
> tioned value other than life.[16]

He adds:

> Our existing world is finished, indisputably, by all accounts, as only we
> are. Our actual life can do nothing further than become conscious of this
> world, piece by piece . . . Life is not a producing but a finding. Our phil-
> osophy even contradicts the supposed productions of other philosophies
> and rejects them. In consequence of our philosophy, this absolute pres-
> ence allows itself to be *examined and judged* in actual life, *just as if* it had
> arisen through an original construction, like the one carried out [in the
> *Wissenschaftslehre*] . . .[17]

The first quotation is a reminder of Fichte's secularist metaphysical views,
his exclusion of transcendent entities. The second quotation, with its
emphasized "as if" formulation, specifically brackets any actual metaphysical superagents, and it makes especially clear that Fichte sees even his own
academic work as primarily a recapitulation, a systematic reordering (in
that sense a "construction") of a perspective on what is already found

---

16 Fichte, "A Crystal Clear Report to the General Public Concerning the Actual Essence of the
   Newest Philosophy: An Attempt to Force the Reader to Understand," trans. J. Botterman
   and W. Rasch, in *Philosophy of German Idealism*, ed. Ernst Behler (New York: Continuum,
   1987), p. 47. Similar passages can be found in Fichte's "On the Foundations of Our Belief
   in a Divine Government" (1798), trans. Paul Edwards, in *Nineteenth Century Philosophy*, pp.
   19–25.
17 Fichte, "Crystal Clear Report," p. 98. This passage expresses a general feature of Fichte's
   program that is well displayed in Zöller, *Fichte's Transcendental Philosophy*. Cf. John Dewey,
   German Philosophy and Politics (New York: Henry Holt, 1915), p. 82: "The idealism in
   question [in Fichte] was not an idealism of another world but of *this* world . . . The
   significance of German philosophy was precisely to make men aware of their nature and
   destiny as the direct and active representatives of absolute creative purpose."

within common experience. He differs from common sense and commonsense philosophers primarily not in *what* he says is "out there" for us to encounter (although he does give this an unusually upbeat, moral form), but on the question of *how* we first gain the right to assert that certainly there are things. Like many classical analytic epistemologists, he wants to focus first on the fundamental question of how someone who does rise to the level of philosophical reflection can overcome doubts about the reference of the "play of representations" within consciousness. I take Fichte's doctrine of the radical primacy of the practical to be directed, among other things, to this basic problem, but to be distinguished by his insistence that ultimately this problem has no resolution at all except from a perspective that is moral and not merely speculative. On this interpretation, Fichte's philosophy remains unique because of its radical methodological position (practical foundationalism), not because it has anything like the odd metaphysical doctrines or limited epistemological objectives that familiar interpretations and first impressions of Fichte, especially in English, all too often suggest.

I will complete the elaboration of this practical approach to Fichte by commenting next on two valuable recent discussions, one by Alain Perrinjaquet (sec. D. 2) and one by Daniel Breazeale (sec. D. 3). Their interpretations come closest to my own approach, even though, at some difficult points, they appear to fall prey to some potentially misleading formulations that require clarification. I will then contrast this approach with important recent accounts offered by Robert Pippin and Allen Wood (secs. E, F). Pippin has reacted to earlier versions of my interpretation by proposing an alternative to a strong emphasis on Fichte's discussion of morality, whereas Wood continues to stress Fichte's practical concerns, but in a way unlike my own, and from a perspective that, like Pippin's, tends to evaluate Fichte's relation to Kant more positively than I would. Clarifying the differences here will provide a convenient way to conclude this chapter by bringing together the themes that make my approach distinctive, since Wood and Pippin give an especially clear presentation of points that underlie many other interpretations as well.

D. 2. Perrinjaquet's Interpretation

Alain Perrinjaquet has presented an especially persuasive interpretation of how moral considerations dominate Fichte's practical foundation for philosophy. Nonetheless, at certain points even some of Perrinjaquet's most helpful remarks are marked by some ambiguities that bedevil

Fichte's own expressions. Perrinjaquet begins quite properly by noting
that for Fichte, "Awareness of the certainty of the first principle of philosophy depends upon a moral attitude,"[18] a point supported by a passage
from the *System of Ethics:* "Certainty is possible for me only insofar as I am a
moral being, for the criterion of all theoretical truth is not itself, in turn,
theoretical . . . but is, instead, a practical criterion, based upon duty" (*SW*,
IV, 169–70). Perrinjaquet then notes that Fichte distinguishes between a
"real" and a "pure" sense of "intellectual intuition." The "real" sense
comes with the moral awareness of ordinary consciousness, and the
"pure" sense comes with the consciousness of the philosopher who reflects upon the moral law and its conditions:

> Consciousness of freedom thus appears on two levels. In the *series of the I* it
> appears as *real* intellectual intuition (consciousness of the moral law, self-
> determination). In the *series of the philosopher* it appears as pure intellectual
> intuition. The latter is possible only thanks to the reality of the former: The
> philosopher would not be able to exert his freedom of reflection and ab-
> straction were he not already free as a human being and had he not at least
> an indistinct consciousness of this freedom. He would not be able to obey
> the 'postulate of philosophy', 'think of yourself' . . .[19]

The proper point of these considerations is to remind us that for Fichte
freedom does not have its original existence at a reflective, theoretical
level – not even at the level of theory about pure practical matters. The
passage can be misleading, however, if one sees in it the dangerous suggestion (found also in Fichte's texts) that somehow a philosopher's thinking about freedom (i.e., his responding to the injunction "think of yourself") *must* itself also be a manifestation of freedom. The difficulty here
comes from the fact that, although in a trivial way one could not "truly"
obey the injunction to "think of oneself"[20] in the sense in which it is

18 Alain Perrinjaquet, "Some Remarks Concerning the Circularity of Philosophy and the
   Evidence of its First Principle in the Jena *Wissenschaftslehre,*" in *Fichte: Historical Contexts/
   Contemporary Controversies,* ed. D. Breazeale and T. Rockmore (Atlantic Highlands, NJ:
   Humanities Press, 1994), p. 80. In addition, Perrinjaquet (p. 83, n. 68 and n. 69; see also
   above at n. 6) refers to works of Fichte's *Atheismusstreit:* "On the Foundations of Our Belief
   in a Divine Government of the Universe" (1798) and "Appeal to the Public" (1799).
19 Perrinjaquet, "Circularity," p. 84.
20 Of course, this injunction to "think of oneself" also plays a fundamental role in Fichte's
   famous argument that there is a kind of self-awareness that is immediate and nonobjective.
   Cf. *SW*, I, pp. 526–7: "a consciousness of the wall is possible only in so far as you are
   conscious of your thinking . . . But if it is claimed that in this self-consciousness I am an
   object to myself, then . . . it [the subject] becomes an object, and requires a new subject,

intended if one were not free – since "injunctions" could be *defined* as meant only for free beings – still, one could, given Fichte's own arguments, *to all appearances* "obey" such an injunction without being absolutely free. That is, if the logical possibility that the dogmatic determinist-realist accepts is in fact true – and nothing has been demonstrated by Fichte to exclude that possibility – then what might happen is that people could reflect on themselves and their thoughts of morality and naturally characterize themselves as free even when no real freedom need have taken place, in either the "ordinary" or reflective series of events. Of course, *if* the original consciousness is free, then the direct reflection on it will be by one and the same being, *and given this condition*, that being will have to be free; but this hypothetical fact can hardly be used to *show*, at the methodological level, that the mere reflective act of "thinking of oneself," or even of expressing a pure "interest" in the practical, can be relied on to reveal freedom.

Matters are made even more complicated by the fact that when Fichte appeals to the idea that there is no speculative refutation of the dogmatist, and that one's philosophy rests on one's actual "interest" (hence his famous dictum that one's philosophy simply reveals what kind of person one is), he almost seems to be saying that this very fact is a proof or indication of freedom. That is, in Perrinjaquet's words, "the dogmatist cannot possibly be *constrained* to adopt the starting point of the [Fichtean] transcendental idealist . . . because the principle of transcendental philosophy cannot be enforced from outside, since it requires an act of freedom – that is, attention to one's freedom."[21] There is a confusing complication here that involves an ambiguity in the notion of "constraint." One bad Fichtean suggestion along this line would be to say that if there were an argument proving one is free, then somehow this itself would wipe out that freedom, for one would be "constrained" to accept the conclusion. This is a confused thought, because even if there were such an argument, it need not follow that the *normative* constraint of "having to accept" the conclusion of the argument involves any kind of *real* constraint that would amount to a "having to act," rather than a free

and so on ad infinitum." For a discussion of the implications of this argument for the theory of apperception, see below Chapter 5, sec. C. 1. Cf. also Manfred Frank, "Intellektuale Anschauung," in *Die Aktualität der Frühromantik*, ed. E. Behler and J. Hörisch (Paderborn: Schöningh, 1987), pp. 96–126. It is striking that sometimes Fichte uses the same basic term, "intellectual intuition," to stand for this immediate but theoretical mode of self-consciousness, and sometimes rather to stand explicitly for moral consciousness.
21 Perrinjaquet, "Circularity," pp. 79–80.

acting, in the original context that the argument is about. Thus, for all we know, one might in fact be able on reflection freely to "adopt" as true a "principle" of freedom merely on the ground of an argument that has a clear appearance of validity rather than simply an appeal to one's "interest." Conversely, one might think that one is, on reflection, simply and freely "adopting" a principle reflecting one's "interest" in freedom, when in fact the adoption could be something that one is after all causally constrained to do in some hidden way.

A further confusion that can arise here concerns a suggestion that since "attention to freedom" and "thinking of oneself" are not "necessary" actions, in the sense that they do not happen "by themselves" in the ordinary prereflective course of experience, they are literally free actions. But the most that follows is that these acts of thought are contingent acts in the sense that one must take an extra step to carry them out, and they can be "free" merely in the extended sense used when one speaks loosely, for example, of "free time." When they are carried out, these acts might reflect and repeat an absolute freedom that we already have – but on the other hand they also might not. From the fact that we are really involved in an act of thinking, one ought not, precisely on Fichte's practical foundationalism, conclude that one must be absolutely free in such a context, even if the content of the thought is itself the idea of absolute freedom. Mere action, being involved in something that has an effect – need not be free action – being an uncaused cause of that effect.

D. 3. Breazeale's Interpretation

Similar points are worth emphasizing with respect to a formulation that occurs in the work of Daniel Breazeale, whose many fine translations and introductions have done the most to make Fichte's writings available in English in their proper context. Breazeale explicitly stresses that Fichte is a "practical foundationalist," a philosopher whose system ultimately rests (as I have been arguing) on an appeal to strong moral considerations. And yet at one point Breazeale is tempted by Fichte's suggestions of an "original positing of self-consciousness" wherein the theoretical and the practical are fully "equiprimordial."

One striking way that Breazeale summarizes this view is in terms of the clever adage "no consciousness without conscience."[22] This adage points

22 Daniel Breazeale, "Why Fichte Now?" *Journal of Philosophy* 88 (1991), p. 526. Cf. Perrinjaquet, "Circularity," p. 87: "self-consciousness would be inexplicable without the demand

to a whole line of Fichtean argument that is deeply ambiguous. The line proceeds by reflecting on the conditions of consciousness, and in particular on the conditions of consciousness in a "full sense" that involves genuine self-consciousness, and then it concludes by arguing that, for this "full sense," morality, and thus freedom, is also required. This kind of argument can appear to be in keeping with the general idea of the "primacy of the practical" because it affirms that "in a sense" we cannot understand our own selves properly without ultimate recourse to a practical, that is to say moral, perspective. It is important, however, to be clear about whether "in a sense" here means "in any sense at all" or rather "fully." If it means we need the practical perspective merely in order to understand ourselves "fully," rather than "in any sense at all," then for basic methodological purposes this kind of argument would be going against the Fichtean notion of the radical primacy of the practical. It would be allowing that "neutral" considerations about consciousness alone *are* sufficient to entail claims about the existence of morality and freedom. The argument would become the direct opposite of Kant's: theory would be the *ratio cognoscendi* of the purely practical, and the purely practical would become the *ratio essendi* of theory (for Kant, the moral law is rather the *ratio cognoscendi* of the fact of absolute freedom; and this freedom is the *ratio essendi* of moral law).[23] Moreover, such an argument is not only un-Kantian; it is intrinsically unpromising and not representative of Fichte's own clearest views. How, after all, could it be held that "consciousness without conscience" is completely *impossible?* Such a consciousness is precisely what the "scoundrel" skeptic or "dogmatic" realist actually maintains in the discussion that Fichte himself generates – and what is actual cannot be impossible.

Fichte does want to show (as Breazeale notes) that morality and freedom are in one sense an "explanatory base" of all consciousness, but this is to be done by showing that the practical perspective is basically *sufficient* to account for ordinary consciousness (i.e., to tell us, supposedly, what ultimately underlies our actual certainty about our projects and their objects), not that it is *immediately necessary* and would have to come with any consciousness that we can imagine. Fichte recognizes that dogmatism also exhibits a possible state of consciousness; the problem for him is simply

made by the moral law." See also Breazeale, "The Theory of Practice and the Practice of Theory: Fichte and the 'Primacy of Practical Reason,'" *International Philosophical Quarterly* 36 (1996): 47–64; and cf. Zöller's use of the notion of "full self-consciousness" in *Fichte's Transcendental Philosophy,* pp. 59–60.

23 Kant, *Critique of Practical Reason,* Preface, n. 1. Cf. above Chapter 1, sec. D. 2.

that it brings along an account of itself that is supposedly quite weak and insufficient. It is true that Fichte states at one point that one would not "perceive the world" if one were not a "practical being,"[24] but in this context he means these words in a peculiar way that does not provide an argument that being practical, that is, being free, is necessary for consciousness or theory as such. Fichte's point is simply that "theory" alone never *proves* a real "world," that is, from a strictly theoretical perspective, one remains stuck, in a classic phenomenalist fashion, with a mere series of representations and not a distinct world. Fichte also holds that if one is a genuine practical being, then one will be led by certainty about one's duties to *believe* that one is dealing with a distinct world, a distinct realm in relation to which one has genuine obligations. But this again is to say at most that the practical perspective, and it alone, is sufficient for what our ordinary consciousness is supposedly committed to; it is not to argue that someone with a traditional "thin" philosophical construal of that consciousness (e.g., a dogmatic phenomenalist) has to accept the practical perspective as a necessary condition for its existence.

There are also problems that remain for Fichte's position even if one were to accept his general idea of a radical primacy of the practical. For example, even if one wanted to heed the call of conscience before anything else, it is unclear how one could do this concretely, on normal perceptual grounds (since theoretical grounds for making existential claims would precisely be bracketed by the radical primacy of the practical), by picking out ordinary human beings as actual grounds of duties because they truly are real persons, and thus deserve respect. Practical reason does not itself say that certain shapes are more relevant than imaginations of angels, or images of barns, and so until one can say "where" other persons are, it is not clear that there is a ground for saying that there really are any external duties deserving one's attention. On the other hand, if it is granted that there is, after all, a sufficient prior and pure epistemological criterion for distinguishing real persons from other items that can (at first) be treated as mere appearances, then the turn to pure practical considerations as fundamental seems unneeded after all; if we can tell what is a real person "by looking," we should be able to tell what is a real barn similarly. Presumably the Fichtean would reply that this line of argument does not take the methodological primacy of the practi-

---

24 Quotations from Breazeale, "Why Fichte Now?" p. 526, and from *J. G. Fichte: Gesamtausgabe der Bayerischen Akademie der Wissenschaften*, ed. R. Lauth, H. Jacobs, and H. Gliwitzky (Stuttgart: Frommann, 1964ff.), I, 4, p. 32. The latter work will hereafter be cited as *GA*.

cal in its full radicality – but once this full radicality is exposed, it becomes all the more perplexing.

E. DOES FICHTE'S IDEALISM AVOID BEING "ONE-SIDED"?

E. 1. Pippin's Interpretation

In a recent brief but highly challenging study, Robert Pippin has taken note of some of my earlier interpretations and gone on to offer an alternative perspective on Fichte's significance. Pippin stresses Fichte's claim in the Second Introduction that "reason is absolutely self-sufficient," and he proposes that this is to be read as signifying that Fichte understands idealism to be defined not by an ontological or pure practical claim but by a general transcendental point that "thoughts can be determined only by other thoughts," that is, that only thoughts and not mere mechanical causes can play an "explanatory" role, providing warrants and norms for judgments.[25] Fichte's idealism, on this intriguing reading, loses its taint as a premature leap to a practical foundationalism and becomes an early anticipation of the contemporary Sellarsian thesis that the "normative domain," the "space of reasons" in a broad sense that is not limited to morality, is itself "autonomous."[26]

Pippin's interpretation certainly brings out important strands within Fichte's thinking, but its attractive points need not be seen as threatening the main thrust of my reading. Pippin is concerned primarily with saving Fichte from being understood in terms of a "subjective, psychological, one-sided, idealism," but this is not the kind of objection that I have been making, insofar as I also read Fichte as holding, at the ontological level, to a genuine affirmation that there is an objective world, and to a position that gives no privilege to psychology or the individual "I" as such but rather stresses what is claimed to be revealed by a general form of reason. And while it is helpful to be reminded of how sensitive Fichte was to the basic epistemological idea that our reason cannot accept "exogenous determination" by either brute empiricist or rationalist givens, this is a point that reflects what I take to be a theme *common* to the whole development of German philosophy from Kant through Hegel, and it does not by

25 Pippin, "Fichte's Alleged Subjective, Psychological, One-Sided Idealism," in *The Reception of Kant's Critical Philosophy: Fichte, Schelling and Hegel*, ed. Sally Sedgwick (Cambridge: Cambridge University Press, 2000), p. 156. Fichte passages as quoted by Pippin and translated by Breazeale, in *Introductions to the Wissenschaftslehre and Other Writings (1797–1800)* (Indianapolis: Hackett, 1994), and cited from *GA*, I, p. 475; see also Pippin, "Fichte," p. 163.
26 Pippin, "Fichte," p. 156.

itself address what has been my main concern, namely identifying the crucial and worrisome points of *difference* that arise after Kant. When one steps back to look for differences, and to move beyond a general invocation of reason and the broadest transcendental considerations, one can still ask specifically how Fichte understands reason in contrast to Kant, and what his arguments imply for old ontological questions that do not disappear simply because there are other topics that can be discussed. I take it to be striking that Fichte does not assume that (what he takes to be) the explanatory inadequacy of "dogmatism" settles these questions, since he readily acknowledges that the dogmatist's ontology remains undefeated from the perspective of speculative reason, and that it matters very much what one's attitude is toward its possible truth.

Because of the way that Fichte goes on to find certainty of existence only by turning to practical considerations, there is a sense in which I do regard his philosophy as "one-sided," but only because of its attitude toward specific kinds of reason, and not in any subjective or psychological sense. This is precisely why I put an emphasis on the *Vocation of Man*, where Fichte clearly does not culminate his philosophy, as would be expected on the alternative reading, with a Sellarsian ode to reason as such. Instead, he devotes the whole final third of the work to stressing the inadequacy of *all* mere thoughts of knowledge or action in general (which can include many ideas of reason), and he explicitly relies on an attitude of "faith" based specifically on moral reason alone. Similarly, even though in the Introductions Fichte often does argue in terms of "reason," there are, as I noted (see above secs. C. 3 and C. 4), several passages there and in other works at the time which show that Fichte has a tendency, once his arguments have been laid out, to use "reason" in an abbreviated manner, signifying considerations that he has indicated are backed ultimately by an appeal to the moral law alone. Moreover, as Pippin notes in his own remarks on the immediate reactions of broadly sympathetic readers such as the early Schelling, Fichte was in fact understood by those closest to him to be not merely an advocate of reason but to be calling for a kind of "practical idealism" that gives limited attention to purely theoretical considerations about nature.[27]

Pippin finds a reply to Schelling's worry in a global and not purely

27 Ibid., p. 159; cf. p. 161, where Schelling is quoted from "Philosophical Letters on Dogmatism and Criticism," in *The Unconditional in Human Knowledge (Four Early Essays 1794–1796)*, ed. and trans. Fritz Marti (Lewisburg, PA: Bucknell University Press, 1980), p. 174; *F. W. J. Schelling, Historische-kritische Ausgabe*, ed. Michael Baumgartner et al. (Stuttgart: Frommann Holzboog, 1976), I, 78.

practical argument Fichte offers against dogmatism, one that claims that those who presuppose "the thoroughgoing validity of the mechanism of cause and effect . . . would directly contradict themselves. What they say stands in direct contradiction to what they do; for to the extent that they *presuppose* mechanism, they at the same time elevate themselves above it."[28] This is a striking passage, but note, first, that if Fichte truly thought that dogmatism itself is "directly contradictory," then he would never have needed to go into the complicated discussions of nontheoretical interests or faith that he introduced repeatedly. Second, if what Fichte meant to appeal to here is not really a "direct contradiction" but some kind of "performative" limitation for his opponents, then it would in any case be a mistake to try to make too much out of this, precisely for the reasons indicated above (at n. 19) in the analysis of Perrinjaquet's interpretation. That is, if the "presupposition" of mere determinism is understood not as an abstract proposition but as a particular thought, then it, like any event of thinking – however "elevated" in content – could still be subject to the natural laws that the determinist hypothesizes; and even if the "presupposition" is understood specifically as a practical "elevating," an act of commitment, it still would be question-begging, for reasons that Fichte himself has stressed, to say this entails that it must be an uncaused act or any proof of our absolute freedom.

   This is not to say that Fichte's remarks have no sense within his own program. The rhetorical point of the passage might be rooted not in any of the confusions just indicated but in a strategy that can be understood as appropriate simply against a peculiar kind of dogmatic opponent committed specifically to the doctrine of the "*thoroughgoing* validity" of mechanism. Taken strictly, this doctrine can be understood to mean something that goes far beyond deterministic realism as such, and to be defined by a specific insistence that a crude mechanical model and nothing else has to be used at all levels of explanation. This is such an extravagant claim that Fichte can easily defeat it, and one might wonder why it is even considered – were it not for the fact that there is some philosophical excuse, ever since Hobbes, for worrying about such an opponent, and sometimes even Kant presented arguments that could only work against such an extreme position. But none of this shows that there is even the beginning of an argument here against other possible determinists who are not so extreme, or against the skeptics who are the direct opponents of the whole idea of a *Wissenschaftslehre*, or, for that matter, against anyone who

28 Pippin, "Fichte," p. 163, quoting from Fichte, *GA*, I, p. 510.

simply finds a lack of warrant for Fichte's crucial idealistic claim to absolute freedom and to a certain ground beyond the veil of ideas to which he has limited our theoretical reason. As long as Fichte calls dogmatic all positions that do not share his own view, these weaker positions remain highly relevant and undefeated forms of "dogmatism."

Fichte unfortunately is not beyond exploiting narrow characterizations of his possible opponents. After making the shocking claim here that "for the idealist nothing is positive but freedom, and being is nothing but a negation of freedom," Fichte shifts, in a passage that Pippin emphasizes, to discussing an opponent to the claim as someone who is now defined as understanding the "I" only as "their own individual person," and as presuming that "reason is present simply in order to assist this person in making his way in the world."[29] Fichte counters: "The relationship between reason and individuality presented in the *Wissenschaftslehre* is just the reverse: Here the only thing that exists is reason, and individuality is something merely incidental." Pippin takes the main point here to be that "the Fichtean frames the problem differently from the outset (he does not answer the same question differently),"[30] and that what Fichte is saying against his opponents is simply a claim about the "unconditioned status of the space of reasons," a reminder that he means "only to state the 'mythic' nature of 'the given.' "[31]

29 Pippin, "Fichte," p. 163, quoting from Fichte, *GA,* I, p. 499; and p. 164, quoting from *GA* I, p. 505; cf. above Chapter 3, n. 65.

30 Pippin, "Fichte," p. 164, quoting from Fichte, *GA,* I, p. 505.

31 Pippin, "Fichte," p. 164. Because of the "long" exposition that is involved in presenting Fichte's notion of rationality and objectivity, Pippin, like Martin (*Objectivity and Ideality,* p. 158, n. 21), suggests that this is an alternative to what I called the "short argument to idealism." However, since I defined that argument simply as one that abstracts from Kantian considerations about the specific limitations imposed by our spatiotemporal form of sensibility (see above Chapter 3), their interpretations still meet the conditions of the kind of argument I had in mind as "short." Some misunderstanding may have arisen on this point because (in the journal version of the paper reprinted above as Chapter 3) I referred to but did not quote an earlier paper with a key passage from Reinhold that speaks in this way directly of a "shorter way" to idealism, and that was the ground for my choice of terms, a ground that has nothing to do with the length of exposition that may be necessary. See above Chapter 2, n. 121, and my "Reinhold and the Short Argument to Idealism," in *Proceedings: Sixth International Kant Congress (1985),* ed. G. Funke and T. Seebohm (Washington: Center for Advanced Research in Phenomenology and University Press of America: 1989), vol. 2, pt. 2, p. 442. Another difficulty with stressing Fichte's invocations of reason is that sometimes he expresses his rejection of things in themselves from the quite different perspective of a kind of concept empiricism (yet another "short argument" approach): "we must derive the entire concept of existence from the form of sensibility, and are thus protected against the claim to any connection with the thing in itself," *Science of Knowledge,* p. 45 (cited in more detail above at Chapter 3, n. 58).

Here I believe it is essential to fix terms in these quotations, and especially to determine exactly what Fichte could mean by "the problem," or
"question," and "the reverse." If "the problem" is now – as Fichte's *last*
quotation would suggest – simply whether strictly individual and instrumental considerations, rather than "the reverse," that is, universal and
categorical uses of reason, are to be taken as primary, then this hardly
needs to be disputed by anyone in the Kantian tradition. Note that here
again Fichte's point can still be understood easily enough in terms of the
idea of pure *practical* reason that I have been stressing, especially because
of its basic criticism of "instrumental" considerations. On the other hand,
if "the problem" is – as the *first* Fichte ("shocking") quotation suggests –
the old question about the certainty of objective existence and absolute
freedom – which certainly seemed to be the central issue of the *Wissenschaftslehre* itself and to deserve some reply – then the new attack on a
"realist" who is forced to take on the special form of an extreme individualist only shifts issues again, and we have to work to determine what this
attack has to say, if anything, about the old question that Fichte raised
himself.

Pippin holds that Fichte here does not "answer the same question
differently," but what he appears to mean by this "question" is simply the
psychological question about how an individual empirical "I" can work its
way out from a set of absolutized instrumental thoughts – a question that I
would also insist is not the defining concern of transcendental philosophers. But even if it is agreed that this psychological question is properly
left behind, there remains an old general question about the relation of
freedom and being. On my interpretation, the unusual attack on individualism at this point in the text can be readily understood as a defensive
moment in Fichte's project to remind readers that his own appeal to
reason as "categorical" is not sheer whimsy but involves some rigorous
general standards within its own framework. In this way it can serve as
another indirect reminder that he understands freedom and reason originally in a pure practical sense, not in a mere individual and psychological
one, and, in particular, that for him we first need to heed the nonsubjec-
tive call of morality and its testimony to our *freedom* and its obligations
before we can posit with certainty that there is *being* outside us. From this
perspective, claims about freedom take on a fundamental precedence in
the order of argument itself (they also have a precedence in the order of
value, but from a Critical perspective this is relatively trivial and does not
account for the details of Fichte's discussion here). Thus, precisely by
using the methodological sense of primacy discussed earlier, one can find

what is at least a relevant (though not necessarily endorsable) meaning in
Fichte's insistence that freedom "precedes" being – a claim that is otherwise well-nigh unintelligible, if one sticks just to the very words in which it
is made. On the other hand, if the attack on individualism is taken only as
an endorsement of reason as such, this cannot *by itself* answer the question
of why one should be specifically a Fichtean idealist in the first place, nor
does it provide a clear sense in which it is literally freedom that is literally
prior to being. There are, after all, countless forms of determinist realism
that can also endorse a general reflective use of reason without being
committed to or even interested in a "thoroughgoing" mechanistic explanatory program, or an absolutizing of individualist and instrumental
considerations.

Whatever interpretation one offers, and whatever acceptable things
Fichte has to say about reason as transcending mere individual and mechanical grounds, this all still leaves him without anything compelling to
say against his most relevant opponents, who can be orthodox Kantians,
and not Hobbesian or Spinozist villains, and who can still hold that in a
basic philosophical (methodological) as well as ontological sense freedom need not and should not be affirmed as *preceding* being. It is, after all,
not dogma but only the global voice of reason itself that makes Kant insist
that the Critical thinker take no shortcut, and that an examination of the
whole range of metaphysical and scientific theories of being (the full
Newtonian, Humean, and Leibnizian traditions, and not only the very
limited positions that Fichte considers) is needed before philosophical
approval can be given to any strong interpretation (let alone a radical one
like Fichte's) of the significance of practical reason. It is no accident for
Kant that the question of the place of freedom and value arises in a world
that is known from the first from the sight of "the starry heavens above."

E. 2. Implications of Fichte's Practical Turn

Given all these difficulties, it is natural to want to return again to contextual considerations to try to dispel the mystery of why Kant's most famous
successors were so reluctant to follow his kind of pursuit of general metaphysical considerations. The obvious answer here is one that has been
long suspected, and for which extensive new research continues to accu-
mulate significant supporting data: the extraordinary cultural conditions
in late eighteenth-century Germany, and especially Tübingen, where
Schelling, Hölderlin, and Hegel were all educated on their way to Jena,
led the most influential new generation of German thinkers (including

writers from very similar backgrounds such as Schiller and Fichte) to suppose that a return to anything like Kantian metaphysics *had* to bring with it the whole reactionary program of his provincial theological apologists.[32] That is, they were more than willing to throw out the baby with the bath water, to dismiss traditional theoretical philosophy in general, and especially the "letter" of Kant's work, because their oppressive seminary circumstances had linked political and theological tyranny so closely that it forced upon them a horror of anything that might lead to a rehabilitation of transcendent religious claims – even if based only on specifically moral arguments that had many components they admired, such as an "ethical commonwealth" as the end goal of human history. Sadly, this is a tendency that continues to this day, usually without any close consideration of Kant's arguments as such, as if Heine's and Nietzsche's *ad hominem* points about Kant's motives could settle all issues at a philosophical level, and as if authoritarian metaphysics teachers are really a force oppressing many intellectuals any more.

In being able to exploit the accidents of the intense sentiments of his time and place, Fichte's most lasting "contribution" was simply the success he achieved by championing the latest philosophical trends while maintaining a public and professional disinterest in the theoretical core of Kant's metaphysics.[33] Thereafter this kind of attitude became a primary influence not only on immediately succeeding generations but also, indi-

32 The philosophical situation at Tübingen was determined by the orthodox theologian, Gottlob Christian Storr (and his assistant Flatt), and the opposition to him that was galvanized by a radical young seminarian, Diez, who went on to play a brief but significant catalytic role in Jena as well. A remarkable feature of the Tübingen situation is that the philosophy position there happened to be unoccupied in the period after 1782 because of illness – a fact that may be very relevant in helping to explain the strange distance to the theoretical tradition that some famous seminarians exhibited. See *Immanuel Carl Diez, Briefwechsel und Kantische Schriften. Wissensbegründung in der Glaubenskrise Tübingen-Jena (1790–1792)*, ed. D. Henrich (Stuttgart: Klett Cotta, 1997), p. lxxxvii. For more on Storr, see also below Chapter 7.

33 It is true that there were well-known "back to Kant" movements in the mid-nineteenth and early twentieth centuries, but insofar as they moved beyond merely historical tasks, they turned out to be limited by the extreme options – epitomized by the famous Cassirer-Heidegger confrontation at Davos – of reading Kant either as merely an apologist for the institutions of liberal culture and modern science or instead as a mysterious Romantic resource (ever invoking the power of "productive imagination") to be deployed against them. Neither approach had the sympathy and patience needed to resuscitate the metaphysical tradition at the core of Kant's work, and in particular the detailed positive arguments of the Analytic. Those arguments were used as a fruitful resource for approaching specific systematic issues in contemporary philosophy only much later in the analytic reformulations that one finds, e.g., in Strawson and Sellars – and, in Germany, in Prauss's and Henrich's early work.

rectly, on most philosophers to this day. The dominant continental (e.g., Foucault, Derrida, Habermas) and American schools (e.g., Quine, Chisholm, Rawls) of our own time are philosophies that are all distressed by the thought of what they assume to be the baleful influence of Kant's *metaphysics,* and so they rush to leave "its ontology behind" and barely attempt a fair reconstruction of it, let alone a refutation.[34] Rorty's work is a particularly striking expression of this confluence of "postmodern" and analytic traditions that otherwise would seem to have nothing to do with one another: the need to overcome the German metaphysical tradition is one thing they can agree on, even if only in what must be a very vague form.[35] This has been a main reason for my putting so much weight on the problematic aspects of Reinhold and Fichte's philosophy, for they initiated a process that has continued to have an enormous influence on philosophy even in circles where there is little direct knowledge of their work. They managed to shift the assessment of Kant's idea of a Critical "philosophy that would come forth as a science" to questions of immediate popularity or the findings of the natural sciences – a level at which Kant, like all great metaphysicians, from Plato to Leibniz, Russell, and, eventually, Lewis, can always seem out of date to the next generation, preoccupied with the movements of its age.

In the last half-century the only major exception to this trend in English appears to have been Wilfrid Sellars, a rare example of a first-class systematic thinker who was also a careful historian, and an especially close reader of the complexities that Kant saw in assertions of freedom. It is his interest in the activities of reason in its broadest sense that has probably done the most, against the polarized pro- and antiscientific currents of the age, to inspire a resurgence of systematic interest in all the idealists and create a broad new audience for important work on difficult themes such as normativity and apperception in the Kantian tradition.[36] While I

---

34 Chisholm's position is unlike the others in this group. He was a very strong advocate of traditional metaphysics and epistemology, and one of the greatest influences in those fields since the midcentury. But although he had a special interest in the idealist tradition (editing Fichte's *Vocation of Man*), he had an erratic concern for history. When he discussed Kant, he strangely misread him as an enemy of his own "personalist" views, as totally denying our subjectivity and substantiality. See my *Kant's Theory of Mind,* chap. II. 8, and "Contemporary German Epistemology," *Inquiry* 25 (1982): 125–38.

35 See, e.g., Rorty's still very applicable "Philosophy in America Today," in *Consequences of Pragmatism* (Minneapolis: University of Minnesota Press, 1982), pp. 211–30.

36 See esp. Wilfrid Sellars, " . . . This I or he or it (the thing) which thinks . . . ," *Proceedings of the American Philosophical Association* 44 (1971): 5–31. Important recent systematic works especially influenced by Sellars's Kantianism include Robert Brandom, *Making It Explicit* (Cambridge, MA: Harvard University Press, 1994); John McDowell, *Mind and World* (Cam-

certainly welcome this development, my main point has been that much of this work can be endorsed without going so far as to assume that most of the truly distinctive claims of Kant's immediate successors, or even Kant's own more ambitious formulations, can be defended as essential to the defense of reason and Critical philosophy as such. The claims have to be tested individually in their precise meaning, and if they all turn out to have severe difficulties, there still remains the more modest Kantian project that was outlined earlier (see above Chapter 1). So far, I have challenged Fichte's unique version of idealism and his radical conception of the primacy of practical reason; in the next chapter I will focus on strong claims, by him and his followers as well as various contemporary Kantians, about the peculiarities of apperception. But first I will consider a different kind of apology for Fichte, one that accepts the primacy of the practical as Fichte's main doctrine but sees this as a way to understand Fichte as improving upon Kant.

F. DOES FICHTE "DEMONSTRATE" WHAT KANT COULD "ONLY POSTULATE"?

F. 1. Wood's Interpretation

Allen Wood has recently offered a more sympathetic interpretation of Fichte that presents Fichte's system as set up precisely to overcome the two "problems" that I listed earlier (see above Chapter 1, sec. B. 3) as the most common complaints that were immediately made about Kant's allegedly incomplete transcendental system: the problem of *skepticism* and the problem of providing a *unity* of theoretical and practical philosophy.[37]

bridge, MA: Harvard University Press, 1994); and McDowell's Woodbridge Lectures, "Having the World in View: Sellars, Kant, and Intentionality," *Journal of Philosophy* 95 (1998): 411–91. Cf. R. Pippin, *Idealism as Modernism: Hegelian Variations* (Cambridge: Cambridge University Press, 1997), chap. 1; and H. E. Allison, "We can act only under the Idea of Freedom," *Proceedings of the American Philosophical Association* 71 (1997): 39–50. P. F. Strawson's work, which also expresses a broadly Kantian systematic perspective, has been most influential and extremely valuable in this period, but for the reasons noted above in Chapter 1, sec. B. 3, it had the unfortunate effect on most readers of reinforcing the image of Kant as concerned primarily with skepticism and empiricism, and it was not much concerned with the important implications of modern science.

37 Allen Wood, "The 'I' as Principle of Practical Philosophy," in *The Reception of Kant's Critical Philosophy: Fichte, Schelling and Hegel*, ed. Sally Sedgwick (Cambridge: Cambridge University Press, 2000), pp. 94–5, 95–6. For an important and massive work that is too recent for me to comment on, and that explores – from the perspective of the very latest German historical research on this era – precisely the same theme of difficulties in philosophy based on an "I," see D. Henrich, *Grundlegung aus dem Ich* (forthcoming).

Wood takes the Fichtean notion of the "I" as a fundamental "practical principle" as the key to resolving both of these problems. He also suggests, in discussing the *transition* in Fichte's presentation of his system between 1794 and 1798, that, contrary to what can seem to be the case, these changes do not point to a major shift. Wood also holds, against other interpreters, that Fichte's reliance on the I as a practical principle is not simply formal but is closely connected with a distinctive Critical approach to *ethics* that is substantive and attractive. My interpretation implies an alternative view on each of these important issues. On the first two issues of skepticism and unity, I will reiterate my position that Fichte does not improve on Kant (secs. F. 2 and F. 3). On the issue of a transition in Fichte's writings, I will argue that after 1794 Fichte's work does involve a significant move in that it gives a much more explicit, even if still problematic, expression to the doctrine of the primacy of the practical (sec. F. 4). Finally, I will note very briefly that Fichte's methodology and practical foundationalism also causes problems for some of Wood's claims on behalf of Fichte's ethical theory (sec. F. 5).

F. 2. Fichte and Kant on Philosophy as a System

Wood's analysis begins with a sympathetic reminder of Fichte's aim to provide an ambitious transcendental philosophy that, unlike Kant's, would be fully "scientific" because it would be absolutely certain, fully systematic, and completely unified – and all this to fulfill the goal of total autonomy. These four points happen to coincide to a considerable degree with the structure of my own analysis, except for the crucial fact that I take them to rest on a background that points to reasons for suspicion of rather than sympathy for Fichte's innovations. More specifically, in Chapter 1 I argued that, while passages indicating a similar-sounding four-part program can be found in Kant's texts, in fact Kant pursued a relatively modest system and ended up addressing these four features (that I discussed under the labels of the public, reflexive, bounded, and autonomous nature of philosophy) in ways that contrast significantly with the approach of his successors. In Chapter 2 I went on to lay out a detailed case that it is actually Reinhold who deserves the main credit – and blame – for insisting on a strong foundational version of transcendental philosophy. In Chapter 3 I began the documentation for the claim that Fichte should be understood as basically responding to, and trying to fulfill, a radical systematic program for philosophy that was much more

clearly spelled out – as Fichte himself noted – in Reinhold's initial ambitious program than anywhere in the *Critique*.

In regard to all these points I now want to emphasize all the more that
Fichte's similarity to and dependence on Reinhold goes beyond abstract
philosophical doctrines and is rooted in pressing practical motivations. As
a technical program considered all by itself, the whole idea of the *Wissenschaftslehre* can appear very bewildering, but one can make considerable
sense of at least its objectives once various long-standing misinterpretations of it are cleared away and the general cultural context of Fichte's
work is appreciated. It is evident that Fichte was motivated to insist on a
special scientific philosophy largely because he, very much like Reinhold,
believed that it was needed for achieving concrete and urgent political
ends. One should never forget Reinhold's remarkable fear that without a
fully *unshakable* Critical philosophy in place nothing could be counted on
to prevent a reversal of the Enlightenment; the very "fate of reason"
supposedly rested on the capacity of the new Critical philosophy to resolve age-old disputes in decisive and basically antimetaphysical fashion.[38]
This Reinholdian spirit lives on vividly in Fichte's naive conviction about
an extraordinarily close interconnection between academic philosophy
and public values. Thus, in his "Crystal Clear Report to the General Public," Fichte insisted:

> As soon as the Science of Knowledge is understood and accepted, public
> administration will blindly grope about and make experiments no more
> than other arts and sciences; it will rather come under firm principles and
> fundamental propositions, because that science established fundamental
> propositions . . . Accordingly, from that moment on, human relations will
> be able to be brought to such a state that it will not only be easily possible,
> but rather almost necessary for people to be order-loving and honorable
> citizens.[39]

In contrast, and in retrospect, most philosophers today would surely regard Fichte's presumption here as a wild inflation of the proper goals,
effects, and value of philosophy. This presumption reveals an ideal that is
not to be resurrected or defended but can only be diagnosed as an all too
understandable fixation in an era when, in addition to all the other crises
of the time, relatively large groups of people, and especially poor clerics

38 See above Chapter 2, sec. A. 4, n. 18.
39 Fichte, "Crystal Clear Report," p. 106.

like Fichte, first desperately aimed to make a living from the suspicious enterprise of critical secular reflection – and hence were intensely motivated to claim that its particular works were absolutely indispensable to society at large.[40]

I have been arguing that Kant offered an alternative to this ambitious foundational project, an alternative that gives philosophy a limited transcendental task and does not forsake the admirable political ideals of autonomy even if it cannot claim to insure their realization. This alternative was sadly neglected from the very first (with, to be sure, exceptions such as the cell of true Kantians in Jena, noted above at Chapter 1, sec. C), and the complicated story of its neglect can only begin to be understood now that a fuller grasp of the shape of the entire Critical era has been gained. In contrast to the foundationalists who succeeded him, Kant offers what I have argued is a much less ambitious but more defensible view of the role of Critical philosophy. This view bypasses the alleged difficulties and ambitious answers that Wood admires in Fichte; it does not accept the assumption that there are inescapable "problems" of skepticism and "unity" that have to be met with a radical philosophical foundationalism, and that are inextricably tied to the advancement of progressive causes. A healthy alternative is exemplified in Kant's frequent appeal to common claims that he assumed no sane person of his time would put in real doubt. Such claims include the fundamentals of mathematics and logic, and the general facts that there is "experience," that is, some warranted determination of empirical objects, and that we acknowledge distinctive and universal demands of morality. Kant understood transcendental philosophy to be an a priori account of common assumptions that seem in fact irresistible, an account that appreciates the metaphysical complexities of alternative explanations, and that offers its own framework as the best way "to save the phenomena" and to keep people from abandoning common sense in the face of modern science and philosophical perplexities. Often Kant's own "account" was quite limited, as when it claimed merely that transcendental idealism would allow us at least to accept – but not "explain" – the combination of absolute freedom, which he presumed morality requires, with the universal causality that he argued

40 See A. J. La Vopa, *Grace, Talent, and Merit: Poor Scholars, Clerical Careers, and Professional Ideology in Eighteenth Century Germany* (Cambridge: Cambridge University Press, 1988), esp. chap. 12, "Radical Visions: Johann Gottlieb Fichte"; and cf. Laurence Dickey, *Hegel: Religion, Economics, and the Politics of Spirit, 1770–1807* (Cambridge: Cambridge University Press, 1987).

"experience" needs for its very objectivity. From the beginning of his career he had maintained that sometimes it is enough if philosophy can introduce a way in which difficult facts that we have always believed to be the case – for example, that we act imputably, or that there is genuine interaction – can at least be held to be not demonstrably impossible upon thorough reflection, and to cohere well with a general metaphysical framework worth serious consideration.[41]

I have called Kant's philosophy "modest" because he was willing to live with such a limited approach, but this is not to deny that many of his specific presumptions and accounts have become highly controversial. His approach clearly does not provide an absolutely self-evident foundation, and so it will hardly satisfy the traditional skeptic or his contemporary devil's advocate. Moreover, one does not even have to be a skeptic to point out that some of Kant's supposed common "facts" are infected by old-fashioned and disputed theories, and that even if they are accepted, the particular account offered for them is overly rigid and surely lacks clear grounding, let alone certainty. Since Kant's own account ultimately was highly metaphysical – the meaning and truth of transcendental idealism is a far reach from common sense – it is after all no wonder that someone like Fichte, seeking irreversible radical change and trained by an outstanding scholar of skepticism (G. E. Schulze), could be inspired by Reinhold's ideal of philosophy to insist on a foundation that, unlike Kant's very controversial system (especially after it had been attacked as incoherent by Jacobi), would appear truly beyond dispute. But, while all these background considerations may help with revealing the *motives* for reactions such as Fichte's radical version of a "philosophy from one principle" – a characterization that was initially applied to Reinhold's first system – it should also be noted that they still do nothing to *justify* Fichte's own monistic and radically practical approach, his short way (in contrast to Kant) with preliminary theoretical and metaphysical considerations. For objections to the very idea of such a methodological monism, one need only recall Kant's work, for he was long familiar with, and for good reason opposed to, earlier attempts to found all philosophy on one principle. He was consistent, for example, in mocking Wolffians who thought that substantive conclusions could be derived from a basic principle of contradiction, that all the powers of the mind could be reduced to one basic faculty of representation, and that ontology in general is based on

41 See above Chapter 1, sec. B. 3.

the idea of "a" first principle of being.[42] No doubt Kant would have also pointed to similar problems with the first principle of the *Wissenschafts-lehre*, the mysterious all-grounding claim that "the I posits itself abso-lutely," for although he did not take the time to criticize Fichte in detail, Kant did take the extraordinary step of explicitly repudiating Fichte's system.[43]

Wood understands the strengths of Kant's system very well, and yet he appears to believe that something can be said in favor of Fichte's first principle, so it is worthwhile exploring what can be made of Wood's apologetic considerations. Wood discusses two more specific formulations of Fichte's principle, or, more precisely, of what it is that is supposed to be certain in the "I" that Fichte puts at the basis of all philosophy. The first of these formulations is the claim that "the self of which we are aware is nothing different from the awareness we have of it."[44] The second for-mulation is that this I has "ubiquity," since we are and always can be aware of it in the original "free act through which the self-awareness [presum-ably of a nonreflective sort] comes about."[45] There are difficulties with each of these formulations, difficulties that I believe Kant surely would have stressed. The first formula has the problem of content; to the extent that it is allowed, to that very extent it must not be assumed to refer to anything other than itself. That is, if the "self" that we are aware of is to be absolutely certain because it is equivalent to the "awareness" of it, then as such it cannot be understood in terms of any deep or nontransparently contained aspects. Such a "self," when it exists, may be a fact not to be denied, but that does not mean that anything substantive follows from it

42 See Kant's remarks as noted in Metaphysik Mrongovius, in *Lectures on Metaphysics/ Immanuel Kant*, ed. and trans. K. Ameriks and S. Naragon (Cambridge: Cambridge University Press, 1997), p. 111. *Kant's gesammelte Schriften* (Berlin: Preussische Akademie der Wissen-schaften/ de Gruyter, 1900–), vol. 29, p. 749. The latter work will hereafter be cited as *AA*.
43 See above Introduction, n. 2, and Chapter 1, n. 15. Kant expressed his view of the *Wissenschaftslehre* in a letter to Tieftrunk, April 5, 1795: "All I know is what the review in the *Allgemeine Literaturzeitung* said . . . the review . . . makes it look to me like a sort of ghost that, when you think you have grasped it, you find that you haven't got hold of any object at all but have only caught yourself and in fact only grasped the hand that tried to catch the ghost. The 'mere self-consciousness,' and indeed, only so far as the mere form of thinking, void of content, is concerned, is consequently of such a nature that reflection on it has nothing to reflect about, nothing to which it could be applied, and this is even supposed to transcend logic – what a marvelous expression this makes on the reader! The title itself (*Wissenschaftslehre*) arouses little expectation of anything valuable." *Correspondence/ Imma-nuel Kant*, ed. and trans. A. Zweig (Cambridge: Cambridge University Press, 1999), p. 545.
44 Wood, "The 'I,'" p. 95. Some of these Fichtean ideas also appear in my discussion of Neuhouser's treatment of apperception; see Chapter 5, sec. C. 2 below.
45 Wood, "The 'I,'" p. 95.

alone, or even that it has to exist. The second formula tries to provide some way out of this difficulty by adding a specific point that this self has the properties of being able to be brought about at any time and freely. These are new claims with substantive content, but taken that way they immediately lose certainty. How do we know that this self can be brought about at *any* time? Reference to the past does not yield certainty, and reference to actually reflecting now is also irrelevant, since this claim is about a capacity rooted in the prereflective self.[46] Moreover, how do we *know*, when an original act of self-consciousness comes about, that it is ever truly free, not determined by anything beyond the immediate act? It is significant that although Kant often focused on the act of thinking, he came to be very careful and backed off from any such tempting but dogmatic assertions. And it is no accident that he saw the futility of claiming to get past skepticism by trying to do without any substantive premises. To get content, one has to start with content, and the advantage Kant claimed is simply that his initial content came from what non-philosophers already accept. In particular, having appreciated Hume, he saw that one cannot just immediately help oneself to certain claims about the existence of absolute freedom, at a philosophical or pre-philosophical level.

F. 3. Fichte and Kant on the Practical

Precisely to cope with these severe problems, problems the theoretical skeptic will press eagerly, Fichteans typically move on to stressing that their disputed formulas must be taken in some "practical" sense. Wood sees that this was done initially with an eye to saving the project of a fully "scientific" first philosophy that maintains a strong unity of reason: "once it is accepted that transcendental philosophy as a doctrine of science must begin with a single fundamental principle . . . the only way to deal with the problem is to discover a first principle that can serve simultaneously as the ground of both theoretical and practical philosophy."[47] Note that one might rather have argued that the very absoluteness of the audacious causal and epistemic aspects of the claim of freedom at the base of this kind of philosophy is enough to provide a *reductio* for the notion of such "a single fundamental principle." One could then fall back on a kind of methodological dualism, of the kind that Kant favored, and allow that the

---

46 Consider specifically the example of the certainty that one is (self-consciously) reading, given in ibid., p. 96.

47 Ibid., pp. 95–6.

claim to absolute freedom is a distinct claim about a "fact of reason" that theoretical philosophy can never demonstrate (neither directly nor from some deep common ground of reason) but at best can only assume from elsewhere – once prior objections to its very possibility are adequately met. If this "postulating" approach, introduced only to serve a limited but compelling and irreducibly practical standpoint, falls short of the project of a radical unity of reason, then, one might well say, so much the worse for any tradition attached to such a project. It is striking that Wood's Fichtean response is just the opposite: he continues to ask how we can save a strong unity of reason by finding something about the I, or some common root of theoretical and practical reason, that would somehow give us certainty and adequate content at once. It is in this way that, in Wood's nondissenting words, "Fichte claims to have demonstrated what Kant had only postulated, that reason can be practical."[48]

The problem here is that the crucial claim at issue, namely that "reason can be practical," is surely something that must be understood at this point in Kant's own terms – for otherwise Fichte simply could not be demonstrating exactly "what Kant . . . postulated." But Kant's own claim is clearly a claim about the reality and efficacy of *pure* practical reason, not a claim about the mere appearance of just any kinds of activity. That is, it is a claim to the effect that morality and its presumed absolute freedom is not a hoax, that we are not mere "turnspits" of however complex a form. But how is it that Fichte "demonstrates" such a strong claim, or even makes a clear attempt at doing so?

Here is what appears to be the best attempt that Wood finds suggested in the text. He reminds us that Fichte has a story to tell about the active-passive distinction, a story that might be taken to imply that this distinction need not be simply assumed, as it is by Kant, but that it can be demonstrated as a general condition of the self's certain self-awareness. In "forming a concept" of itself, the self supposedly must be aware of a nonself that it posits as a contrast with itself, and as not to be abolished, so that in constantly "practically striving" with it, self-consciousness can be maintained.[49] This is an interesting story, and it points to a central function that a general kind of "practical" activity, one not already understood as moral, *might* have in the life of the self. But there are many things that this story still does *not* do. It does not show that the conditions of the process of forming a concept of a self, whatever they are, are themselves

48 Ibid., p. 98.
49 Ibid., p. 97.

absolutely certain – especially since, precisely on Fichte's own view, such a reflective activity is not primary. It does not show that the "not-self" that is posited in this process is anything more than an idea within the self, that is, it is not shown that this "passivity" involves an "other" in ultimate reality and not simply in immediate intention. It does not show that the "practical striving" involved here has implications specifically for the reality of the pure practical reason that is ultimately supposed to be "demonstrated." And most importantly, it does not begin to show that the activity involved, whatever it contrasts with, and however it is oriented, is an absolutely free activity, undetermined from outside. But until it can give support to all these claims, it has not even begun to look like a worked-out "demonstration" from a single principle that "reason is practical" in the relevant sense.

It is striking that Kant also has a story to tell about the active-passive distinction, one that offers a multilayered account of its presence in theoretical and practical contexts. In theoretical philosophy, he stresses that the receptivity of our intuition is not in total contrast with the spontaneity of our understanding, because there is an a priori form of intuition that contrasts with the mere receptivity of sensation. Similarly, in our willing, a slavish attention to the ends of sensibility may at first seem to indicate mere passivity, but for Kant this attention is never simply a product of sensibility. Rather it is always grounded in our active intentionality and our autonomous capacity to give ourselves heteronomous ends. Above all, there is what Kant calls the "optical illusion" of moral respect, "which may be easily looked upon as something that we passively feel."[50] Although psychologically and normatively this feeling can appear to be something that is simply imposed upon us, it turns out, for the Critical philosophy, to be something that can be best understood as ultimately a sign of our spontaneity in both an executive and a legislative sense. Fichte's philosophy, and most of the whole era of German idealism, can be seen as a massive attempt to work out the implications of this model of an "optical illusion" of passivity by going as far as possible to argue that whatever seems to be a given of nature is in some hidden sense the product of an autonomous mind. Unlike his successors, however, Kant himself very much appreciated the limits of this approach, and he was eventually quite clear that none of these considerations about activity should be taken by itself to provide a strict demonstration of absolute freedom in any context. It is an illusion of our own to assume that we are absolutely passive in

50 Kant, *Critique of Practical Reason*, p. 116.

various ways, but it is equally a mistake to jump into immediately accepting claims that we are absolutely spontaneous.

The subtlety and originality of Kant's approach contrasts sharply with the attempt that was just evaluated to make a demonstration out of Fichte's story of the genesis of the active-passive distinction in self-consciousness. Beyond this story, Wood provides an extra citation meant to bear on the claim that the self is genuinely free and not simply active in some not clearly relevant sense. In an initial attempt to reformulate the *Wissenschaftslehre*, Fichte says at one point that one can "directly note activity and freedom in this thinking," that is, in the transition from one thought to another.[51] If this is a "demonstration," and not merely another shorthand reference to another line of considerations, it is certainly a very brief and dogmatic one, and a Kantian cannot help but immediately ask, just how did this kind of apparently psychological claim about "freedom" get in here, especially when one is supposed to be allowing only claims that are certain? Even if we are *not aware* that we are being determined, why *must* we presume – and how can we ever "*directly* note" – that we are *not* being determined?[52]

At this point it is appropriate to look at another transition of thought – this time the transition in Fichte's own style of presentation of his system, which on my interpretation was developed precisely as the weight of these obvious difficulties began to be appreciated.

F. 4. Fichte's Transition

Following Neuhouser and others,[53] Wood notes that in the new Introductions for the *Wissenschaftslehre* in 1797 Fichte moved toward a different

---

51 Wood, "The 'I,' " p. 96. The passage is from Fichte's "Chapter One of 'Attempt at a New Presentation of the Wissenschaftslehre,' " in J. G. Fichte, *Introductions*, p. 106 (*SW*, I, p. 522).

52 This point is made explicitly by Kant, as noted in "Metaphysik K3" in *Lectures on Metaphysics*, p. 490 (*AA*, vol. 29, p. 1022), and is discussed in K. Ameriks, "Kant on Spontaneity: Some New Data," *Proceedings of the VII International Kant-Kongress 1990* (Berlin: de Gruyter, 1991), pp. 436–46. Fichte earlier showed an explicit sensitivity to this problem when he responded to Reinhold's treatment of the will (in letters 6–8 of vol. 2 of his *Briefe über die Kantische Philosophie* [Leipzig: Göschen, 1792]) by inserting the chapter "On the General Theory of the Will" in the second edition (1793) of his *Attempt at a Critique of All Revelation*, trans. G. Green (Cambridge: Cambridge University Press, 1978), p. 45. See above Chapter 2, sec. D. 6; and cf. Alessandro Lazzari, "Fichtes Entwicklung von der zweiten Auflage der Offenbarungskritik bis zur Rezeption von Schulzes 'Aenesidemus,' " *Fichte-Studien* 9 (1997): 182–96.

53 See the works cited above at n. 1. The possibility that by 1796 Fichte was reacting specifically to criticisms of his earlier foundationalism here by trying to incorporate some of Hölderlin's ideas is explored in Violetta Waibel, "Hölderlins frühe Fichte-Kritik und ihre Wirkung auf den Gang der Ausarbeitung der Wissenschaftslehre," *Revue Internationale de*

way of expressing the foundation of his philosophy. In the famous original formulation in sec. 5 of the *Wissenschaftslehre* (1794), Fichte spoke of aiming to demonstrate that "reason cannot even be theoretical unless it is practical."[54] This passage resembles announcements of bold programs in Fichte's early reviews, programs devoted to the ambitious idea that any mere state of awareness, or perhaps self-awareness, brings with it enough to provide a *proof* that "reason is practical." However, Wood allows that by 1797, "whereas the earlier system made the practical power of reason into an object of demonstration, the later system grounds itself directly on the original act (*Tathandlung*) through which the free I posits itself."[55] In this way it seems the "first principle" becomes an initial "postulate" after all – but one not backed, like Kant's, by a *prior* analysis of theoretical reason – and it no longer claims to provide the supposedly absolute "demonstration" that overcomes the need for all postulates.

After drawing attention to this transition, Wood appears to play it down somewhat by saying that in both stages "the I . . . was always regarded as fundamentally a practical rather than a theoretical principle."[56] Methodologically, this claim can lead to some significant misunderstandings. It is true that in both stages of his thought here Fichte claims to give a major role to what he understands as a practical aspect of the I. But in a situation where epistemic and foundational relations have been made the main focus, as they clearly have been by Fichte's own concern for "science," everything hangs on the *order* of considerations. It is one thing to start, as Fichte apparently does initially, with something not explicitly characterized as practical, from which we are to try to move *toward* the purely practical as the conclusion of a "demonstration"; and it is something else to start expressly, as Fichte does later, with something *already* clearly characterized as practical (a *Tathandlung*) in a fundamental sense. Very loosely speaking, both procedures could be described, because of their ultimate goals, as sympathetic to a "primacy of the practical," but in the *methodological* order, the order of reasoning (as opposed to the order of being or value), Fichte's first procedure precisely does not yet give primacy to the practical. Rather, it aims to demonstrate "the practical" from something else that is given as absolutely first for us.

Philosophie 197 (1996): 430–60; and Jürgen Stolzenberg, "Selbstbewusstsein: Ein Problem der Philosophie nach Kant, Zum Verhältnis Reinhold-Hölderlin-Fichte," *Revue Internationale de Philosophie* 197 (1996): 461–82.

54 Cited at Wood, "The 'I,'" p. 99, from *SW,* I, p. 264. Cf. above Chapter 3, n. 39; and Fichte's 1793 "Rezension Creuzer," *GA,* I, 2, p. 28.

55 Wood, "The 'I,'" pp. 100–101.

56 Ibid., pp. 101–2.

Although Fichte's transition to an explicitly practical starting point gives up on the suggested starting points found in his earliest and most ambitious outlines of a fully scientific philosophy, this shift is quite understandable on my interpretation. The shift responds directly to appreciating the difficulties noted earlier with his original project. For those who were asking exactly how does one know that one really is free, the Fichtean now can say that this is not claimed to be a matter of "demonstration" at all, it is simply something that comes with one's practical orientation – an idealist just is the kind of person who *believes* in his or her freedom and works *from* that "interest." Such a standpoint is formulated most perspicuously in works such as Fichte's *Vocation of Man* (1800), which, as I have noted, focuses right on the very kind of experiences that Fichte had mentioned before – the nonmorally defined "acts" of mere thinking and planning – and then concludes that while these might well seem to prove one's freedom, they really do no such thing; freedom is affirmed only as a matter of "faith" (see above at n. 9). In all his later expositions, Fichte provides reminders of the basic position that not just any "practical" premise can work as a starting point, that only contexts in which one is sensitive to a categorical moral "ought" bring with them the claim of absolute freedom.

In what seems to be an attempt to tone down the implications of this shift, Wood points out various ways in which Fichte is not resorting to a "blind leap of faith."[57] Wood reminds us how, in the Introductions, Fichte argues that the idealist philosophy of freedom has the advantages of appearing to fit our immediate experience of our subjectivity and of being able to offer some explanations from its perspective – something that "dogmatism" and its mysteriously posited thing in itself cannot do. While Fichte's claims here could surely be challenged, it must be granted that his arguments do at least *aim* to show that there is something even nonpractical to be said for freedom, and apparently nothing specific – given his characterization of a hamstrung "mechanist" opponent – to be said against it.[58] Nonetheless, on Fichte's own account the considerations do *not* refute skepticism, and so, contra Wood, they still do not vindicate the idea of what is called an "*absolutely certain* first principle."[59]

57 Ibid., p. 99.
58 This point is developed in a helpful paper by Andrew Lamb, "Positions of Fichte on the Certainty of his Philosophy," *Idealistic Studies* 28 (1998): 193–215. Cf. my analysis above at n. 12.
59 Wood, "The 'I,'" p. 99.

It is true that Fichte's considerations are not idiosyncratic or "blind," for they rely to a large extent on the familiar universal perspective of Kantian pure practical reason. Nonetheless, it should be stressed again that they do give up on the general autonomy of reason in one key respect by drastically narrowing its options. When Kant resorted to the "fact of reason" to let in the claim of freedom, he did so only after a prior theoretical investigation that aimed to show how, despite appearances, a thoroughly deterministic framework was not metaphysically required for us. Without such an investigation, he conceded that the move to "practical faith" would be illegitimate, irresponsible in the face of all that was (for better or worse) commonly accepted as known.[60] Fichte unfortunately has no room for such an extended prior investigation, since he presumes that any consideration from the mere "theoretical standpoint" can be quickly dismissed as a dead end and outweighed by our pure practical interest. This presumption appears to discount further theoretical investigations simply because it is locked into the extreme Jacobian presumptions that all pure epistemological theories must start from a premise of inner representations from which there is no sound theoretical route to an external world, and that all deterministic theories must be based on some kind of absurd metaphysical notion of a thing in itself. But surely this is to sell theory much too short, and to take a precipitous if not entirely blind leap to the practical. The dramatic language of faith that Fichte came to rely on in the last part of the *Vocation of Man* appears to rest on little more than badly exaggerated worries about certain odd conceptions of the thing in itself and a hasty thought that more theory could give us, at best, only extra reasons for fearing an undermining of our concerns for freedom and "being" rather than for finding – as with Kant – a removal of the objections to them. Ironically, an absolute Fichtean faith in freedom can itself become a form of bad dogmatism, keeping us from the "freedom" of an open-minded attempt to make sense of sophisticated forms of determinism, one of which might after all be true and not as harmful to our dignity as Fichte feared.

F. 5. Methodological Implications

Wood contends in the end that Fichte's principle of the I is to be supported because it is "not originally and fundamentally a cognitive standpoint at all . . . [and] no clear content can be given to the idea of a self

60 See above at n. 4.

understood only theoretically."[61] Here too there are highly controversial claims about the practical, claims typical of contemporary neo-Kantian pragmatism. Wood claims, for example, that even identity of the self over time is not a "deep metaphysical fact" but rather rests on the "fact that my body is the fundamental vehicle of my agency."[62] But how is it that reference to a "body," of all things, no longer counts as "cognitive"? And why should even the mere "requirements of agency" (conceived of in terms of either representations or physical beings, but not yet in terms that presuppose the validity of morality) have to bring in a noncognitive perspective? To act, we typically do need to plan and to think of ends, that is, to think of what we believe we can do and of what we think that we should do, and all these thoughts can themselves be gathered "cognitively," as Kant notes, as just so many speculations or pieces of "technical" knowledge (i.e., as still broadly theoretical, even if it is *about* action).[63] That is, as Fichte himself emphasized in the *Vocation of Man,* even the most vivid concern with images of the body, plans, and impressions of action still seems possible without accepting that "reason is practical" in the deep and relevant sense that alone brings with it absolute agency and moral freedom.

These worries do not directly affect the claims of Wood and others that details in Fichte's *System of Ethics* and *Natural Right* provide a rich normative content to supplement Kant's system in various significant ways, especially with their proposal that we regard the development of moral knowledge as involving a process of mutual recognition and a "quest for systematic agreement among moral conceptions."[64] It is not at all clear, however, that this account follows from, rather than at best simply "fits," Fichte's general reflections on an active fundamental I. The empirical nature of the method that comes to be stressed in the notion of "systematic agreement" here, and that Wood regards as a virtue, is very difficult to reconcile with Fichte's strongly foundational notion of philosophy as a science. Most importantly, as Wood also indicates, and as I documented earlier (see above sec. C. 4), the *central* passages of these two famous

---

61 Wood, "The 'I,'" pp. 102–3.
62 Ibid., p. 103; cf. Martin, *Idealism and Objectivity,* p. 140. This claim is explicitly linked to Christine Korsgaard's recent work, *Creating the Kingdom of Ends* (Cambridge: Cambridge University Press, 1996), chap. 13. See above Chapter 1, n. 52, and for a contrasting and more metaphysical view of the problem of personal identity in Kant, see my *Kant's Theory of Mind* (Oxford: Clarendon Press, 1982), chap. IV.
63 Kant, *Critique of Judgment,* Introduction, sec. 1.
64 Wood, "The 'I,'" p. 105.

books do nothing to take back Fichte's a priori notion of a radical primacy of the practical but instead give that notion a classical expression.

To the extent that this notion remains highly problematic, the major methodological shift from Kant to Fichte remains anything other than a matter of clear philosophical progress, however attractive it may have seemed at first, and however influential it has become again. It is no wonder that the successor who put Fichte in the shade, namely Hegel, began by directly presenting his own perspective (1802–3) in a work on the relation of "faith and knowledge,"[65] and that he energetically reversed the radical methodological principle of the primacy of the practical while helping himself to many of the innovative details of Fichte's normative doctrines.[66] It is hardly surprising that Hegel believed it was time for philosophers to take a more expansive look at what theoretical reason could accomplish, and especially to overcome the representationalist presumptions that characterized the blind alleys of the Reinhold-to-Fichte period – a period that Hegel unfortunately took to include, in its antecedents, not only the Lockean tradition but also Kant. One way that Hegel's all-inclusive system can be understood is as a synthesis that combines as much as it can from the form of the systematic foundational program that Reinhold proposed with the matter of the concrete intersubjective principles that Fichte introduced. Hegel's work is much too massive to consider in its entirety, but in the final chapters I will present the beginnings of an evaluation of it as basically a reaction to Kant in these terms, that is, as above all a grand attempt to recover the sovereignty of the autonomy of reason from a perspective that in its method is neither dualistic, as in Kant, nor basically practical, as in Fichte, but rather, as in Reinhold, all-encompassingly theoretical.

65 Hegel, *Faith and Knowledge,* ed. and trans. H. S. Harris and Walter Cerf (Albany: State University of New York Press, 1977).
66 See Ludwig Siep, *Anerkennung als Prinzip der praktischen Philosophie* (München: Alber, 1979).

5

KANT, FICHTE, AND APPERCEPTION

A. FICHTE'S LEGACY AND CONTEMPORARY THEORIES OF APPERCEPTION

The Fichtean strand in the development of post-Kantian philosophy is rooted from the very start in a fundamental duality in Fichte's creative use of the basic Kantian notion of the "I think."[1] On the one hand, when Fichte reinterpreted this "fact of consciousness" as an original "act" (*Tathandlung* rather than *Tatsache*), he eventually incorporated it into a popular – but, as I have argued, questionable – radicalization of the doctrine of the "primacy of *practical* reason," a radicalization that put pure practical philosophy at the base of all philosophy.[2] On the other hand, Fichte also used his "active" understanding of the "I think" as part of a

---

1 Günter Zöller's *Fichte's Transcendental Philosophy: The Original Duplicity of Intelligence and Will* (Cambridge: Cambridge University Press, 1998) discusses a duality that is close to but not the same as the one I am stressing here.

2 See above Chapters 2–4. While on my interpretation it was Reinhold who first gave this Kantian doctrine a revised form and fundamental role, it was Fichte who took the crucial step of completely "purifying" this role by entirely jettisoning things in themselves and thus removing the important remaining "orthodox" theoretical and metaphysical components in Reinhold's version of the Critical philosophy. See the end of this chapter for examples of how this step becomes important again in evaluating some contemporary accounts of apperception.

reconceptualization (especially in his earliest works) of the nature of pure *theoretical* reason. It is this second side of Fichte's influence, which is independent of action in an ordinary practical or moral sense, that I will be focusing on here.

Although Kant is also well known for having discussed thinking, even in its purest theoretical sense, as an "activity" rooted in the unique spontaneity of subjectivity, he did not directly develop a complete account of subjectivity as such. Following immediately upon Reinhold's focus on a general faculty of representation (*Vorstellungsvermögen*), Fichte insisted on such an account, and from the beginning he put a special stress on the bare notion of self-consciousness as a synthetic activity of apperception that is indispensable to "scientific philosophy" as such, that is, to anything like a *Wissenschaftslehre* or systematic theory of subjectivity. This idea was picked up by Fichte's *immediate* successors, Schelling and Hegel,[3] but it has also been stressed repeatedly in the best *contemporary* interpretations of Fichte, and these interpretations have motivated, or paralleled, much of the best contemporary literature on the "active" aspect of Kant's own theoretical doctrine of apperception as well. In this chapter I will discuss several of the most important of these recent interpretations of apperception, interpretations that can be understood as quite Fichtean in spirit, either explicitly or implicitly. The evaluation of these interpretations should indicate the continuing power – and limits – of what I take to be a major aspect of the strong Fichtean turn in philosophy after Kant.

The most influential approach to Kantian apperception from the perspective of an emphasis on Fichte's development of the notion of self-consciousness has been worked out by Dieter Henrich and his students, especially in the extensive studies by Manfred Frank.[4] A strikingly similar approach has also found favor in America, notably in Frederick Neu-

---

3 See Robert Pippin, *Hegel's Idealism: The Satisfactions of Self-Consciousness* (Cambridge: Cambridge University Press, 1989), and cf. his "Fichte's Alleged Subjective, Psychological, One-Sided Idealism," in *The Reception of Kant's Critical Philosophy: Fichte, Schelling and Hegel*, ed. Sally Sedgwick (Cambridge: Cambridge University Press, 2000).

4 See especially Dieter Henrich, *Fichtes ursprüngliche Einsicht* (Frankfurt: Klostermann, 1967); *Identität und Objektivität* (Heidelberg: Carl Winter, 1976), translated in *The Unity of Reason: Essays in Kant's Philosophy*, ed. R. Velkley (Cambridge, MA: Harvard University Press, 1994), pp. 123–208; and "The Identity of the Subject in the Transcendental Deduction," in *Reading Kant*, ed. E. Schaper and W. Vossenkuhl (Oxford: Blackwell, 1989), pp. 250–80. See also Manfred Frank, "Fragmente zu einer Geschichte der Selbstbewusstseinstheorien von Kant bis Sartre," in *Selbstbewusstseinstheorien von Fichte bis Sartre*, ed. M. Frank (Frankfurt: Suhrkamp, 1991), pp. 415–599. Frank goes on to combine his interest in Fichte with a criticism of developments in German idealism that move away from the reservations expressed by Jena's early Romantics. Cf. above Chapter 1, n. 18.

houser's *Fichte's Theory of Subjectivity,* which defends a Fichtean notion of "self-positing" that resembles aspects of Kant's concept of apperception, especially as it has been interpreted recently in influential work by Henry Allison and Robert Pippin.[5] Most of these writers are sympathetic to post-Kantian philosophy, but it is also striking that broadly similar emphases on apperception can be found even in more empirically oriented studies that show no interest in this tradition. For example, C. T. Powell's *Kant's Theory of Self-Consciousness,* which can be seen as one more indication of the strong influence of P. F. Strawson's interpretation of Kant, continues to be dominated by issues set by the strategy of focusing on using Kant's notion of apperception (now understood in terms of determining a set of conditions for the "self-ascribability" of representations) to respond to problems of Humean skepticism.[6] A different kind of indebtedness to British empiricism, with a broader concern for a variety of concrete activities of consciousness, can be found in interpreters such as Patricia Kitcher,[7] who focuses on the Kantian notion of synthesis in an attempt to resolve issues arising from the latest research in psychology, or what is now called "cognitive science."[8]

5 See Frederick Neuhouser, *Fichte's Theory of Subjectivity* (Cambridge: Cambridge University Press, 1990); Henry E. Allison, *Kant's Theory of Freedom* (Cambridge: Cambridge University Press, 1990), and *Idealism and Freedom* (Cambridge: Cambridge University Press, 1997); and Robert Pippin, *Hegel's Idealism,* chap. 2. Cf. also Wayne Martin, *Idealism and Objectivity: Understanding Fichte's Jena Project* (Stanford: Stanford University Press, 1997), and Daniel Breazeale's introductions to his editions of *Fichte: Early Philosophical Writings* (Ithaca: Cornell University Press, 1988), *Fichte: Foundations of Transcendental Philosophy (Wissenschaftslehre) nova methodo 1796/99* (Ithaca: Cornell University Press, 1992), and *Fichte: Introductions to the Wissenschaftslehre and Other Writings* (1797–1800) (Indianapolis: Hackett, 1994).

6 Charles T. Powell, *Kant's Theory of Self-Consciousness* (Oxford: Oxford University Press, 1990). Cf. P. F. Strawson, *The Bounds of Sense* (London: Methuen, 1966), and, more recently, Q. Cassam, *Self and World* (Oxford: Oxford University Press, 1996).

7 Patricia Kitcher, *Kant's Transcendental Psychology* (Oxford: Oxford University Press, 1990). Cf. Andrew Brook, *Kant and the Mind* (Cambridge: Cambridge University Press, 1994). I discuss aspects of Brook's interpretation (and contrast it with recent work by Colin McGinn) in "Kant and Mind: Mere Immaterialism," *Proceedings of the Eighth International Kant Congress 1995,* ed. H. Robinson (Milwaukee: Marquette University Press, 1995), vol. 1, pp. 675–90. This is reprinted as the Postscript in my *Kant's Theory of Mind* (Oxford: Oxford University Press, 2d rev. ed., 2000).

8 For other overviews of treatments of Kant's theory of the self, see esp. Günter Zöller, "Main Developments in Recent Scholarship on the Critique of Pure Reason," *Philosophy and Phenomenological Research* 53 (1993), pp. 445–66; Gary Hatfield, "Empirical, Rational, and Transcendental Psychology: Psychology as Science and as Philosophy," in *The Cambridge Companion to Kant,* ed. Paul Guyer (Cambridge: Cambridge University Press, 1992), pp. 200–27; Eric Watkins, "Recent Developments in Kant Scholarship: Kant's Philosophy of Mind," *Eidos* 12 (1995): 83–107; and K. Ameriks, "The First Edition Paralogisms of Pure Reason," in *Immanuel Kant: Kritik der reinen Vernunft,* ed. Georg Mohr and Marcus Willaschek (Berlin: Akademie Verlag, 1998), pp. 369–88.

Although Powell and Kitcher, unlike Henrich and Neuhouser, make no reference to the post-Kantian German tradition, they still can be regarded as Fichtean in a "broad and implicit" sense for two reasons: (i) like Fichte, they continue to stress, in as concrete a manner as possible, the *active* dimension of apperception, and (ii) they use this notion to focus on *skepticism*, a problem that was also central to Fichte's work, and that was made acute by the modern philosophical tradition that culminated in Hume's work and that Powell and Kitcher are still trying to overcome. Although Fichte himself makes relatively few direct references to Hume,[9] there can be no doubt that Hume's problems were central to Fichte's thought as well. His concern for these problems comes not so much from Kant as from Jacobi, whose book *David Hume on Faith, or Idealism and Realism, a Dialogue* (1787) was very clearly one of the most important influences on Fichte and his whole generation.[10]

In criticizing these sets of contemporary interpretations, I will be arguing that they suffer from going to opposite extremes: the more empirically oriented accounts (Powell, Kitcher) downplay Kant's ultimate concern with a real, but not empirically determinable, subject underlying apperception, whereas the explicitly Fichtean accounts (Henrich, Neuhouser) tend, despite their own intentions, to interpret apperception in overly Cartesian and reflective terms. These weaknesses reflect a pair of natural misunderstandings arising in the wake of Kant's famous reference to the "I think" that must "be able to accompany all consciousness": one can lose sight of the ineliminable self-reference in this "I think" by reducing apperception to a mere function or general feature of empirical synthesis; or one can exaggerate the self that is involved by turning it into something that has a constant and necessary grasp of itself as such. More broadly speaking, these two opposed errors recapitulate the functionalist-empiricist and the Cartesian rationalist transfigurations of Kant's notion of the "I think" that have characterized much of philosophy from Kant's time to our own.[11] It is almost as if a "metaparalogism" continues to haunt us after the first *Critique*, for there is something about the very idea of the self that tends to lead philosophers (even philosophers operating right

9 See, e.g., Fichte's references to Hume in his "*Aenesidemus* Review" and in his letter to Hufeland, Aug. 3, 1795, in *Fichte: Early Philosophical Writings*, pp. 67, 71, 405.

10 Jacobi's Hume book is translated now in George di Giovanni's massive collection, *The Main Philosophical Writings and the Novel Allwill, Friedrich Heinrich Jacobi* (Montreal: McGill University Press, 1994), pp. 253–338. Cf. D. Breazeale, "Fichte on Skepticism," *Journal of the History of Philosophy* 29 (1991): 427–53.

11 Cf. Henry E. Allison, "On Naturalizing Kant's Transcendental Psychology," in his *Idealism and Freedom*, pp. 53–66; and David Carr, *The Paradox of Subjectivity* (Oxford: Oxford University Press, 1998).

after the benefit of Kant's Critical distinctions) repeatedly to make either much too little of the self, by prematurely blocking off metaphysical issues, or much too much of the self, by inflating epistemological claims about it.

B. REVIEW OF KANT'S NOTION OF APPERCEPTION

B. 1. The Original Synthetic Unity of Transcendental Apperception

In all these schools of interpretation the manifold ambiguity of Kant's doctrine of the "transcendental unity of apperception" plays a central role. Some aspects of this doctrine are clear enough. Kant speaks of this unity as "transcendental" because he takes it to be a *necessary* condition of all our experience. He calls it a unity of "apperception" because it is the condition that all items of that experience must be able to be accompanied by the representation "*I* think." And he speaks of this apperception as involving a "unity" in order to highlight the fact that this "I" has a kind of formal simplicity or *self-sameness* that contrasts with the multiplicity of items that are its possible objects. Moreover, it is called an "original synthetic" unity because it is *not derivable* from any one of the representations by themselves, and because even as a group the representations do not "combine themselves."

This minimal gloss on Kant's terms is common ground for all interpreters, but the intrinsic complexity of the doctrine of apperception still allows for several different points of departure. Having already given considerable attention to the nonempirical (that is, moral and metaphysical) issues that I believe are central to the ultimate understanding of the Kantian self, I will now withdraw from these issues as much as possible in order to concentrate instead on its purely apperceptive aspect, for it is this aspect that is dominant in the current Fichtean interpretations under discussion here. After a brief general review of Kant's own doctrine (sec. B. 2), I will offer a criticism of the explicit Fichtean interpretations (sec. C), and then a criticism of the more empiricist interpretations that also reflect some of Fichte's main interests (sec. D).

B. 2. The Strong Apperception Thesis

In the most fundamental claim of his doctrine of apperception, Kant says there is an "I think" that is "transcendental" precisely because it necessarily can accompany all of one's representations.[12] Much attention has been focused on the phrase "I think" here, but equal attention needs to be given to what it is that this "I think" is supposed to be accompanying. Exactly what is it that this "I think" thinks of? One might believe that here Kant is speaking directly of objects, psychological objects at least. But for at least two reasons that cannot be exactly right.

The first reason is that to say "I think" is to use a phrase that calls out for completion with a that-clause rather than a mere object term; we say "I think *that* this is how it feels . . ." rather than merely "I think *x*" or "I think *x, y.*"[13] Second, although it might seem that Kant means to attach the *transcendental* "I think" directly to representations as such, his real claim is about one's "own" representations, that is, representations that have the quality of not being, as he says, "nothing to me."[14] Although this is often forgotten, Kant's doctrine is not that all representation requires apperception, for he holds that there are whole species of beings (e.g., dogs, and no doubt cats as well) who have representation but not apperception, and there are probably whole layers of human existence (e.g., our "peripheral" or subconscious or infantile representations) that have a similar form. Thus, Kant's claim is only that representations that are "something to" one, are what must be able to be accompanied by the transcendental "I think." And this means that his doctrine of apperception is precisely *not* a claim that each human *representation as such,* that is, just as a representation, must be susceptible to apperception. And yet it is his view that all "relevant" representations (representations that are not "nothing to" one) must *already* have some kind of personal quality. This point has been missed largely because interpretations tend to follow Reinhold's and Fichte's tendency to speak merely in terms of representation as such, a tendency that remains very strong in empiricist and analytic traditions (see above Chapter 1, sec. B. 2, and Chapter 2, sec. B. 3).

I propose that the simplest way to begin to understand the "personal" quality of consciousness here is to presume that the individual representations in question are already at least *implicitly* of the form "I think that so and so . . ." It might at first seem that this would make redundant the

---

12 Kant, *Critique of Pure Reason,* B 131. All quotations of this work are from the Norman Kemp Smith translation (London: Macmillan, 1929), with the first and second editions designated as A and B, respectively, followed by page numbers.

13 Cf. Ernst Tugendhat, *Self-Consciousness and Self-Determination,* trans. Paul Stern (Cambridge, MA: MIT Press, 1986).

14 Kant, *Critique of Pure Reason,* B 132; cf. my "Kant and Guyer on Apperception," *Archiv für Geschichte der Philosophie* 65 (1983): 174–86, and, on the ambiguities of apperception in general, my *Kant's Theory of Mind,* chap. VII. B.

"transcendental" "I think," the "I think" that necessarily can accompany all the representations that are "something to" one. However, a transcendental "I think" is worth introducing because it has a special collective function, for even if in fact the same "I" is distributively involved in the set:

(E) I think that x, I think that y, I think that z . . . ;

nevertheless, (E) is not the same as:

(T) I think that (I think that x, I think that y, I think that z . . .).

The difference here is not merely that (T) is more complex than any part of (E) or even the whole set (E). There are at least two extra features of (T) that are noteworthy. The first is that it implicitly includes the claim (which may or may not be a correct claim) that all the uses of "I" within it are coreferential; that is, I believe Kant understands (T) to include the claim that the I which thinks that x, *is the same as* the I which thinks that y, etc., as well as the thought that this is the very same I which thinks *that* I thinks that x, etc. A second and much more controversial point is that, given the a priori status of transcendental apperception, it seems that Kant understands the *possibility* of (T) to be a truth condition of the components of (E). More exactly, I take Kant's view to be that, for any of our thoughts contained in sets such as (E), there are corresponding thoughts such as (T), although, given the psychological limits of finite minds, this need not involve the "real possibility" of one all-inclusive thought (T) which contains all (E)-thoughts. That is, he believes that for any component of an (E)-set, there needs to be at least *some* possible (T)-thought which contains that component, but there need not be one really possible (T)-thought that includes *all* such components. At most, what he calls for is roughly what Dieter Henrich has spoken of as "the *coordination* of all possible 'I think'-instances."[15]

It is not immediately clear from a non-Kantian perspective why someone would insist that (E), empirical apperception, requires (T), transcendental apperception. (This terminology can be a little confusing since of course an instance of [T] could also be an example of what Kant would call "empirical apperception" – a term that he uses in a variety of ways that I will abstract from here – but the point to keep in mind is that the specific capacity for thoughts at least as complex as [T] is what is crucial for

15 Henrich, "The Identity of the Subject," pp. 270–1.

introducing the notion of transcendental apperception.) One ground could be the meaning of "I" in these contexts, for, Kant may be reasoning, what could it mean to be an I which is a correlate of any of the "first-level" thoughts "I think that *x*," etc., if that I *could not* be identical with other I's, such as those referred to in (T)? But if the full meaning of (T) is used here, then this amounts to what suddenly appears to be a fairly substantive claim, namely that a "real subject" of thought could not be such that it could have only one instantiation, *or* even such that some of its multiple instantiations could not be recognized by it as such, that is, as instantiations of one and the same subject. The latter part of this claim is striking because, if one allows, as it has just been noted that Kant does, that there are representations in beings incapable of thoughts, then for parallel reasons one could also suppose (with a little sympathy for something like the old idea of a "chain of being") that there are or could be thoughts in beings incapable of thoughts of thoughts. In Kant's terms, such beings could be said to have "empirical" but not "transcendental" apperception (hence the designations "E" and "T").

It can sound sadly dogmatic to insist such beings are impossible, or to ascribe such an insistence to Kant, but can one avoid such dogmatism and still hold onto Kant's doctrine of apperception? One response would be to concede the remote possibility of such beings and to stress that Kant's doctrine is meant primarily as a doctrine for *us;* we know that we (at least) do in fact have more than punctual, uncollected, "merely empirical" apperception. Nonetheless, just as we may still have some representations without even empirical apperception, it can also seem that, even if we have some thoughts that are also parts of thoughts like (T), we still could also have some other ("first-level") thoughts without any possible thought of those thoughts, let alone a collective "transcendental" thought (a set or sequence of thoughts like [T]) that connects the whole set of such ("first-level," that is, "[E]-level") thoughts. To deny that this could happen is to hold for us what I will call the *Strong Apperception Thesis* (SAT), that is, the thesis that *all* one's empirical apperception requires transcendental apperception.

B. 3. The Significance of the Strong Apperception Thesis

It might seem that very little depends on such an esoteric thesis, and yet I believe one very appropriate perspective that can be developed on the mainstream of most recent work on apperception is to see it as focusing on precisely this point, that is, as building on SAT and as contending that an insistence on this kind of possible self-consciousness for *all our* consciousness is the very cornerstone of Kant's philosophy. To fill out this perspective, I will distinguish two closely related sets of substantive claims that recent explicitly Fichtean interpretations of apperception (in Henrich and Neuhouser) have attempted to connect with SAT.

The first set of interpretive claims is dominated by a thesis that I will call the *Cartesian Claim*. This is the claim that SAT is used by Kant to ground a "Cartesian" or a priori grasp of our continuing personal identity, a grasp that is then claimed to be essential to a defeat of skepticism through an a priori proof of the objectivity of our representations. The second set of claims I will call the *Anti-Reflection Claim*. This is defined by the compound thesis that Kant's understanding of SAT is accompanied by an account of self-consciousness that Henrich calls the *Reflection Theory*, that this is a fundamentally inadequate theory, and that it has to be replaced by a nonreflective account inspired by what Henrich calls "Fichte's original insight." I have argued earlier against the Cartesian Claim,[16] so what I will emphasize here will be difficulties in the Anti-Reflection Claim. A group of arguments similar to my own against the Anti-Reflection Claim is contained in a critical discussion by Dieter Sturma.[17] I will endorse Sturma's points and then go on to defend a less Fichtean account of self-consciousness that I take to be closer to, even if not identical with (because it explicitly backs off from a commitment to SAT), an orthodox reading of Kant's own doctrine of apperception. I will then use these results in criticizing Frederick Neuhouser's recent quasi-Henrichian arguments that Kant supposedly failed to see how the notions involved in SAT should lead us to follow Fichte in reconceiving the theoretical subject as a "self-positing" being. In conclusion, I will also argue against recent analytic interpretations (in Kitcher and Powell) that resemble Henrich's in their commitment to arguments that supposedly defeat Hume's arguments for skepticism about the self (here again I interpret Kant not as meaning to provide conclusive arguments against these arguments but rather as falling back on apologetics and common sense; cf. above Chapter 1, sec. C).

16 See my "Recent Work on Kant's Theoretical Philosophy," *American Philosophical Quarterly* 19 (1982): 1–24; and "Kant and Guyer on Apperception." Cf. Paul Guyer, "Kant on Apperception and A Priori Synthesis," *American Philosophical Quarterly* 17 (1980): 205–12; "Review of D. Henrich, *Identität und Objektivität*," *Journal of Philosophy* 76 (1979): 151–67.

17 Dieter Sturma, *Kant über Selbstbewusstsein* (Hildesheim: Olms, 1985).

B. 4. Critical Evaluation of the Strong Apperception Thesis

The evaluation of SAT itself clearly hinges on how one understands the "possibility" that it denies. Understood as restricted to humans, SAT insists on the claim that any "I think that x" episodes that we have must be able to be connected with other such episodes in the transcendental way that was discussed earlier (when analyzing what was called "[T]"). I presume that if the issue here were one of *mere logical* possibility, then it would be extremely odd to reject such a claim, and yet it would also be uninteresting to uphold it. Since in some sense anything can always be made more complex than it is, any particular empirical apperception should always be able to be inflated into an aspect of a higher-level apperception. But SAT is meant to imply more than this triviality; it implies that there is something about the very *type* of "thing" that empirical apperception is that *it* requires some *real*, even if implicit, constant connection to transcendental apperception. A similar idea about "types" clearly appears to be behind Kant's notion that if mere animal awareness were "inflated" into apperception this should be described not as a mere enrichment but as a leap into a different kind of awareness. This is to say that *as* "mere animal" awareness it necessarily lacks the "real potential" for apperceptive representation, just as, for Kant, mere human awareness lacks the real potential for intellectual intuition.

It can appear very difficult to determine how one is even to go about beginning to settle the question of whether or not all our empirical apperception does have such a "real potential" relation to transcendental apperception. The whole question may seem to be a matter of the most speculative psychology. Of course, one could assume a strong "realist" attitude to this issue, and hold that there is some hidden truth here, such that the potential is either there or it is not. But this attitude does not do much by itself to help one to decide how to evaluate SAT. A more "Critical" approach would be to ask how a use of SAT might help in the resolution of other philosophical issues. If it turns out that affirming SAT appears to be, as some interpreters suggest, the only way to make sense of various distinctive features of our self-awareness, this can build a strong indirect case for it and for affirming the disputed "real potential." On the other hand, it may be true, as I will be arguing, that if we keep in mind all the distinctions (and then some) that were developed along the way in introducing SAT, then there can be a more modest way to understand our self-awareness, such that one can employ a basically Kantian notion of apperception without going so far as to *insist* on SAT itself, let alone stronger claims that others have attached to it.

C. PROBLEMS IN CURRENT EXPLICITLY FICHTEAN ACCOUNTS OF APPERCEPTION

C. 1. Henrich's Account

One source of resistance to a modest doctrine of apperception may come from an interpretation of the Cartesian Claim, promoted, for example, by Dieter Henrich, that *separate and prior* awareness of the identity of the self as an enduring object (a person) underlies and discloses the conditions sufficient for the objective unity of experience that is asserted in the transcendental deduction. In fact, however, what Kant claims about "objective unity" is only that any objective assertion about one's own particular unity must meet the general necessary conditions of any objective unity; for a set of representations to be ascribed to *my* (one, objective) consciousness, they must meet whatever are the conditions for any *one* (objective) consciousness.[18] This is not the inverse and absurd claim that for any representations to be ascribed to one consciousness they must be ascribed specifically to my particular consciousness or my self. And even though Kant's doctrine of apperception (*Critique of Pure Reason*, sec. 19) also says that any objective unity requires the possibility of the correlative unity of "a" consciousness, his Paralogisms teach that this unity of consciousness reveals a formal unity, not necessarily the unity of a particular objective self. Nonetheless, current interpreters often propose Cartesian arguments that attempt to demonstrate the objectivity of our experience as a consequence of knowledge of one's own personal identity or simplicity, a strategy that oddly presumes a privileged status for such knowledge.[19] Whatever the attraction of such arguments for the project of defeating skepticism, they seem quite contrary to Kant's argument in the deduction.

It cannot be denied that there are some textual reasons why some interpreters have taken SAT to be central to Kant's account of self-consciousness and to the whole project of the transcendental deduction. Henrich finds the "central thought" of this project in the A-edition statement that "the mind could never think its identity in the manifoldness of

---

18 Kant, *Critique of Pure Reason*, B 132; cf. Sturma, *Kant*, pp. 43–5, 70, and my "Kant and Guyer on Apperception."

19 See Sturma, *Kant*, p. 123, for instances of this presumption in Henrich and Fichte.

its representations, and indeed think this identity a priori, if it did not have before its eyes the identity of its act, whereby it subordinates all synthesis of apprehension . . . to a transcendental unity."[20] Henrich's interpretation of this "central thought" has many aspects, but the most important aspect for our purposes here is a claim he makes that goes even further than SAT: "in every instance of self-consciousness there is a reference to the totality of all other instances of self-consciousness. And it is in this reference that the knowledge of the identity of the subject consists; which *knowledge* thus likewise necessarily occurs with every instance of self-consciousness."[21] This last claim appears especially questionable, and the remarkable thing is that Henrich himself strongly criticizes a natural, even if futile, line of support for the claim, namely the Reflection Theory. According to Henrich, Kant understood the subject's alleged "constant relation to itself" in terms of the Reflection Theory's thesis that "this relation to the self is brought about by the subject making an object of itself."[22] Although Henrich seems to accept SAT by itself as a valuable component of the transcendental deduction, he assails this extra Reflection Theory as a very inadequate account of *self*-consciousness.

Henrich's main criticism of the theory[23] is that it generates a vicious circle, presupposing self-consciousness rather than giving an "explanation" of its "origin." According to Henrich, this is because the reflection in which a subject makes an object of itself must, in order for it to be intentional and effective, already understand that the representations it is reflecting upon are its own (since it is precisely seeking out "its" experiences). The reflection itself can hardly be what *first* brings about self-consciousness.

This is an interesting point, but even if one accepts it and acknowledges that Kant did not directly state or fully appreciate it, it does nothing to show that Kant himself actually held the Reflection Theory. Moreover, there are various considerations that suggest that Kant might well not have been interested in the Reflection Theory. First, he might have been satisfied with the phenomenological point that a person simply will not be presented with instances of experience *to reflect upon* (which is not the

20 Kant, *Critique of Pure Reason,* A 108, cited in Henrich, "The Identity of the Subject," p. 262. This is a passage central to his earlier and longer interpretation in *Identität und Objektivität.*
21 Henrich, "The Identity of the Subject," p. 271 (my emphasis).
22 Henrich calls this "the only case of an identity of activity and what is acted upon" ("den einzigen Fall von einer Identität von Tätigkeit und Getätigtem"). *Fichtes ursprüngliche Einsicht,* p. 192, cited in Sturma, *Kant,* p. 109.
23 Henrich's other main criticism is that it doesn't allow for full "identity" (*Gleichheit*) of self-consciousness with itself. For a critique of this charge, see Sturma, *Kant,* p. 110.

same as saying that it could not *have* any "nonpersonal" layers of awareness) that do *not already* "come to" one (*before* one even begins to "seek"
them "intentionally and effectively") with what we have called a "personal
quality," an implicit "I think" in the original experience. Secondly, SAT
itself can be taken to presume original experiences that are already instances of a kind of self-consciousness, for it is precisely a thesis about how
such first-level "personal" experiences ("I think . . .") must, *in addition* to
existing, supposedly be tied to a *higher* level of self-consciousness. As was
noted above, for Kant this cannot be a thesis that all one's mere representations as such contain self-consciousness; rather it is a thesis about what
else is needed by what are *already* in some sense one's self-conscious
representations.

Thus, SAT by itself does not lead to the Reflection Theory, and, in the
absence of any proof that Kant subscribed to such a theory, it can be
concluded that the problems of the Reflection Theory, severe as they may
be, do not show that here Henrich has any valid critique of Kant. Henrich's critique illegitimately presumes that Kant means to or should be
attempting to give an explanation of how self-consciousness "origi-
nates."[24] Once this extravagant demand is dropped, there is no clear
reason to believe Kant's doctrine of apperception requires radical modification, in the way Henrich proposes, by something closer to Fichte's
philosophy. Ironically, Henrich's discussion seems more appropriate for
classical *non*-Kantian theories, theories that (unlike Kant's) presume that
there is some kind of objective "criterion" or marker attaching to a set of
experiences (e.g., spatiotemporal proximity, or "connection" with a particular body), such that, once one finds that marker present, one can
suddenly identify the experiences as one's own.

There is another irony here. Henrich thinks that it is an *improvement
upon Kant* to replace the Reflection Theory with a doctrine of "self-
familiarity," that is, the idea that there are (perhaps throughout all one's
mental life) representations that are "one's own" *prior* to any explicit
reflection.[25] The irony is that, as Sturma notes, this doctrine can be
regarded as simply exploiting a point central to Kant's own famous claim
that the transcendental "I think" expresses a special representation that it

24 Sturma, *Kant*, p. 111. Henrich appears to appreciate this point in his later "The Identity of
the Subject."
25 Henrich, "Selbstbewusstsein: Kritische Einleitung einer Theorie," in *Hermeneutik und
Dialektik*, ed. R. Bubner (Tübingen: Klostermann, 1972), p. 267, cited in Sturma, *Kant*, p.
111n.

is *possible* to attach to all "our" representations,[26] for this stress on the "possible" shows that Kant sees that there are representations that do not become "ours" by means of an *actual* ever-present act of reflection. This Kantian point can be expressed in terms of Henrich's own notion of "self-familiarity"; in Sturma's provocative terminology, the point is that there is at least one level of our awareness that is primitively "self-referential" but not "cognitive." This level of awareness is not originally obtained by a reflective use of objective criteria, and it does not "locate" the self in any specific empirical way.[27] Consider what happens, for example, when a person says, "I think something is going on here." This can be said quite properly even when the person uses no "criterion" to "identify" himself.

It turns out by a further irony that, except for some incidental terminological complications, this view can be brought quite close to the "original insight" in the "Fichtean" theory that Henrich advocates and expresses in terms of a "self-less consciousness belonging to the self."[28] That is, not only are the "improvements" to be made on Kant present already in Kant himself, but the inspiration for these "improvements," the *valid* "Fichtean" ideas to which Henrich calls attention, are (as Sturma argues) also already present in Kant. What Fichte proposed is that the "I" be understood as "positing itself absolutely *as* self-positing."[29] I believe that the valid kernel in this difficult claim can be broken down into two plausible ideas, namely that self-representation is primitive (hence the I "posits itself," that is, its representation cannot be *derived* from the observation of something else, as in the "classical non-Kantian theories"), and that the self which is represented *understands* this and sees itself as in this sense spontaneous (hence "*as* self-positing").[30] Both these points surely appear

26 Sturma, *Kant*, p. 111n.

27 See ibid., *Kant*, pp. 56, 117, on how the unique "self-referential" character of the "I" makes it a "quasi-object," something concrete but something for which our access is not limited to our knowledge of any specific spatiotemporal location.

28 Henrich, "Selbstbewusstsein," p. 280: "a selfless consciousness of self" ("selbstlosen Bewusstseins vom Selbst"). Cited at Sturma, *Kant*, p. 111n.

29 Sturma, *Kant*, p.116; the quotation is also in Henrich, *Fichtes ursprüngliche Einsicht*, p. 21, and comes from Fichte's *Sämtliche Werke* I, ed. I. H. Fichte (Berlin: Veit, 1845–6), p. 528. This is not to say that Kant thematizes self-consciousness as such in the way that later writers do, but the obvious reason for this is that they have the advantage of being able to take advantage of his pathbreaking work.

30 However, I do not think it is valid to say that *each* instance of self-awareness must see itself this way. That is an extra and dubious claim (tied to certain ideas about "constant" self-awareness that are challenged below in my discussion of Neuhouser). All I mean to endorse is the idea *that at some points* in its existence a theoretical subject like us (in contrast to

to be central to Kant's own theory. Why then do Fichte and Henrich present them as challenges to Kant? A clue may come from Fichte's expression of his dissatisfaction (which also lies behind Henrich's analysis) with Kant. Fichte says:

> But again this consciousness of our [prior] consciousness we are [supposedly, according to Kant] conscious of only by making it into an object, and thereby we attain a consciousness of the consciousness of our consciousness, so forth into infinity – But our consciousness is not explained thereby . . .[31]

The mistake here – which Fichte imputes and which there is no evidence that Kant commits – is to presume that, because we may get *cognitive access* to our consciousness only by making a reflective object out of it, this is what *makes it* "our" consciousness in the first place.[32] The presumption can be corrected by seeing that it can be true of a state of awareness that, without any objective reflection on the self having taken place, the state is *structured* by the form "I think that *x*,"[33] and therefore is already in a personal, even if implicit, sense an instance of "our" consciousness. In that sense it is an instance of a kind of "self-consciousness" even if it is not expressly consciousness directed to "a self" or explicitly a "consciousness of consciousness."[34] Instead of working as a point against Kant, all this rather just recalls his notion of "first-level" representations that are specifically "one's own," that is, not "nothing to me." One could also draw upon SAT here, and argue that such a first-level state is structured by an "I think" because there appears to be no point in calling the original state

a being with mere awareness) must be able at least implicitly to understand that it has some kind of spontaneity. To this extent I may be departing from what Fichte means in saying the self "absolutely" posits itself as self-positing.

31 Cited in Sturma, *Kant*, p. 118, from J. G. Fichte, *Gesamtausgabe der Bayerischen Akademie der Wissenschaften*, ed. R. Lauth, H. Jacobs, and H. Gliwitzky (Stuttgart: Frommann-Holzboog, 1964–5), IV, 2, 30.

32 Although Henrich emphasizes the influence of this "Reflection Theory," he of course means to criticize rather than endorse it. But some analytic philosophers still seem sympathetic to such a theory, e.g., D. Dennett, "Toward a Cognitive Theory of Consciousness," in *Perception and Cognition: Issues in the Foundations of Psychology, Minnesota Studies in the Philosophy of Science* 9 (1978); cf. D. Rosenthal, "Two Concepts of Consciousness," *Philosophical Studies* 94 (1991): 329–59. By trying to reduce consciousness to reflection, this approach gains a handy operational tool at the cost of losing the basic phenomenon at issue.

33 Cf. Sturma's helpful distinction between "logical" and "descriptive" elements of an explication of self-consciousness (*Kant*, p. 119).

34 Cf. ibid., p. 25, who points out the problems in restricting self-consciousness either to such "rationalist" self-as-pure-object episodes or to mere "Humean" reflective episodes (mere consciousness of consciousness).

"one's own" if it *could not* be connected with other similar states that can be (even if they need not actually be) reflectively, that is, "transcendentally," represented. However, even *without insisting* on SAT – that is, without assuming that *all* such "I think" states must be "really" accessible – I believe we could fall back on the mere idea of "self-familiarity" that Henrich introduces as if it were a corrective to Kant and that Sturma develops as just an explication of Kant.[35] Either way, one can give a sense to regarding a simple "I think that *x*" (e.g., "I think that it is warm")[36] state as something that in one sense is *already* a kind of self-consciousness – since it directly expresses a thinking self's activity – even if it is precisely not a reflection upon a distinct "object-self."

C. 2. Neuhouser's Account

A related but distinct line of thought can be found in Neuhouser's impressive reconstruction of Fichte's discussion of apperception. Like Henrich, Neuhouser attempts to isolate a nonpractical sense in which, for at least a while, Fichte takes the representation of the I and its "self-positing" to be "absolute." Neuhouser, however, goes far beyond what I have called the "valid kernel" of Fichte's discussion, and focuses on passages where Fichte says, "The I exists only insofar as it is conscious of itself."[37] This surely appears to say more than that the representation of the self is not derivable from other representations, or that it involves some grasp of this nonderivability. It rather appears to be an *ontological* claim, a claim that the I and self-consciousness are necessarily coexistent. If this is not taken as a mere stipulation, it is a controversial claim, one that does not follow directly even from SAT. SAT, after all, is a claim about how

35 Ibid., p. 10. A similar point is often made by M. Frank; see e.g., "Is Subjectivity a Non-Thing, an Absurdity [*Unding*]? On some Difficulties in Naturalistic Reductions of Self-Consciousness," in *The Modern Subject*, ed. Karl Ameriks and Dieter Sturma (Albany: State University of New York, 1995), pp. 177–98.
36 Cf. what Gerold Prauss in *Erscheinung bei Kant* (Berlin: de Gruyter, 1971) calls *Erscheinungsurteile*, e.g., "it appears to me that it is warm." However, contrary to what Roderick Chisholm (an editor, not coincidentally, of an English version of Fichte's *Vocation of Man*) has suggested, I believe we should not transform "I think *x* is red" into "I think I am appeared to redly." Rather, "I am under the impression of being appeared to redly" is enough; a second level "I" should not be introduced here. See my "Recent Work on Kant's Theoretical Philosophy," and "Contemporary German Epistemology," *Inquiry* 25 (1982): 125–38.
37 Neuhouser, *Fichte's Theory*, p. 46, cited from Fichte, *Sämtliche Werke* I, p. 97. In Neuhouser's own words, "The I is 'self-grounded' in the sense that its act of intuition constitutes its being."

one kind of awareness involves another kind; it does not entail that an I could not exist when there is not the first kind of awareness.[38]

Neuhouser himself concedes that if Fichte did at first intend the doctrine of self-positing to express an ontological thesis about the theoretical subject, he also appears to have backed off from this kind of argument to emphasize practical or broadly moral senses in which the subject is self-positing.[39] However, Neuhouser argues that there are many ambiguities and shifts in Fichte's early work, and that in the late 1790s Fichte was at times still stressing distinctive features of *theoretical* subjectivity. Neuhouser isolates three strong senses in which this subject is said by Fichte (during this period) to be self-positing. The first kind of self-positing involves the subject's "*non-representational* self-awareness," the second concerns its self-positing as a "*transcendental* condition," and the third has to do with the subject's "*self-constituting* existence." What remains to be determined is whether any of these three notions involves a valid sense of self-positing that points to a crucial supplement of or corrective to Kant's account of apperception.

Neuhouser expresses the first, "non-representational," Fichtean sense of self-positing in the claim that "the subject is *at all times* present within consciousness but . . . its mode of being *present to* itself is fundamentally different from the way it is conscious of objects."[40] I read this claim as insisting on a "constancy" or "ubiquity" of self-presentation that is inherently controversial, that is contrary to Kant's suggestion that we could exist during states that are "nothing to" us, and that is not even necessary for SAT. The constancy claim is an ontological leap beyond the thesis of self-familiarity. It is a claim not merely about *how* we are self-aware; it is already a claim that we cannot exist except when self-aware in a certain way.

This claim might seem more plausible when it is kept in mind that the self-awareness Fichte discusses is meant as a concomitant of straightforward consciousness, and precisely not as a matter of explicit, reflective

---

38 One explanation of this controversial claim would be that Fichte and Neuhouser (to the extent that he is sympathetic to Fichte) have simply forgotten or rejected Kant's notion of nonapperceived (i.e., not even merely empirically apperceived) representations, which one could have even if they are "nothing to" one. Neuhouser cites the relevant passage from Kant (B 132), but without noting the import I have been stressing (*Fichte's Theory*, p. 97).

39 Neuhouser, *Fichte's Theory*, p. 52. See above, Chapters 3–4 and below at n. 54 for my proposal that Fichte's idea here is best understood in terms that are ultimately moral.

40 Neuhouser, *Fichte's Theory*, p. 69 (my emphases).

KANT, FICHTE, AND APPERCEPTION

self-consciousness.[41] It would be absurd to contend that we must always be in the latter kind of state, and this is something Fichte himself wants to emphasize. Fichte expresses his view most directly when he says:

> a consciousness of the wall is possible only in so far as you are conscious of your thinking [NB, not merely "conscious of the wall"] . . . But if it is claimed that in this self-consciousness I am an object to myself, then . . . it [the subject] too becomes an object, and requires a new subject, and so on ad infinitum . . . consciousness cannot be accounted for in this manner.[42]

The unobjectionable aspect of this passage is its reminder of the difficulties noted earlier with the theories that accept the Reflection Theory in attempting to account for "first-level" self-awareness simply by means of objective reflection. The objectionable aspect is that (because of its insistence that you are "conscious 'of'- and not merely 'in' – your thinking") the passage can be used (as in Neuhouser's discussion) to back a claim that there is "a self-awareness that is involved in *every* representational state."[43] Despite all efforts to resist talk of constant explicit or "objective" self-consciousness, Fichte and Neuhouser still insist at times on what seems to be a kind of constant self-awareness that is unnecessarily complex and reflexive; an awareness that is "present to itself." This goes beyond both the doctrine of self-familiarity (as interpreted by Sturma and myself) and SAT to assert some kind of actual (simultaneous) dual awareness. Although sometimes their point appears to be merely that the I is a "component" of all consciousness (and even this is controversial, on common broad construals of "consciousness"), at other times the I is said to be a perpetual theme: "every consciousness of an object x involves . . . an outward, object directed consciousness (a consciousness of x), and an inward, self-referential awareness (a consciousness that I am conscious of x)."[44] Note that this claim is stronger than an expression of SAT, for it is

41 It can be argued that something like this view can be found in Reinhold's theory of consciousness; and in fact Schulze argued against Reinhold's theory that it in effect had much the same flaws as the Reflection Theory (cf. Neuhouser, *Fichte's Theory*, pp. 71–2). This may be another instance where Kant has been faulted, in the twentieth as well as the eighteenth century, by those who mistakenly assimilate his philosophy to Reinhold's. Cf. above Chapter 3.

42 Fichte, *Sämtliche Werke* I, 526–7, *Gesamtausgabe* IV, 2, 30; cited at Neuhouser, *Fichte's Theory*, p. 73.

43 Neuhouser, *Fichte's Theory*, pp. 73–4 (my emphasis). Neuhouser explicitly contends that Fichte is concerned with more than a relation to a merely possible consciousness.

44 Neuhouser, *Fichte's Theory*, p. 79–80; cf. above at n. 40, and Neuhouser's talk of "ever-present" awareness that one is conscious. A similar tendency is found occasionally in

speaking of an *actual* consciousness of consciousness, not merely of a "real potential." The claim of such an actual consciousness seems unnecessary and inaccurate, and it encourages an absurd regress. Yet the claim is made repeatedly; for example: "When I say that I represent something, this is *equivalent* to the following: 'I am aware that I have a representation of this object.'"[45] But surely, absurdities result if "equivalent" is taken literally here; one needs only to begin to make the called-for substitutions.

Again, there is an abundance of ironies, for not only does this position appear to take us back into a kind of complexity from which the attack on the Reflection Theory was meant to liberate us, but it also seems that the way out of this complexity is ready at hand in Neuhouser's own stress on the idea that we have "easy and immediate access" to our own awarenesses.[46] This access can be explained simply by the structure of those awarenesses; since they are awarenesses of the form "I think that *x*," no wonder they can be and will be called up that way upon reflection. But this does not mean that they always must be *already* of the form "I think that I think that *x*."

Unfortunately, this "constant" form is affirmed on the Fichtean analysis. But how could staunch opponents of the Reflection Theory, of all people, make such an odd affirmation? The Fichteans defend themselves by emphasizing two ideas: first, the initial "think" – in "I think that I think that *x*" – is "non-discursive," and second, the theme of this thinking is not an "object" but an "activity." The claim is that there is an "ever present" "intellectual intuition," whereby I know something (namely, *that* "I think that *x*") "because I do it,"[47] and what I know is not a thing but something else, my activity.[48] But the former idea – that doing is knowing – is myste-

---

Pippin's work; cf. my analysis in "Recent Work on Hegel: The Rehabilitation of an Epistemologist?" *Philosophy and Phenomenological Research* 52 (1992): 196.

45 Cited at Neuhouser, *Fichte's Theory*, p. 77.

46 Ibid., p. 82; cf. p. 88.

47 Ibid., p. 83.

48 Cf. Sturma's point (*Kant*, p. 117) that instead of taking self-familiarity, as Fichte does, as *both* intuitive (immediate) and conceptual (cognitive), we would be better to take it as "neither/nor." My way of putting it would be to say that, as general or transcendental, this special self-familiarity is not entirely immediate (it needs something, anything, through which we are familiar to ourselves), but, as particular or empirical, it is still not a cognition of a particular empirical situation. This is consistent with Sturma's talk of the self as a "quasi-object" or Kant's own talk of our special familiarity with the self as involving both a "pure representation" and an "indeterminate empirical representation." See my "From Kant to Frank: The Ineliminable Subject," in *The Modern Subject*, pp. 217–30; and cf. Robert Hanna, "How Do We Know Necessary Truths? Kant's Answer," *European Journal of Philosophy* 6 (1998): 126.

rious, since doing by itself is not tantamount to theoretical knowing (only the latter can be epistemically evaluated; and Fichte himself argues that even an impression of action is not a theoretical proof that one is really acting), and the latter idea – that what is known is an activity – is irrelevant, since this does not show that the items known (and hence "true") are not correlates of that-clauses, states of affairs rather than mere things or activities.

So much for the first ("non-representational") sense in which Neuhouser elaborates Fichte's notion of the I as "self-positing." The second sense concerns the idea of self-positing as a "transcendental condition of consciousness," that is, of empirical knowledge. Neuhouser discusses several Fichtean texts that develop a line of argument close to what was earlier called the Cartesian Claim, namely that a special sort of (actual and not just potential) self-awareness is present a priori and required to make sense of the subject's knowledge of its identity over time, which in turn is supposedly necessary for its knowledge of external objects. Neuhouser does an excellent job of retracing Fichte's thoughts along this line, but then he concedes, quite properly, that this line "can be shown to rest on a serious misconception of the [transcendental] deduction's strategy."[49] The misconception involves failing to see that for Kant the *transcendental* role of the "I think" in the deduction has to do with its being the correlate of representations that are related to it as objective and category-governed – and not with any direct relation between a constant intellectual intuition and individual representations.

Neuhouser is right in arguing that although Kant speaks of representations that must be able to be taken as "my own," Kant does not mean to account for them in Fichte's way. However, Neuhouser goes a bit too far in explaining the difference this way: "What makes this condition possible for Kant [that representations count as mine] is not an original awareness of each of them as my own, but the joining together of these representations in accord with the categories."[50] Here, unfortunately, Neuhouser could be taken to be implying that Kant is proposing sufficient rather than necessary conditions for the warranted ascription of states to a particular subject. But if Kant were proposing such sufficient conditions, he would after all be offering what is really a non-Kantian theory of consciousness's origin, a theory that is subject to the objections to the Reflection Theory. Fortunately, we need not ascribe this strange view to Kant,

49 Neuhouser, *Fichte's Theory,* p. 98.
50 Ibid., p. 99.

and yet we can still accept Neuhouser's own conclusion that the "transcendental" role that Fichte may envision for his doctrine of a "self-
positing" theoretical subject does nothing to force a revision of Kant's
doctrine of apperception.

Fichte's third sense of self-positing concerns the subject as "self-
constituting existence." The main idea is that if the I is thought of not as a
thing that acts or has a power to act, but simply as the activity of self-
positing itself, then one need not postulate a "pre-existing noumenal
ground" for one's states of consciousness.[51] As in other issues, one can
understand the motivation for this Fichtean point as a response to obscurities in the metaphysics of quasi-Kantians such as Reinhold, the invocation of literally unthinkable things in themselves.[52] But the basic issue
can be discussed independently of any invocation of "noumenal
grounds." The issue is whether it is true that "what does not exist for itself
is not an I,"[53] and that this I cannot have any kind of ground outside itself.

Both claims are mysterious and appear to conflate epistemic and metaphysical issues. This seems especially clear for the second claim, that the
self can have no ground outside it. It may be true that the conception of
any ground that the self actually invokes to explain itself must be part of
the self's epistemic state; but this hardly means that such a ground, any

51 Ibid., p. 109–10.
52 This, however, is definitely not to go so far as Neuhouser does in claiming (*Fichte's Theory*,
     pp. 104–5) that the notion of a noumenal cause is incoherent. Cf. above Chapters 2 and 3.
     Nor can I follow Martin's similar acceptance of Fichte's idea that it would be incoherent for
     things in themselves to "possess properties" at all because "Kant insists that the schema of
     thing and property (of substance and accident) is part of the framework of human under-
     standing" (*Idealism and Objectivity*, p. 62). This would make nonsense of all of Kant's mere
     discussion of such matters as the arguments of rational theology. What Kant holds to be
     limited specifically to "human understanding" is not at all a so-called schema of thing and
     property but rather only the *temporal schematization* of the pure categories of substance and
     accident in the form of the Analogies. A similar point is made clearly in Zöller, *Fichte's
     Transcendental Philosophy*, pp. 13–14.
53 Fichte, *Sämtliche Werke*, I, 97, cited at Neuhouser, *Fichte's Theory*, p. 111. Cf. Neuhouser's
     formulation, *Fichte's Theory*, p. 116: "The I is essentially a self-referring activity that, only in
     referring to itself, is constituted as an existent." Similarly, Wayne Martin points out that for
     the purposes of Fichte's theory of objectivity, a thesis about constant self-awareness is not
     needed (*Idealism and Objectivity*, p. 155, n. 27), but at another point he seems to equate the
     I with the activity of "immediate self-identification," so that, in the case of the I, "being and
     self-positing are essentially co-extensive" (ibid., p. 98) – which makes one wonder if this
     means that we go out of existence altogether in the moments in between ordinary explicit
     self-identification. Martin does speak not only about "states" of self-positing but also about
     a mere "capacity," but, as with Kant's SAT, one can wonder what underlies the certainty of
     even the fallback claim about a constant real capacity here.

more than the correlate of any other conception we have, could not exist on its own and have an effect upon us. The first claim involves the old issue of whether the self and its self-awareness are necessarily coextensive. Obviously, a being with no representations at all would hardly deserve the title of a subject or self, but Fichte's claim must be more than that, it must be the claim that there is *no state* of a self that does not actually involve self-awareness. This claim could be affirmed as a matter of definition, but that would rob it of significance. The motivation behind the claim appears to be to counter the idea that a self involves a cluster of very different properties, such that in some sense the self could persist as long as just some of those properties remained – that is, even in the absence of self-awareness, for example, in deep sleep.

There may well be something important about why this idea strikes us as odd. Perhaps a "nutritive" or "vegetative" being without any thought has been called a soul or self by some, but we can see that this is a strained idea. Similarly, it is not clear that there is a self even with a being that has many representations but *none* at all that are "something to" the being. But it would certainly would seem that there could be a self, even an ordinary human self, that persists even through *some* intervals of states that are "nothing to it." Moreover, it must be kept in mind that (as was re-marked above at n. 45) the kind of self-awareness which the Fichtean affirms as constantly necessary is even stronger than mere empirical ap-perception or the mere "real potential" central to SAT. And for just this reason the *Fichtean* version of the self-positing thesis is especially question-able, for it is all too easy to imagine that even if all our states are states that are "something to us," this need not involve the kind of "dual awareness" that the Fichtean insists upon. Hence a self-constitution theory of the subject becomes plausible only to the extent that one *retreats* from what is distinctive about the Fichtean doctrine of apperception. That is, the more reflexive one makes the kind of awareness that is claimed to be distinctive of us, the less ground there is for insisting that we could not exist for a moment without such complexity.[54] And this is to say that the distinctively Fichtean aspects of self-positing that Neuhouser distinguishes still do not point to a convincing need to revise Kant's own account of apperception.

---

54 It is in large part out of an attempt to find a more charitable interpretation of Fichte on this point that I have proposed (see above Chapter 3, n. 31) that his idea that the self can only exist "for itself" is best construed as a doctrine about the *moral* self, since it does imme-diately seem odd to think of a self that is subject to moral claims that it does not at all understand as presented "for" or to itself.

D. SIMILAR PROBLEMS IN OTHER CURRENT
ACCOUNTS OF APPERCEPTION

D. 1. Kitcher's Account

If one turns to the mainline American tradition, and in particular to Patricia Kitcher's well-known *Kant's Transcendental Psychology* (hereafter *PK*), one finds an interpretation that appreciates many of these points insofar as it approaches Kant's notion of apperception in a way that does not overemphasize features of self-awareness. Instead, Kitcher proposes that Kantian self-consciousness be understood primarily in terms of a "system" of mental states that process and combine information. While this approach avoids difficulties in views that, in a Fichtean manner, try to build too much onto SAT, there remain exegetic and intrinsic problems with Kitcher's positive account of apperception, problems that stem from still claiming too quickly to be able to defeat Humean skepticism.

Kitcher's main concern is with aspects of apperception that do not bear directly on the nature of the self. On her account, apperception is to be understood as a very general cognitive task of synthesizing data for knowledge, a task that involves various connections that go beyond the mere associative relations of what is derived from sensation. Kant's "transcendental psychology" is taken to be an account of the specific kinds of cognitive capacities that these connections require, for example, forms of intuition and schematization (*PK*, p. 209). Kitcher recognizes that the emphasis (within Kant's transcendental deduction) on the unity of apperception can sometimes make it appear as if Kant is concerned originally with the self as such and is arguing from conditions for knowledge of one's self to structures of the world at large. But, as her analysis of the B deduction shows, Kant's argument is rather that "synthetic connection and so the categories are crucial for the entire range of our cognitive capacities and not just for our ability to ascribe states to ourselves. Moreover, the categories and synthetic connection are not sufficient for self-ascription" (*PK*, p. 127; cf. pp. 92–4).[55]

---

55 This point goes beyond Neuhouser's interpretation, cited above at n. 50. As C. T. Powell (*Kant's Theory*, pp. 39–45) has noted, J. L. Mackie and Leslie Stevenson have made similar points by arguing that there could be subjects capable of experience but not self-ascription. I see these interpreters as mistaken only in presuming that a Kantian could not accept their point, and I find Powell's reply, his insistence on the necessity of the capacity for self-ascription, to be unpersuasive and unneeded. Powell's main claim, that the very notion of

Although the main argument of the deduction, according to Kitcher, thus does not concern the self specifically (but rather the general application of the categories to our empirical domain), the notion of apperception that is central to that argument can still be examined for its implications about the self. In particular, Kitcher proposes that Kant uses the phenomenon of apperception to establish a real unity of self, one that defeats Hume's skepticism while at the same time not going so far as to make the mistake of claiming to know a "metaphysical" subject. Transcendental psychology provides a set of positive descriptions of a "thinking, or better, knowing, self" (*PK*, p. 22), a self that Kitcher insists is nothing more than the phenomenal self, even though the method she says one must use in learning how to describe it is philosophical and not straightforwardly empirical. The method proceeds by determining what is needed for our epistemic tasks given certain "facts" about our mode of cognition, for example, that one aspect of it (sensibility) is characterized by receptivity rather than spontaneity. Since these "facts" are so general, they can be said to underlie experience rather than to be found "in" it, and because the determination of what they involve gives us "general specifications for a mind capable of performing various cognitive tasks," the knowledge that is generated can be called philosophical even if it "has striking affinities with empirical psychology" (*PK*, p. 26).

One advantage of Kitcher's discussion is that she stresses throughout that Kant's direct concern is not with "experience" in any loose and primitive sense, but specifically with "cognitive" experience, that is, representation that can be "something to" somebody and involves representing objects and making judgments (*PK*, pp. 134–5). Also, unlike those who insist on SAT, Kitcher sees that Kant need not assume that reflexive awareness is an "inseparable component" of what it is to perceive, remember, and so on (*PK*, p. 107). She allows that we need not be capable of direct

---

making a judgment must always bring with it not only the possibility of being mistaken, *but also* the real potential for regarding the experience as one's own, is very close to SAT, and has the same problems as that thesis. In other words, a "theoretical wanton" might not be rational, in a full-blooded sense, but might still exist. For similar reasons, I am skeptical of Martin's attempt (*Idealism and Objectivity*, p. 134) to develop a Fichtean argument that all consciousness of objects by itself requires some kind of "striving," some kind of practical frustration and satisfaction of norms. Objectivity may require judgment and the norms of truth and falsehood, but it is not immediately clear that norms of "activity" are required. This is not to deny the point that Kant and interpreters such as Pippin stress, that once we engage specifically in the higher activities of reason, more complex and broadly practical norms of reflective judgment are needed.

reflection on *each one* of our own mental states, although she adds – and here she still may be going too far – that they all need to be indirectly "connectable" to our actual present consciousness by some string of thoughts (*PK*, pp. 103, 113, 118–19; at *PK*, pp. 119, 134, and 138, she claims that each conscious state must have an epistemic impact on others; and at *PK*, p. 136, she recommends determining the "size" of the self by what it has access to at any moment). In any case, by stressing that Kant does allow for some precognitive states, or layers of such states within cognitive consciousness, Kitcher also has room for the possibility that the self is more than its cognitive states and that there may be a point in attaching a state to a real subject when it is only a state of obscurely desiring, moving, or dreaming, that is, even at a time when no conscious cognition is going on. (She allows "non-representative sensations," *PK*, pp. 68, 114; cf. also pp. 136–8 on parts of one's life that may fail to leave "traces.") Nonetheless, even if the self extends beyond its higher mental states, the question remains of what specifically constitutes this mental unity of a real subject. That is, one can ask not only "objective" questions about what the general structures of cognizable objects must be (or what must be the specific structures of bodies, in order for mental states to be ascribed to them in a way that others can accept) but also "subjective" questions about what general structure or capacities we must have in order to be able to know such objects.

The main subjective issue that concerns Kitcher here is the need to prove, against Hume's "inner" skepticism, that the mind does have a real unity. She contends that Kant's notion of apperception provides the necessary proof: since a state of apperception is a complex unified representation, one that involves other prior representations, the resultant unity of apperception testifies to an "existential dependence" of our mental states. She concludes that since there must be such a necessary real relation presumed in any cognitive representation (i.e., any representation with a content about putative objects), there is a non-question-begging argument that shows that the self is itself a real unity, contrary to all that the Humean is allowed to say on his own principles.

Here are some objections to this intriguing argument. One objection is that the Humean already has all that Kitcher claims, since on one version of Hume's own account association is itself a causal process involving real relations between states of mind. One response Kitcher has to this gambit is to translate Hume's text (*PK*, p. 250, n. 35; cf. Hume's famous phrase "if the first object had not been, the second never had existed") into a weaker claim that says only that various sequences of mental states have occurred in constant conjunction. But whether or not Hume should be taken to mean only the weaker claim, one can still object that it is not clear exactly what kind of stronger claim can be warranted by the phenomenon of apperception as opposed to association. Certainly, association itself, like apperception, could be (and usually is) understood as involving a real dependence of mental states. Thus it can be argued that I would not be able associatively to imagine a pink object if I had not actually seen something like it, say a pale red one; and, similarly, one could say, as Kitcher would want to, that I could not have the apperception "I think that the cat is on the mat" without having had actual past "cat" and "mat" thoughts. But then whatever one thinks are the substantive claims about the mind that follow from apperception, it could be contended that just as much follows already from association.

On the other hand, one could also contend, skeptically, that at any moment I need not have prior and separately existing "cat" and "mat" thoughts; I could just perceive or project all these thoughts at the same time (a similar argument, incidentally, could be used to challenge SAT). It is true that Kant speaks of the synthesis of apperception as drawing upon given "prior" thoughts, but a skeptic could contend that the actual existence of such past thoughts is not necessary. After all, that past existence is not even clearly relevant, for suppose one rather had at this moment a thought that was not exactly the same as the prior one, but rather something quite close to it that just happened to "fly into one's head." There is no reason to think that this must impugn the content of the particular apperceptive thought. On Kitcher's own account, what really counts is the *content* of the states that are combined in apperception (cf. *PK*, p. 103), so it is not clear that where the content comes from really should matter. Kitcher speaks of the need for a judgment to be "generated" from particular intuitions (*PK*, p. 110), but there is no proof that this could not be a logical construction rather than a process of temporally separated states. After all, even if there is a complex causal background to a present thought, one needs a complex present thought in any case.

One could even allow that a present thought has some relation to a past idea, as in Kant's own example of the analogy of the mind with a series of elastic balls that transmit properties over time without ever forming a real unity. Kant's point is precisely that there could be "a series of substances of which the first transmits its state together with its consciousness to the second . . . and yet it would not have been the same person in all these states."⁵⁶ So for Kant himself a "real unity" of mind over time does not turn out to be entailed by just any individual apperceptive act as such. And for any state of mind that is claimed to require a real connection of distinct temporal states, it should be possible to substitute one very complex present state, one that need not be really connected with anything outside it; the content should be all the same. (I bracket "twin earth" and "swampman" problems in order to avoid anachronisms here.) Of course, one could counter that this is to make too much of skeptical hypotheses that neither Kant nor we really take seriously. But unfortunately for Kitcher's argument, this would be a fair response for any context except the present one, where the claim is nothing other than to be able to present an argument with premises that even a skeptic would have to accept. It is true that if one were facing a skeptic who presumes that all a mind could contain at any moment were absolutely isolated *and simple* ideas (cf. *PK*, p. 115), then the "fact" of apperception would be hard to account for – but that peculiar atomistic presumption does not have to be endorsed in the skepticism that is relevant here.

In sum, if the mind does require a real unity, apperception alone, as Kitcher understands it, does not seem sufficient to establish this. It is significant that a key passage at A 121 that she cites (*PK*, p. 79) stresses that our cognitive representations require something more than association not because otherwise they would be wholly without content, but because they would give us mere "accidental heaps." Kant's reply to Hume thus appears to turn on an appeal to a necessity and not to a mere unity. (At *PK*, p. 102, Kitcher cites A 107, which makes a similar claim, and she notes the distinction between establishing actual connections and necessary ones, but she does not note the implications of the possibility that Kant's notion of apperception is tied to claims of necessity.) Kitcher knows that Kant makes this extra claim, but she plays it down because she is so suspicious of it. She may be right that the claim has problems, but without it, Kitcher has a much harder time of trying to show what it is specifically about transcendental apperception that yields special knowledge about the self that the Humean cannot have.

Another response Kitcher might take would be to claim that all along the "real unity" of mind that she finds proven by the phenomenon of apperception is something that she, as a Kantian, precisely does not want

---

56 Kant, *Critique or Pure Reason*, A 364n. Note that this passage does suggest Kant is thinking in terms of sameness of person as requiring at least sameness of substance.

to be understood as the identity of an enduring thing, rather than as merely a continuity of a certain kind of causal process. The arguments of the Paralogisms might be understood in this light as meant to liberate us from thinking of the self as a mysterious substratum or noumenal substance. But even if one does not want to get involved with such mysterious thoughts, there are intrinsic and textual difficulties (as C. T. Powell has argued)[57] in letting the self that exercises apperception become, in Kitcher's own provocative words, "no more than contentually interconnected systems of cognitive states" (PK, p. 122).

A natural way to try to save the self as such would be to bring it in as what Kitcher calls the "combiner," a self actually generating the system of thoughts. However, unlike interpreters such as Prauss, Allison, and Pippin, Kitcher resists appealing to a spontaneous "combiner" self as the ground of apperception. This resistance is understandable if one wants to focus on skepticism, but I find unclear Kitcher's reason for dismissing such an absolute claim as not even "coherent" (PK, p. 122). She contends, "acts or processes of synthesis could not be performed by agents. They are unconscious activities" (PK, p. 122; I have not been able to follow her other claim, that making the self the "combiner" would involve an absurd appeal to "faculty identity"). This seems unclear because, even if there are various kinds of "unconscious" syntheses, apperception, the paradigmatic combining synthesis, surely can be and is conscious. Of course, it may be that the *absolute spontaneity* of the combining act of the agent of apperception is not determinable by consciousness alone. I have argued that such an appeal is controversial for reasons that Kant himself stressed,[58] but that is another issue. Problems about the scope of our freedom or consciousness need not affect the common and Kantian belief that the self is more than a mere system.

Another advantage that is alleged to arise from not appealing to an underlying self is that the supposedly obscure metaphysical notion of a "perfect bond" (i.e., a substantial one) between one's states could be replaced by an explanatory appeal to mere "synthetic connections" of states (PK, p. 125). But this appeal simply does not guarantee a true "unity" of self, since then there is nothing to prevent many states from belonging to various selves; "synthetic connections" can be organized in all sorts of ways. Kitcher thus appears to be inviting a Parfitian conclusion that persons should not be thought of in terms of strict identity. However,

---

57 Powell, *Kant's Theory*, p. 18.
58 See above Chapter 1, and my "Kant and Hegel on Freedom: On Two New Interpretations," *Inquiry* 35 (1992): 219–35.

she surprisingly resists Parfit's contention that there is "no fact of the matter about personal identity," and she counters that "synthetic connection is a deep fact about mental life; it underlies mental capacities that enable us to be persons" (*PK*, p. 133). This move seems to be a flight from the original question of what is required for the unity of a particular person, and amounts to a shift to the very different question of what kind of capacities cognizers in general need. This may be, as she says, an important "preliminary" question, but it does not resolve the original issue at all, and for that issue a real enduring self, a substance, can still be the natural solution.

D. 2. Powell's Account

Recent work on these topics has continued to develop exponentially, but not necessarily by resolving fundamental difficulties. To illustrate briefly how persistent the old problems remain, I will conclude with an observation on C. T. Powell's *Kant's Theory of Self-Consciousness,* a helpful study that typifies current analytic approaches to Kant that are closer to Strawson's general epistemological concerns than to the specific problems of cognitive science. The remarkable fact is that although Powell criticizes Kitcher's belief that she has found an argument to defeat Hume, Powell continues to believe that we can get a result from Kant that, although weaker than Kitcher's conclusion, still does defeat Hume's questions about the unity of consciousness. The claimed result is that although apperception does not prove strict identity of a self "throughout" a number of mental states, nor even that there certainly are real connections between distinct states over time, still we must "consider" these states to be connected.[59] Thus, experience must supposedly be thought of "as if" it is in a single consciousness (note the parallel to current interpretations that claim it is enough if we must act "as if" we are free),[60] and to this extent Powell believes Hume is defeated. Powell, like Kitcher, concedes that the main argument of Kant's transcendental deduction could be written without reference to apperception (which Powell understands in terms of the Strawsonian idea of finding conditions of "self-ascription" that require "objectivity"). He points out that the deduction could rather be understood as going simply from the conceptualizability of experience to its objectivity (because the former involves corrigibility, hence the possibility of a mistake, hence the idea of something distinct to be mistaken about).

59 Powell, *Kant's Theory*, p. 18.
60 Ibid., p. 56. Cf. above Chapter 1, sec. D.

Nonetheless, Powell insists that the discussion of apperception has this value: it shows us, contra Hume, that experience must be "systematic" and "represented *as* of" one subject.[61]

It remains unclear to me why it is claimed that experience "must" be like this, even if in fact it usually is. As was pointed out above in disputing SAT, it could be supposed that there are awarenesses that do not really connect with others "systematically," or that for some reason cannot actually come to our reflection as "of" one subject (even though *once* they enter reflection, they appear this way). Even if it were true that whenever we do represent our experience we regard it as being of "a" subject, the Humean could still contend that this is merely an understandable fiction. So although Powell goes a step further than Kitcher, backing off from literal "real connection" claims to psychological claims such as "we cannot but think in terms of a deep unity," the skeptic still seems unrebutted. This need not be a severe problem in itself, but it is a problem for those who claim to have a philosophical refutation of Hume.

D. 3. Apperception and the Self

I will end by remarking on a common and long-standing exegetical problem concerning Kantian apperception. Kitcher argues that since apperception is a phenomenal aspect of the self, it can be nothing more than that, that is, it *could not* be the sign of an absolutely free and, say, nonspatiotemporal side of the self (*PK*, p. 140). The problem here is the strong claim that we can understand apperception "only" (*PK*, p. 140) as phenomenal. This common contemporary view can be seen as a repetition of Fichte's hasty rejection of things in themselves as totally senseless. As a response to the Critical philosophy, this simply begs the question by ruling out from the beginning Kant's great confidence that investigations of space and time show that we have to affirm theoretically that there is something more to what underlies experience (and hence apperception) than what is phenomenal – and that investigations of morality oblige us to believe that this "something more" includes a self.[62] The major current interpretations of Kant on the self ignore this point and continue to rush to old and questionable extremes – on the one hand, to overly bold assertions that there is a strong unity throughout experience such as the

---

61 Powell, *Kant's Theory*, p. 62. I pass over other objections I have to Powell's approach to the deduction.

62 For more details on Kant's view here and its relation to contemporary theories of mind, see my "Kant and Mind: Mere Immaterialism."

Cartesian Claim asserts, and that this points to a kind of self-consciousness that is pivotal to the whole deduction; or, on the other hand, to overly bold denials of any possible underlying substantial unity of self, a unity that may at least cohere with, if not point to, the metaphysical nature of the self that Kant believed was essential for his whole Critical system, and especially the metaphysical preconditions of its crucial practical component. Despite all the focus in current schools of interpretation on the "functional" character of reflection and apperception, Kant himself is clear enough that he does, after all, also want to say something nonfunctional about what the "nature" or the stuff of the self is, namely that it definitely is not material, because it, like everything else, cannot be spatiotemporal in its ultimate essence. In his view it does not constitute itself through reflection or synthesis, but rather, like everything else, simply exists as the (not further theoretically determinable by us) nonmaterial thing in itself that it is, no matter how we characterize it for empirical theoretical purposes. Nothing in this relatively modest Kantian view is vulnerable to any of the problems in the stable of now well-flogged horses such as the Cartesian Claim, the Reflection Theory, or the dogmatic assertion of an intuition of spiritual beings.

PART IV

HEGEL

6

HEGEL'S CRITIQUE OF KANT'S
THEORETICAL PHILOSOPHY

Pre-Hegelian Prologue

Given the preceding investigations, the inevitable next question is: How did German philosophy proceed right after Fichte's innovations? For the most part, I have compared Fichte not with his immediate successors but with interpreters and like-minded philosophers of our own time. This was a response to the fact that the general philosophical orientation that Fichte took over from Reinhold has recently enjoyed a very significant growth in popularity. Even philosophers who have a fairly casual understanding of Kant are still tempted, for example, by the notion of making idealism more attractive by using something like the "short argument" that Reinhold introduced and that Fichte took over in his own way (see above Chapter 3). Similarly, there has been a tendency to follow Reinhold and Fichte's move of making the notion of apperception absolutely central, and of emphasizing aspects of it that have little to do directly with Kant's own understanding of apperception – which is dependent on the notion of specific forms of judgment and the capacity to provide what are first of all general principles for objects of experience rather than specific insights into self-consciousness or our absolute freedom (see above Chapter 5). Both of these moves radicalize the notion of autonomy by suggesting a philosphical program that uses the bare notion of human thought as such as a sufficient foundation for determining the basic structures of all meaningful reality. Metaphysically, this post-Kantian program rejects the restricted idealism of Kant's own system, which (unlike idealisms gained by a global "short argument") is limited to a thesis about *our* specific kind of theoretical knowledge – and thus to determinations that are dependent upon our underivable intuitions of space and time and that do not provide us with reality "in itself." Epistemologically, this post-Kantian program also departs from the non-Cartesian pattern of Kant's deductions, which begin not with private representations but instead with common judgments (see above Chapter 1). In sum, post-Kantian theoretical philosophy takes a radically self-oriented turn, and in its "strong," "imperialistic," and "humanistic" foundationalism (see above Introduction), it makes the realm of immediate human self-determination nothing less than the absolute measure of all being and the sufficient ground of all knowing.

This movement toward radical autonomy gathers momentum in the practical philosophy and metaphilosophy of the very first post-Kantians. Whereas Reinhold gives primacy to concrete practical ends but initially leaves some kind of room for components of Kant's transcendent metaphysics (as required by a literal reading of the postulates), Fichte's commitment to the radical primacy of practical reason makes a clean break away from any neutral mode of knowing that would be a precondition for our absolute sense of pure moral commitment (see above Chapter 4). The *Vocation of Man* rests on a faith that literally everything must be thought of as an instrument for the goal of complete human self-determination.

These doctrines of Jena's very first years as a philosophical center define an impressive and influential moral vision. It has already inspired so many writers that I felt there was no need to trumpet its positive aspects any further, and so I have been drawing attention to its relatively neglected defects. In particular, I have argued that there are deep problems with this movement in both its general and its particular claims.

At the most general philosophical level, I have faulted the movement for indirectly encouraging the current swing back and forth between representationalist preoccupations and extreme pragmatist trends. These trends have not only continually tended to block a patient reexamination of the benefits of a more balanced, objective, and modest system such as Kant's, they have also helped, I suspect, to maintain the splintering of late modern philosophy into camps that do little to bridge the gap between private idealistic visions and an analytically rigorous but narrow focus on the latest scientific developments. Whether or not one is convinced by the specifics of Kant's Critical philosophy, one can regret the eclipse of his kind of "synoptic vision," his insistence that philosophy attempt to offer a balanced and systematic account of both its modern interests in liberation and its traditional interests in metaphysics.

At a more specific level, I have faulted the post-Kantians and their admirers for being too quick in bypassing, misunderstanding, or dismissing crucial steps in complicated Kantian arguments concerning transcendental idealism, transcendental apperception, and transcendental freedom. My counterattacks here have not amounted to an argument establishing the validity of Kant's own claims, or even of slightly more "modest" and modernized versions of them. For the time being, I have been aiming primarily at simply making room for more of a dialectical balance in our own era, so that the feverish interest in autonomy in the reigning liberal consensus – as well as the suspicion of this notion in other camps – does not block out the full range of options that deserve to be heard. It would be most ironic and unfortunate if dedicated advocates of the era of autonomy do not themselves make a full effort to look closely at their own roots – and such a look surely must involve a patient reconsideration of Kant on his own terms.

There are some obvious objections that remain to the way that I have developed this prolegomenon to a rehabilitation of orthodox Kantianism. One objection would be to note that, even if my analysis is granted, my bemoaning of the representational, foundational, and ultimately "one-sided" practical orientation of post-Kantianism so far does not even begin to cover all the options within this rich movement. There remain several other important figures to consider, such as Hölderlin and Schelling, and, above all, there is the towering presence of Hegel, whose system exhibits features that seem to be precisely the opposite of representationalism, foundationalism, and a radical primacy of "pure" practical reason (even if, as I indicated very briefly at the end of Chapter 3, there are ways to connect Hegel with analogs to these doctrines). This point is well taken, and is precisely why I indicated earlier that it is important to realize that there are many options worth exploring, especially among the "early Romantics" (see above Chapter 1, sec. C. 2). Insightful as the Romantic alternatives may be, however, they cannot be said to have been very *influential* so far (see above Chapter 1, sec. C. 1). The concluding part of this book is therefore devoted to an examination of Hegel, who, for better or worse, is clearly the dominant philosopher of the post-Fichtean era. My study here does not pretend to be anything like an evaluation of the full Hegelian system, or even of the most recent interpretations of it (see below Chapter 8, n. 1). I will attend simply to those most fundamental aspects of Hegel's work that amount to a *direct* challenge to the Kantian theses that I have singled out as defining the era of the philosophy of autonomy. This means that, in theoretical philosophy, it will be essential to investigate how Hegel approaches the question of the base, development, bounds, and goal of philosophy in terms of reacting to the fundamental Kantian doctrines of the transcendental deduction, transcendental idealism, and transcendental freedom (see the remainder of this chapter). In Hegel's practical philosophy there is a near-endless variety of relevant topics to explore, but here, too, I will limit my study to only a few of the most basic issues. I have chosen to structure the analysis in terms of the main points that Hegel introduces himself, that is, the objections that Kantian morality cannot account for the possibility, content, and motivation of morality. The last issue will be given the most emphasis because it appears to involve the most significant otherwise-undiscussed differences between Hegel and Kant, and it introduces an especially interesting new understanding of the central notion of autonomy. I will carry out the analysis "straight through," by focusing simply on Kant and Hegel (and some of Hegel's contemporary admirers), and then in a brief postscript (Chapter 8) I will explain how my findings on Hegel fit in with the general account that I have been offering of the era.

First, however, there is another serious objection to my approach that should be acknowledged and kept in mind for the final accounting. The objection consists in noting that even if it is not fair to demand a full vindication of Kant's own system, the fact is that most of the problems that I have stressed seem to have roots within Kant's own writings, and so it is not clear that his approach will prove to be much better than that of his successors. If post-Kantians insisted too much on a "certain" foundation, if they called for unrealistically rigorous "deductions," if they desired an excessively strong "unity" of reason, and if they hastily heaped scorn on earlier otherworldly metaphysics, they certainly could point to many passages in Kant to inspire them. Moreover, if, as I have charged, they failed to provide a convincing set of theoretical deductions, or, above all, a clear and satisfying deduction of freedom to undergird the whole idea of a system of autonomy, it cannot be denied that, in some sense, similar objections can be raised against Kant. So has it all been a matter of special pleading, or of shading in one side of the picture simply because it has been relatively neglected by others?

At this point, the issues do very much come down to a matter of the *details*. There is no point in denying the close connection in general between Kant and the post-Kantians. I have been trying precisely to emphasize this connection in order to make intelligible developments after Kant that otherwise can seem very bizarre and unmotivated. But the fact that Kant's statements and the cultural surroundings of his era could naturally lead to a more radical version of his thought cannot excuse, let alone justify, post-Kantian positions that are clearly more suspect than Kant's own views simply because they are obviously so much more extreme. It is hard enough to show the ideality, or deduce the necessity, of the propositions that Kant was arguing for, but it is obvious that the post-Kantians were *trying* to argue for much, much more, and hence they must face the consequences of the fallacies that have been pointed out. There no doubt are also flaws to be found in Kant's own less ambitious arguments, but these difficulties do not immediately cast into question the general idea of a modest reconstruction of a Kantian system that would aim to show, for example, simply that there is some sort of philosophically specifiable structure to our common experience, and that there may be specific reasons for introducing a line somewhere between what we can theoretically know in principle and what exists "in itself." This kind of system is hardly an uncontested option in current philosophy, but it still seems to have a lot more going for it even in current discussion than the forgotten details of the grandiose idealist systems, which are understandably largely ignored even by most philosophers sympathetic to their authors.

I have noted earlier (see above Chapter 1, n. 23) that one could compare this general "modest" kind of approach to Kant with the work that P. F. Strawson and others have carried out in our own era under the heading of a "metaphysics of experience," that is, a philosophical attempt to give a "descriptive" account of the basic concepts without which we *cannot* make our way cognitively, especially in perception. I have criticized, for historical and systematic reasons, those versions of this approach that remain fixed on trying to "deduce" the concept of objectivity as such. This approach usually involves trying (always vainly, as far as I can tell) to show that even someone who is initially a skeptic eventually cannot do without introducing "objectivity" if it is to be possible even to make any sense of the immediate self-ascribability of its inner awarenesses (I will not say "experiences," since, as I have repeatedly noted, this is not the proper Kantian term for this level of consciousness). Given the difficulties of this specific approach, it seems better to opt out of the game of imagining how to answer a radical skeptic, and instead ask simply what particular principles there are that seem most difficult for us to do without if we are to hold on to our claims to a public world *at all*. These principles might be close analogs of the Kantian principles of the Transcendental Analytic, or they might be rather different, and look, for example, more like Chisholm's general epistemological rules. There are two things, however, that I believe they will not be like. The first is that they cannot be simply the latest principles of our most fundamental natural sciences (cf. above Chapter 1, n. 23). This is because we are looking for necessary principles, principles that would hold for worlds where empirical knowledge can take place even if physical conditions are quite different from those in our particular world. The other thing that I strongly suspect these principles will not be is *direct* analogs of anything like the idealist systems that Schelling, Hegel, and others constructed. On this point my confidence is rooted in more contingent considerations, primarily the "test of time," the fact that fairly soon after the publication of these systems their detailed content ceased playing an active role in major philosophical discussions.

This point is consistent with allowing that there are *terms* in post-Kantian philosophy that have played an important historical role on their own and that can function as crucial catalysts for the process of the self-interpretation of our era and its history – as carried out, for example, by the interesting work of innumerable left- and right-wing Hegelians. It is also likely that these terms have had, and will continue to have, an enormously productive *heuristic* role even for "ground level" theoretical philosophy. The role of Fichtean-Hegelian terms such as "recognition," "dialectic," and "practice" may be just as "objectively" useful for the present and future of our theoretical discussions as hallowed terms such as "picture theory" and "language game." But these "metaterms" do not seem to be at quite the same level as categories. The only way for me to begin to build up confidence that they, or something like them in the Hegelian repertoire, might function on the same level as Kant's categories, as objective "necessary conditions of *all* human experience," is first to test some of Hegel's *direct* discussions of the relatively simple Kantian categories. These discussions may not be a fair indication of the full potential of the Hegelian system, but they are a natural place to start and the appropriate topic for this section, given my primary focus on the issue of the basic shape of the immediate reception of *Kant's* theory. The final concept in the list of categories discussed here turns out to be the concept of freedom, which is also the keystone of the discussion of the Hegelian reaction to Kant's practical philosophy. The concluding Postscript will return to this topic, and to the central question of how Kant's Critical philosophy in general is to be evaluated if one acknowledges, as I have, that, Kant, like his successors, does not present an entirely clear foundation for the all-important claim that human beings actually have autonomy.

A. KANT'S TRANSCENDENTAL DEDUCTION AND TRANSCENDENTAL IDEALISM

Ivan Soll has remarked that "Hegel's entire program and conception of philosophy depended upon refuting Kant's limitation of reason."[1] But while Soll discusses Hegel's attempts in this regard, he admits he has not "attempted to corroborate or criticize Hegel's interpretation of Kant."[2] Soll is not alone here, for even with the great renewal of interest in Hegel today,[3] there is room for a more critical discussion of Hegel's treatment of Kant, especially with regard to the difficult core of that treatment, namely, the rejection of the two central components of Kant's theoretical philosophy: the transcendental deduction of the categories and the doctrine of transcendental idealism.[4] After reviewing the relation between these two components in Kant's own view (in sec. A), I distinguish and evaluate Hegel's three types of objections to Kant's deduction (in secs. B–D) and his three types of objections to Kant's idealism (in secs. E–H). I argue that these objections all fail because of a closely related set of errors, errors that are understandable because they concern some of the most difficult issues in Kant's philosophy. I also contend that these errors illustrate certain general patterns of approaching transcendental philosophy that are still very influential, and hence an especially appropriate route "back to Kant" in our own time is via the reexamination of Hegel's critique of that philosophy.[5]

Hegel's treatment of Kant's transcendental deduction turns out to be so closely connected to his objections to transcendental idealism that before any assessment can be made of his specific attacks, it is necessary to

---

1 Ivan Soll, *An Introduction to Hegel's Metaphysics* (Chicago: University of Chicago Press, 1969), pp. 48–9.
2 Ibid., p. xiv.
3 See, e.g., Charles Taylor, *Hegel* (Cambridge: Cambridge University Press, 1975); Richard Bernstein, "Why Hegel Now?" *Review of Metaphysics* 31 (1977): 29–60; William Maker, "Understanding Hegel Today," *Journal of the History of Philosophy* 19 (1981): 343–75.
4 See esp. John Smith, "Hegel's Critique of Kant," *Review of Metaphysics* 26 (1973): 438–60; Ingtraud Görland, *Die Kantkritik des jungen Hegels* (Frankfurt: Klostermann, 1966); and Klaus Düsing, *Das Problem der Subjektivität in Hegels Logik* (Bonn: Bouvier, 1976), pp. 109–20.
5 In addition, I believe this evaluation is the precondition for any thorough assessment of Hegel's even more influential objections to Kant's practical philosophy, especially since, as Soll emphasizes, Hegel's conceptions of truth and freedom give a unique unity to his theoretical and practical philosophy (*Introduction*, pp. 73ff.). See below Chapter 7.

review the essentials of the general relation of Kant's deduction to his idealism.[6] The point of Kant's deduction is basically the central claim of the Transcendental Analytic of the *Critique of Pure Reason,* namely that (1) there are determinable a priori principles for spatiotemporal experience, principles involving categories such as substance and causality. The point of Kant's idealism is basically the central claim of the Transcendental Dialectic of the *Critique,* namely that (2) metaphysically the spatiotemporal realm has a nonultimate status, so that whatever we or other beings such as God may be in themselves, such things in themselves cannot have intrinsic material properties. If we combine these points and add that (3) our objective theoretical knowledge[7] cannot transcend the realm governed by the principles of the Analytic, we then get the lesson of the *Critique* as a whole, a doctrine that has been called Kant's *restriction thesis,* namely that (4) although our knowledge has a priori structure, it is all only phenomenal.

Understood simply in these terms, the central claims of the Analytic and the Dialectic are independent in meaning, and in fact there are many philosophers who have accepted only the one or the other. However, the claims are not completely separated in the *Critique,* for already in the deduction of the categories (as in the transcendental exposition of space) Kant discusses both points. That is, he first establishes the content and validity of certain a priori propositions, and then he asserts the transcendental ideality of what is covered by those propositions.[8] But while this means that to a certain extent the Dialectic is anticipated earlier in the *Critique,* the fact remains that the ideality of Kant's principles is not a part of the argument *toward* their validity but is rather an explanation offered only after they have been shown to be valid and therefore seen as in need of a metaphysical account. Moreover, Kant indicates that it is the Dialectic that nails down the strong claim that our (objective theoretical) knowledge is absolutely limited to spatiotemporal properties and that affirming

6 Cf. R. Walker, *Kant* (London: Routledge and Kegan Paul, 1978), pp. 11–23; K. Ameriks, "Recent Work on Kant's Theoretical Philosophy," *American Philosophical Quarterly* 19 (1982): 1–24.

7 By "knowledge" I will generally mean (without always making it explicit hereafter), as Kant does, "objective" or determinate as opposed to merely analytic or formal knowledge, and "theoretical" as opposed to practical knowledge, where practical knowledge is any knowledge based on some premise asserting an obligation.

8 See, e.g., B 41, B 146. All citations of Kant's *Critique of Pure Reason* (London: Macmillan, 1929) refer to the first or second editions as A or B, respectively, followed by page numbers. Cf. K. Ameriks, "Kant's Transcendental Deduction as a Regressive Argument," *Kant-Studien* 69 (1978): 273–87.

the ideality of the spatiotemporal gives us not merely a "best" account but rather an absolutely necessary one.[9] More specifically, while the Aesthetic argues that there are a variety of particular difficulties with each of the traditional accounts of space and time (the Newtonian, Leibnizian, and Berkeleyan), and that there is the general problem that none of them "makes intelligible" synthetic a priori knowledge, it is only in the Antinomies that Kant shows transcendental idealism is inescapable because without it we are left in contradiction. This is Kant's ultimate ground for (2), and it is only via this claim and (3)[10] that he concludes with his restriction thesis. Hence for Kant the restriction thesis can be neither conflated with nor wholly cut off from the deduction: the deduction alone does not prove the spatiotemporal data we deal with are only phenomenal, and the Antinomies alone do not prove that the realm of these data exhausts what we can know.

Hegel was not very clear about these relations between Kant's basic arguments. For example, he says repeatedly that in using the term "transcendental" in the proof of the categories, Kant means to be expressing their ideality.[11] This is simply to overlook the two stages in the deduction noted earlier, and to miss the fact that in such typical phrases as "the transcendental deduction" the term "transcendental" distinguishes not the metaphysical status of the elements deduced but rather the manner of their being deduced, namely as conditions necessary for experience.[12] Thus, to say that a unity of apperception is transcendental is not to mean that it must attach to what is beyond experience and intrinsically non-

---

9 B xix.
10 The basis for (3) is Kant's doctrine of judgment, i.e., that our objective knowledge requires both concepts and intuitions, and therefore if the principles of the Analytic govern the whole domain of our intuition then our objective knowledge cannot transcend that domain. See A 51/ B75–6, A 68/ B 93–4, B 146–50.
11 "That Unity . . . Kant called transcendental only; and he meant thereby that the unity was only in our mind." *Encyclopedia,* sec. 42 Zusatz 2, VIII: 118, Wallace, p. 70. Page references to Hegel's texts will always include the volume and page number from the recent *Theorie-Werkausgabe* (Frankfurt: Suhrkamp, 1970), and, when appropriate, by the author and page of an English translation, in this case *Hegel's Logic,* by William Wallace (Oxford: Oxford University Press, 1975). Cf. Hegel, *Vorlesungen über die Geschichte der Philosophie,* XX:338: "The transcendental consists in disclosing these [categorial] determinations to be in subjective thinking." Some recent commentators have reversed Hegel's idea, i.e., they have equated Kant's deduction and idealism in such a way that the idealism is reduced to a mere expression of the argument of the deduction, whereas Hegel reduces Kant's deduction to an argument for idealism. See Ameriks, "Recent Work," p. 5.
12 By "experience" I will generally mean, as Kant does, putative empirical knowledge, and not precognitive consciousness. See B 161, B 218–19, and Walker, *Kant,* p. 10.

spatiotemporal, but is just to say that it is a kind of apperception necessary for experience.

Some historical considerations may help account for Hegel's confusion here.[13] We know that in his crucial formative years Hegel neglected close study of the central theoretical components of Kant's philosophy,[14] and when he did approach them it was through the perspective of someone already indoctrinated by the interpretations of Fichte and Schelling – interpretations that give a very peculiar slant to Kant's work. Thus Fichte's route to the restriction thesis[15] rests on crude representationalist worries[16] and ignores the specific arguments of the deduction and the Antinomies. Hegel followed Fichte's lead in skipping over these arguments, and even in his latest and most systematic accounts of Kant there is no patient analysis of these texts and hence no clear statement of the two stages in Kant's argument. Fortunately, though, Hegel did not accept Fichte's representationalist starting point. He appears to have been spurred to idealism rather by Schelling's view that it is the notion of freedom that immediately demonstrates that our ordinary knowledge is merely phenomenal.[17] Thus Hegel argues that the items within the world are merely phenomenal simply in the sense that they do not have their ground in themselves (as an absolutely free being supposedly does).[18] In

13 See H. S. Harris, *Hegel's Development: Towards the Sunlight 1770–1801* (Oxford: Oxford University Press, 1972), esp. pp. xx, 68, 79, 107.

14 See *Briefe von und an Hegel*, ed. J. Hoffmeister (Hamburg: Felix Meiner, 1969, 3d ed.), vol. 1, p. 16; and G. Lukács, *The Young Hegel*, trans. R. Livingstone (Cambridge, MA: MIT Press, 1966), p. 6: "From the Berne period there is not a single remark that would suggest more than a superficial interest in the problems of the *Critique of Pure Reason* and with epistemology in the narrower sense."

15 Note that here I am referring only to Fichte's conception of *theoretical* philosophy.

16 See especially Fichte's *Vocation of Man*, ed. Roderick Chisholm (Indianapolis: Bobbs-Merrill, 1956). The "doubt" that Fichte generates at the beginning of his book rests clearly on a reduction of thoughts to mental images, so that perception becomes a mere series of private pictures.

17 F. W. Schelling, *Werke* (Stuttgart: J. G. Cotta, 1856), vol. 1, p. 340. Cf. Hegel, I: 234. Note that whereas Fichte and Schelling agree that our practical feeling of freedom itself proves idealism, Kant argues that unless one can first make room for the theoretical possibility of idealism, the impression of freedom must be given up as an illusion (B xix). Note also that Hegel, like Fichte, seems to believe that allowing things in themselves would threaten our freedom, as if our receptivity vis-à-vis some things would have to entail ultimate passivity.

18 See Hegel, *Encyclopedia*, sec. 45 Zusatz, VIII:122, Wallace, p. 73: "The things immediately known are mere appearances – in other words, the ground of their being is not in themselves but in something else." The same point is made at sec. 50, VIII:13, Wallace, p. 82; but the translation is misleading. Hegel is not saying, "the being which the world has is only a semblance, no real being" – as if it only appeared that the world exists, but it really does not. On the contrary, he is saying, "the world does [indeed] have being, but only the being

this way Hegel can manage to hold onto the metaphysical downgrading of space and time[19] that is at the heart of transcendental idealism, while avoiding commitment to Kant's restriction thesis or any of the specific arguments to it. As a consequence, however, it becomes all the easier for Hegel to miss what is really involved in Kant's deduction and idealism.[20]

B. HEGEL VERSUS KANT: THE "I" IN THE DEDUCTION

We can now begin to consider the three major weaknesses that Hegel finds in Kant's deduction: (sec. B) the treatment of the "I," (sec. C) the account of necessity in our knowledge, and (sec. D) the notion that a preliminary study of knowing is feasible.

The first objection demonstrates Fichte's influence, for Hegel repeatedly remarks that Fichte is to be given credit for being more consistent and rigorous, for at least trying to deduce all of the categories from the I.[21] This objection also reveals how uncertain Hegel could be about Kant himself, for when he first expresses his ideal conception of the deduction, he hesitates saying Kant did not see this ideal. In "principle or spirit," if not in "form," Kant is allowed to have understood the fundamental truth that all reality is related to and founded in an I, an absolute mind.[22] Or, to note two other ways Hegel has of expressing this fundamental truth, it is

of appearance." That is, its being is founded on something, namely, the self-grounding reason which Hegel calls God.

19 Cf. Hegel's downgrading of matter at II:104, *The Difference Between the Fichtean and the Schellingian System of Philosophy*, trans. J. P. Surber (Resida, CA: Ridgeway Press, 1978), p. 80. Cf. also his approval of the idea that spatio-temporal causal relations have only the being of appearances, at II:338, *Faith and Knowledge*, trans. Walter Cerf and H. S. Harris (Albany: State University of New York Press, 1977), p. 101.

20 Here I suspect Hegel was influenced by the tendency of those like Reinhold, who stated that his philosophy would "finally provide full confirmation for the essential results of the *Critique of Pure Reason* independently of those profound meditations through which they have been established in Kant's own works." *Versuch einer neuen Theorie des menschlichen Vorstellungsvermögens* (1789) (reprint ed., Darmstadt: Wissenschaftliche Buchgesellschaft, 1963), pp. 67–8. The remark is cited and translated by Daniel Breazeale in "Reinhold's Elementary Philosophy," *Review of Metaphysics* 35 (1982): 789.

21 Hegel, *Encyclopedia*, sec. 42, VIII:117, Wallace, p. 69; ibid., sec. 60 Zusatz 2, VIII:141, Wallace, p. 94; *Science of Logic*, VI:505, trans. W. H. Johnston and L. G. Struthers (2 vols., London: George Allen and Unwin, 1929), vol. 2, p. 431–2; XX:386–401. It is clear that Fichte in turn owes this project – as well as another concept central to Hegel's critique, namely the rejection of the thing in itself – to the influence of Reinhold and G. E. Schulze. See above at n. 20 and below at n. 87; and D. Breazeale, "Fichte's *Aenisidemus* Review and the Transformation of German Idealism," *Review of Metaphysics* 34 (1981): 545–68.

22 Hegel, II:10, Surber, p. 1.

said that the "principle of the deduction" is just the Fichtean notion of "genuine idealism" (which is supposed to reject any distinct "thing in itself"),[23] and that this is the same as the "general principle of speculation," the principle of the absolute (and not merely formal) identity of subject and object.[24] Very soon, however, Hegel changed his estimate of Kant, and although he continued to hold to the fallacy noted earlier, the idea that a transcendental deduction must by itself be an argument for idealism, he came to recognize that even in the very "spirit" of his work Kant himself was not directed toward the form of idealism that does without things in themselves.[25] Hegel then charged Kant with internal inconsistency, for he held that the principle of Kant's own deduction (the I) demanded such idealism, despite whatever Kant himself said.

Before we evaluate Hegel on this point it should be made clear that in calling for a deduction tied directly to absolute idealism and based entirely on a simple, mental starting point (the pure representation of the I), Hegel did not mean to insist on a Cartesian or egoistic basis for philosophy. On the contrary, he stressed that it is precisely a virtue of his view, as *opposed* to what he now understands as the "subjective" or "psychological" idealism of Kant, that there is no suggestion that the form of reality arises from our imposition, as if it were literally up to us, as finite, particular minds, to determine the categories that obtain.[26] Unfortunately, while this claim shows Hegel's own view is at least not as radical as some have feared, it reveals but another injustice to Kant, who would have been only too happy to agree that such a subjective idealism is inappropriate. It is precisely for this reason that Kant stresses (as Hegel may see elsewhere)[27] that the form of the individual empirical ego is just as limited to the condition of mere phenomenality as is the rest of the spatiotemporal realm, and that the phenomenality of this realm rests ultimately on the distinctive quantitative features of space and time, features that are a priori and not imposed by humans in any imaginable sense.[28]

---

23 Hegel, II:9, Surber, p. 1. Hegel goes on to argue that Fichte himself did not hold true to this idealism.

24 Hegel, II:10–11, Surber, p. 2; cf. Hegel, II:338, Cerf and Harris, p. 101.

25 Hegel thus goes on to say that Kant's principle of speculation is not that of absolute idealism but rather its very opposite, the separation of thought and being (Hegel, II:338, Cerf and Harris, p. 101).

26 Hegel, *Encyclopedia*, sec. 42 Zusatz 1, VIII:118, Wallace, p. 69. Cf. II:309–11, 315, Cerf and Harris, pp. 74–5, 79.

27 Hegel, IV:440.

28 Hegel denies our being in a receptive relation to space and time at Hegel II:305, Cerf and Harris, pp. 69–70. For a critique, cf. Düsing, *Das Problem*, p. 118.

Thus if it is wrong to begin with to connect Kant's deduction *directly* with idealism, it is even more unfair to connect it at all with a *subjective* version of idealism.

This all still leaves it unclear just why Hegel believed one should devote the deduction to an argument for absolute idealism. In general terms, I believe the answer here rests on the idea that *if* the categories of things in themselves were completely determinable from what is involved in a pure representation of the I, then this would demonstrate the basic subject-object identity to which Hegel is committed. Then the world would not be the mere image of a particular self, as in egoistic idealism (solipsism), nor would its ultimate features be beyond the reach of all such selves, as in Kantian idealism,[29] but it would rather be distinct from us and yet (in essence) wholly accessible to our mind. Expressed simply in these terms, Hegel's position is not all that implausible, although for it to be distinguishable from ordinary realism, as Hegel surely takes it to be, he also needs to show how the "pure" representation with which he wants the deduction to begin can have some kind of mental or subjective meaning without being identical with the notion of a mere empirical ego. Here everything rests on precisely what Hegel understands by the pure representation of the I.

Insofar as Hegel criticizes Kant for not having moved properly *from* this notion, it would seem that one could find out what the notion is simply by looking at what Kant says. Yet the fact that Kant reaches conclusions very different from what Hegel expects already suggests that Kant's own starting point may be unlike Hegel's, and what has already been seen of Hegel's interpretation would support such a suggestion. Further confirmation for it can be found in the fact that at one point Hegel takes the notion of the I to stand for an absolute identity that is expressed not in what is called the "shallowness"[30] of the argument of the deduction itself, but rather in Kant's reference to the "productive imagination," which is said to be the ground of both the "subjective I" and the "objective world."[31] Elsewhere Hegel identifies this faculty with a unity that is the "absolute identity of self-consciousness, which posits judgment [and so the unity of subject and predicate, 'particular and universal'] absolutely

29 Once again, the restriction to theoretical knowledge should be kept in mind.
30 Hegel, II:304, Cerf and Harris, p. 69.
31 Hegel, II:308, Cerf and Harris, p. 73. Except for the identification of productive imagination with speculative reason, a similar view can be found in M. Heidegger, *Kant und das
   Problem der Metaphysik* (Bonn: Cohen, 1929). This view has been decisively challenged by D.
   Henrich, "Über die Einheit der Subjektivität," *Philosophische Rundschau* 3 (1955): 28–69.

out of itself."[32] Hegel thus moves far beyond the text, for Kant himself
(unlike Fichte) does not speak of such a "positing" absolute consciousness, nor does he hypostatize the productive imagination. Although it
sounds quite forbidding, "productive imagination" in the *Critique* can be
understood as a term that stands for little more than the fact that there
are a priori (and hence "productive" rather than "reproductive" or merely
contingent) rules that govern particular forms of sensibility (hence "imagination" rather than abstract thought).[33]

Hegel senses this restraint in Kant's own talk, and he charges that it
leaves Kant with the absurd picture of an empty (not literally "productive") I confronting an absolutely distinct manifold of data, which as such
would retain an unsurpassable primacy vis-à-vis the mind.[34] The picture is
called absurd because Hegel thinks that the I and the manifold make
sense only as components abstracted from a successful synthesis. As far as
I can see, it is only with a question-begging assumption of absolute idealism that Hegel can force on Kant the kind of all-encompassing "productive" representation of the I that he does. Thus the question is really not
why Kant fails to move from a "genuinely idealistic" representation of the
I to a full idealistic system (directly deducing categories applying to things
in themselves) – for he really never does have such a starting point, it is
rather why Hegel would think that we all should have such a starting point
and that this is at least in some way strongly hinted at by what Kant has to
say.

The main clue for handling this complex question has to do with some
basic ambiguities in the notion of apperception in the pure representation of the I. For Hegel, as for Kant, the notion of a pure representation of
the I is most commonly expressed as the notion of a necessary synthetic

---

32 Hegel, II:306, Cerf and Harris, p. 71. Hegel here is playing on the components of the term
    "Urteil." At this point he also makes the bizarre suggestion that this "speculative unity" is
    Kant's solution to the problem of synthetic a priori judgment. As Düsing points out (*Das
    Problem*, pp. 110–15), Hegel seems unaware that since such unity can also be found in
    analytic judgments it can hardly be the solution to Kant's problem. Hegel appears to have
    conflated the psychological and logical meanings of synthesis in judgments. Cf. Hegel
    VI:254, 505, Johnston and Struthers, vol. 2, pp. 218, 431–2; and Hegel XX:389.
33 Cf. K. Ameriks, "Kant and Guyer on Apperception," *Archiv für Geschichte der Philosophie* 65
    (1983): 175–86.
34 Hegel, II:306, Cerf and Harris, p. 71. Cf. Hegel, VI:258, 261, Johnston and Struthers, vol. 2,
    pp. 221, 225. In his late lectures Hegel makes the remarkable proposal that Kant's doctrine
    of the schematism points to an intuitive intellect ("ein anschauender intuitiver Verstand,
    oder verständiges Anschauen"), but he allows that Kant himself did not comprehend
    matters this way (XX:348).

unity of apperception. However, by saying there is necessary synthetic unity of apperception, one could mean either:

(i) (a) all representations[35] must be able to *belong* to one self-consciousness;

    (b) since there is a manifold of such representations, the unity here can be called synthetic, even when it involves analytic relations among the contents of the representations;

    (c) and since it is a unity within (and potentially for) a self-conscious being, it can be called apperceptive, even if there is at no point an actual all-encompassing thought of the form "I think . . .";

or:

(ii) (a) all representations in our cognition are components of judgment and express an objective unity of terms, which can always be formulated, "I think . . . is . . .";

    (b) since there is a manifold . . . representations (as above);

    (c) and since it is a unity . . . "I think . . ." (as above).

Note that (i) stresses a condition on thoughts as representations simply had by us, whereas (ii) stresses a condition on them as cognitive elements, that is, states that at least make a claim that can be true or false. They emphasize in turn what I will call the *possessive* and the *epistemic* relation of representations to consciousness. Keeping these relations distinct is important, especially in view of the fact that Kant may mean eventually to argue that for us the sets of items to which they apply turn out to be coextensive and necessarily related. That is, he may want to show that all the representations we can possess must be cognitive either directly, as in judgments of experience such as "*x* is *y*," or indirectly, as in judgments of perception, such as "*x* seems to be *y*," which necessarily can be embedded in the cognition "It *is* the case that I think *x* is *y*."[36]

These distinctions have great consequences for the issue of the applicability of the categories. An argument that moves first from only the epistemic sense of apperception would show that the categories are necessary insofar as they are necessary for judgment (as in Kant's "metaphysical

35 I believe this principle should be restricted to representations for a mind like ours, but in fact those who employ this understanding of apperception often neglect to make this restriction.

36 That this is Kant's position is argued in Ameriks, "Recent Work," pp. 14–18.

deduction"). If one then holds, as Kant does, that our (determining) judgments depend on given intuitions, and so on particular forms of sensibility, a belief in the ideality of those forms will block using the categories that are deduced (via the epistemic relation) to determine things in themselves. On the other hand, if one believes categories are deducible from the mere possessive sense of apperception, then there will be no such original restriction of the categories derived and not even a clear need for consideration of what is involved in the conditions of judgment. In other words, one will be in a natural position to be an absolute idealist and to be perplexed, as Hegel was, by any "restriction thesis." (Note also that this kind of understanding of apperception can meet the need discussed earlier for some kind of mental element without immediate subjectivistic consequences.)

I contend this line of thought represents not only a path Hegel could have taken but the one he actually took.[37] He explicitly commits himself to the crucial conflation necessary for this line when he defines pure apperception as the "act by which the 'I' makes the materials [of representation] 'mine.' "[38] Elsewhere he contends similarly that the "specific ground of the categories is declared by the critical system to lie in the primary *identity* of the 'I' in thought – what Kant calls the transcendental unity of self-consciousness."[39]

This conflation is not unprovoked by Kant's language. In addition to the complicated close connection ultimately existing between what is covered by the two senses of apperception,[40] there is the fact that Kant sometimes speaks as if his principle of apperception had an ontological meaning, as if the point is how all our possible representations are necessarily related to our *being* one and the same thinker having them. Fortunately, Kant also says enough elsewhere to indicate the difficulties with resting the deduction on the possessive sense of apperception.[41] In the

---

37 Here I am passing over the contrast between Hegel's radical (the one that emphasizes productive imagination) and tame (the one that speaks merely of the possessive sense) models of the I, and I take myself to be doing him a favor by concentrating on the tame model. There is of course a close relation between these models, since it appears that for Hegel the primordial subject-object, particular-universal relation is instantiated when one generates one's thought and considers it to be one's own and subject to the principle of apperception. Cf. Hegel, VI:255, Johnston and Struthers, vol. 2, p. 219. See also below at n. 45.

38 Hegel, *Encyclopedia*, sec. 42 Zusatz 1, VIII:118, Wallace, p. 69. Here Hegel speaks of a remarkable "Tätigkeit des Vermeinigens [activity of making something mine]."

39 Hegel, *Encyclopedia*, sec. 42, VIII:116, Wallace, p. 68 (my emphasis).

40 See above at n. 36.

41 See K. Ameriks, *Kant's Theory of Mind* (Oxford: Oxford University Press, 1982), pp. 137–42.

Paralogisms he indicates that the argument would go through even on the hypothesis that there is an ultimate plurality of substances underlying the act in which thought is synthetically united.[42] And within the deduction itself, he stresses that it is the epistemic condition of the "objective unity of apperception" that is really the premise of his argument,[43] and not the mere fact that representations belong to one consciousness, as obtains in a subjective unity of associative relations.

A further difficulty with stressing the possessive sense is that it is unclear just what can be meant by saying it is an act of ours that makes our representations our own. As Hegel himself indicates, in mocking talk of representations being merely "accompanied" by a mind,[44] we have no relevant notion of a representation that is not a representation had by a mind. The dependent nature of representations makes them ready to belong to us quite independent of whatever we do. Moreover, if there were some act by which representations were made capable of being ours, it is remarkable that the very principle of apperception (on this reading) implies that there is no special effect or limitation that this action would involve – any and all representations are subject to it, and by being put into relation with oneself they themselves are not supposed to change. (I suspect this fact is related to the earlier point that Hegel stressed about the manifold having to be wholly amenable to us. This is obviously true in the sense that there is nothing data would have that would block them a priori from *this* kind of "act" of mind.) On the other hand, if it is said that what is meant by the act of apperception is simply the familiar procedure of explicitly bringing some specific train of representations to mind and giving them a feature of vivacity that other representations would lack, it must be countered that this is to invoke an empirical notion of apperception that is precisely what was to be excluded by the notion of a pure representation of the I. Such apperception might be responsible for a quite intelligible relation to representations, but it would have no chance of claiming a priori to be applicable to all representations and would fail the requirements of both transcendental philosophy and absolute idealism.

So far, Hegel's criticism of Kant appears at best to trade on a conflation of the substantive but not absolutely universal applicability of the epistemic form of the principle of apperception with the genuinely universal,

42 A 364.
43 B 139–40.
44 Hegel, *Encyclopedia*, sec. 20, VIII:74, Wallace, p. 31; VI:254, Johnston and Struthers, vol. 2, p. 218; XX:343.

but only apparently substantive character of the possessive form of the principle. This is not the whole story, for in his last treatment of Kant, Hegel gives a more detailed attempt to spell out the kind of action that he takes to be involved in apperception, admitting that it is "not exactly" explained this way by Kant himself:

> I am the entirely universal, the completely indeterminable, abstract. Insofar as I set an empirical content in the I, i.e., apperceive it, it must come into this simplicity of the I. In order for a content to be able to enter into the One [*das Eine*], the simplicity of the I, it itself must be made simple and infected by simplicity. A content in consciousness thus becomes One, becomes my content. I am I, am One. Thus the thought is put into a unity and so becomes one . . . What thought produces is a unity, and thus it produces itself, for it is one . . . Whatever I touch must be able to allow itself to be forced into these forms [of the synthesis of apperception] of unity.[45]

In this argument Hegel expresses a combination of his earlier radical interpretation of the I in terms of a productive power and his later possessive conception of apperception, a combination that he may have always had in mind but never made so clear before. The I is now given a very specific power, one that is to go beyond the mere designating of a representation as one's own. Apperception is said to involve the imposing of a form on the representation, the form of simplicity, which is what then allows the representation to become one's own. Unfortunately, the mere notion of simplifying a thought remains as mysterious as that of directly making it mine. Once again, it is not explained how anything is really given to the thought that it does not already have. On the other hand, if some ordinary action is proposed, such as somehow making the thought simple by giving it a special vivid or personal tone, then this again conflicts with the necessary universal scope that is to be attached to apperception. One way out of this impasse would be to switch from discussing about what must be done to *a* thought or representation to make it simple to discussing the conditions for making a manifold or "congeries" of data simple in the sense of being united.[46] But then another dilemma returns, for it seems that either these conditions can be spelled out in minimal terms that, as Hume indicated, require no reference to an I, let alone absolute idealism, or one focuses on a richer kind of unity, such as that of judgment, thereby bringing in the epistemic sense of apperception that

45 Hegel, XX:344.
46 Hegel, XX:347; *Encyclopedia*, sec. 42, VIII:116, Wallace, p. 68.

Hegel avoids here in suggesting and Kant's approach is distinct from his own.[47]

Although Hegel's first objection thus fails because it rests on an interpretation that is inaccurate as well as intrinsically inadequate (given the limited consequences of the Hegelian notion of apperception), it should be noted that it at least fits into the mainstream of recent interpretations of transcendental arguments, and especially of the many quasi-Strawsonian reconstructions of the deduction that abstract from the features that eventually led Kant to an espousal of transcendental idealism.[48] In this way Hegel's attack expresses a very influential and understandable response to Kant that in principle, if not in origin, is largely detachable from any peculiar metaphysics. Moreover, even if Hegel may have gone too far in calling for a dialectical argument from one category to all the others, and even if he is unfair in charging Kant with a merely "historical" and "psychological" method in the metaphysical deduction,[49] one cannot help but feel that Hegel has at least a stronger sense of the need for a complete and fully persuasive metaphysical deduction, and *to this extent* his call for a more rigorous proof of the categories is well taken.

C. HEGEL VERSUS KANT: NECESSITY AND THE DEDUCTION

The considerations advanced so far make it relatively easy to deal with Hegel's second objection, namely that with Kant the "universality and necessity we find in cognition . . . remains a presupposition after all; . . . Kant did no more than offer an explanation of this fact."[50] The heart of this objection is the idea that Kant's main point is just the picture of imposition, that the deduction amounts merely to a metaphysical story of how the categories are imposed by us and so do not have absolute reality. Here again Hegel is conflating the argument of the deduction proper with (his understanding of) Kant's doctrine of idealism, a conflation made understandable by the just-noted fact that Hegel missed Kant's own

47 Hegel may appear to approach Kant here when he links possessing with conceiving, but unfortunately he uses the former to understand the latter, rather than vice versa: "In order to recognize what a notion is, one is to consider the notion of the I" (VI:255, Johnston and Struthers, vol. 2, p. 219). My translation.

48 See Ameriks, "Recent Work," p. 13. Cf. below at n. 54.

49 See, e.g., Hegel, VI:289, Johnston and Struthers, vol. 2, p. 247; and XX:346. Hegel is well challenged here by Smith, "Hegel's Critique," pp. 445–8.

50 Hegel, *Encyclopedia*, sec. 40, VIII:113, Wallace, p. 65; cf. XX:336.

argument to the categories. This conflation may also have been encouraged by the fact that in Kant's *Prolegomena* the "necessity in cognition" is in
effect taken as a presupposition.[51] We know, however, that the method of
the *Prolegomena* is not that of the *Critique* itself,[52] and in any case a mere
glance at arguments such as the second Analogy shows Kant is out to
derive a principle of necessity rather than simply to assume one.[53]

Hegel does not attend to these textual points, and in any event he may
have been unwilling to give them much weight. Given our analysis of the
first objection, it seems likely that for any argument other than one that
defeats skepticism and partial idealism (by deducing the structure of the
world from what is given in the possessive sense of the representation of
the "I"), he would incline to the view that we are at the level of mere
presupposition and "explanation" rather than of the demonstration of
genuine necessity. The ascription of such a view seems even more proper
if one considers how high in general Hegel's requirements are for what
counts as a proof, and if one recalls how even many contemporary interpreters of transcendental arguments have tended to assume that apart
from a refutation of skepticism Kant's deduction loses epistemological
force and can have only an odd metaphysical meaning.[54] Hegel explicitly
shares this assumption when he states that with the presupposition of "a
thing that senses and a thing that is sensed, all [true] philosophy is driven
from the field."[55] There is no appreciation here for the Kantian idea of an
argument that begins with certain commonsense presuppositions and
then moves to unearth their dependence on various controversial principles that are to constitute a necessary conceptual framework.

In sum, whereas Kant presents a relatively modest argument from (a)
the nature of empirical judgment to (b) a list of valid categories and then
to (c) a system of transcendental idealism, Hegel desires a radical deduction that would begin with something prior to (a), such as (aa) a pure

51 *Kant's gesammelte Schriften* (Berlin: Preussische Akademie der Wissenschaften/ de Gruyter,
   1900–), vol. 4, p. 279. Hereafter *AA*.
52 See ibid., p. 274.
53 See A 176/ B 218, A 189/ B 232. Here my interpretation contrasts with Smith, "Hegel's
   Critique," p. 459. My defense of Kant here is also meant to meet at least the first two points
   of J. Habermas's (*Erkenntnis und Interesse* [Frankfurt: Suhrkamp, 1968]) neo-Hegelian
   challenge to transcendental philosophy for assuming (1) a normative concept of experience (science), (2) an a priori identity of the ego, and (3) a sharp theory-praxis distinction.
   I have just tried to show that these first two points (in reverse order) are not inherent in
   Kant's strategy.
54 See above at n. 48.
55 Hegel, II:338, Cerf and Harris, p. 101 (my translation).

possessive or "simple-making" power of apperception, and that would go beyond (c) to (d) a system of absolute idealism. Not finding such a radical argument worked out in the *Critique,* Hegel scolds Kant for not moving directly from (aa) to (b), and then for supposedly not moving to (b) at all but only moving from it to (c). In missing the basic structure of Kant's argument, Hegel, like many other interpreters, also misses the important ancillary considerations that are to make possible the transitions from (a) to (b) and from (b) to (c). The omission in regard to the latter inference will be stressed later; the main oversights in regard to the former concern not only the epistemic sense of apperception but also the use of the pure forms of intuition, which is crucial to Kant's conclusion that the categories have a fully universal applicability within our experience.[56]

D. HEGEL VERSUS KANT: ON PRELIMINARY KNOWLEDGE

Hegel's third objection to Kant does not appear to be so closely related to details of the deduction, for in Hegel's original presentation it is stated as a very general problem that applies just as well to Locke.[57] The objection is directed against all philosophers who try to set down the scope and limits of knowledge by first examining our cognitive faculties and forget thereby that such a preliminary inquiry is itself a part of the process of knowledge. In the *Phenomenology* Kant's name is not mentioned when this objection is made in its most famous form, but it is obvious that it is the *Critique* that Hegel means to refer to when he attacks the project of a preliminary inquiry as motivated by a conception of knowledge as a "medium" or "instrument" to be examined beforehand for its reliability.[58] The problems that such a critical philosophy is taken to emphasize, that the medium of our cognition may, as passive, be obscure or partial, and that the instruments of our knowledge may, as active, be distorting, are surely meant to correspond to Kant's conception of our a priori forms of sensibility and understanding.[59]

Hegel's explanation of the difficulty with this conception is very indi-

---

56 This point was first made clear in D. Henrich, "The Proof-Structure of Kant's Transcendental Deduction," *Review of Metaphysics* 22 (1969): 640–59. Cf. above at n. 36.

57 Hegel, II:304, Cerf and Harris, p. 69. In general, Hegel links Kant closely to empiricism.

58 Hegel, III:68, *Phenomenology of Mind,* trans. J. Baillie (New York: Harper, 1967), p. 131.

59 Ibid. Cf. Richard Norman, *Hegel's Phenomenology* (London: Chatto and Windus, 1976), pp. 19–27; and G. Kortian, *Metacritique,* trans. J. Raffan (Cambridge: Cambridge University Press, 1980), pp. 34–41.

rect; his favorite way of expressing it is that the critical philosopher commits the error of "refusing to enter the water until you have learnt to
swim."[60] If that is the difficulty involved, then it appears it could be
expressed less metaphorically in terms of what Roderick Chisholm has
discussed as the "problem of the criterion."[61] Roughly speaking, it seems
that in order properly to advance a cognitive claim, one first ought to
know that the claim meets the conditions for being a cognition, and yet it
also seems that one cannot know that (i.e., what the conditions for being
such a cognition are) unless one already knows some particular things.

Chisholm has chosen to resolve this problem by a *particularist* rather
than a *methodist* route. He says there are some particular things we know
prior to knowing the general criterion that makes them knowledge, and it
is through reflecting on these given particular cases that we then can
develop a formulation of what the general criterion is.[62] In contrast, a
critical philosopher would appear to be a methodist who urges withholding on particular knowledge claims – perhaps because he is aware of the
difficulties just noted with our cognitive "instruments" – until he has
ascertained certain general principles. On the basis of these principles,
and an examination of our capacity for satisfying them, his preliminary
inquiry can then be developed into a full account of the structure and
scope of our knowledge.

This may well seem to be precisely what Kant was up to in producing a
deduction of a priori principles and then an idealistic account of their
scope. And if one does believe this is what Kant was up to, then it is natural
to challenge Kant by in effect invoking the problem of the criterion and
asking how one could hope to deduce general principles without already
admitting some knowledge claims, that is, by asking how Kant intended to
learn how to swim without being already wet.[63] However, if one works
instead with the construal of Kant's project developed in opposition to
Hegel's in the first part of our analysis, then there is no such problem at
this point. For on that construal the deduction is not out to give a methodist resolution of the general problem of a criterion for knowledge, for it

60 Hegel, *Encyclopedia*, sec. 41 Zusatz, VIII:114, Wallace, p. 66. Cf. ibid., sec. 10, VIII:54, Wallace, p. 14; II:154; XVI:58ff.; XX:334
61 See Roderick Chisholm, *The Foundations of Knowing* (Minneapolis: University of Minnesota Press, 1982), p. 63.
62 Ibid., pp. 69ff.
63 Cf. Hegel, *Encyclopedia*, sec. 41 Zusatz, VIII:114, Wallace, p. 66: "True, indeed, the forms of thought should be subjected to a scrutiny before they are used; yet what is this scrutiny but ipso facto a cognition?"

rather assumes that there are some warranted statements[64] (e.g., "there is something happening at *t*") and asks only about the a priori principles required by such statements. Hence if there is no more to Hegel's third objection than what has just been developed, it can be dismissed (as a direct critique of Kant) in the same way that the previous objections were.

It turns out that there is something more to the third objection, for Hegel stresses that closely intertwined with (what we have called) the problem of the criterion one finds the basic error of treating knowledge, or our cognitive faculty, as an instrument. The difficulty (or deep water) Kant supposedly gets into here is most frequently explained by Hegel by saying that in assuming such a "tool" conception of knowledge Kant overlooked the great difference between it and real tools.[65] Whereas an ordinary tool can be tested independently to see if it is proper (e.g., to check a hammer we don't have to use it, let alone hit it with a hammer), our cognition is such that it seems there is no test for it that does not itself appeal to the use of our cognition. Thus there is something fundamentally questionable about assuming cognition is a mere tool, and once we have dropped this assumption, we have dropped what Hegel gives as the motivation for the critical philosophy (namely the idea of checking beforehand how this tool works).

Unfortunately, this new way of formulating Hegel's objection involves the misleading suggestion that the tool conception of knowledge (as just explained) is a *presupposition* of Kant's philosophy. Perhaps it does function this way for some philosophers, but in Kant's case it must be reiterated that the talk of forms of intuition and understanding is meant precisely as the conclusion rather than the starting point of his argument. Kant no doubt believes it would be wrong to assume that our empirical representations directly reveal things in themselves,[66] for the ground of such an assumption is hardly evident, and he also surely believes that the history of metaphysical controversies warrants some initial withholding about the reliability of reason when it goes beyond the empirical realm, but all this does not mean that *from the start* he is saying that what we have to work with are *only our* forms of access to objects. On the contrary, once these forms are discovered and elaborated it becomes an extra point to

64 Actually, all it needs to do is ask what follows if there are such statements, but I am sure that Kant, like the rest of us, believed there really are such. On the similarities between Chisholm and Kant here, see K. Ameriks, "Current German Epistemology," *Inquiry* 25 (1982): 125–38.

65 See the passages cited above at n. 60.

66 See especially *AA*, vol. 4, p. 282.

show that they are only our forms, only our instruments for trying to get at something in itself quite distinct from us.

Here one might insist that Hegel's objection is independent of *when* one holds that there is such a thing as a tool of cognition distinct from things in themselves (what Hegel calls "the Absolute"). For as long as it is true that knowledge cannot be like an ordinary tool, then this would seem to be enough to make improper any talk of knowledge as a medium or instrument, and so even if Critical philosophy is not off base at the beginning it is ultimately off base. The Kantian's reply to this point is that all he is *ever* committed to is an *analogy* between cognitions and tools, an analogy with a particular meaning *resulting* from an argument to a particular kind of independence of things from our mind. More specifically, he can reply that while the reflexive capacity of our faculty of cognition in general and the absolutely universal scope of a certain part of that faculty do make it quite unlike an ordinary tool, it is also true that this part of our cognitive faculty can use the principle of contradiction to test other parts, and the results of that test can imply that *those* parts have limited scope and *to that extent* are like media or mere tools. So if (as in the Antinomies) there are contradictions arising when certain propositions of common sense are combined with a particular metaphysical thesis such as the thesis of transcendental realism, then the Critical philosopher (who, once again, does not have to be committed to an absolutely presuppositionless starting point) can assert the negation of the metaphysical thesis. And if it happens that a consequence of that negation is the assertion of a gap between what we can empirically determine about items and what can be true about them in themselves, then it is appropriate to say that in a sense our empirical cognitive faculty is like a tool, one that reaches so far and only so far.

One can, of course, challenge the specific arguments made in the process of demonstrating the alleged contradictions, but any such objection is no longer one to the mere idea of cognition as a tool but is rather an objection only to a particular kind of justification for one form of this idea. One can also seek some general way to oppose Kant's *entire* attempt to make a meaningful distinction between what our cognitive faculties can determine and what things are in themselves, and in fact this is just what Hegel does in his second major group of objections to Kant's theoretical philosophy, the critique of Kantian idealism. There is a striking argument along this line that could also be considered another variant of the third objection to the deduction, namely that if one were to try to assert on its basis that all we have are principles that apply only to phenomena, then this bare assertion itself would conflict with the restriction thesis, for the assertion would not be merely about how things appear to our tools of cognition but would rather be a claim about what is absolutely the case.[67] The Kantian's reply to this charge must be that it was never claimed that there is nothing we can know that is absolutely true. Rather, the point of Kant's thesis is only that the determination of things requires intuition and that the predications (and all that rests on them) of the intuitive qualities given via our forms of sensibility cannot characterize things in themselves. The bare assertion "our sensible qualities must have such and such principles and cannot as such characterize things in themselves" conflicts with the restriction thesis only if it gives determinate knowledge of things in themselves. This it does not do, for although it gives a kind of absolute knowledge, this is quite negative and indeterminate and not inconsistent with any thesis Kant wants to hold.

The most famous Hegelian treatment of this reply is in the *Phenomenology*'s introductory attack on Critical philosophy, where Hegel suggests Kant's inquiry gives news that is not so much illicit as vacuous:

> It seems . . . a remedy . . . to remove from the result the part which, in our idea of the Absolute received through that instrument, belongs to the instrument, and thus to get the truth in its purity. But this improvement would, as a matter of fact, only bring us back to the point where we were before . . . The thing stands before us once more just as it was previous to all this trouble, which, as we now see, was superfluous.[68]

This statement is easily recognizable as referring to the Kantian project of excluding space and time from the noumenal realm, but its objection is most surprising. It precludes the Kantian from making any use of the concept of determinate negation, which in its simplest form is just the thought that the well-grounded denial of a particular view leaves us not with a mere empty result but rather some increase in our own understanding. Thus, when a Kantian denies the spatiotemporality of things in themselves he admittedly does not determine positively what such things are like, but he surely has improved his understanding by overcoming a serious misconception (transcendental realism).

67 See Hegel's statement, "If they cannot be determinations of the *Thing in itself*, they can still less be determinations of the Understanding, to which we must allow at the very least the dignity of a Thing in itself" (V:40, Johnston and Struthers, vol. 1, p. 57). Cf. P. F. Strawson, *The Bounds of Sense* (London: Methuen, 1966), p. 39; and Ameriks, *Kant's Theory*, pp. 280ff.
68 Hegel, III:69, Baillie, p. 132.

It may be that Hegel's statement is to be understood dialectically, that it means not that the Kantian can get nothing from his discovery of the limits of our forms of knowledge, but rather that either he must say he is getting nothing from this, or he must admit to claiming some genuine knowledge, and then it can be shown that this admission leads to difficulties. Thus Hegel goes on to argue:

> Or again, if the examination of knowledge, which we represent as a medium, makes us acquainted with the law its refraction, it is likewise useless to eliminate this refraction from the result. For knowledge is not the divergence of the ray, but the ray itself by which the truth comes into contact with us; and if this be removed the bare direction or the empty place would alone be indicated . . . More especially it [the Critical philosophy] takes for granted that the Absolute stands on one side, and that knowledge on the other side, by itself and cut off from the Absolute, is still something real; in other words, that knowledge, which, by being outside the Absolute, is certainly outside truth, is nevertheless true . . . [The Critical philosophy proceeds by] making the distinction that a knowledge which does not indeed know the Absolute as science wants to do, is nonetheless true too; and that knowledge in general, though it may possibly be incapable of grasping the Absolute, can still be capable of truth of another kind. But we shall see as we proceed that random talk like this leads in the long run to a confused distinction between an absolute truth and a truth of some other sort.[69]

Here the basic objection is that *either* the *Critique* leaves us with a "bare direction," an "empty place," *or* it should admit to a knowledge that is "itself something real." Note, however, that for all that has been explicitly argued, the knowledge that supposedly must be admitted, and admitted as an embarrassment to Kant, is not said to be the general claim "we know only the form of our 'tool,' the 'law of refraction,' not the thing in itself," but is rather the set of claims made through this tool. In other words, it is being urged that the particular content of our sensible knowledge (the "ray itself," or knowledge "by itself and [supposedly] cut off from the Absolute") must be admitted as a part of the Absolute, that is, as a part of what is absolutely true.

By itself such urging is hardly persuasive, for the aim of the Antinomies is precisely to argue in detail against it. It is most likely, though, that Hegel did not mean his claim to be persuasive here,[70] for it occurs in what is only a brief Introduction, and that the issue is to be settled only when Hegel

69 Hegel, III:69–70, Baillie, pp. 132–3.
70 Note that Hegel says, "we shall see as we proceed" (ibid.).

considers the Antinomies itself more directly and systematically. We will focus on these considerations in the next section, but first it should be made clear how much rests on them. The fact is that although Hegel repeated his general attack on Kant many times and therefore had ample opportunity to flesh out his grounds for rejecting the Critical philosophy *tout court*, he never offered anything more rigorous at this level than the passages just examined. The talk of "tools," "rays," and "swimming" are about all that can be found apart from what is in the sections dealing specifically with the Antinomies.

It is true that the latter part of the long quoted passage introduces one new line of argument, but it is not strong enough to bear very much weight. The argument is that the mere admission (which Kant is certainly willing to make) that there are empirical truths counts against the restriction thesis and the phenomenal-noumenal distinction tied up with it. Supposedly, the distinction between "empirical truth" and "truth of another kind" is only so much "random talk," "words which presuppose a meaning that has to be got at."[71] This is not a petty issue, for surely the Kantian must say something about the different kinds of truths that he considers, namely transcendental formal truths about the structure of our empirical cognition, absolute formal truths about the structure of understanding as such, empirical material truths about the items of our sensibility, and noumenal material truths about the character of things in themselves. But I see no problem here as long as Kant gives, as he surely does, some indication about how these truths are to be distinguished, such as by different procedures of verification (respectively: transcendental arguments, formal logic, science, intellectual intuition), and as long as it is clear that these distinctions need not be meant to imply that truth itself is of different kinds (rather than that there simply are different kinds of items that are found true and different routes to them).

It is hard to determine Kant's opinion on the character of truth itself, as opposed to that of knowledge or its objects,[72] but there is no reason this should amount to a weakness specific to Critical philosophy. At most, Hegel can chide Kant for not being quite open enough about the limitations of "empirical truth," since for Kant it is after all the case that what is empirically true of *x,* for example that its existence is temporally limited,

71 Ibid. Cf. Hegel V:39, Johnston and Struthers, vol. 1, p. 57: "a true knowledge which did not know the object of knowledge as it is in itself would be equally absurd."
72 See Gerold Prauss, "Zum Wahrheitsproblem bei Kant," *Kant-Studien* 60 (1969): 166–82; and Hans Wagner, "Zu Kants Auffassung bezüglich des Verhältnisses zwischen Formal-und Transzendental Logik," *Kant-Studien* 68 (1977): 71–6.

does not entail, as one might suppose, a correspondent or basing (in a Leibnizian way) fact true of *x* in itself. On the contrary, the noumenal truth about *x*, for example that its existence is without temporal limits, can be quite the opposite of what we would empirically assert and of what anyone could analyze out of such assertions. But this just means that for Kant our empirical truth is truth only in a particular irreducible but limited context,[73] and this should not be a thought that, in our linguistic age, must be held to put Kant into special difficulty.[74] Thus, even if in some deep sense "truth is one," there is, for all Hegel says, still an understandable point and meaning to the distinctions between the different kinds of truths that the Kantian wants to introduce; it is hardly all "random talk."[75]

E. HEGEL VERSUS KANT'S IDEALISM: ON THE THING IN ITSELF

As we turn now to assess Hegel's second group of objections, his rejection of Kant's transcendental idealism, it must be admitted that this has already been in view for some time because of the way Hegel tended to connect it with his first group of objections to Kant's theoretical philosophy. Nonetheless, we have yet to look at Hegel's more direct attacks on the Kantian notion of the thing in itself and on the specific arguments of the Transcendental Dialectic, wherein Kant tries to complete his case for the restriction thesis.

The general perspective from which all these attacks start is Hegel's own absolute idealism, which was discussed earlier as being remarkably like a highly confident realism, a belief in the in-principle transparency of all reality to our rational faculty.[76] Of course, Hegel also builds into this

---

73 There is, of course, no such limitation on the nonempirical statement that our empirical truth is limited.

74 Consider, for example, W. Sellars's discussion of truth as semantic assertability in *Science and Metaphysics* (London: Routledge and Kegan Paul, 1968).

75 At one point Hegel himself seems to appreciate this in laying out the different senses of "objectivity" in Kant (*Encyclopedia*, sec. 41 Zusatz 3,VIII:115–16, Wallace, pp. 67–8). When he regrets that Kant does not allow insight into noumenal (what Hegel calls "true") objectivity, the real essence of things, his discussion implies Kant's view is lacking only in justification, not sense.

76 To this extent Hegel is remarkably close to what Michael Dummett calls Frege's objectivism: "In saying that what is objective is not independent of reason, Frege does not mean that its existence depends on our thinking . . . He means that it cannot be apprehended save by, or by reference to, rational thought." "Objectivity and Reality in Lotze and Frege," *Inquiry* 25 (1982) 111. Frege's own language is remarkably Hegelian: "By objectivity I

idealism a set of teleological details that are not so easy to accept, for the world is said necessarily to be not only open to reason, but also so open to it that it is just as if a supernatural Idea, in the fullest providential sense, generated reality and all its basic forms (a level of contingency is allowed by Hegel, but that there is such a level is something that is itself due to the Idea). Important as the more exuberant aspects of idealism were to Hegel, they will not concern us, for our question is simply whether there is any *minimal* way in which Hegel demonstrates that the restrictions Kant imposes on reason must be rejected.

Unfortunately, it is not always easy to keep apart the minimal and the exuberant sides of Hegel's critique. For example, in trying to embarrass the Kantian about the status of empirical truths, what Hegel eventually wants to emphasize is that he (Hegel) has the best explanation of how "the ray itself," the domain of appearances, has a kind of truth that is part of the Absolute. That is, for Hegel the truth of appearances (and, in *a* sense, their "untruth") is their very nature as mere appearances, the fact that, as merely sensible and finite,[77] they require an ultimate explanation in a self-grounded notion of reason.[78] Appearances have truth insofar as they are grounded in reason in a way that can be revealed either from the bottom up, as in the *Phenomenology,* where limited conceptions of limited things lead us to an all-embracing explanation, or from the top down, as in the *Logic,* where the sequence of basic logical categories unfolds in such a way as to disclose the structure of the empirical world. For the Kantian, however, the gap between appearances and things in themselves is absolute, for in neither direction are we able to derive the (particular positive) qualities of the one from those of the other. Similarly, the truth of the empirical lies not in its being grounded in an ultimately final explanation, a known Idea, but rather in an internal consistency with the

understand an independence from our sensation, intuition, ideation . . . but not independence from reason, for to answer the question what things are independent of reason would be as much as to judge without judging, to wash the fur without getting it wet." Cited by Dummett, ibid., p. 110, from *Die Grundlagen der Arithmetik* (Breslau, 1884), sec. 26.

77 Note that a mathematically infinite magnitude, such as the domain of even numbers, is still metaphysically finite for Hegel, since it has an essential reference to another, in this case the domain of odd numbers. For Hegel, to be truly infinite is to be wholly self-grounded. Thus when Hegel lists the infinite items that he insists (contra Kant) can be known by us, namely freedom, spirit, and God, these all ultimately designate the same thing, the absolutely self-sufficient whole. See the equations of infinity and reason in these terms at *Encyclopedia,* sec. 45, VIII:121, Wallace, p. 72; and V:52, Johnston and Struthers, vol. 1, p. 67. For a fine treatment of Hegel's view of the infinite, see Paul Guyer, "Hegel, Leibniz, and the Contradiction in the Finite," *Philosophy and Phenomenological Research* 40 (1979): 75–98.

78 See Hegel, *Encyclopedia,* sec. 131 Zusatz, VIII:262–3, Wallace, p. 187.

limited (though a priori structured) procedures of our empirical inquiries.

What this means is that apart from the general opposition to Kant's distinction of truth levels, reviewed in the previous section, Hegel's ultimate objection to Kant rests on a very elaborate claim about how appearances and reality entail each other. There is no way to test this claim now, and so I will admit to be challenging Hegel only with respect to those aspects of his critique that are detachable from the details of his own positive metaphysical system. Such a challenge will no doubt strike an orthodox Hegelian as incomplete and unfair, but I will assume there are understandable reasons for it, and that if a Hegelian is really to hope somehow to break into contemporary discussions in theoretical philosophy it must be by some arguments that do not already require appeal to the more elaborate parts of the Hegelian system. Moreover, I presume Hegel himself would not have to regard my tactic as wholly unfair, for, as our many quotations from the early Jena publications have shown, Hegel clearly formulated his basic critique of Kant before developing his own system, and (as the parallel citations from much later texts show) what he formulated then remained to the end the core of his direct critique.

There remain to be examined three basic aspects of this critique: the general attack on the conception of a thing in itself; the general treatment of Kant's basic argument for idealism in the Antinomies; and the specific treatment of individual doctrines in the Transcendental Dialectic that are developed in line with transcendental idealism.

The first kind of objection comes in various forms, but these all appear to rest on the presumption that Kant's categories are to be equated with their sensible meaning.[79] Thus the restriction thesis is read in such a way as to imply that since we cannot apply the categories beyond the sensible and phenomenal conditions spelled out in the Schematism and Principles, the domain of things in themselves is wholly, and absurdly, blocked from our thought: "reality is absolutely beyond the Notion,"[80] "the object, as a thing in itself, simply remains a something beyond thought."[81] Time

---

79 It is notable that another way in which Hegel expresses the principle of true idealism is in terms of the idea that related items have no sense in isolation, and he takes as an expression of this view Kant's doctrine that concepts and intuitions alone are each insufficient (II:302–3, Cerf and Harris, p. 68). Here Hegel (like many current interpreters) already seems to have missed the fact that for Kant concepts can have some meaning even if, without intuition, they are "empty." See J. Nolan, "Kant on Meaning: Two Studies," Kant-Studien 70 (1979): 113–30; and J. Smith, "Hegel's Critique," pp. 450ff.

80 Hegel, VI:266, Johnston and Struthers, vol. 2, p. 227.

81 Hegel, V:37, Johnston and Struthers, vol. 1, p. 55.

and again Hegel asserts that the essence of Kant's idealism is its "subjectivity," its wholly limiting the categories to *our* mind, so that whereas for Jacobi the categories are limited because they apply to a conditioned and finite domain, for Kant the limitation comes directly from their source in a merely psychological concept of the self.[82]

The traditional Kantian would reply that such charges wholly miss the essential distinction between the pure and the schematized meaning of the categories. On the basis of this distinction the Kantian can say that (contra Jacobi) what goes beyond the sensible is not a wholly amorphous domain but rather something that can be allowed some sort of conceptual order. This order is one that holds for all thinkers, and it can even be made determinate by us as long as we have another type of data than the spatiotemporal to make use of, as in fact occurs with our moral faculty.[83] So even if schematized categories, such as those found in our rule of temporal causality, are not to be applied to things in themselves, such things need not be wholly beyond thought, and in fact Kant believes we *must* think them in accord with a kind of pure, moral causality.

Hegel's objection can also be countered by noting again that he misses the two-step form of Kant's deduction, for if ideality were attached to the categories as such, then obviously any deduction of categories would immediately be limited to mere appearances. But Kant sees that precisely because the source of the categories (for him) rests on a capacity for judgment that does not immediately have such limits, extra considerations are needed to get to the restriction thesis. Were this not so, there would be no need for his focus on the fact that our use of the categories involves particular forms of sensibility, or for the argument of the Antinomies about the specific limitations of these forms.[84]

Hegel is not unaware of this Kantian response, for he tries to block it by remarking, "it is no escape to turn around and explain that reason falls

---

82 See esp. Hegel, V:59, Johnston and Struthers, vol. 1, p. 73; VI:261, Johnston and Struthers, vol. 2, p. 224; *Encyclopedia*, sec. 42 Zusatz 3, VIII:118–19, Wallace, p. 70; *Encyclopedia*, sec. 62, VIII:149, Wallace, p. 96; XVIII:318; XX:322, 350.

83 See above at n. 79, and *AA*, vol. 5, pp. 484–5, and vol. 8, p. 136.

84 It is true that Kant notes his deduction assumes the passive nature of our intuition (B 145), and so is not claimed to apply for knowers such as God, who might cognize things by an active intuition. But even this means only that God might not need to use the categories (in synthesizing a "given" manifold), not that they lack a pure meaning that applies, in some way that we cannot determine theoretically, to things in themselves such as even God and his powers. This point is borne out in detail in Kant, *Lectures in Rational Theology*, trans. A. Wood and G. Clark (Ithaca: Cornell University Press, 1978); and A. Wood, *Kant's Rational Theology* (Ithaca: Cornell University Press, 1978).

into contradictions only by applying the categories."[85] This suggests an acceptance that the Kantian need not believe that things in themselves are directly unreasonable, and therefore fully "beyond thought." Nonetheless, Hegel does not allow this point to make any difference, for he adds immediately, "application of the categories is maintained to be necessary, and reason is not supposed to be equipped with any other forms but categories for the purpose of cognition. But cognition is determining and determinate thinking: so that if reason be merely empty indeterminate thought, it thinks nothing."[86] This charge involves serious confusions. Hegel appears to conflate the fact that (for Kant) the applicability of the categories is necessary in that it is indispensable for our empirical *cognition* (see quote above) with the idea that somehow without such an application the categories themselves would be senseless. There is no basis for concluding that without applying the categories reason is absolutely empty, it "thinks nothing." When I consider God as the ground of the world, I do not cognize him in accord with the principle of the Second Analogy, I do not apply the category of causality in its schematized meaning, and yet I still have something other than a "merely empty" representation. In particular, I can be thinking – perhaps without justification, but still with sense – that somehow God stands in at least that general relation to the world in which any necessary real condition of a thing's being stands to that being.

There are two other texts that can help explain why Hegel did not appreciate this point. In one passage he remarks that "transcendental idealism, carried more consistently to its logical conclusion, has recognized the emptiness of that spectre of the thing in itself."[87] This implies Hegel may have begun by simply accepting the verdict of his contemporaries, that is, accepting the famous critique of Jacobi and Fichte (the philosophers who carried transcendental idealism to "its logical conclusion") that Kant could not consistently use causality as a principle of experience and as a principle that holds for a relation involving things in themselves. But this charge, just like Hegel's own, rests on a refusal to distinguish between pure and empirical meanings of the categories. As long as the latter (the temporal meaning of causality) is not applied to the noumenal, and as long as the former is not used to make any determinate

---

85 Hegel, *Encyclopedia*, sec. 48, VIII:127, Wallace, p. 77.
86 Ibid.
87 Hegel, V:41, Johnston and Struthers, vol. 1, p. 58. Cf. Hegel, II:338, Cerf and Harris, p. 101. A contrary view is expressed by Soll, *An Introduction*, p. 81.

claims about particular objects, there is no direct contradiction of Kant's principles.[88]

In a second text Hegel makes a claim that also leads into the second of his objections to Kant's idealism, the objections concerning the general argument of the Antinomies. On Hegel's reading the argument is that "insofar as it is determined by the categories, the infinite entangles itself in contradictions."[89] On this reading the restrictions Kant is laying down for pure reason are required by reason all by itself, and the specific features of space and time become wholly secondary. *If* one accepts this reading, then it is natural to say (as in Hegel's objection to Kant's idealism) that for Kant objects must be absolutely beyond thought, that things in themselves must be above the contradictory faculties of the mind. It then becomes natural to object, as Hegel does repeatedly, that Kant is being too hard on reason,[90] for it does seem too much to think that reason itself is a contradictory faculty.

This objection is unfair because Kant's Antinomies are not about the contradictions of reason as such, the entanglements that arise from the mere concept of the infinite. On the contrary, the chapter is about how the infinite or unconditional (supposedly) cannot be *determined* to be present in the *empirical* realm. Where such determination is not considered necessary, where there is nothing demonstrably inconsistent about an endless (and supposedly indeterminate) series of complex, or dependent, or contingent items, Kant proposes it is enough to say that there *may* be something unconditioned found in a realm of things in themselves. Thus there may be both simple, free, and necessarily existent noumenal beings, as well as complex, determined, and contingent sensible characters.[91] None of these topics are taken to force one to transcendental idealism; they simply encourage it as an option to be kept in mind. On the other hand, when Kant discusses space and time, there is no room even to entertain a separate noumenal character. Whereas the Third

---

88 This obviously raises the so-called problem of double affection. See Ameriks, *Kant's Theory*, pp. 284–6; and M. Westphal, "In Defense of the Thing in Itself," *Kant-Studien* 59 (1968): 135–41.

89 Hegel, XX:353. Cf. Hegel, V:39, Johnston and Struthers, vol. 1, p. 56, where Kant is attacked for the error of supposing it is reason that is in contradiction with itself, and for not realizing that the contradictions arise "just from the lifting of Reason above the limitations of the Understanding."

90 Hegel, *Encyclopedia*, sec. 48, VIII:126, Wallace, p. 77. Cf. Hegel, XX:359.

91 Actually, although this is his official solution for these topics, Kant says precious little about precisely why he does not accept the dogmatic arguments to the effect that the absence of a simple, or free, or necessary being in noumena would be contradictory. All too often he merely points out how it would be a mistake to assert such beings must exist phenomenally.

Antinomy, for example, can introduce the idea of noumenal freedom, there is no idea of a separate noumenal finitude or infinitude of the spatiotemporal dimensions of the world for the First Antinomy to encourage.

In his basic argument Kant presumes that if spatiotemporal relations were transcendentally real, then the world would have to have either a determinate and infinite[92] or a determinate and finite spatiotemporal magnitude.[93] The particular arguments of the First Antinomy are advanced to show that neither of these disjuncts is possible, and precisely rather than assert that reason itself is contradictory, Kant concludes only that the premise of transcendental realism *must* be given up (unfortunately he does not consider giving up instead what he presumes to follow from this premise, i.e., the supposedly exhaustive disjuncts). None of the steps to this conclusion, questionable as they may be, invoke the claim that the notion of the infinite itself entangles us in contradictions, and Kant even seems willing to allow an infinite future. There is no assertion of a single and basic difficulty with reason; rather, there is a sequence of very different considerations about space and time that supposedly lead to conclusions about the world's dimensions that in turn involve a certain limited restriction of reason.

Hegel never acknowledged the role and structure of the basic argument of the First Antinomy. In a letter of 1812, he explains that as far as he is concerned the content of the Antinomies should be explicated logically without any reference to cosmology: "indeed, all further content about the world, matter, etc., is a useless ballast, a confusing image [*Nebelbild*] of the imagination."[94] The same view is expressed in the *Logic,* where Hegel makes no basic distinction between the various Antinomies and asserts that all concepts of the sensible world involve contradictions – because they are about mere particulars, not because they are concepts of reason.[95] His casual attitude to the text may again explain why Hegel's second objection to Kant's idealism, like his first, applies only against an absurd idea – in the one case, that of an unthinkable object, in the other,

92 See A 529–31/ B 557–9.

93 See A 503–7/ B 531–5. For Kant's difficulties with the notion of infinity, see J. Bennett, *Kant's Dialectic* (Cambridge: Cambridge University Press, 1974), pp. 114–42. Cf. Hegel, V:283ff., Johnston and Struthers, vol. 1, pp. 259ff.

94 Hegel, IV:407; cf. ibid., IV:414.

95 Hegel, V:217, Johnston and Struthers, vol. 1, p. 205; VI:361, Johnston and Struthers, vol. 2, p. 309.

that of an internally incoherent reason – which is not at all a part of that idealism.

F. HEGEL VERSUS KANT'S IDEALISM: ON THE ANTINOMY OF SPACE AND TIME

Similar problems arise as we move from Hegel's general treatment of the Antinomies to his third and last group of objections to Kant's idealism, those that concern the individual treatment of the specific topics of the Dialectic. In each case Hegel urges that Kant has failed to be idealistic in the genuine sense in that he has remained fixed on a choice between abstractly opposed alternatives and has overlooked further options within the knowable realm. Expressed in these general terms his objection points to what is no doubt a proper criticism of Kant, and yet as one looks more closely at exactly how Hegel works out his own critique, it becomes more difficult to approve of it.

Hegel's tendencies are already revealed in his early essay, *Faith and Knowledge,* which gives an overview of the entire Kantian philosophy and emphasizes how Kant has missed a "positive" mediating solution to the Antinomies.[96] The First Antinomy is described as arising simply because "being-other is posited as well as being, i.e., the contradiction in its absolute insuperability. Hence one side of the antinomy must consist in positing the determinate point, and the refutation in positing the opposite, the being-other . . ."[97] This is an elliptical way of saying that we seem forced to posit a first point of space and time, and then also a point beyond that. Nothing is said here to challenge the specifics of the route taken to this dilemma. Instead, Hegel again expresses his general disappointment with Kant's going on to insist on transcendental idealism, and he stresses that Kant's arguments are difficult to reconcile with his later talk about an "endless progress" in our moral life.[98] Correct as he is on the latter point, Hegel's discussion adds nothing to solve the particular theoretical problem at stake.

A few years later, while teaching in Nuremberg, Hegel provided his students with a more detailed treatment of the Antinomies, which at least includes a synopsis of the various arguments as well as the claim that the problem can be resolved because the concepts of a limited and an endless

96 Hegel, II:320, Cerf and Harris, p. 84.
97 Hegel, II:319, Cerf and Harris, p. 83.
98 Hegel, II:320, Cerf and Harris, p. 84.

time (and space) each involve the other, for the limited is what can be transcended, and the endless is what transcends limits.[99] In contrast to these interdependent and hence insufficient concepts, Hegel introduces the notion of an all inclusive or "true infinity," which concerns not the temporal as such but rather reason, whose reflexivity "penetrates the concept and essence of the world."[100] This is, of course, one of Hegel's favorite ideas – that reflection has the peculiar kind of endlessness suggested by the form of a circle, ever turning upon itself, whereas the nonspiritual has a merely linear form (and "bad infinity"). But whatever the value of this idea, it too simply bypasses the original problem, the factual question of the world's physical dimensions, which remains even if there is the kind of necessary relation Hegel stresses between the *concepts* of the limited and the endless.

Similarly frustrating is the treatment in the *Encyclopedia,* where the First Antinomy is described simply as implying "recognition of the doctrine that space and time present a discrete as well as a continuous aspect . . . We can go beyond every definite space and beyond every definite time, but it is no less correct that space and time are real and actual only when they are defined or specialized into 'here' and 'now.' "[101] Here the subject has changed again – and in a third new way – for there is no reason to presume that any party to the Antinomy would have to dispute the "discreteness" of time and space in the way that it is introduced here. The question at issue, though, is how large the world is, and to this Hegel is giving either a strange dogmatic answer, namely that we really can go beyond "every definite" point, or no answer at all. In his final lectures Hegel takes the same ambivalent line. He repeats the points made in Nuremberg and concludes that "the world, as the universe, is the whole; it is thus a universal Idea, and therefore can be determined either as limited or unlimited."[102]

G. HEGEL VERSUS KANT'S IDEALISM: ON THE ANTINOMY OF FREEDOM

The distinctive role of the First Antinomy makes Hegel's indirect approach to it especially disturbing, and all the more so because he might

99 Hegel, IV:185–6; cf. V:275, Johnston and Struthers, vol. 1, p. 252 ("the thesis and the antithesis . . . ").
100 Hegel, IV:386.
101 Hegel, *Encyclopedia,* sec. 48 Zusatz, VIII:129, Wallace, p. 79. Cf. *Encyclopedia,* sec. 100, VIII:212–13, Wallace, p. 100.
102 Hegel, XX:357.

well have made specific objections (e.g., to the exhaustiveness of the basic disjunction Kant poses) that would have blocked Kant's argument to transcendental idealism. Hegel's treatment of the other Antinomies is even briefer, and the evaluation of the treatment is even more difficult. Since Hegel believes that the argument of the Second Antinomy is basically the same as that of the First,[103] and that that of the Fourth is basically the same as that of the Third,[104] we shall examine only his treatment of the Third Antinomy.

Hegel's basic position is that "freedom and necessity, as understood by abstract thinkers, are not independently real, as these thinkers suppose, but merely ideal factors (moments) in the true freedom."[105] This might be read as an expression of the traditional compatibilist position, and one might imagine Hegel pressing against Kant the charge that the whole need and motivation for the project of trying to clear a way for transcendental idealism disappears if there can be an account of human action and morality that allows metaphysical necessity. Thus one might imagine Hegel challenging Kant by pointing out how little Kant had said directly against such a position, and how much Hegel and others had said in their accounts of action and morality without invoking transcendental freedom.[106] In fact, however, Hegel does not take this route, and instead he declares again that both thesis and antithesis can be true, that both (absolute) freedom and necessity hold, though only as part of a larger truth.

Precisely what Hegel has in mind here is difficult to determine, for he does not opt for the Kantian solution, that what can hold is both *transcendental freedom* and *phenomenal necessity,* nor, I believe, for the compatibilist position that a lack of transcendental freedom still leaves a merely *phenomenal* but adequate kind of *freedom* (viz., rational self-determination) that is consistent with *absolute necessity.* It is true that sometimes it appears that all Hegel has in mind by our freedom is the ordinary self-determination of the compatibilist, or our participation in the broader self-determination of the rational course of the world as a whole.[107] In fact, however, he also implies (as a part of his general strategy of adopting a synthesis that includes both of the opposing theses) that we do have the absolute free-

103 Hegel, IV:187–9; cf. V:217ff., Johnston and Struthers, vol. 1, pp. 205ff.; Hegel, VI:171, Johnston and Struthers, vol. 2, pp. 146; XX:357.

104 Hegel, IV:192; XX:357–8.

105 Hegel, *Encyclopedia,* sec. 48 Zusatz, VIII:129, Wallace, p. 79; cf. sec. 35 Zusatz, VIII:102, Wallace p. 55–6.

106 See Ameriks, *Kant's Theory,* pp. 185–233.

107 See the sketch for "a proof that the will is free" in Hegel's *Philosophy of Right,* secs. 4–5, VII:48–50, trans. T. M. Knox (Oxford: Clarendon Press, 1952), pp. 21–2.

dom that concerns the Kantian, the "ability to abstract from everything whatever," the negative freedom to be completely undetermined (in some contexts) by anything outside one.[108] What Hegel argues is not that such freedom is unrequired but rather that it is insufficient, that, as Kant indicated, we want not only the ability to choose as an uncaused cause but also the ability to choose in this way to follow a rational law. His dispute with Kant arises only with the issue of how such a law is to be understood, for Hegel believes that it can and must be explained in a much less formal way than Kant would accept.

What is disturbing about Hegel's position is that, while he does appear to allow that absolute or "negative freedom" is at least part of what man has, he does not put any effort into arguing for the possibility of such freedom (he appears to think it is obvious on introspection).[109] Kant's doctrine of transcendental idealism is at least addressed to this issue, and it at least takes seriously the deterministic implications of science and social life. Thus Kant uses the Third Antinomy to introduce the idea that, despite universal natural necessity, there may be some uncaused causality. Of course his argument may be faulty, and it still provides no theoretical reason to affirm that *we* have such causality, but at least it makes a start toward the argument needed. Hegel, however, simply tries to have the best of both worlds, that is, he builds on the metaphysical doctrine of our absolute negative freedom, while impugning traditional metaphysics and dismissing all particular arguments to the doctrine,

There is thus in all of Hegel's systematic and textual discussions a kind of strategic silence about the basic issue of the existence of absolute freedom. In the first Jena writings, for example, he presents no details of the discussions in the Third Antinomy and simply declares, "Freedom and necessity are ideal factors, and thus are not in real opposition . . . Freedom is the character of the Absolute when the Absolute is posited as something inner . . . Necessity is the character of the Absolute insofar as it is observed as something external . . . Free will [*Willkür*] and accident,

108 Ibid. I believe this point is not stressed enough in R. Schacht's fine essay, "Hegel on Freedom," in *Hegel: A Collection of Critical Essays*, ed. A. MacIntyre (Garden City, NY: Doubleday Anchor, 1972), pp. 289–328. For example, Schacht says, "The experience of freedom is taken by Hegel . . . to reflect the fact that what are commonly referred to as the laws of nature do not govern the whole of phenomenal reality" (ibid., p. 301). Schacht does not point out how important this claim is and how nonetheless Hegel fails to say it clearly and fails to offer justification.

109 Cf. above at n. 107; and Hegel's *Philosophy of Mind* (in the *Encyclopedia*), secs. 473–82, X: 295–302, trans. W. Wallace and A. V. Miller (Oxford: Clarendon Press, 1971), pp. 234–40.

which have a place only in subordinate standpoints, are banished from the concept of the science of the Absolute."[110] The first part of this statement sidesteps the fundamental point that in one sense freedom and necessity must be in "real opposition," for to hold to transcendental or negative freedom is to hold to the existence of uncaused causality, and to hold to transcendental or absolute necessity is to assert the direct denial of this. The latter part of Hegel's statement, the remarks about an arbitrary free will (*Willkür*), might suggest that Hegel is coming down on the side of the denial of negative freedom. But the remarks do not settle the matter, for we know Hegel eventually leaves room for the existence of even the accidental, and the fact that such matters are not considered part of the *concept* of an absolute science hardly means they cannot exist at all. It seems rather that once more Hegel's point is that even if there is such freedom, it by itself is not the highest state.

In later work Hegel expresses a slightly different but equally undecisive position. In Nuremberg he introduces the idea that the "true solution" of the Antinomy is in the relation of community or interaction (*Wechselwirkung*). Each item in such a relation is a cause and in that sense is said to be free,[111] and yet each is also an effect, and in that sense is subject to necessity. But clearly, whether such a relation exists or can be proved would not by itself settle the issue of human freedom. The fundamental question remains of whether and on what basis we can believe in some uncaused causality on our part. In the *Logic*,[112] as in the *Lectures on the History of Philosophy*,[113] no new ideas are introduced on this issue, and Hegel implies that the matter has already been dealt with satisfactorily. The arguments of the Antinomy are dismissed as "proving" their own claims only by finding opposed views to be contrary to these original claims. Thus the arguments are held to be entirely question-begging: the determinist disproves freedom only by finding it inconsistent with determinism, and vice versa. Here Hegel entirely misses the underlying aim of

---

110 Hegel, II:108, Surber, p. 83. In *Faith and Knowledge* Hegel does go on to review Kant's discussion briefly, but he reduces it to the idea that "when they are thought without any communion at all freedom and necessity do not conflict" (II:320, Cerf and Harris, p. 84). This is a very inaccurate expression of Kant's position, since for Kant the freedom of the intelligible character has responsibility for, and so is "in communion with" the necessity of the empirical character. See A 551/ B 579.

111 Hegel, IV:190. Hegel speaks here of an "absolute causality of freedom." Cf. VI:237–40, Johnston and Struthers, vol. 2, pp. 203–5.

112 Hegel, VI:441–2, Johnston and Struthers, vol. 2, p. 377. Cf. Hegel, II:320, Cerf and Harris, p. 84.

113 Hegel, XX:357.

Kant's discussion, the exposure of the dogmatic assumption that for the law of causality to hold at all it must hold in a metaphysically absolute sense as a temporal rule. Once this supposition is dropped, we are left not with question-begging claims but rather with consistent demonstrations (given Kant's Analytic) that it would be improper to assert there *can* be a *temporal* free causality, and improper to assert there *cannot* be a *non*temporal free causality.

Hegel does not consider, let alone use, this solution, nor does he ever show precisely how anything short of this solution would be satisfactory. The most natural formulation of his own position is that he wants to continue to assert our freedom in the traditional sense but simply has no interest in or means for backing that assertion. A less charitable reading would have him asserting that the contradiction of freedom and necessity is not a mere appearance arising from the introduction of dogmatic premises and the misapplication of our reason but is rather a truth about our nature as finite things, that is, just what one should expect from items that are only finite.[114] I will presume, however, that when Hegel seems to be talking in this way we are to say not that he is ascribing a literally contradictory relation to things but rather that he has in mind some kind of lesser and at least comprehensible contrast like that between what he calls the continuity and discreteness of space and time. But of course this is only to say that at best Hegel's treatment of the Third Antinomy is no better than that of the First; it leaves the original question, as well as Kant's treatment of it, untouched.

H. HEGEL VERSUS KANT'S IDEALISM: ON THE PARALOGISMS

A similar and final example of Hegel's treatment of Kant can be found in his discussion of the Paralogisms. The main issue that Hegel discusses here, the soul's simplicity, is treated just like the issues of the Antinomies (not inappropriately, for I suspect Kant originally meant to treat it under the Second Antinomy). We are to see how both sides of the debate can be affirmed, for the soul is both simple and complex: "Thus, for example, while the soul may be admitted to be simple self-sameness, it is at the same time active and institutes distinctions in its own nature."[115] Here again we find a shift from the original issue, for neither party to the traditional question need dispute that the soul involves some "distinctions." The

114 See, e.g., Hegel, XX:359.
115 Hegel, *Encyclopedia*, sec. 47 Zusatz, VIII:126, Wallace, p. 76.

question is rather whether it is a simple being or a complex of beings; whichever it is, it can involve "distinctions" and need not be what Hegel calls "a mere dead thing." To talk about the soul as simple *and* something else besides is to ignore discussing how we are to resolve the original question of whether the soul is simple at all.

In the same paragraph in which he appears to encourage the assumption of the soul's simplicity, Hegel also seems to say that such an assumption is false, that "predicates like simplicity, permanence, etc. are inapplicable to the soul."[116] Taken literally, this implies Hegel thinks that what is simple and complex is not even simple, which is of course an absurd thought. Taken more charitably, his position must be that what is simple and complex in a sense, is *not merely* simple, that is, is not "a dead thing," and in that sense *alone* is not to be said to be simple. But again, it would seem there is no need to make this point, for no party to the Paralogism holds such a "dead" view. In fact, however, Hegel ascribes something very like this position to Kant. Hegel gives the name "dogmatic subjectivism" to the Kantian position that supposedly holds that the soul (qua simple) is only a form, in contrast to the rationalist position of "dogmatic objectivism," which holds that the soul can be described in terms of transcendent objective (material as opposed to merely formal) predicates.[117] Later Hegel implied that Kant's view is that if the self is not a mere sensible thing, then it is not something actual at all.[118] Thus Hegel explains that whereas Kant thought the terms "being, thing, substance" are "too high" for the self, on his own view they are "too low."[119]

Hegel's critique of Kant gives some sense to his comments about the soul, but the critique itself is very questionable. In particular, (a) Hegel implies that Kant denies the existence and substantiality of the soul,[120] something that Kant does not do (what Kant does is criticize *certain* ways of arguing about the soul); and (b) Hegel fails to explain on what basis he means to defend such assertions, given those who argue (*partly* under the influence of Kant) that the soul might be a mere complex of material

---

116 Ibid.
117 Hegel, II:319, Cerf and Harris, p. 83.
118 Hegel, XX:355.
119 Hegel, XX:356.
120 See Hegel, *Encyclopedia*, sec. 47, VIII:125, Wallace, p. 75: "That the soul cannot be described as the substantial, simple, self-same . . . Kant argues." A similar error is made by R. Chisholm, *Person and Object* (London: Allen & Unwin, 1976), p. 42. For a critique, see K. Ameriks, "Chisholm's Paralogisms," *Idealistic Studies* 11 (1981): 100–2, and "Kant's First Paralogism," *Akten des V Internationalen Kant-Kongresses*, ed. G. Funke (Bonn: Bouvier, 1981), vol. 1, pp. 485–92.

parts with rational functions. Once again, in the context of urging us to go beyond two opposed and limited positions – that the soul is a mere thing, just like any other, and that it is a mere form, not a thing at all – to a reconciling higher view, Hegel wholly fails to focus on the arguments behind either of the original positions (that the soul is simple or it is not) and falls into a dogmatic acceptance of one of them (simplicity).

In one important respect Hegel's handling of the Paralogisms differs from his treatment of the rest of the Dialectic, for this chapter has a different relation to the doctrine of transcendental idealism. In the Anti-nomies, Hegel's failure to read Kant closely had as it most important consequence that it left him without a direct counter to transcendental idealism. In the Paralogisms, Hegel's failure has only the immediate con-sequence that he misperceives the complexity of Kant's position, and so fails to see the depth of Kant's critique of the tradition (a critique that would also apply to Hegel) as well as the tolerance within Kant's positive view (which *allows* that the self may have all the complexity Hegel asserts). But a further consequence of Hegel's approach here is that he misses the epistemological complement to Kant's critique of the metaphysical doctrines of rational psychology. Kant's Paralogisms implies not only a questioning of certain kinds of specific claims about the soul but also a challenge to the basic method on which such claims were based, namely via an appeal to an allegedly privileged inner perception. The main locus of this challenge is in the doctrine of apperception and the Refutation of Idealism, where Kant argues that our self-knowledge not only requires judgment and general rules but also is parasitic upon spatial data and external objects. Hegel practically ignores this argument, and when he does come to it he seriously misrepresents it, saying that its point is that temporal determination requires reference to something permanent in *oneself*.[121] Thus Hegel misses Kant's most significant challenge to the metaphysical tradition, the challenge to explain how mere self-reflection can give us determinate knowledge without reference to a public realm. Hegel did challenge the Cartesian tradition in many ways, but he often remained bound to its presumption that self-perception (as in the meta-physical articulation of the forms of *Geist*) has a special privilege. In this respect his treatment of the Paralogisms involves his most serious under-estimation of Kant's work, and in this way his critique of the Dialectic suffers from the same weakness as his critique of the Analytic: an overcon-fidence about what is obvious from the mere representation of the "I."

121 Hegel, XX:348–9.

7

THE HEGELIAN CRITIQUE OF KANTIAN MORALITY

Important work on the Hegelian critique of Kantian morality can now be found in at least three different domains. The first is the field of current English-language ethical theory, where after an influential neo-Hegelian attack on Kant by Bernard Williams and others, Kantians have now begun to mount a sharp counterattack. The second is the domain of English-language Kant scholarship proper, from Paton and Knox[1] to Gregor and Hill, where exegetes have tried diligently but without true popular success to put down the cruder misconceptions about Kant. The third sphere is the German scene, where after the great historical researches of scholars such as Henrich and Schmucker, a number of younger philosophers have attempted to combine traditional exegesis with an extensive systematic

---

1 Here I am thinking specifically of T. M. Knox, "Hegel's Attitude to Kant's Ethics," *Kant-Studien* 49 (1957–8): 70–81, an account that is probably closest to mine except for two points. First, I think Knox misses Hegel's intention when he concludes that "what Hegel is saying here is not that Kant's analysis of duty and moral experience is mistaken, but that there is an experience of a different kind that transcends it" (p. 76). I take it that Hegel rather thinks there is such a thing as positive moral experience, and so his analysis of the Kantian position as precluding that is meant as a *reductio*. Secondly, I believe Knox underestimates the significance of the concept of love *within* ethics in Kant's work. Knox says, "For Kant as for Hegel, there is a higher sphere than that of law, a sphere where the law is 'fulfilled' by the love of God. This sphere is visualized by both of them as a religious sphere" (p. 77). But I will argue that for Kant (as for Hegel) love as such is primarily neither love of God for us nor love of God by us, but rather ethical love of human beings for one another.

309

and analytic treatment of the Hegelian challenge. I believe it is only by considering all these perspectives together – and by realizing how closely related they are – that we can properly estimate the force and value of Hegel's challenge. As a first step toward such a consideration, I will briefly outline what appear to be the three main points at issue, and then by focusing on one of them, I will show how to a great extent Kant can be vindicated. Obviously, a complete evaluation of this matter must await a thorough examination of Kant's entire practical philosophy as well as an explanation of how Hegel's critique fits in with the general objective of his own massive system.[2]

A. THREE DISPUTES: THE POSSIBILITY, CONTENT, AND MOTIVATION OF MORALITY

In their briefest form, the three major difficulties that Hegel develops are these. First, according to Kant, morality requires absolute freedom, and yet such freedom is (supposedly) not to be had in the empirical or phenomenal realm, and thus morality is regarded as possible only on the condition that transcendental idealism is accepted. For Hegel, this is to say that the very *possibility* of Kantian morality absurdly rests on an obscure, otherworldly, and unacceptable metaphysics. Second, Kant proposes that the principles of morality rest on the categorical imperative, and what this requires is to be determined by testing maxims to see if they can be consistently and universally willed. For Hegel, this is to say that the very *content* of Kantian morality absurdly rests on a test that is too empty to prescribe any significant specific form of action without also unacceptably permitting practically any other form of action. Third, Kant is taken to hold that only action from duty can have moral worth, and thus, since the ground of duty is defined independently of all our natural inclinations, it seems that Kantian morality leaves the very *motivation* of moral activity unexplainable. For Hegel, this is to say that even if action on Kantian principles is metaphysically possible and specifiable, we would absurdly be left with no moving reason to act on such a morality, and we may even be left with a morality that leads us to work against or to undermine the good that is given in our nature.

There are, of course, other charges that one could press against Kant, most notably that ultimately he leaves the very obligatory ground of the

2 For further limitations of this study, see above Chapter 6, Prologue.

moral law dependent on an "inscrutable" "fact of reason."[3] But whatever extra difficulties there may be, the three problems mentioned surely appear weighty enough to merit Hegel's emphasis,[4] especially since it is fairly obvious how he might have thought his own philosophy provides an immediate solution. Thus, when Hegel introduces his notion of *Sittlichkeit*[5] or custom (or "ethos") in the *Phenomenology of Spirit,* he straightway explains how it handles the problems of the possibility, content, and motivation of morality. First, since a social ethos could not be in place unless it is practiced and supported by individuals, action in accord with such an ethos obviously has to be possible, and no recourse to a peculiar metaphysics is needed to establish this. Second, since an ethos is what it is precisely in virtue of an easily recognizable content that can guide and distinguish the action of a particular people, there can be no problem in principle about its being abstract and empty of content. Third, since individuals inevitably develop their desires through maturing within their

3 The seriousness of this problem is brought out in D. Henrich's "Der Begriff der sittlichen Einsicht und Kants Lehre von Faktum der Vernunft," *in Kant: Zur Deutung seiner Theorie von Erkennen und Handeln,* ed. G. Prauss (Cologne: Kiepenhauer und Witsch, 1973), pp. 223–54, and "Die Deduktion des Sittengesetzes," in *Denken im Schatten des Nihilismus,* ed. A. Schwan (Darmstadt: Wissenschaftliche Buchgesellschaft, 1975), pp. 55–112; R. Bittner, *Moralisches Gebot oder Autonomie* (Freiburg: Karl Alber, 1983), pp. 140–5; and K. Ameriks, "Kant's Deduction of Freedom and Morality," *Journal of the History of Philosophy* 19 (1981): 53–79. Omission of this point can appear unfair to Hegel, for a large part of his critique of Kantian moral law as "alien" to us rests on his displeasure with its appearing as a mere given "fact" rather than a systematically justified principle. But it is not clear that at this sheer theoretical level – at which Kant is reduced to having to rely on a "fact" rather than a proof – Hegel has much better to offer.

4 It is no accident, then, that recent commentators such as Rawls have in effect divided the evaluation of Kant's theory into just these issues. See, e.g., Rawls's lectures at Johns Hopkins, August 1983, which distinguish these problems: "(a) The categorical imperative must not be interpreted as merely formal, but as having sufficient structure and *content* to provide at least some rough guidelines for practical moral deliberation; (b) the categorical imperative must represent the Moral Law as a principle of autonomy, so that from our consciousness of this law as supremely authoritative and regulative for us we can recognize our *freedom;* (c) our consciousness of the Moral Law as supremely *authoritative* for us as reasonable and rational agents must be found in our everyday moral thought, feeling and conduct; and the Moral Law must be a principle recognized, at least implicitly, by ordinary human reason; (d) our consciousness of the Moral Law as supremely authoritative for us must be so deeply rooted in our person as reasonable and rational beings that this law by itself can be, when fully grasped and understood, a sufficient *motive* for us to act from it, whatever our natural desires" (Lecture II, pp. 1–2; the fourth condition that Rawls lists, namely authoritativeness, is touched on in my previous note).

5 For a remark by Kant on the ordinary meaning of *Sittlichkeit* see his *Lectures on Ethics,* trans. Louis Infeld (New York: Bobbs-Merrill, 1963), p. 73. Cf. K.-H. Ilting, *Naturrecht und Sittlichkeit* (Stuttgart: Klett-Cotta, 1983), p. 244.

particular ethos, they will naturally tend to develop a self that values what the ethos promotes, so that in doing what it calls for they will be fulfilling a call in their own self and will have a thoroughly intelligible motivation to morality.

Hegel's own inimitable outline of these points – but with the problem of content placed before that of possibility – is as follows:

> [i] The spiritual being [*Sittlichkeit*] thus exists first of all for self-conscious-ness as law which has an intrinsic being; the universality associated with testing the law, a merely formal, not an essential universality, is now behind us . . . [ii] Again, it is not a commandment, which only ought to be; it is and is valid; it is the universal "I" of the category, the "I" which is immediately a category, and the world is of this reality. [iii] But since this existent law is valid unconditionally, the obedience of self-consciousness is not the serving of a master whose commands were arbitrary, and in which it would not recognize itself. On the contrary, laws are the thoughts of its own absolute consciousness, thoughts which are immediately its own.[6]

A simpler formulation of these same points, and also a confirmation of the idea that they are not incidental but central to the structure of the Hegelian view, can be found in Bradley's famous summary (again with the content problem preceding the possibility problem):

> Let us now in detail compare the advantage of our present view with the defects of "duty for duty's sake." The objections which we found fatal to that view may be stated as follows: [i] the universal was abstract. There was no content which belonged to it and was one with it; and the consequence was that either nothing could be willed, or what was willed was willed not be-cause of the universal but capriciously. [ii] The universal was "subjective." It certainly gave itself out as "objective," in the sense of being independent of this or that person, but still it was not real in the world. It did not come to us as what was, it came as what (merely) was to be, an inner nature in moral persons, which has no power to carry itself out and transform the world . . . [iii] The universal left a part of ourselves outside it. However much we tried

---

6 Hegel, *Phenomenology of Spirit*, trans. A. V. Miller (Oxford: Oxford University Press, 1977), pp. 260–1. Cf. his *Natural Law*, trans. T. M. Knox (Philadelphia: University of Pennsylvania Press, 1975), pp. 112–13, and *Philosophy of Mind*, trans. A. V. Miller (Oxford: Oxford University Press, 1971), sec. 514: "The consciously free substance, in which the absolute 'ought' is no less an 'is,' has actuality as the spirit of a nation . . . The person performs his duty as *his own* and as something which *is;* and in this necessity *he* has himself and his actual freedom." Here we get the motivation and possibility points explicitly and the content point implicitly. Cf. L. Siep, "Was heisst Aufhebung der Moralität in Sittlichkeit in Hegels Rechts-philosophie?" *Hegel-Studien* 17 (1980): 86.

to be good, however determined we were to make our will one with the good will, yet we never succeeded. There was always something left in us which was in contradiction with the good.[7]

Although these passages should be adequate to give some idea of why and where Hegel thinks he bested Kant, by themselves, of course, they barely set the stage for an evaluation of the Hegelian critique. The first point, for example, has weight only so long as Hegel can supplement it by a superior account of what Kant thought was central to establishing the possibility of morality, namely human freedom. Without a direct attack on either (a) Kant's claim that an absolute kind of freedom is requisite for morality or (b) the claim that such freedom cannot be had empirically, the actuality, and thus the demonstrable possibility of *Sittlichkeit* does nothing to show the possibility of genuine morality (in the broad and ordinary sense required to avoid begging the question). Elsewhere I have argued that Hegel has surprisingly little to offer in the way of a direct attack here,[8] but it is well known that he did develop a complex alternative notion of freedom as reflective agreement with the dialectical path of reason and spirit. This notion is a weighty indirect challenge to the Kantian conception, but it brings with it metaphysical features that to many today would make it as objectionable as transcendental idealism.

The second issue, the content of morality, is also something of a standoff. If the tests for usage of the categorical imperative are taken to exclude any reference to empirical matters,[9] or even the general concepts, given in the later formulations, of man as an end in himself and a member of a kingdom of ends, then of course Kantian morality has an abstractness that contrasts with the detailed prescriptions of *Sittlichkeit*. This fact is of limited significance, though, since the use of these exclusions, common as it is by Hegel, is manifestly unfair. What Hegel can argue is that even if considerable content were derivable in a nonarbitrary manner from the categorical imperative[10] (something that is not clearly achieved in the *Metaphysics of Morals*), it still would seem clear that an ethos, since it must

7 F. H. Bradley, *Ethical Studies* (Indianapolis: Bobbs-Merrill, 1951), p. 111.
8 See above Chapter 6, sec. G.
9 That some reference to the empirical is relevant to the categorical imperative is nicely argued in A. Buchanan, "Categorical Imperatives and Moral Principles," *Philosophical Studies* 31 (1977): 248–60.
10 See Ping-cheung Lo, "A Critical Re-evaluation of the Alleged 'Empty Formalism' of Kantian Ethics," *Ethics* 91 (1981): 181–201; and O. O'Neill, "Consistency in Action," in *Morality and Universalizability*, ed. Nelson T. Potter and Mark Timmons (Dordrecht: Reidel, 1985), pp. 159–86.

exist precisely as a functioning guide, will remain more specific and more recognizable by people at large than a typical formal construction of duties devised by a Kantian. But the crucial point here is that this superior concreteness can be a real advantage only if the content is *correct*. At this point, rather than lapsing into social relativism, as he is all too often still charged with having done,[11] Hegel tends to fall back on bounds set by pure morality: our commitment to *Sittlichkeit* is to be restrained by a Kantian respect for man as an end in himself.[12] In this way Hegel can properly criticize ancient slave culture as well as the similarly objectionable *Sittlichkeit* of some modern societies, but only at the price of relying on what seem to be the very abstract principles he meant to transcend.

Given these and other similar difficulties with the much belabored first two points of Hegel's critique, I shall focus on the third point, the problem of motivation, especially since it is on this issue that Hegel has in effect been followed by the most interesting recent critics of Kant, and because it is here that Kant's own views have an important and often unappreciated complexity. There are actually two intricately connected problems here,[13] but rather than dealing purely with one or the other, I will be considering them together. One problem is how to understand moral motivation at all if it is as disconnected from our natural inclinations as Kant indicates. The second problem is how Kant can handle the large domain of moral values that appear to fall outside the common concept of duty, in particular the values of an attractive life, with a healthy fund of altruistic emotions and a direct concern for specific individuals. (This problem is stressed by Williams, Stocker, and Blum.)[14] Current

11 E.g., A. Donagan, *The Theory of Morality* (Chicago: University of Chicago Press, 1977), pp. 12–17.

12 I am thinking especially of the primacy of "abstract right" in Hegel's *Philosophy of Right*. See W. H. Walsh, "Hegelian Ethics," in *New Studies in Ethics*, vol. I, ed. W. D. Hudson (London: Macmillan, 1974), pp. 431–2; Siep, "Aufhebung," p. 93; and M. Riedel, *Studien zu Hegels Rechtsphilosophie* (Frankfurt: Suhrkamp, 1969), p. 72. Cf. Andreas Wildt, *Autonomie und Anerkennung* (Stuttgart: Klett-Cotta, 1982), who argues that Hegel is best construed as not faulting Kant's ethics for lacking all content, and that Hegel's major concern is not to doubt the inviolability of legal duties but to display the social conditions in which alone adherence to them has an understandable motivation (pp. 27–8, 41–2, 96ff.; see also pp. 18, 149, and below at n. 69).

13 The two problems are closely linked by Wildt, *Autonomie*, p. 147.

14 See B. Williams, "Persons, Character and Morality," in *The Identities of Persons*, ed. A. Rorty (Berkeley: University of California Press, 1976), pp. 197–216, and "Morality and the Emotions," in *Morality and Moral Reasoning*, ed. J. Casey (London: Methuen, 1971), pp. 1–24; Michael Stocker, "The Schizophrenia of Modern Ethical Theories," *Journal of Philosophy* 63 (1976): 453–66; and L. Blum, *Friendship, Altruism, and Morality* (London: Routledge and Kegan Paul, 1980). Similar charges focusing on the examples of gratitude and friend-

critics emphasize the latter problem by charging that Kant's emphasis on purity, and in particular on what he calls strict or perfect duties, leads not only to a neglect but also to a distortion of other values, so that the acts of benevolence, friendship, development of talent, and so forth, that Kant lumps under the heading of "imperfect duty," become poisoned by what Williams has called the curse of having "one thought too many."[15] That is, the Kantian who insists on first checking his general rule for perfect obligations before reacting in a crisis with a saving "human gesture" infects himself in such a way that he *never* can give the gesture with its proper spontaneity.

On this point a curious convergence has emerged among current English-language and German-language interpreters of Kant. While the English-speaking philosophers express the problem in roughly the terms just used but without discussing Kant in detail, recent German expositors – Andreas Wildt, Rüdiger Bittner, and Gerold Prauss[16] – go on at length to try to explain why and to what extent Kant's own development led him to minimize attention to acts that are praiseworthy but fall outside of the model of strict duty. Prauss, for example, argues that full recognition of such acts was hindered by an excessive desire to hold together freedom and morality, a desire that went back to both Kant's general tendency to see nonmoral freedom as chaotic and his special frustration in finding a nonmoral basis for absolute freedom. Wildt, on the other hand, argues that Kant was simply preoccupied with the relatively clear rights that can be sanctioned as if on the basis of legal duties, and so his interpretation in effect gives a deeper meaning to Thomas Hill's point that "it is as if Kant started to work out a moral theory on the model of legal-like duties and then discovering that there is more to morality than duty, still retained the old labels for types of duty rather than spoil the symmetry of his theory by changing to more natural expressions."[17] In particular, Wildt charges Kant with overlooking the fact that although there can be moral obligations to acts of gratitude, forgiveness, and sacrifice, these acts, *unlike* legal or strict obligations, are not suitable to be

---

ship were raised by C. D. Broad, *Five Types of Ethical Theory* (London: Routledge and Kegan Paul, 1930); and H. Reiner, *Die philosophische Ethik* (Heidelberg: Quelle Meyer, 1964). For a defense of the *nonmoral* value of a "well-balanced" life, see S. Wolf, "Moral Saints," *Journal of Philosophy* 79 (1982): 419–39.

15 Williams, "Morality and the Emotions," p. 23.

16 See Wildt, *Autonomie*, pp. 16–17, 124–34; Bittner, *Moralisches Gebot*, pp. 124–67; and G. Prauss, *Kant über Freiheit als Autonomie* (Frankfurt: Klostermann, 1983), pp. 262–3.

17 T. Hill, "Kant on Imperfect Duty and Supererogation, *Kant-Studien* 62 (1971): 74.

demanded by the benefiting parties.[18] Bittner also argues for a need to move beyond a juridical model of moral evaluation (to what he calls a "dietetic" of counsels of "wisdom"), but his interpretation is more like Prauss's insofar as he sees Kant as having been most concerned with autonomy and the basic deduction of morality. Yet, while Prauss thinks the notion of autonomy can be used to justify even more than just the strictly moral, Bittner claims, in a manner reminiscent of Robert Paul Wolff, that it cannot even justify strict obligation, for autonomy requires adherence only to self-legislated laws, whereas obligations supposedly are commands that must have force even – and especially – over those who feel unwilling to "legislate" them.

These interpretations differ in many details, but it is striking that although these writers are not on the whole very sympathetic to Hegel, they all discuss him in this context. Little effort is needed to see that the moral concerns which interest both the English speakers and the Germans – especially a concern for saving the nonlegalistic aspects of autonomy – correspond nicely to what Hegel meant to cover with his notion of *Sittlichkeit*. The social ethos not only generates a climate for the respect of perfect duty but also is meant to preserve our autonomy while providing all the concrete components of the full moral life – for example, the virtues of gratitude, forgiveness, solidarity – that the Kantian emphasis on such duty seems to neglect or undermine. Moreover, given Hegel's acute analysis of the interdependence of individual thought, work, and feeling on the one hand, and the ideology, labor, and desire-generating mechanisms of society on the other,[19] it is natural to turn to *Sittlichkeit* for explaining the crucial relation between individual motives and the social values left out by the concept of perfect duty and whatever can be plausibly deduced from it.[20]

Before any evaluation of Hegel's proposals can be given, it must be made clear that it is unfair to suppose, as some earlier interpreters have, that Kant's problem is that he has no concept of the supererogatory or

---

18 Wildt, *Autonomie*, pp. 131–41. Wildt here is arguing that Kant has no room for what G. R. Grice calls "ultra obligations" (*The Grounds of Moral Judgment* [Cambridge: Cambridge University Press, 1967], pp. 155–6). I will be arguing that Wildt is wrong on this point because he too quickly dismisses Kant's postulates and duties of love (see esp. *Autonomie*, pp. 131, 155).

19 See Hegel, *Phenomenology*, p. 213, and *Philosophy of Mind*, sec. 524–5.

20 It is thus fitting that although Donagan gives Hegel's notion of *Sittlichkeit* a sharp critique (see above at n. 11), he goes on to build his own theory around the categories Hegel emphasized: abstract right, family, civil society, intention and purpose, culpability, conscience.

allows no value in meritorious but (what we would ordinarily call) non-obligatory action. On this point neo-Hegelian critics of Kantianism were generally attacking a straw man and simply neglecting what Kant and his careful expositors really hold.[21] The crucial question is not so much whether Kant says there is moral value in what goes beyond strict obligation; rather it is how he proposes to explain our interest in such value. In particular, how can he accommodate the obvious pressures to interpret such interest as resting on an acknowledgment of the primacy of our affective nature – and perhaps the *Sittlichkeit* that interacts with it – while not sacrificing his own rationalistic conception of autonomy? To approach this issue we need an overview of Kant's general treatment of the problem of motivation and of what this implies for such matters as particular altruistic emotions.

B. KANT ON MORAL MOTIVATION

It is well known that since the beginning of his serious work in ethics, Kant gave the problem of motivation a central position, and in fact he was so insistent on it that he at first inclined to a kind of moral sense theory. Moreover, even when he moved beyond such a theory because of his commitment to the necessary character of moral rules, he was very concerned that the intellectualistic orientation that this commitment required (since it put the basis of morality in reason rather than sense) should not be allowed to conflict with the fundamental principle of the universal accessibility and applicability of morality. Whatever it is that morality requires, a complex intellectual capacity should not be needed to perceive what these requirements are. Obligation must reach down to the common man, and so every rationalist morality is condemned that does not allow the common man both to see what is right and to move toward realizing that right.[22]

---

21 See Hill, "Imperfect Duty"; David Heyd, "Beyond the Call of Duty in Kant's Ethics," *Kant-Studien* 71 (1980): 308–24; P. Eisenberg, "From the Forbidden to the Supererogatory, the Basic Categories in Kant's 'Tugendlehre,'" *American Philosophical Quarterly* 3 (1966): 255–69; Mary Gregor, *Laws of Freedom* (New York: Barnes and Noble, 1963); Prauss, *Autonomie*, pp. 259–60.

22 See e.g., Kant, *Lectures*, p. 74, and "On the Proverb: That May Be True in Theory but Is of No Practical Use," trans. T. Humphrey, in *Perpetual Peace and Other Essays* (Indianapolis: Hackett, 1983), p. 70 [287–8]. In this chapter, immediately following references to pages of English translations of Kant, references in parentheses are given to pages in the *Akademieausgabe* (*AA*): *Kant's gesammelte Schriften* (Berlin: Preussische Akademie der Wissenschaften/ de Gruyter, 1900–). Cf. W. Kersting, "Kann die Kritik der praktischen Vernunft populär sein?" *Studia Leibnitiana* 15 (1983): 82–93.

Here we must pass over Kant's striking claim that the categorical imperative solves the first problem and makes proper recognition of what is right within the reach of all. This still does not solve the second problem, what he calls "the philosopher's stone": how "to give to this judgment of the understanding a compelling force."[23] At first he even suggests that unless we know there is something in us that really can respond to this judgment, the judgment itself loses its claim: "We are forever hearing sermons about what ought be done from people who do not stop to consider whether what they preach can be done . . . We must know whether mankind is capable of performing what is demanded of him."[24] After some halfhearted attempts at building this capability into the judgmental faculty itself (so that, for example, the intellectual horror of inconsistency or formlessness is said to stimulate action),[25] Kant's general line in his early Critical work is to say that only religiosity gives man the needed impetus to be moral. Although "the pre-eminent consideration in morality is purity of disposition," this consideration "would lose its force if there existed no being to take notice of it."[26] Or, more precisely, unless we believe there is "a Being to give vigor and reality to the moral laws," these laws will not be "springs to action" and morality will be empty to us.[27] Hence, "without religion obligation is motiveless. Religion supplies the conditions under which the binding force of the laws can be thought."[28]

These remarks are in tension with the ultimate critical doctrine of autonomy, and later Kant is much clearer about keeping the sheer validity of the moral law free from jeopardy by motivational problems.[29] In place of a direct reference to religion, he inserts an account of "respect" as a

---

23 Kant, *Lectures*, p. 45. Cf. Kant's letter to Herz, end of 1773 (*AA*, vol. 10, p. 154), and R6867, R6915, R6972, R6988 (*AA*, vol. 17, *Reflexionen*).

24 Kant, *Lectures*, p. 3.

25 See Henrich, "Der Begriff," pp. 239–47; H. Allison, "The Concept of Freedom in Kant's Semi-critical Ethics," *Archiv für Geschichte der Philosophie*, 68 (1986): 96–115; and K. Ward, *The Development of Kant's View of Ethics* (Oxford: Basil Blackwell, 1972), pp. 58–60. For a residue of this view, cf. Kant, *Critique of Practical Reason*, trans. L. W. Beck (Indianapolis: Bobbs-Merrill 1956), p. 164 (*AA*, 160).

26 Kant, *Lectures*, p. 80.

27 Kant, *Lectures*, p. 82; cf. ibid., pp. 40, 77–8, and *Critique of Pure Reason*, A 811 /B 839, A 813/ B 871, A 816/ B 844. All citations of Kant's *Critique of Pure Reason* (London: Macmillan, 1929) refer to the first or second editions as A or B, respectively, followed by page numbers. Cf. K. Düsing, "Die Rezeption der kantischen Postulatenlehre in den frühen philosophischen Entwürfen Schellings und Hegels," *Hegel-Studien*, Beiheft 9 (1973): 53–90.

28 Kant, *Lectures*, p. 82; cf. ibid., p. 54 (*AA*, vol. 20, p. 28).

29 See e.g., Kant, *Critique of Judgment*, sec. 87.

unique "a priori feeling," which is generated by a pure judgment that acknowledges the claim of the moral law, and then in turn acts as the phenomenal "spring" to action from appreciation of that law. But what is most noteworthy here is that even after these significant revisions, Kant continues to attend to the issue of motivation. Respect by itself is not claimed to be *in fact* sufficient to move *man* to morality, and a pure moral attitude unsupplemented by religious hope is not allowed to be sufficient to *keep* man devoted to morality in the long run and in its full breadth.[30]

These final positions are remarkable because even if one regards the theory of respect as a kind of *deus ex machina* that responds to the "philosopher's stone" by simply inventing a source of action in the form of a mysterious intermediary between the noumenal and phenomenal realms, the fact is that once such an intermediary is in place, it is at first unclear why anything else should be added. It may seem a matter of theft rather than honest toil to posit respect as the force that allows us to move to morality, but if one does accept Kant's metaphysics so far (in particular the division between phenomenal and noumenal aspects of the self), and also accepts that moral actions cannot be simply intellectually caused (i.e., by a mere act of judgment) but require some kind of subjective psychological cause, then there is no special reason to disallow respect. But once it is allowed in this way, it would seem that it could do *whatever* is needed for Kant to "solve" the problem of motivation. So why does Kant get entangled in saying even more than respect is needed?

To move toward an answer here, we should recall that when Kant invented the special moral meaning of the term "respect,"[31] he took it to signal not only a causal place in his complex metaphysics of action but also a specific kind of attitude with a distinctive content. It not only stands for the "whatever it is that is needed" in feeling to get man to move morally; in addition, it signifies a particular way of so moving – a way that can leave room for extra intermediaries with a different content but a somewhat similar function. The specific content that Kant has in mind for respect involves the negative feeling of a check to one's inclinations by the standard of the law. Now, while such a feeling can have for Kant an obvious and special appropriateness to "action from duty," and can even

---

30 Ibid. Cf. Kant, *Religion Within the Limits of Reason Alone*, trans. T. M. Green and H. H. Hudson (New York, 1960), pp. 5–6. (*AA*, 6–7).

31 On the unusual meaning (for his time) that Kant gave to the term *Achtung*, see Henrich, "Das Problem der Grundlegung der Ethik bei Kant und im spekulativen Idealismus," in *Sein und Ethos*, ed. P. Engelhardt (Mainz: Matthias Grünewald, 1963), p. 373.

be requisite for any such action, there is no need to think such a feeling *dominates* all such actions. Rather, given the kind of complex and imperfect phenomenal nature that we always observe man to have, it could well be that other attitudes are present and – even if they are secondary to respect – must be present when we act morally.[32] In other words, once we get into allowing some phenomenal effects to have a noumenal backing, there is not much to restrain us from thinking that a whole range of such effects, and in particular a whole range of moral feelings, can have such a backing.

For these reasons, I propose that a Kantian can accept the details of a thoroughly naturalistic psychology, can isolate the whole range of attitudes that in fact turn out to be central in a good human life, and then can claim that *all* these attitudes (and not just respect) have their ultimate source in a noumenal acceptance of pure duty.[33] Such a move has the virtue of blocking the unfortunate picture, which Kant himself sometimes encourages, of noumenal dutifulness and phenomenal inclination in its entirety pushing against each other in an absurd quasi-physical battle in a veritable no-man's-land. Kant's ultimate position here, once he worked out his notion of an elective *Willkür* that selects between the *maxims* of *both* duty and inclination, does not involve such reciprocal interaction. It is a position that allows only noumenal influence on the phenomenal and leaves no pure a priori bounds on where that influence takes place.[34] All this is compatible with allowing that in fact the proper effect of the noumenal self will be a rather circumscribed set of (phenomenal) motivating feelings. And in fact, rather than always restricting this set to one effect, the feeling of pure respect, or expanding it to include the whole domain of human emotions, Kant in his late work focuses on a specific set of emotions, the normal accompaniments of respect, which are the attitudes of love and (moral) hope and the virtues that flow from these.

This theory is not an incoherent one, but the difficulty in justifying it can well explain Kant's own frequent reminders about our ignorance of

---

32 See Kant, *Religion*, pp. 6–7n. (*AA*, 6–7n.): "In this end [the highest good] if directly presented him by reason alone, man seeks something that he can *love;* therefore the law, which merely arouses his *respect* . . . does yet extend itself . . . because of the moral law's being taken in relation to the natural characteristic of man."

33 I take this view to be supported by Kant's notion that the source of all our "empirical character" rests in our "intelligible character." See *Critique of Pure Reason*, A 539/B 637.

34 On the need to go beyond the "pure" a priori, see, e.g., Kant, *Metaphysical Principles of Virtue*, trans. J. Ellington (Indianapolis: Bobbs-Merrill, 1964), p. 16 (*AA*, 217): "We shall often have to take as our object the special nature of man, which we can know only by experience."

the nature of the ultimate source of our own actions.[35] Here I take him to be making not the trivial point that our overt phenomenal sense of generosity, for example, may be but a screen for a covert but phenomenal sense of selfishness. Rather, the point is that whatever our phenomenal (i.e., empirically accessible) personality may appear to be to us, this could be rooted in a surprising noumenal character. The opacity here can infect not only judgments about an individual but also the whole domain of moral anthropology. In some ultimate sense, we remain uncertain as to whether our deepest feelings of benevolence and our concern for perfection really have a sincere basis and a genuine moral worth. And yet we can also believe that if in fact the actions that conform to the moral law tend to have as their common accompaniments certain kinds of feelings, then the practical presumption is that these feelings are rooted in a proper moral self. Of course – as Kant insists all too unforgettably – if there is a specific reason to think a person would go along with these feelings *even at the cost of violating duty,* then this presumption is to be overridden in particular cases.[36] While Kant thus stresses it is "risky" to see benevolent feeling as a "cooperating" factor in our moral life,[37] this still does not rule out the idea that in fact it may be an essential feeling for us to have if we are to be expected to be moral. And this is just what Kant himself recognizes in his late emphasis on our need for love and hope.

This view is especially clear in a footnote in the *Religion:* "a heart which is happy in the performance of its duty . . . is a mark of genuineness in the virtuous disposition . . . a joyous frame of mind [is] that without which man is never certain of having really attained a love of the good, i.e., of having incorporated it in his maxim."[38] But without going to the late work, one can use even the most notorious Kantian texts to defend the idea that Kant has a positive place for a broad range of moral emotions. Consider the second *Critique,* for example, where he makes his point about "risk" and explains repeatedly that respect is to be the "sole mode

---

35 See e.g., ibid., pp. 44 (*AA,* 387), 51 (*AA,* 392), 111 (*AA,* 446–7); cf. *Foundations of the Metaphysics of Morals,* trans. L.W. Beck (Indianapolis: Bobbs-Merrill, 1959), p. 23 (*AA,* 407), and "Theory and Practice," in *Perpetual Peace,* p. 64 (*AA,* 279–80).

36 Here I agree with Barbara Herman, "On the Value of Acting from the Motive of Duty," *Philosophical Review* 90 (1981): 359–82.

37 Kant, *Critique of Practical Reason,* p. 75 (*AA,* 73).

38 Kant, *Religion,* p. 19n. (*AA,* 23n.); cf. *Metaphysics of Virtue,* p. 154–5 (*AA,* 484–5): "What is done not with pleasure but as mere compulsory service has no inner worth for him who so responds to his duty . . . The discipline that man practices on himself can therefore become meritorious and exemplary only through the cheer which accompanies it."

of determining" the self morally, the "sole genuine moral feeling."[39] These phrases make sense if we see that when Kant is concerned here with contrasting love and respect, what he is really contrasting are agents who think of themselves as acting out of *sheer* love as opposed to those acting out of respect. This contrast by no means impugns love as such. Kant's point is simply this:

> If a rational creature would ever reach the stage of *thoroughly* liking to do all moral laws, it would mean that there was no *possibility* of there being in him a desire which could tempt him to deviate from them . . . [Man] can never be *wholly* free from desires and inclinations which . . . do not *of themselves* agree with the moral law . . . *Consequently* it is . . . necessary to base the intention of the creature's maxims on moral constraint and not on ready willingness, i.e., to base it on respect . . . and not on love, which apprehends *no* inward reluctance.[40]

The crucial point is that love is rejected here as a basis for morality only insofar as it designates an attitude that would know no *possibility* of even a temptation to deviation. To insist that respect must always be present, then, is just to insist that one not fool oneself into thinking one can act by not only *actually* liking to do the right, but by also never being even inclined to go against the right. Surely, given our moral situation, it is hard to criticize the stress on respect over love *in this sense.*[41]

While respect must always be present as an ultimate subjective ground in the morality of nonholy beings like us, there is still room for love, in some sense other than the extreme one just used for the contrast with respect, to be frequently present as a penultimate subjective ground. In fact, a less extreme sense of "love" is introduced by Kant in a number of places. Thus, in this same discussion, Kant endorses the "kernel of all laws," the command to strive toward the disposition of "practical love," where "to love one's neighbor means to *like* to practice all duties toward

39 Kant, *Critique of Practical Reason*, pp. 84 (*AA*, 81), 88 (*AA*, 85).

40 Ibid., pp. 86–7 (*AA*, 83–4). Here as elsewhere the emphasis is mine.

41 A similar exegesis can be given to the very negative remarks (noted by L. Hinman, in "On the Purity of Our Moral Motives: A Critique of Kant's Account of the Emotions and Acting for the Sake of Duty," *Monist* 66 [1983]: 251–66) about "passion" in *Anthropology From a Pragmatic Point of View*, trans. M. Gregor (The Hague: Nijhoff, 1974), sec. 81. What Kant is rejecting there is not what we ordinarily mean by passion, in a broad sense that includes all kinds of feelings, and thus also the happiness consequent upon being morally motivated, but is rather just passion as an extreme *policy* of subordinating moral *maxims* to quasi-addictive drives.

him."[42] Here love is not the opposite but rather the natural supplement of respect, and so it is quite consistent for Kant later to say that "if we ask about the subjective basis of actions . . . then is love, as the free integration of the will of another into one's maxims, an indispensable addition to human nature's imperfection . . . [Duty] cannot be counted on to any great degree unless the command is accompanied by love."[43] In addition to the general attitude of love, Kant can allow that in particular circumstances there is a specific extra spur that we can properly need to get moving toward being moral. Kant speaks, for example, of the duty to see and experience the discomfort of the plight of the poor, "for this feeling, though painful, nevertheless is one of the impulses placed in us by nature for effecting what the representation of duty might not accomplish by itself."[44] By the time of the *Metaphysics of Morals*, Kant uses the term "love" to cover the attitudes necessary for the achievement of all imperfect duties of "widest latitude" (e.g., beneficence, sympathy) while "respect" is used in a new sense for the feeling present only in the acceptance of more narrow ethical duties (e.g., avoidance of pride and mockery). With these meanings they become equal in significance, for Kant insists love and respect "are basically, according to the law, always combined in one duty, although in such a way that sometimes the one duty and sometimes the other is the subjective principle, to which the other is joined as accessory . . . Should *one* of these great moral forces sink, 'so then would nothingness . . . drink up the whole realm.' "[45]

To give some indication of how well this Kantian theory can accommodate those who would stress the moral value of a broad range of emotions, and hence the imperfect duties typically realized by them, it is helpful to consider atypical recent criticism of Kant's views here, namely Lawrence Hinman's discussion of Kant on the purity of moral motives. Hinman concludes with three major charges against Kant. The first is that the significance of respect should be understood not (as Kant wishes) in noumenal terms but simply in terms of its being a feeling that can be generated only in a rational being. Once this is done, other motives, such as compassion and regret, that also require a grounding in a rational being, can be given an equivalent significance. Second, Kant is faulted for

---

42 Kant, *Critique of Practical Reason*, p. 86 (*AA*, 83). As Prauss notes, in stressing the term *gern* Kant is explicitly invoking a moral value that cannot be commanded, since he also says we cannot be made to like anything (*Autonomie*, pp. 252–5). Cf. Wildt, *Autonomie*, p. 186 for a different interpretation.

43 Kant, "The End of All Things," in *Perpetual Peace*, p. 101 (*AA*, 338).

44 Kant, *Metaphysics of Virtue*, p. 122 (*AA*, 457).

45 Ibid., pp. 112–13 (*AA*, 448–9). Cf. Hill, "Imperfect Duty," p. 66.

holding to the intractability of the emotions, for not seeing that they can be educated and morally transformed. Third, Kant (and here Hinman speaks of a "clear break") is faulted for not seeing how "having certain emotions may in some cases be necessary to moral understanding and even to moral action."[46] These charges correspond to similar and perhaps more familiar points made by Bernard Williams and Lawrence Blum,[47] but I will focus on Hinman's discussion because it is the most sensitive to Kant's own writings. The striking fact is that even with this sensitivity, Hinman falls prey to the popular picture of Kant and fails to see the natural ways in which a Kantian can respond to all these points.

On the first point, there is no reason why a Kantian could not welcome an appreciation of the fact that there are a number of emotions that are important and depend on our rationality. This does nothing to undermine the special status of respect, for the worth of these motives still rests on their incorporation of respect in its major function, even if the phenomenological aspects of respect may on occasion be overshadowed by the other specific emotions. Thus, compassion and regret lose their moral worth if they arise without any basic moral sensitivity, without respect for strict obligation and a sense of how we are beings who cannot expect to be always inclined to the right.[48] Only insofar as respect in this sense is an implicit element in these emotions do they avoid becoming indulgent or morbid. As for Hinman's second point, there is admittedly a difference of emphasis to be noted. Kant may not speak as directly and clearly as one would like about training the emotions, but he does reiterate that we are under the burden of having to *cultivate* our virtue, and he gives numerous particular reminders, in the style of our last point, about how various emotions benefit from a tempering by respect.[49] He may not always add that after such tempering they then can become essential components of

---

46 L. Hinman, "Purity," p. 265.

47 Cf. above at n. 14, and esp. Williams's charges that for Kant, "the emotions are too capricious; they are passively experienced; a man's proneness to experience them or not is the product of natural causation, and (in that sense) fortuitously distributed" ("Morality and the Emotions," p. 21). I think Kant can meet all these charges, although the last criticism points to serious problems such as the difficulty with change of character explained at the end of this chapter, and the idea of the universal accessibility of the moral noted at the beginning of the last section.

48 Similar points are very well made in B. Herman, "Rules, Motives, and Helping Actions," *Philosophical Studies* 45 (1984): 369–77; M. Baron, "The Alleged Moral Repugnance of Acting from Duty," *Journal of Philosophy* 81 (1984): 197–220; and D. Richards, "Rights and Autonomy," *Ethics* 82 (1981), pp. 15–16.

49 On cultivation, see Kant, *Metaphysics of Virtue*, pp. 51 (*AA*, 392), 57 (*AA*, 395), 145 (*AA*, 477), as well as *Anthropology*, sec. 14, and *Critique of Practical Reason*, Part II. On tempering, see *Metaphysics of Virtue*, pp. 87, (*AA*, 426), 137 (*AA*, 471). Cf. the discussion of "how virtues are generally established" by role playing in the *Anthropology*, sec. 14.

our moral life, but there is no reason why he cannot say that. Consider, for example, the statement that "beneficence will produce in you the love of mankind (as a readiness of *inclination* toward beneficence in general)."[50] Also relevant are his remarks on the effect of aesthetic pleasure: a "feeling in man which is indeed not of itself already moral but which . . . still does much to promote a state of sensibility favorable to morals."[51] These claims speak to Hinman's third point, as does the earlier quote about our indirect duty to feel for the poor. Moreover, Kant stresses that "I can benefit no one . . . according to my own concepts of happiness, but only according to the concepts of him whom I think of benefiting."[52] This reminder can be used to meet the commonsense idea Hinman is relying on, namely that if to do someone good in a particular situation requires that the other person see us as having a certain attitude or feeling, then we should do what we can to help develop such a feeling. Thus it is significant that Kant adds: "a *merely heartfelt* benevolence on the part of the benefactor, without physical results, deserves to be called a duty of virtue."[53]

C. KANT ON MORAL MOTIVATION AND RELIGION

The Kantian reply to Hinman would apply equally to what is a large part – but only a part – of Hegel's opposition to Kant on the motivation problem. The notion of *Sittlichkeit* outlined earlier indicates that Hegel shares the current belief that our feelings require a phenomenal explication, that they can be cultivated, and that this cultivation can make them an essential part of our moral life. But it was not directly in these terms that Hegel initially attacked Kant, and so in order to evaluate that attack, we

50 Kant, *Metaphysics of Virtue*, p. 61 (*AA*, 402). Cf. ibid., p. 140 (*AA*, 473): "social graces . . . promote the moral feeling itself."
51 Ibid., p. 106 (*AA*, 443); cf. *Anthropology*, sec. 75.
52 Kant, *Metaphysics of Virtue*, p. 119 (*AA*, 454). I think this passage applies nicely to the controversy between Stocker and Baron. See above at n. 14 and n. 48, and Williams, "Morality and the Emotions," p. 22: "Is it certain that one who receives good treatment . . . thinks the better of the giver, if he knows it to be the result of the application of principle, rather than the product of an emotional response?" Williams unfairly presumes that the moral man cannot have emotional responses that are also proper in principle. An objection very similar to Williams's seems to be at the heart of Henrich's opposition to Kant, for even after carefully noting the ways in which Schiller could not say that for Kant emotions can't be present in moral action, Henrich still takes the Hegelian view that Kant fails to be true to the "real intent" of morality, which presumably involves a kind of *direct* concern ("Das Problem," p. 372; cf. Wildt, *Autonomie*, pp. 41–2).
53 Kant, *Metaphysics of Virtue*, p. 119 (*AA*, 455); cf. p. 137 (*AA*, 470–1). Cf. A. J. Simmons, *Moral Principles and Political Obligations* (Princeton: Princeton University Press, 1979), pp. 164–7; and B. Herman, "The Practice of Moral Judgment," *Journal of Philosophy* 82 (1985): 369–77.

need to review Kant's development again with an eye to laying out more precisely those features which generated Hegel's specific response.

Broadly speaking, we can see Kant as having moved toward a more and more complicated story of the interrelations and intermediaries between the *ground,* the *motive,* and the *instantiation* of good action. His first picture is that an intention governed by rationality will issue in good action (or at least good effort) as long as the ever-present force of hedonistic inclination is met by a counterforce of religious confidence. In place of this crude interaction model, we then get the idea of an elective noumenal will that can decide between either rational-moral *or* hedonistic-immoral maxims, and that allows the former to be effected phenomenally by producing the feeling of respect. On this basis, the second part of the second *Critique* gives a quick treatment of the problem of turning the "objective" or rationally grounded principle of morality into a "subjective" one,[54] that is, one that is effective in human life. In contrast to Kant's own earlier stress on religion, as well as to classical references to inspiring models of magnanimity, the influence of pure moral ideals is stressed. Virtue is claimed to be not only the proper but also the "strongest incentive" to good action,[55] and it is said that over time respect of itself creates a "liking" for morality, a feeling that in turn generates further moral action.[56]

Elsewhere, however, especially in the *Religion* book and the *Metaphysics of Morals,* Kant gives full recognition to the fact that for us respect cannot be the whole phenomenal spring to morality. Whereas at times he had suggested love, for example, is either an incidental, amoral, and "pathological" affect or just a pattern of behavior equivalent to what might be inspired by respect alone,[57] Kant now indicates that it can be present as a moral *attitude,* a distinct psychological intermediary, probably behind all *our* good actions, and especially the fulfillment of the larger part of our "broad" duties.[58] In place of a single sense of respect, Kant introduces a variety of vital feelings that accompany our moral life – feelings of joy, sympathy, self-respect, moral contentment and displeasure, aesthetic awe, and religious hope.[59]

54 Kant, *Critique of Practical Reason,* p. 155 (*AA,* 151).
55 Ibid., p. 156 (*AA,* 152).
56 Ibid., p. 164 (*AA,* 160).
57 Kant, *Foundations,* p. 16 (*AA,* 399); Blum fixes on this passage (*Friendship,* p. 28).
58 See above at n. 45.
59 See Kant, *Metaphysics of Virtue,* pp. 33 (*AA,* 377), 49–50 (*AA,* 391), 65–6 (*AA,* 406); "Theory and Practice," p. 67n. (*AA,* 283n.), and Henrich, "Das Problem," p. 380.

The last plays a special role for Kant, and it is now no longer an independent and heteronomous counterforce to the threat of inclination but rather is seen as just the indispensable phenomenal articulation, given our psychology, of the pure elective *commitment* to morality. More specifically, Kant ends by insisting that, given our "weak" nature, the "ethical commonwealth" we are obliged to build "can be realized . . . only in the form of a church."[60] "Pure [i.e., merely respectful] faith cannot be relied on."[61] Rather, "some historical ecclesiastical faith or other . . . must be utilized" if a sufficient "interest" in morality is to be expected.[62] Although such historical elements are indispensable, they have to be critically regarded, and over time their secondary nature is to become more and more evident in a process that Kant calls the "Annäherung des Reich Gottes"[63] – an obvious secularization of the orthodox notion of the Coming of the Kingdom of God. In the section of the *Religion* devoted to this process, Kant elaborates on the development of critical moral faith within the individual, and he challenges traditional doctrines of atonement by insisting that one "must first improve his way of life . . . if he is to have even the slightest hope of a higher gain."[64] That is, though we naturally work with the idea of receiving some special benefit from God, and especially relief from guilt, we can legitimately hope for help in this regard only after we reform our self, not vice versa.[65]

However peripheral these conceptions may seem to some Kantians, they were absolutely central to Hegel. We know that the Kantian works he studied most were the second *Critique*, the *Religion* book, and the *Metaphysics of Morals* (for which he wrote a lost commentary).[66] And it is also clear that once Hegel got over an initial infatuation with the idea of duty for duty's sake, he gave most of his attention explicitly to the motivational issue of making "objective" principles "subjective," and to the need to supplement the attitude of respect with an attitude of love.[67] But to both of these points he added even more complications than Kant. While he agreed with Kant's later writings that the power to make morality "subjective" is tied to the influence of religion, he immediately noted that "re-

60 Kant, *Religion*, p. 91 (*AA*, 101).
61 Ibid., p. 94 (*AA*, 103).
62 Ibid., p. 100 (*AA*, 109).
63 Ibid., p. 105 (*AA*, 115).
64 Ibid., p. 107 (*AA*, 117).
65 Ibid., pp. 107–9 (*AA*, 116–18); cf. *Lectures*, p. 92.
66 See Knox, "Hegel's Attitude," p. 77.
67 Hegel, *Early Theological Writings*, trans. T. M. Knox (Chicago: University of Chicago Press, 1948), p. 145.

ligion is not the first thing that can put down roots in the mind, it must
have a cultivated ground there before it can flourish."[68] As a consequence, he studied the historical and social conditions that surrounded
the rise and fall of ancient religious communities and the ultimate effect
of these conditions on the morality of their participants.[69] In this way
Hegel encouraged canceling through the Kantian intermediaries between these conditions and moral action, for if something richer than
respect is needed here, and if this in turn requires a special social setting,
then the analysis of this setting by itself could give the crucial conditions
for morality. Religion and psychology as such become incidental, for once
we know the intersubjective basis for these subjective motivating factors,
we know the true phenomenal springs of our action.

   This point had been implicitly conceded by Kant when he insisted on
an ecclesiastical component for the "ethical commonwealth" and when
he allowed that the triggering of moral sensitivity is a function of our
environment: a man exposed to the poor is moved by sympathy to help; a
man reduced to poverty himself suffers special temptations to immorality.[70] Hegel used such facts to license a focus on the phenomenal rather
than the noumenal conditions of morality. He insisted we are "to take
[men] as they are"[71] and to expect only those accomplishments that a
man's station makes possible. This focus made Kant's doctrine of transcendental freedom idle. It by no means refuted or even directly con-
fronted it,[72] but it did reveal a genuine problem for Kantians, namely that
the very phenomenal causality that Kant himself established makes it
possible to trim our expectations of people to the patterns revealed by
past social conditioning.

   An even more significant and complex break with Kant concerned not
the cause but the form and content of the crucial attitude of love. Like
Kant, Hegel claimed to find this attitude specially exemplified in the
character of Jesus, but eventually he developed a quite distinctive concep-

---

68 Hegel, "The Tübingen Essay of 1793," trans. H. S. Harris, in *Hegel's Development: Toward the
     Sunlight, 1770–1801* (Oxford: Oxford University Press, 1972), p. 485.
69. See ibid., p. 486, where Hegel takes his project to be "to inquire what institutions are
     requisite that the doctrines and the force of religion should enter into the web of human
     feelings." Cf. ibid., p. 508; and O. Marquard, "Hegel und das Sollen," *Philosophisches
     Jahrbuch* 65 (1964–5): 112–13.
70 Kant, *Metaphysics of Virtue*, p. 46 (*AA*, 388).
71 Hegel, "Tübingen," in Harris, *Development*, p. 496.
72 On the defensible coherence of Kant's position here, see A. Wood, "Kant's Compatibilism,"
     in *Self and Nature in Kant's Philosophy*, ed. A. Wood (Ithaca: Cornell University Press, 1984),
     pp. 73–101.

tion of the attitude and used it to attack Kant and to reverse his own early radical critique of Christianity. Hegel's radicality here can probably be best explained as a reaction to Storr, his orthodox teacher in Tübingen, who tried to bend Kant's notion of practical faith to traditional purposes. If Kant could argue that as a matter of psychological necessity, even the good man will need to commit himself to the hope of some appropriate reward from God, Storr could argue that such a man would also be most sensitive to his own guilt, and so would equally require a commitment to the specific Christian hope of redemption and forgiveness. Hegel directly challenged this psychological argument from his own typical sociohistorical perspective, and he claimed that the Christian tradition that used the doctrines Storr defended actually frustrated rather than satisfied the "true needs" of man.[73] Hegel had laid down three criteria a religion should meet to accommodate these needs and to fulfill the essential function of making "objective" principles "subjective": it must satisfy the *reason*, the *heart*, and the *public* interest of man.[74] On these grounds, traditional Christianity, especially in contrast to Greek religion, was condemned in detail because of its irrational mysteries, its gloomy festivals, and its private, antigovernmental nature.[75]

After developing his own notion of love, however, Hegel came very close to in effect, repealing these severe charges.[76] He argued that the attitude of sharing and acceptance that Christian love involved gave it a higher *rationality* and *appeal*[77] than anything in the notion of strict duty. Whereas duty comes in the form of an alienating command,[78] a command to discipline one's whole natural self, love teaches full acceptance of one's own nature and unity with rather than judgment of others.[79] In this way the Hegelian conception of love also introduces a content that is meant to go beyond Kant's ethics: love realizes the capacity for forgive-

---

73 Hegel, *Early Writings*, p. 72.

74 Hegel, "Tübingen," in Harris, *Development*, p. 499.

75 Ibid., p. 505; cf. *Early Writings*, pp. 106, 283ff.

76 See esp. D. Henrich, "Hegel und Hölderlin," in *Hegel in Kontext* (Frankfurt: Suhrkamp, 1975), pp. 9–40.

77 The rationality involved the metaphysical truths that Hegel saw metaphorically present in the structure of love; the appeal involved the extra sensitivity (which Hegel came to appreciate more over time) that Christianity developed for man's inward feelings, his reflexivity.

78 Hegel, *Early Writings*, p. 225: "[Jesus preaches] not particular subjection under a law of one's own, the self-coercion of Kantian virtue, but virtues without lordship." Cf. below at n. 106.

79 Hegel, *Early Writings*, p. 226: "Over against dutiful fidelity and the right to divorce a wife, Jesus sets love . . . In face of love . . . there can be no talk of leave or rights."

ness, which in turn makes possible the experience of mutual reconciliation, something not derivable from respect.[80] In his insistence on man's
need for this experience, Hegel returns to a position that appears to be
closer to Storr than Kant: "man cannot bear this disquiet, from the terrify-
ing reality of evil and the immutability of the law, he can fly to grace
alone."[81] But of course Kant is to be both transcended and incorporated.
The emphasis on "grace" at first seems more traditional than the Kantian
attitude to atonement,[82] but it is essential that the grace Hegel intends is a
phenomenal and not a noumenal matter. It is the forgiveness granted by
other humans in this world that counts, and this is described as a matter
of "life" and self-generated "fate," a process wherein we are motivated not
by "fear of an alien being"[83] but by a "longing for what was lost," the
communal harmony that preceded transgression.[84] The "spirit of love,"
the "living bond" that achieves this independence from what is alien, is
described as the "highest freedom," and so by his own very roundabout
route Hegel wants to maintain the autonomy Kant cherished.

After his early writings, from which all these remarks have been taken,
Hegel developed his concept of love further until it became the high
point of the *Phenomenology,* the crucial alternative to what Hegel depicts as
the subjectivity and hypocrisy of Kantian morality and its immediate successors.[85] In this way a very positive connection was established between
ethics and Christianity but nothing was said to show that the third (the
"public") and not only the first two of Hegel's criteria could be met.
Hence it can be argued that the central question of his later work is to find
an enlightened form of Christianity that is dominated by the experience
of love and yet also realizes the affirmative relation to the state that had
marked other ancient religions. As with Kant, the mere attitude of neither

80 Ibid., p. 227. To be sure, Kant says, "reconciliation is a duty of man" (*Metaphysics of Virtue,* p.
126 [*AA,* 461], but although he may have influenced Hegel here, it is fair to say Kant hardly
makes reconciliation a preeminent value as Hegel does. More influential was probably
Schiller's remark that a merely dominated enemy can rise again, but a reconciled one is
truly overcome: "Der bloss *niedergeworfene* Feind kann wieder aufstehen, aber der *versöhnte*
ist wahrhaft überwunden." *Schriften 4* (Frankfurt: Suhrkamp, 1966), p. 170 (from "Über
Anmut und Würde," 1793).
81 Hegel, *Early Writings,* p. 227; cf. Harris, *Development,* p. 320: "He is ready now to concede
Storr's claim that the upshot of rational theology is the recognition that we are absolutely
dependent on God's grace."
82 See above, at n. 64, but note that in a parallel to Kant, Hegel insists one is to forgive others
first before being forgiven (*Early Writings,* p. 237).
83 Hegel, *Early Writings.* p. 231.
84 Ibid., p. 230.
85 See esp. Hegel, *Phenomenology,* VI: C. c., "Conscience, the Beautiful Soul, Evil and its
Forgiveness."

respect nor love is of the highest value in life; highest is our fulfillment in an "ethical commonwealth" that integrates the appeal and intensity of religious commitment with the rationality and overarching unity of a political structure that exerts authority and yet respects individual autonomy.[86]

D. HEGEL'S ALTERNATIVE: AUTONOMY AND DEVELOPMENT WITHIN SECULAR BOUNDS

From Hegel's perspective the major flaw of love by itself was already captured in the insistence of the *Early Writings* that "enmities like those he [Jesus] sought to transcend can be overcome only by valor; they cannot be reconciled by love."[87] In this way Hegel indicated that for him the experience of active sacrifice was preeminent. Rather than follow out how his views on this experience developed through Hegel's later ideas on patriotism and politics, I will devote the concluding part of this chapter to showing how an examination of his earliest thoughts on this experience can be combined with the material reviewed so far in order to help substantiate two points. The first is that the early Hegelian account of love and sacrifice anticipates the chief aspects of his critique of the Kantian account of motivation as well as of the current critique of that account. The second point is that despite Kant's ability to turn back this critique, there are other weaknesses in Kant's account, as just reviewed, that Hegel realized, although less clearly, and that do amount to a significant problem.

Hegel's chief response to Kant is dominated by the thought that here he must oppose "Kant's profound reduction of what he calls a command (love God first and thy neighbor as thyself) to his moral imperative."[88] Oblivious to the ways in which, as we have noted, Kant ultimately does not claim such a *reduction*, Hegel interprets and advocates Jesus's teaching of love "in a sense quite different from that of the 'shalt' of a moral imperative."[89] In place of a "thou shalt," which "presupposes a cleavage," an opposition of duty and inclination,[90] Hegel speaks of a "correspondence

---

86 Cf. Hegel, *Early Writings*, p. 278: "a nation of men united to one another by relations of love."

87 Ibid., p. 205; cf., Wildt, *Autonomie*, p. 192.

88 Hegel, *Early Writings*, p. 213.

89 Ibid.

90 Ibid., p. 212. Hegel again is obviously very much influenced by Schiller's "Anmut und Würde." See M. Brelage, *Studien zur Transzendental-philosophie* (Berlin: de Gruyter, 1965), p. 242.

of inclination with law,"[91] wherein the "moral disposition" "*ceases to be universal,* opposed to inclination."[92] "Against commands . . . Jesus set . . . a *human* urge and a human need,"[93] the need to unite with others in a beautiful way. The "fortuitous"[94] unity of human nature and the good is already the target of this attack, and it remains at the heart of Hegel's most intense critique of Kant, the dismissal of the postulates in the *Phenomenology.*[95]

Before commenting on that critique, we can already note how much Hegel here anticipates the contemporary charges cited earlier. His concern with the particular and the "human," for example, almost exactly matches Williams's talk of the priority of the "human gesture" over the invocation of general principle. In response to such talk, consider an example of sacrifice of the kind that, ironically, both Williams and Kant invoke: the spontaneous rescue of someone who is drowning. Against Williams, Herman and Baron have recently shown how it is a mistake to think that action on Kantian principle precludes properly having a strong and spontaneous inclination here, say the inclination to save one's wife because she is one's wife.[96] We are not obliged by Kant to hold only to what strict duty enjoins, nor need we have the thought of such duty foremost in our mind at the time of our action.[97] But what moral worth does require is some implicit sensitivity to not being *so* immediately helpful that one would be willing to act at the cost of violating what is clearly owed as a matter of strict duty. Thus, Kant reminds us, for the man who bravely "seeks to save others in a shipwreck," even without their being his special relations, "there still remain some scruples as to whether it is so perfect a duty to devote oneself spontaneously and unbidden."[98]

What Kant had in mind here is a possible violation of a duty to oneself (thus his scruples are about a case even more magnanimous than Williams's), but although this does not directly apply to Williams's exam-

91 Hegel, *Early Writings,* p. 214.
92 Ibid., p. 215.
93 Ibid., p. 206.
94 Ibid., p. 216; cf. B. Herman, "Impartiality and Integrity," *Monist* 66 (1983): 235.
95 Hegel, *Phenomenology* VI: C. b., "Dissemblance or Duplicity." Cf. below at n. 104.
96 Cf. Baron, "Repugnance"; and Herman, "Impartiality and Integrity," pp. 246–7.
97 It might be thought no one would still raise this as a key objection against Kant, but it has been stressed recently, both in English (by Blum, *Friendship,* p. 99) and German (by T. Baumeister, *Hegels frühe Kritik an Kants Ethik* [Heidelberg: Winter, 1976], p. 91). Cf. Hegel, "Tübingen," in Harris, *Development,* p. 496: "love . . . does not do good action because it has calculated."
98 Kant, *Critique of Practical Reason,* p. 162 (*AA,* 158).

ple, indirectly it is relevant, for what Kant is concerned with ultimately is the dangerous "pretension"[99] of the do-gooder, the indulgence of one who would lose *all* sight of the *possibility* that what would seem to be the best of reactions can still go against what ought to be. And surely it is just this lack of humility that undercuts the sympathy we might have for Hegel's enthusiasm, for however brave or loving the good heart appears to be, it surely can do wrong. Hegel himself showed awareness of this problem by later giving primacy to the rules of *Sittlichkeit,* but this move concedes that although *in general* the well-taught heart of the common man can be an adequate guide[100] – something that really is not in dispute – in difficult situations we must be ready to appeal to the strict duties that provide the essential skeleton for any particular *Sittlichkeit.* On occasion then, we must forgo Hegelian love, whereas we can always honor Kantian love, that is, genuine benevolence that is based on (and limited by) and yet goes beyond sheer respect.

Similar points can be made when one looks directly at Hegel's own discussion of sacrifice and at the critique of Kant's postulates alluded to earlier. These points come together in a remarkable fragment that is unfortunately not included in the translated *Early Theological Writings.*[101] As Harris explains in his excellent gloss, Hegel here is challenging the principle underlying the postulate that "virtue deserves happiness," for he thinks that here "the moral will exists in a mind dominated by *sensible* desires, [and] its command is interpreted as the condition of sensible happiness."[102] This challenge points back to the influence of Schelling, who first emphasized that the Kantian "highest good" was really too low an ideal for a being of reason like man,[103] and forward to Hegel's critique in the *Phenomenology,* where the component of happiness in the highest good is claimed to introduce "dissemblance," inconsistency and hypocrisy

---

99   Ibid., p. 160 (*AA,* 157).

100 Thus it is unclear how Blum's point that "in normal contexts" we give no thought to general principles should count against Kant (*Friendship,* pp. 62–3). Similarly, Kant can accept Williams's last claim: "The capacity for creative moral response has the advantage of being, if not equally, at least widely distributed" ("Morality and the Emotions," p. 24).

101 See Hegel, *Early Writings,* p. 167, n. 43, and *Hegels theologische Jugendschriften,* ed. H. Nohl (Tübingen: J. C. B. Mohr, 1907), pp. 237–40. Cf. Harris, *Development,* pp. 182–4, 190–4, 224–9, and *Jugendschriften,* pp. 70–1, 361–2.

102 Harris, *Development,* p. 227; cf. his "The Young Hegel and the Postulates of Practical Reason," in *Hegel and the Philosophy of Religion,* ed. D. Christensen (The Hague: Nijhoff, 1960), p. 73.

103 See F. Schelling, *The Unconditional in Human Knowledge,* trans. F. Marti (Lewisburg, PA: Bucknell University Press, 1980), pp. 96–7.

for the Kantian.[104] As an alternative, Hegel proposes that (in Harris's words) "where reason itself attains its full and proper mastery over the mind, a man may sacrifice his whole sensible existence (his life) for an ideal of honor or patriotism."[105] The ground for the supreme value of this action is put clearly by Hegel himself when he says that such a hero "has a purpose whose realization depends entirely on him, and thus stands in need of no alien assistance."[106] The concern voiced here parallels the view one finds Kantians, and Kant himself on occasion, expressing when pressed about why man really has a special "dignity" and is an end in himself.[107] The answer often given is that through his will man has something that he alone completely controls, and this self-control is of unique and absolute value. But although Hegel is thus again continuing in his own way to give precedence to autonomy, it is important to see that this autonomy comes in at two levels and with a complexity that makes it rather unlike what matters in the drowning example.

The first aspect of autonomy, and the one that Hegel is stressing here and in similar fragments at this time, is that, as Harris puts it, "If we sacrifice something in doing our duty, the *voluntary abandonment* of our right is just what constitutes the sacrifice, and to suppose that we have only postponed the satisfaction destroys the fundamental moral dignity of the free act."[108] The act of heroism, then, is a free and simultaneous renunciation of comfort and of right. In Hegel's example the right concerns one's reward, whereas in the drowning case it is either, as in Kant's discussion, the right to one's own life, or, as in Williams's discussion, the right of others to our aid. A more significant difference, though, is that in the latter cases the Kantian will reply that, all things being equal, it is not clear that right should be sacrificed, whereas in the first case he would say the introduction of the notion of rights is unfair to begin with.[109] The

---

104 This critique is developed in J. Robinson, *Duty and Hypocrisy in Hegel's Phenomenology of Mind* (Toronto: University of Toronto Press, 1977); and David Hoy, "Hegel's Morals," *Dialogue* 20 (1981): 84–102.

105 Harris, *Development*, p. 227. Cf. Baumeister, *Hegels Kritik*, p. 33.

106 Hegel, *Jugendschriften*, p. 239 (my translation).

107 See, e.g., J. Atwell, "The Uniqueness of a Good Will," in *Akten des IV. Internationaler Kant-Kongresses*, ed. G. Funke (Berlin, 1974), pp. 479–84, and Kant, *AA*, vol. 17, R7206. Here Hegel is closer to Kant than are the "neo-Hegelians"; thus this point is objected to by Williams, "Morality and the Emotions," p. 22.

108 Harris, *Development*, p. 192.

109 See Kant, *Metaphysics of Virtue*, p. 159 (*AA*, 489): "Reward from the Supreme Being, however, cannot be derived at all from justice toward beings who have no rights and nothing but duties to him, but can be derived only from love and beneficence." As for punishment, Kant goes on to indicate universal damnation is not to be expected, since it

Kantian postulate does not rest on a *right* to reward for virtue, nor, for this matter, need it involve a sensible reward; it rests not on insisting on what one deserves but on aiming at what can be legitimately hoped – and hence "renunciation" here is an unnecessary gesture.[110]

To this extent, Hegel's early reaction to the postulates is seriously flawed, and although this cannot be established here, I think seeing this flaw can prepare us to admit that similar crude misinterpretations plague his later more elaborate discussions – as, for example, when he suggests that the Kantian who seeks perfection must ultimately and incoherently seek the elimination of morality itself, for this supposedly requires imperfection as the occasion for its work.[111] This claim is unfair because it is not morality but only duty, that is, obligation for less than holy creatures, that requires imperfection, and so there is nothing incoherent about a person striving morally to approximate the elimination of duty in this sense.

There is, however, a second aspect to the autonomy involved in Hegel's concept of heroism, and although it is not spelled out so much in his early work, it leads to a more interesting objection. The second aspect comes out when we ask why the Hegelian hero is not simply an indulgent fool, one who has, to be sure, oriented himself to something entirely within his control, but something tainted nonetheless to the extent that the cause for which he sacrifices himself is unworthy. As Kant reminds us, sacrifice as such can hardly be an overriding value, so what really must recommend the hero here is not his choosing his own life but rather his voluntarily laying down his own fate for the benefit of a community. But surely this is a cause of sufficient value only to the extent the community is rational and requires this kind of sacrifice in order to maintain itself as such. In serving human autonomy in general, then, the hero merits our praise, but at this point the example loses its force against Kant, for such praise is most

"seems to contradict the principles of practical reason, according to which the creation of the world would have been foregone if it were to have yielded a product so contrary to the aim of the Creator, which can only have love as its ground." Ibid., p. 161 (*AA*, 490–1); cf. *Religion*, p. 137n. (*AA*, 146n.).

110 This is not to deny that the postulates leave room for misuse and misunderstanding, as Kant notes at *Metaphysics of Virtue*, pp. 33–5 (*AA*, 377–8), and "Theory and Practice," p. 65 (*AA*, 281). A very radical critique of the postulates, which I cannot take up here, is to be found in A. Wood, "The Immorality of Moral Faith," in *Proceedings: Sixth International Kant Congress 1985*, ed. G. Funke and T. Seebohm (Washington: Center for Advanced Research in Phenomenology and University Press of America: 1989), vol. 2, part 2, pp. 417–37.

111 Hegel, *Phenomenology*, p. 378. Another similarly unfair charge arises at ibid., p. 374, where Hegel implies the highest good is an absurd goal since imperfect men are in no position to demand happiness. But a "demand" is irrelevant here, and in any case even imperfect men could hope for some reward in proportion to the good they have done.

intelligible with a Kantian postulate that one's work does in the long run serve the good. Thus, just as Kant criticizes the pretentious individual, working simply out of love, who in effect cloaks himself in holiness and insists his immediate inclinations are not to be questioned, so here he can criticize the historical agent who presumes to be able to know, and not just hope, that his immediate service is for the good.

Hegel's fragment ends by touching on (and then breaking off at) the last and probably the most intractable problem here, namely the unease the conscientious man feels about the punishments he would have to think he deserves if there is an afterlife to be postulated.[112] We have already seen how Hegel struggled with this problem, first rejecting all notions of atonement, then recognizing a need for grace, and finally building the notion of forgiveness and reconciliation into the center of his ethical system while giving it a basically secular (and perhaps political) significance. This development is continuous with the concerns that first motivated the fragment just studied, for as others have noted, the fragment appears to be connected to a letter to Schelling of August 1795 in which Hegel wrote, "I once had the notion of making clear to myself in an essay what it might mean *to draw near* to God [*was es heissen könne, sich Gott zu nähern*], and thought there to find the satisfaction of the postulate that practical reason governs the world of appearances, and of the other postulates."[113] I take the source of this project to be that strange chapter of Kant's *Religion*, noted earlier, devoted to the "Coming [*Annäherung*] of the Kingdom of God." In that chapter, Kant in effect replaces *God's coming*, in the orthodox sense, with the project of *our coming* nearer to an ideal commonwealth, and he focuses especially on what each individual can do to develop toward his own ideal ethical state.

Hegel takes up these transformations and goes one step further by eventually insisting that the divine is already present in our self-development; it *is* and is not a mere "ought to be." He not only rejects Kant's critical hesitancy about the actual state of human nature and history, but he also banishes any thought that some extra help even might come from a separate deity once we make our own improvement. I suspect a major reason he rejected this thought is that he could make no sense of Kant's idea of how this improvement, this "getting nearer to God," was to work. The question Kant poses is "how can man . . . make himself a new man, well pleasing to God,"[114] and the Kantian answer is: only first "through a

112 Hegel, *Jugendschriften*, p. 239; cf. Harris, *Development*, pp. 227–8.
113 Harris, *Development*, p. 204, n. 2; cf. ibid., p. 224, n. 4.
114 Kant, *Religion*, p. 108 (*AA*, 117).

revolution in the man's disposition,"[115] a "restoration of the original disposition to good in us."[116] With his doctrine of radical evil, Kant suggests that "nearing" God must require not simply doing the good that one can do, qua what one's noumenal will and character has *already elected* to do. It means that one must recognize that he has at this point a disposition to evil, and so he is "under the necessity of a . . . revolution in his cast of mind."[117] But this talk of change, "revolution," and "nearing," is extremely difficult to follow, and not just because of the general difficulties with Kant's transcendental idealism and the notion of timeless noumenal character. The problem is exacerbated here because of a crucial feature of Kant's ethical theory, namely that an attitude, like any object, can have worth only if it is sought with the proper intention. But now if the attitude in question is one's *general* "cast of mind," then to say that one is to overturn this is to say that one must do the overturning with a good intent. But this is something that is *ex hypothesi* impossible, for what one lacks is precisely the requisite intent; if one had that, one would already be of the right "cast of mind" and would need no "revolution."

Thus either it must be conceded that an "approach to God" is literally impossible, that one is always as close in one's real self as one will ever be (unless, of course, one goes back to a doctrine of substitutionary atonement that precedes one's self-improvement), and so one is an imperfect self with a mixed phenomenal character that only appears to undergo a supposedly vital change, or one holds that one's phenomenal changes, conditioned by environment, *Sittlichkeit,* and so forth, just are ultimate, in which case there is a real "nearing" process and not a charade. I submit that Hegel took the latter option and in this one instance may be improved on Kant, although I am not so sure he did it for the right reasons. In any case, in one of his earliest discussions of this topic, Hegel did directly link his rejection of the highest good argument to the doctrine of radical evil, which he felt was its basis in both Kant and orthodoxy: "[It is conceded that] the good man deserves happiness, he can demand it with right. But it is also presumed that it is impossible to *become* a good man."[118] If Hegel had only spent more effort on developing this last point, his critique of Kant would have had more substance.

115 Ibid., p. 43 (*AA*, 47).
116 Ibid., p. 42 (*AA*, 46).
117 Ibid., p. 43 (*AA*, 47).
118 Hegel, *Jugendschriften,* p. 63 (my translation).

8

THE UNRESOLVED FATE OF
AUTONOMY

In these final very brief remarks, I will not be adding any significant new historical details, or trying to sum up all the main points covered so far. Instead, I will attempt merely to provide a final perspective on this study as a whole, so as to forestall some understandable possible misunderstandings of its basic objectives and underlying contentions.

This study began with a reminder of Kant's own sharp public repudiation in 1798 of his first successors. Kant himself could not have known or foreseen the details that I have uncovered in examining the main stages in the later development in German idealism. But Kant was certainly familiar with his own philosophy, and he was expressly disinclined to follow the route of the *Elementarphilosophie* of Reinhold or what he could make out of the *Wissenschaftslehre* of Fichte. Most interpreters would surely agree that, if he had the chance, Kant would have also kept a similar distance from Hegel. I have offered an extended argument about *why* Kant would have been right to do so, since on my account there is a basic structure to Kant's philosophy that undergoes significant modification in Reinhold's work, and these modifications then determine, albeit in a now largely forgotten way, major features and corresponding weaknesses in the better-known systems of both Fichte and Hegel. But my account can hardly claim to be an exhaustive study of the issue. Like any investigation of this length, it must be very incomplete, but is it also unfair or misleading? This charge is obviously most worrisome with respect to the treatment of Hegel, since Hegel is the most complex of all these writers, and yet my discussion of him here has given him the least space.

In reply to this worry I would stress, first, that although the previous two chapters give only a partial presentation of Hegel's philosophy, they do seek to address the most basic points of Hegel's direct criticism of the fundamentals of Kant's theoretical and practical philosophy. Obviously there is more to be said; the comparison of Kant and Hegel continues to be carried out with ever-growing intensity in the current literature, and by now it has certainly reached a point that defies overview. Elsewhere, however, I have offered critical evaluations of several of the more important recent contributions to this immense discussion, and these evaluations reiterate the argument that establishing specific ways in which Hegel *improved* on Kant's approach is much more difficult than is commonly recognized.[1] Documenting this point further here would involve getting into detailed skirmishes with the secondary literature that would deflect from the main issues of this book, which concern the character of the *immediate* reaction to Kant.

In stressing various overlooked ways in which post-Kantians have committed what seem to me to be to some serious philosophical errors with many long-term effects, I do not mean to deny that one could write a quite different story, as many scholars have, emphasizing much more positive developments in philosophy after Kant. It is obvious that there are many important *new* issues that Hegel and the other idealists introduce to philosophy, and on which they make invaluable contributions, contributions that so far I have not given even a passing acknowledgment – for example, Reinhold's late work on language and phenomenology, Fichte's pathbreaking social doctrines, Hegel's notion of alienation or his work in aesthetics. I have by no means been trying to argue that the road in German philosophy after Kant – not even the main highway from Jena to Berlin – is one that goes steadily downhill. I have even noted that there

1 See my "Hegel and Idealism," *Monist* 74 (1991): 386–402; "Recent Work on Hegel: The Rehabilitation of an Epistemologist?" *Philosophy and Phenomenological Research* 52 (1992): 177–202; "*Hegel's Theory of Mental Activity*, by W. de Vries," *Philosophical Review* 101 (1992): 399–401; "Kant and Hegel on Freedom: Two New Interpretations," *Inquiry*, 35 (1992): 219–32; "*Hegel, Kant, and the Structure of the Object* by R. Stern," *Bulletin of the Hegel Society of Great Britain* no. 27–8 (1993): 58–60; "Probleme der Moralität bei Kant und Hegel," in *Das Recht der Vernunft: Kant und Hegel über Denken, Erkennen und Handeln*, ed. C. Fricke et al. (Stuttgart: Frommann Holzboog, 1995), pp. 263–89. On problems raised in Chapter 7 above with respect to Kant's account of moral motivation, cf. also my "Kant on the Good Will," in *Grundlegung zur Metaphysik der Sitten*, ed. O. Höffe (Frankfurt: Klostermann, 1989), pp. 45–65, and "On Paul Guyer's 'Kant and the Experience of Freedom,'" *Philosophy and Phenomenological Research* 55 (1995): 361–7.

are weaknesses and ambiguities in Kant's work that were doubtless at least a catalyst for the very errors of the idealists that I have stressed. The key question that remains is simply, given the specific finding of the last two chapters, what are the most basic conclusions to be drawn about how Hegel's system stands with respect to the fundamental changes in theoretical philosophy and practical philosophy that Reinhold and Fichte introduced because of their overriding concern with autonomy?

With respect to theoretical philosophy, it is significant that Hegel himself is not at all tempted by the representationalism that Reinhold and Fichte carried over from Jacobi. He remains very interested in skepticism, but he is not concerned primarily with the problem of the external world. He comes into the discussion late enough to appreciate the problems arising from anything like Reinhold's suggestion that philosophy could base itself on a single "principle of consciousness." Above all, he rejects the desperate strategy of moving from the theoretical weaknesses of the representationalist starting point to insisting on a purely practical foundation for philosophy. Like Kant, he instead takes the weaknesses of a subjective theoretical starting point to be a good reason for seeking a better theoretical method rather than a reason for moving immediately to moral and practical considerations, especially ones that make strong categorical claims all on their own.

These are all important differences, but my point has been that they take place within a model of philosophy that inherits more that is distinctive of the post-Kantians than of Kant himself. This is because Hegel's system remains a monistic whole. It is equipped with a conception of the base, development, boundary, and ultimate goal of philosophy that agrees with Reinhold's and Fichte's most fundamental departures from Kant. Like Fichte and Reinhold, Hegel insists on absolute certainty for philosophy, and hence he continues the attack on Kant's reliance on the contingent starting point of common experience (see above Chapter 6, sec. C). Like them, he also resists making a fundamental distinction between space and time and other notions, and thus he rejects the major organizing principle in the development of Kant's theoretical philosophy. If space and time are rooted in pure notions, it is no wonder that there is no room in Hegel's system for the ultimate contingency of human knowledge. It is not easy to say if Hegel is wrong on this very difficult issue, but it is clear at the very least that he continues to follow the Reinhold-Fichte pattern of thinking that philosophy can develop simply by deducing features from concepts alone, without allowing an irreducible role in philosophy for our specific kind of sensible intuition. A similar insistence on radical rather than modest systematicity is carried over in Hegel's Fichtean desire to have a linearly deduced set of categories, rather than accepting anything like a "given" table from "common logic." Also, insofar as Hegel's idealism does not rest on the specific limitations of space and time, its metaphysics resembles the post-Kantian systems and the perspective of the "short argument" much more than Kant's own transcendental idealism. It is no wonder that Hegel does without the thing in itself altogether, and that he has no interest at all in a literal reading of the Kantian postulates and the meaningfulness (whatever one thinks of their theoretical justifiability) of traditional doctrines in rational theology and psychology.

In the metaphysical dimension of practical philosophy, it is also clear that Hegel remains closer to the post-Kantians than to Kant on the fundamental issue of autonomy. Although Reinhold and Fichte remained interested in a traditional libertarian view, they expressly did not follow Kant in working out a metaphysical dimension in which uncaused causation could take place. This left their position more mysterious than Kant's own. Hegel shared Fichte's disinterest in the metaphysics of uncaused causes, but he resisted Fichte's "practical" libertarianism as well as the Fichtean thought that backing off from libertarianism would make one a bad "dogmatist." As I have noted (see above Chapter 6, sec. G and Chapter 7, sec. A), he was willing to risk a position that, despite many unclarities, ultimately seems closer to compatibilism than any of the other classical options. The crucial point is that Hegel seems willing to allow that the "freedom" of human beings need not involve a truly absolute spontaneity of their own (here he is, ironically, closest to his Berlin archenemy, Schleiermacher). This move gives him a crucial advantage over Kant and the other post-Kantians insofar as they adhere without qualification to a language of absolute freedom but must admit that they have no strict proof for their most basic commitment.[2]

There are only a few basic options left at this point. The Kantian option, as I understand it, is to endorse libertarianism, to accept what seem to be the findings of the best of modern science, and to see if there can be some way of constructing a rational metaphysics that leaves room for both. Kant's transcendental idealism is at least a consistent option within this framework.

---

2 I abstract from developments in Schelling's later philosophy, which puts a special emphasis on the issue of freedom. See Dieter Sturma, "Präreflexive Freiheit und menschliche Selbstbestimmung," in *F. W. Schelling. Über das Wesen der menschlichen Freiheit*, ed. Otfried Höffe and Annemarie Piper (Berlin: Akademie Verlag, 1995), pp. 146–69.

Another option is to insist explicitly on the fundamental importance of absolute freedom, but to undercut all theoretical grounds for making sense of such a doctrine. On my account, this manifestly unattractive position is precisely what Reinhold and Fichte held, even though Fichte and his school thought it was actually Kant who was caught in absurdity. The decisive issue here is simply whether Kant's transcendental idealism is clearly incoherent in its own terms, a claim that I have denied.

But I have also stressed the fact that even if Kant's option may be preferable to that of his immediate successors, it does not follow that his philosophy is without problems. In other words, we are back again at the "fact of reason" and Kant's embarrassing lack of a nonpractical evidence base for the absolute freedom that he puts so much weight upon. Given the emphasis that Kant himself puts on evidence, on what is truly clear to common sense, and on not relying on practical considerations alone, he has painted himself into a difficult corner – at least for an era in which libertarianism and common sense do not clearly overlap, if they ever did.

It may appear that by emphasizing this point, I have taken away much of the force of my extensive attempt to rehabilitate Kant. But to say that it would be much better if Kant had a non-question-begging ground – and not only a "not clearly incoherent conceptual space" – for his belief in freedom, is not to say that he has an untenable position. Such a claim depends on what the alternatives are. Kant's position looks awkward simply because he draws special attention to the difficulty of the issue. He does not run away into a practical foundationalism or presume that we can make categorical metaphysical assertions ("I really am *absolutely* free" or "I *absolutely* cannot help but regard myself as free") without some meaningful metaphysical space for such manifestly nonphysical claims. In the end, I do not see my account, critical though it is, as in any way undercutting Kant's position. Kant's view is epistemologically still much more sophisticated than what one can find in earlier geniuses such as Descartes or Leibniz, and in every way it is much better thought out than that of his immediate successors.

But Hegel presents us with at least one more option. I have stressed that on the issue of freedom, like other sensitive issues, Hegel "plays it safe" and seems to use the language of freedom while not being always open about the deterministic implications of his system and the need to address more directly the issue of whether he is really espousing compatibilism. To this extent, Hegel seems to be methodologically less admirable than Kant. The investigations in Chapter 6 of his theoretical discussions of Kant provide evidence that his doctrine of freedom, like his treatment of other basic issues, could be rooted not in hidden depth but simply in some bad and unfair arguments. But the investigations in Chapter 7 reveal that at the origins of Hegel's philosophy there are some complex and impressive considerations about precisely one of the most difficult aspects of the whole Kantian doctrine of freedom – the problem of making comprehensible how it could be at all attractive to think of oneself as so "free" that one could freely commit one's whole "cast of mind" against morality, and yet find something *in oneself* that would allow for an autonomous "revolution" back toward morality. From Hegel's perspective, Kant's discussion of "moral conversion" in traditional metaphysical terms departs too much from understandable natural senses of "autonomy,"[3] senses where the fulfilled self is (as Bradley put it) not one that "is fallen from heaven." Hegel is still attracted to the overriding value of some kind of autonomy, but one without the commitment to libertarianism that defined Reinhold and Fichte. His alternative is to redefine the self-determining "self" in explicitly social and historical terms, and to emphasize the autonomy of reason as an immanent whole.

This leaves us with at least two consistent options that seem more feasible than the halfway houses of Fichte and Reinhold. The first is Kant's coherent but somewhat mysterious libertarian autonomy – mysterious because it accepts not only absolute freedom, but also phenomenal determinism and radical evil. The second is Hegel's nonlibertarian "autonomy." This position is also not inconsistent or absurd, but it could be much more forthright in its admission of determinism, and much more honest about the fact that "autonomy" can be mysterious even without involving noumenal freedom or conversion from radical evil. If we are not absolutely spontaneous in being the absolute cause of our actions, some other story must be given about how we are following not only a "law" of some kind but a law truly of "our" own. This is the challenge Hegelianism must meet to keep its post-Kantian version of autonomy from ultimately suffering the same fate as that of the other post-Kantians, the fate of becoming a word for a power of the "self" that has no recognizable ultimate location for the individual, and that is in that sense a self in name only.

---

3 For a fine contemporary defense of Kant here, see John E. Hare, *The Moral Gap: Kantian Ethics, Human Limits, and God's Assistance* (Oxford: Clarendon Press, 1996); and for some problems in Kant, see Phillip L. Quinn, "Original Sin, Radical Evil and Moral Identity," *Faith and Philosophy* 1 (1984): 188–202.

NAME INDEX

SUBJECT INDEX